Science 5-11

This fully updated fourth edition of the bestselling textbook *Science 5-11* provides a comprehensive introduction to current research and professional practice for teaching science in the primary school.

Chapters are organised into five sections, first introducing theory and practice, then providing specific guidance on teaching topics in biology, chemistry and physics, and finally discussing supporting science across the whole school. Updates to the new edition include:

- Responding to recent changes in the Initial Teacher Education framework, discussion about cognitive science is integrated throughout.
- Supporting all children's engagement in science by suggesting inclusive and creative ways of building and consolidating knowledge including making connections between topics and with the wider world.
- New discussion on planning to support pupil progression in scientific knowledge throughout their time at primary school, building on Early Years and preparing for transition to secondary school.

Presenting current research and outlining guidance on best practice, *Science 5-11* provides a guide to the subject knowledge, curriculum requirements and pedagogical techniques to successfully teach science within the primary school.

Kendra McMahon is Reader in Education, Bath Spa University.

Alan Howe was the former Head of Department for Education Studies, Bath Spa University. He is lead author of 'Science 5-11' editions 1, 2 and 3.

Christopher Collier is Senior Lecturer in Education, Bath Spa University.

Sarah Earle is Professor of Primary Science Education, Bath Spa University.

Dan Davies is Director of Higher Education Management Programmes at the University of Bath.

Darren McKay is Senior Lecturer in Education, Bath Spa University.

Kerry-Anne Barber is Senior Lecturer in Education, Bath Spa University.

Lisa Ziegler is Senior Lecturer in Education, Bath Spa University.

The *5-11* series combines academic rigor with practical classroom experience in a tried and tested approach which has proved indispensable to both trainee PGCE students and to practicing teachers. Bringing the best and latest research knowledge to core subject areas, this series addresses the key issues surrounding the teaching of these subjects in the primary curriculum. The series aims to stay up to date by reflecting changes in government policy and is closely related to the changing curriculum for the primary core subjects.

Each book contains lesson planning guidance and methods to develop pupils' understanding as well as offering creative and innovative ways to teach subjects in the primary classroom.

Titles in this series include:

Physical Education 5-11, Jonathan Doherty and Peter Brennan

History 5-11, Hilary Cooper

Modern Foreign Languages 5-11, Jane Jones and Simon Coffey

English 5-11, David Waugh and Wendy Jolliffe

Science 5-11, Kendra McMahon, Alan Howe, Christopher Collier, Sarah Earle, Dan Davies, Darren McKay, Kerry-Anne Barber and Lisa Ziegler

Maths 5-11, Caroline Clissold

Religious Education 5-11, Imran Mogra

Science 5-11
A Guide for Teachers
Fourth Edition

Kendra McMahon, Alan Howe,
Christopher Collier, Sarah Earle,
Dan Davies, Darren McKay,
Kerry-Anne Barber and Lisa Ziegler

LONDON AND NEW YORK

Designed cover image: © Getty Images

First published 2025
by Routledge
4 Park Square, Milton Park, Abingdon, Oxon OX14 4RN

and by Routledge
605 Third Avenue, New York, NY 10158

Routledge is an imprint of the Taylor & Francis Group, an informa business

© 2025 Kendra McMahon, Alan Howe, Christopher Collier, Sarah Earle, Dan Davies, Darren McKay, Kerry-Anne Barber and Lisa Ziegler

The right of Kendra McMahon, Alan Howe, Chris Collier, Sarah Earle, Dan Davies, Darren McKay, Kerry-Anne Barber and Lisa Ziegler to be identified as authors of this work has been asserted in accordance with sections 77 and 78 of the Copyright, Designs and Patents Act 1988.

All rights reserved. No part of this book may be reprinted or reproduced or utilised in any form or by any electronic, mechanical, or other means, now known or hereafter invented, including photocopying and recording, or in any information storage or retrieval system, without permission in writing from the publishers.

Trademark notice: Product or corporate names may be trademarks or registered trademarks, and are used only for identification and explanation without intent to infringe.

British Library Cataloguing-in-Publication Data
A catalogue record for this book is available from the British Library

Library of Congress Cataloging-in-Publication Data
Names: McMahon, Kendra, author. | Howe, Alan (Alan Robin), author. | Collier, Chris, author. | Earle, Sarah, author. | Davies, Dan (Daniel John), 1962- author. | McKay, Darren, author. | Barber, Kerry-Ann, author. | Ziegler, Lisa, author.
Title: Science 5-11 : a guide for teachers / Kendra McMahon, Alan Howe, Chris Collier, Sarah Earle, Dan Davies, Darren McKay, Kerry-Ann Barber, and Lisa Ziegler.
Other titles: Science five to eleven
Description: 4th edition. | Abingdon, Oxon ; New York, NY : Routledge, 2025. | Series: Primary 5-11 | Third edition published in 2017. | Includes bibliographical references and index.
Identifiers: LCCN 2024016152 (print) | LCCN 2024016153 (ebook) | ISBN 9781032377681 (hbk) | ISBN 9781032377704 (pbk) | ISBN 9781003341833 (ebk)
Subjects: LCSH: Science--Study and teaching (Preschool)--Great Britain. | Science--Study and teaching (Elementary)--Great Britain. | Science--Experiments.
Classification: LCC LB1585.5.G7 S34 2025 (print) | LCC LB1585.5.G7 (ebook) | DDC 372.35/044--dc23/eng/20240629
LC record available at https://lccn.loc.gov/2024016152
LC ebook record available at https://lccn.loc.gov/2024016153

ISBN: 978-1-032-37768-1 (hbk)
ISBN: 978-1-032-37770-4 (pbk)
ISBN: 978-1-003-34183-3 (ebk)

DOI: 10.4324/9781003341833

Typeset in Bembo
by SPi Technologies Private Limited, India (Straive)

Contents

Acknowledgments		*vi*
Introduction		1
SECTION 1	Teaching science: theory and practice	5
SECTION 2	Teaching biology topics	43
	2.1 Living things and their habitats	47
	2.2 Plants	69
	2.3 Animals including humans	89
SECTION 3	Teaching chemistry topics	115
	3.1 Everyday materials and their properties	117
	3.2 Changing materials	138
SECTION 4	Teaching physics topics	157
	4.1 Earth and space	159
	4.2 Light and sound	175
	4.3 Electricity	191
	4.4 Forces and magnets	207
SECTION 5	Supporting science across the school	223
	5.1 A whole-school approach to assessment	225
	5.2 Subject leadership	234
	5.3 Transitions	243
Index		*249*

Acknowledgments

The authors would like to thank all the colleagues, teachers and children who have provided ideas and inspiration for each edition of this book. For this fourth edition, thanks go to:

> Milo McKay-Moore for his fantastic drawings;
> Children and staff at Widcombe Infant School, Bath;
> Carol Sampey, children and other staff at Shaw Primary School, Melksham;
> Kate Porter, children and other staff at Worlebury St. Paul's Primary School, Weston-super-Mare;
> Pauline Rodger, children and other staff at Holt Primary School, Wiltshire;
> Asima Qureshi, children and other staff at Meadowbrook Primary School;
> South Gloucestershire; children and staff at Chandag Infants' School, Keynsham;
> Children and staff at Northleaze CE Primary School, Long Ashton;
> All participants of the 'Teacher Assessment in Primary Science' project and the Primary Science Teaching Trust.

In writing this book we have drawn on our wide range of experiences and expertise gathered from a variety of perspectives: as primary teachers, advisory teachers, university tutors and teacher trainers. We warmly welcome new authors to the collaborative writing team for this edition.

We must also acknowledge that this book would not have been possible if we had not been fortunate enough to work within a science education community that is creative, dedicated and generous. We have drawn ideas together from past colleagues, students, trainees and teachers, as well as from published sources. We hope we have acknowledged everyone and offended no one in the process.

After leading three successful editions of this book, Alan Howe has handed over the baton. We wholeheartedly thank Alan for his leadership, generosity and trust.

Introduction

Science education seems more important than ever as we write this fourth edition. We are in a time of global heating - now undeniably a climate crisis. We recently experienced the global pandemic of Covid-19. There are global concerns about health with rising levels of obesity. In a world of fake news we want science education to enable children to be confident in being critical of what they read and identifying reliable sources of information. We want a science education that hits the sweet spot between realizing that scientific knowledge is always tentative and recognizing when we have good grounds for confidence in it.

We can offer opportunities for children to take action in their own lives and to influence others. Perhaps children could write to food manufacturers to ask them why there is a particular additive in their favourite product. Perhaps they could support local insect populations. They might present a play in school assembly with the aim of persuading others not to vape. We want children to understand that scientific knowledge can be powerful, but not to feel overwhelmed with responsibility (that is the job of adults and governments).

Hands-on experience of the stuff of the world is at the heart of primary science education and we want children wonder and puzzle as they look at extraordinary beetles, smell lilac, taste lemons, feel the invisible forces between magnets and listen to the sounds of a guitar. We live in an amazing world and the more we enjoy it, the more we appreciate it and care for it.

This fourth edition responds to developments in the scientific understanding of how we learn. In England, policy has recently been influenced by the cognitive psychology of memory and we consider the implications of that for primary science. However, a broader range of research is being carried out under the umbrella of 'the learning sciences' and in this book we draw on that. We have considered how educational neuroscience can help us to understand the mechanisms of learning. We have taken the view that this scientific perspective on learning is useful but needs to be considered alongside the rich body of educational research and theory. We also draw on the professional knowledge of teachers and teacher educators and the wisdom of the wider primary science community.

This new edition responds to research into 'science capital' - how children think about science and who they know in science-related occupations has a big influence whether children see science as 'for me'. We have considered how science topics can connect with a diversity of social and cultural experiences and perspectives and we suggest possible ways of making connections with children's lives.

We know that primary teachers constantly reflect on their teaching and wonder if they are 'good' at their job. We suggest the following criteria are useful to answer that question and they inform subsequent chapters. Good science teachers:

- have clear personal aims for science teaching;
- have an understanding of the nature of science;
- have an understanding of the 'processes of science' and how science creates knowledge – that ideas are tentative, and are based on interpretation of evidence;

- have sufficient understanding of the 'big ideas' of science to see where learning is leading and to avoid giving misleading information;
- value children's existing ideas;
- have a knowledge of some common alternative ideas that children hold;
- have a repertoire of teaching strategies they can use responsively and creatively;
- feel excited about teaching science.

We intend that this book will be a valuable starting point for anyone who wishes to teach science in a creative and inspiring way. Students in initial teacher training and primary teachers who are relatively new to the profession will find here a framework for teaching science that is both relevant and engaging for primary children. This framework is grounded in personal experience, theory and research, in line with our commitment to evidence-informed practice. It will be introduced in the first chapter and developed in subsequent chapters as we consider what it means for teaching various topics within the primary science curriculum. We hope that the book will also be useful for those who are more experienced practitioners. Rather than present a prescriptive model for teaching science, we explain approaches and strategies that teachers can adopt, develop and use creatively with the children in their own classes. Teachers who have the additional responsibility of being science subject leaders may also find it useful in helping them with supporting colleagues, and in reflecting on progression across the whole primary school. We focus on their role in Chapter 5.2.

Organisation of the book

We have divided the book into five sections. In Section 1 we consider the aims of primary science, introduce our view of the nature of science and explore the central role of scientific enquiry. We introduce perspectives on learning in science, and feature of this fourth edition is that we consider the contribution that cognitive science can make to our understanding of learning. The level of discussion and debate within the section are a good starting point for students who are studying at 'Masters' level. There is a full discussion of the importance of talk, specifically dialogue, between teachers and learners. Sections 2, 3 and 4 take in turn the teaching of Biology, Chemistry and Physics. Within each section you will find chapters on a range of science topics, such as 'living things', 'materials and their properties' and 'electricity'. Here we explore in depth the issues for teaching and learning in that topic.

For ease of reference, each topic-based chapter will follow a similar pattern.

Purpose of this chapter

A series of bullet points will set out the aims of the chapter for the reader.

Introduction

In the introduction to each chapter we will explain the relevance of the topic for primary children, and in terms of developing the 'big ideas' of science.

Planning for Progression

What are the key concepts that are to be developed rom the early years to the beginning of secondary school within this conceptual area? A table will summarise the subject knowledge related to those 'key ideas' for teachers to access at a glance. We also give you some 'teachers' self-assessment questions' to test your own subject knowledge.

Engage

Situating the topic

Teachers are always keen to make learning as relevant and engaging as possible for their class. The context within which scientific ideas are presented is vitally important in motivating children and ensuring that the ideas connect with their own lives sufficiently to make sense. This includes identifying opportunities for cross-curricular planning.

Breaking down barriers

We also provide suggestions for how to introduce children to the topic in question in ways that will excite their interest and be meaningful and relevant for them. Across the chapters we introduce a diverse range of scientists and offer suggestions for promoting equity in science education.

Activating Children's ideas

In this sub-section we select and exemplify those strategies for activating and eliciting children's existing ideas that are most appropriate for the topic. We also explore common alternative ideas that children may hold, preparing teachers for what they might encounter in their own classrooms. This will draw on a range of established research and literature.

Build

Constructing new knowledge

This section explains what topic-specific strategies could build children's understanding and how these might be adapted for different learners.

Working scientifically

Working scientifically contributes to constructing new knowledge and in some chapters these two headings will be taken together. Here we focus on the particular aspects of practical work and types of scientific enquiry that could be developed through this topic, drawing on the categories identified in Section 1.

Monitoring and Feedback

Here we identify suitable strategies for formative assessment and feedback, often connected with those used for activating children's ideas.

Consolidate

Retrieving and Applying

Here we suggest strategies could be used for rehearsing new knowledge to consolidate it and to build that knowledge into complex schemas by extending and elaborating it. Where relevant we identify opportunities for action on environmental sustainability.

Reviewing

There are two purposes for reviewing – for children to reflect on their learning and strengthen their metacognition (becoming more aware of their own learning processes) and also for the teacher to make summative assessment judgments.

Classroom management

Primary teachers often find the organisational aspects of science, particularly practical work, a challenge. In this section we offer advice and raise awareness of health and safety issues relating to the topic.

Summary

A brief resume of the chapter contents.

Discussion questions

1. These are intended to further develop your thinking and understanding of the chapter content. Some aim to promote critical thinking at 'Masters' level.

Further Reading

At the end of each chapter we suggest further reading.

References

In this fourth edition, the references to research for each chapter are listed at the end of that chapter.

Section 5 is designed to support teachers in thinking beyond the classroom to issues that impact on the whole school. This is addressed to all teachers but is of particular relevance to subject leaders, headteachers and those with a role in developing a school's strategic direction. Three key aspects are discussed: assessment, subject leadership and transitions.

Throughout this book we take a constructivist view of learning, recognising that children build their own ideas; it is just not possible to pour ready-made ideas into a brain. The complex role of the teacher involves giving children access to rich experiences, helping them to notice phenomena, valuing their questions and ideas and offering explanations that draw on scientific knowledge. We hope that this book helps primary teachers to build or extend their repertoire of strategies for doing that. We see scientific knowledge as a cultural legacy and an ongoing conversation that we are handing over to the next generation. The message is not 'This is right - you'd better learn it perfectly.', but 'This is where we've got to so far - over to you'. It is in that same spirit we hand over our ideas to the readers of this book.

SECTION 1

Teaching science: theory and practice

Purpose of this section

In this section we lay out some of the key principles, values and theories that underpin the other sections of the book. After reading this chapter you should have:

- reflected on the aims and purposes of teaching science in the primary school;
- an understanding of the nature of science;
- an understanding of some theories of learning in relation to science;
- considered the implications of research and theory for the pedagogy of science.

What are the aims of primary science?

We believe that every person must have a good science education so that they can participate in society as a scientifically literate individual and make informed choices about their world and their future. We know that lifelong attitudes and enthusiasms can be initiated by powerful experiences during childhood, and we believe primary educators have an important responsibility to ensure that children's experiences of science are positive. It is not the main aim of primary science to produce biochemists, engineers, doctors, ecologists, astronomers and wildlife photographers, yet these may be the future professions of the young children sat on the carpet or at their desks in front of you. There may be other children who already have begun to develop a sense that science is 'difficult', 'boring' or 'not for me'. Individuals will have a greater or lesser need for an understanding of particular aspects of science in their everyday lives, depending on their roles and interests, and primary science provides the broad foundation for lifelong learning, but primary science also has an even broader agenda. We also believe no group, for example females, should be excluded by the ways in which science is presented in school. Teachers have a responsibility to enable all children to access a full science education. Stereotypes about science and scientists must be actively challenged.

Looking beyond the need of the individual, we argue that an important aim of science education is establishing 'scientific literacy' across the population. Science is not something scientists do in isolation from the rest of society. It requires funding, and so the providers of these funds must consider the research to be worthwhile. In many cases science is supported by public money, via taxation. Science is also subject to government regulation, such as ethical guidance for the use of animal experiments and standards for testing medicines. So it is not just scientists that need to make decisions about science and the directions in which science goes. In our roles as consumers, parents, citizens and voters, everyone has a stake in science and, arguably, a responsibility for it. In a scientifically literate society people would engage with science issues that affect our lives and take an active part through democratic processes and personal decisions. In our experience, primary-aged children begin to develop viewpoints on issues that have an ethical and scientific basis, such as how farm animals should be treated and how habitats should be protected. It is likely they will need to think about many such complex issues and participate in debates as they grow up.

In England, there is concern that the status of science in some primary schools has been lower since national tests in science were removed in 2009 (Ofsted 2023) and a suggestion that this may account for the reduced the performance of secondary pupils in the 'Trends in international mathematics and science study' (TIMSS) in 2019 (Richardson et al. 2020). We are glad to see this recognition of the value of primary science and hope this will support all schools to give science its status as a core subject in the curriculum. However, science in primary schools is more than just a foundation for what pupils learn at secondary school.

We believe that the most important aim of primary science is to foster children's deep appreciation of the world around – what is sometimes referred to as 'awe and wonder'. We do this by encouraging a keen eye for observation and a keen mind for questioning. We might see that having to 'introduce' the scientific world to children is a great responsibility. In fact, it is also a great pleasure. As children introduce us to the world as they see it, we learn too. Through science, children will develop an understanding of how natural phenomena, living things and the environment are closely related. This is worthwhile because the world is fascinating, it can amaze, and such encounters enrich our lives.

Here we have outlined some of the beliefs and values that give the authors a passion for science and science teaching. What will your reasons be for teaching science?

What is science?

Arguably, some of our above aims could be achieved through art, through literature, or through more everyday experiences such as going out for a woodland walk. So, what is it that makes the scientific study of the world a distinct and valuable approach? Science provides a unique way of making sense of the world by offering a way of responding to many of those 'why?' questions that children have and providing some plausible (but often tentative) answers. Science emphasises knowledge gained through observation and investigation (i.e. it is empirical) but also values evidence, reasoning and critique. Osborne (2015) argues that science is fundamentally about developing ideas. It provides people with a means of engaging with the world in their everyday life, which is empowering rather than fatalistic or superstitious. There are other ways of understanding the world too – the arts, humanities and sciences are not in opposition or on different 'sides', rather they can be complementary ways of looking at the world.

Scientific knowledge is tentative; the explanations are the best we have at the moment, but there is always the possibility that these theories will be challenged or replaced in the light of new ideas and evidence. If children are to really understand science, this fundamental view of the nature of science must run through all of science teaching. Science is not standing still – ideas are changing, new evidence is being produced, and creative thinking generates new questions and explanations. Critical thinking tests explanations. What are the effects of global heating on animal migration? What are the long-term impacts of COVID-19 on our health? What is the effect on children of increased screen time? At any one time, scientists may disagree about explanations, and different studies may provide conflicting evidence yet the argument that science should be studied as one of the great cultural achievements of modern times is a compelling one.

Scientific knowledge could be defined as the ideas any individual constructs as a result of scientific reasoning. Ask yourself 'What happens to your food after you have swallowed it?', 'Where does the Sun go at night?', 'Why are house bricks heavier than balloons?' Now consider where these ideas came from. We all engage in scientific reasoning as we try to make sense of what we see.

Osborne (2015, p. 17) identifies types or styles of reasoning that could be summarised for primary education as: experimenting, sorting/classifying, pattern-seeking, hypothesising and mathematical reasoning. Osborne also identifies a sixth type, that of 'historical-based thinking' (p. 17) which encompasses the 'evolution' of big ideas of science over the centuries. This reasoning has resulted in a body of knowledge that is held by the scientific community as a whole, including inherent tensions, contradictions and uncertainties. This presents particular challenges for teaching science that we hope to address in subsequent chapters. We need to consider how this tentativeness can be communicated, while at the same time acknowledging the value of the existing body of knowledge. We also need to help children get to grips with ideas that have developed over thousands of years.

The timescale for changes in the better-established concepts in science seems to be sufficiently long that there is a fairly stable body of knowledge that primary children can get to grips with that is likely to remain useful for years to come. The National Curriculum (NC) for England is one attempt to select aspects that might be relevant and accessible for primary-aged children, and this book is largely based on that selection. Other authors (Harlen 2015) have emphasised the importance of the 'big ideas' in science – concepts such as particle theory, energy, evolution and the formation of the Earth – that unify different branches of science, and are powerful 'explanatory stories' in how, as a culture, we currently make sense of the world. We also draw your attention to these big ideas in turn in subsequent chapters, and so will sometimes go beyond the prescription of the local NC.

There has been a recent trend towards people being more sceptical about 'experts' and having a lack of trust in their pronouncements. It is reasonable to be sceptical about who is defined as or appoints themselves as an 'expert'. We should question their sources of funding, their credentials and their vested interests. Indeed, scientific attitudes include questioning what others say. However, when there is a rejection of scientific reasoning, it can be due to unrealistic expectations of the kind of answers science can generate. It does not always produce certainties, though findings have sometimes been presented as such in media headlines that announce miracle cures or predict impending doom. If teachers see scientific ideas as indisputable facts, and present them as such, they are misleading children and giving them a false understanding of the nature of science. Weighing evidence, understanding probability and assessing risk are all part of understanding how to make judgements and taking decisions based on scientific evidence. However, teachers also need to understand the weight of evidence that is available to challenge the claims of those who use 'an expert' or 'a scientist' to bolster an entirely unscientific worldview.

A critical understanding of how ideas are based on evidence requires an understanding of the processes of science, such as the use of controlled tests and the implications of sampling procedures. It also requires an understanding of why scientists do the things they do: they might repeat experiments because errors may occur at any time; they sample carefully in an attempt to eliminate bias; they present findings to peers to invite scrutiny and argument. This critical understanding of the nature of science can begin in the primary school as children carry out their own scientific enquiries.

The language used to discuss science knowledge can be confusing as a range of different terms are used for similar ideas. The English NC (DfE 2013) distinguishes between 'conceptual understanding' and 'working scientifically'. Examples of conceptual understanding include identifying and naming common plants, knowing that some materials dissolve in a liquid and that light is reflected from a surface. Working scientifically encompasses the nature of science (NoS), the processes and methods of science. In England, the view of science held by Ofsted, the body that inspects schools, has a significant influence. Ofsted's review of science education research (Ofsted 2021) used the terms 'substantive knowledge' and 'disciplinary knowledge'. They argue for developing substantive knowledge that is a set of interrelated concepts rather than disconnected facts. In this view disciplinary knowledge encompasses knowing the range of ways in which scientists answer questions, knowing how to use scientific equipment and how to make measurements, how to analyse the data that has been collected and to communicate findings. It also includes understanding the complex relationship between evidence and explanations – what others have termed understanding the 'nature of science' (abbreviated to NoS). We agree with their emphasis that substantive and disciplinary knowledge should be seen as intertwined, not separate.

Looking at the different school curricula of different nations reminds us that what goes into a curriculum is a human choice! The curriculum for Wales (Welsh Government and Curriculum for Wales 2021) brings science and technology together as an area of learning and emphasises curiosity as a key aim. The science curriculum for the Canadian province of Saskatchewan explicitly values the knowledge of indigenous peoples as part of a bigger social aim for truth and reconciliation. For example, it says pupils in Grade 4 (8- to 9-year-olds) should 'Draw upon facets of Indigenous worldviews, such as the Medicine Wheel or circle of life, to examine understanding about the interdependence of plants and animals in various habitats and communities.'(Saskatchewan Ministry of Education 2011).

In summary, science is a combination of the big ideas (content knowledge), doing science (procedural knowledge) and understanding the practice of science (epistemic knowledge). In England, Ofsted uses the term 'substantive knowledge' instead of content knowledge and combines procedural and epistemic knowledge under the label 'disciplinary knowledge'. If 'real' science is a heady mix of intellectual and practical activity undertaken by individuals and communities, then science in school should reflect this creativity, criticality and sometimes 'fuzzy' process rather than pretend science is a linear path or simple recipe for getting answers for questions. Osborne (2015) succinctly summarises teaching science as involving 'doing, talking, reading, writing and representing' (p. 18). In this book we present a view of science as a blend of thinking, doing, using skills, developing concepts and adopting attitudes that should remain intertwined during teaching. Below we will explore the research and theories that lead us to these conclusions.

Learning in science – constructivist theories

To make decisions about how to teach, we need to think about how children learn. Constructivist theories of learning and socio-cultural views of learning have significantly influenced approaches to science education. More recently these have been reconsidered to take account of research in cognitive psychology and neuroscience.

Constructivist theories view learning as a process by which an individual actively constructs ideas, rather than as a process of 'transmission' in which concepts or ideas are received fully formed and copied in the mind of the learner.

Versions of constructivism based on the work of Piaget emphasise the importance of interaction with the physical world and see young children as behaving like scientists – making and testing hypotheses about the environment: for example, 'This toy will fall to the floor if I drop it.' In this view of learning science, the practical hands-on experiences become the most important element, and the teacher's role is to provide a rich environment for the child to explore. If we reflect on our own learning, few people would deny the power of handling objects, feeling and seeing something happen in giving us a depth of understanding. It is also understood that play is a vital element of learning and different kinds of play contribute to children's learning in science in different ways. Running around a woodland breaking sticks or throwing different pebbles into a pond could be defined as exploratory or *epistemic* play that results in knowledge of things. Working out how to make a swing go higher with friends in the playground might be problem-solving play and lead to an understanding of procedures for conducting other experiments. Play that involves inventing a game with rules (ludic play) – e.g. snail racing or hide and seek – can also lead to learning of a scientific nature.

Much of how we teach science today is founded on some 'classic' research conducted in the 1980s when science became compulsory for children in primary school. In this research there is a great deal of evidence (Driver et al. 1985, Science Processes and Concept Exploration Project – various authors 1989–1998,) that when children construct their own ideas and explanations about the world, their explanations are different from accepted scientific views. These are sometimes called 'alternative frameworks', sometimes less respectfully labelled as 'misconceptions'. Constructivists believe children are innately motivated to make sense of the world around them, so it is not surprising that their early attempts to explain are incomplete – they are based on very limited experiences. Realising that children are developing ideas about the world, even in the absence of being 'taught', and that their ideas are not random or thoughtless but are logical interpretations based on limited knowledge, are important insights for teachers to understand. Piaget (1929) also introduced the term 'schema' to describe mental structures that link multiple representations of ideas. Although not every child will construct the same ideas, or schemas, researchers have noticed that there are some common patterns in the emerging alternative frameworks, and being aware of these is useful to teachers. These common patterns may reflect similarities in the social environment in which children grow up. We outline some ways in which children think about scientific phenomena in subsequent chapters.

Social-constructivist views of learning in science (Ollerenshaw and Ritchie 1997; Harlen and Qualter 2018) also emphasise the central role of practical investigations in developing children's ideas but, in addition, they stress the importance of learning with and from others – both peers and adults. They argue that children will develop their existing ideas when they encounter new evidence, which could be in the form of new physical experiences or new ideas from other people. This new evidence may confirm or conflict with their existing ideas, or develop new ideas, but if they are not to be rejected as meaningless then children must be able to make some sense of experiences by connecting them to their existing understanding. They may be able to make links without support, or it may need the intervention of someone else to help them (a *more knowledgeable other* as Vygotsky (1978) identified). Ideas that do not make sense and that are not linked with other ideas, are those that are easily forgotten. Younger children need more support with this process of making connections with prior learning as the brain area (prefrontal regions) that are responsible for doing this are slow to mature (Howard-Jones et al. 2020, p. 454); this means that teachers need to help them to 'activate' their existing ideas.

The above theories lead us to conclude that *talking* is a vital part of learning in science and a special kind of talk is particularly valuable – where meanings are negotiated through *dialogue* (more about this below). Talk should happen among children, and between children and the teacher. Teacher's questioning is important as it helps the teacher to find out what children's ideas are and to try to get at the reasoning behind those ideas. The process of talking about observations and evidence and relating it to other experiences helps to make sense of the world. In this view of learning, as well as recognising that ideas are developed within individual minds, a socio-cultural approach sets out to understand how ideas are developed *between* minds. Vygotsky (1978) proposed the existence of an individual and a social plane, 'intramental' and 'intermental' planes. His theory is that learning occurs when concepts developed on the social plane, the intermental plane, between people are then internalised by individuals to their 'intramental space'. Other authors (Rogoff 1990) use the term *appropriated* instead of internalised to make the point that this is an active process for the learner which transforms the ideas of the social plane, not a copying process, which would take us back to a transmission view of learning.

Socio-cultural views of learning in science also stress the importance of the cultural context for learning. In this view, the way that people interact is thought to be important. For learning to occur, there needs to be a genuine two-way process of interpretation and meaning making, where the ideas of all participants are respected and given equal value. During this exchange the ideas of each person may develop and change. One implication of this is that teachers need to be aware of making assumptions about children's understanding of the language they use. The teacher needs to make an effort to understand children in their own terms, not just expect them to see things from the teacher's perspective. Bruner (1996) explains that to teach others we need to use our 'theory of mind' – we need to imagine what it is that another person is thinking.

Each person brings their own cultural position to the process of creating a dialogue, and this can present barriers to shared understanding. If a teacher presented putting sugar in tea as an example of dissolving, he might assume that people put sugar in a cup of tea after it was made, while in some African and Indian communities the common practice is to boil tea, sugar, water and milk together in a kettle. The scientific version of what dissolving means wouldn't change, but the way in which children made sense of the example might be different. A teacher might assume that the children understand that because they are doing science, the word 'table' is being used to refer to a chart for recording results, rather than a piece of furniture. Words with an everyday meaning can also have a particular scientific meaning: force, solid and fruit are further examples of this.

In the classroom the teacher has a great deal of power in determining what counts as the 'right' knowledge. Children may come to accept the 'correct' teacher's view, but not really connect it with their own deeper understandings, so it becomes compartmentalised as 'school knowledge' and kept as separate from their everyday or common-sense views of the world. Another possibility, if the teacher's view is meaningless to the child in terms of their own existing knowledge and understanding, is that they either fail to 'get it right' in school or learn to produce the 'right answer' by rote. So, for the teacher, the art is to make scientifically accepted ideas meaningful in terms of the child's existing ideas. To do this, the teacher needs to understand both the child's existing constructions and the scientific body of knowledge to be taught. This is a challenge for any teacher! The chapters of this book attempt to support teachers in this process of examining examples of children's ideas, presenting the ideas currently held by scientists, and providing a repertoire of teaching strategies that relate them. This is not a 'top-down process': by helping children to actively engage with scientific ideas and language, they can become part of science, rather than passive receivers of it. In each chapter we emphasise the importance of the context: is it interesting, meaningful and relevant? What different experiences might different children bring to it? Might there be any aspects of the topic that are beyond the children's experience?

Children working together in groups without an adult present can come to a shared understanding about what they are doing and observing and how they are explaining their experiences. This can be very productive in that there is an immediate connection with existing ideas and often children can help make sense of ideas to each other in terms of a shared language and set of experiences that a teacher would not have access to. With the teacher's dominant presence removed, children are free to have a more open-ended exploration of what is taking place. However, there is no guarantee that the understandings they reach will be in line with the scientific view! There may be dominant children in the group who are persuasive and convince the others that their explanations are correct when others may have ideas that fit better with accepted ideas and evidence. The view taken in this book is not only that scientific processes are useful in supporting children's learning, and we strongly support the importance of providing first-hand experiences and extending the evidence available to children, but also that there are a range of other strategies that can be used to create a shared understanding of scientific concepts. Different areas of the curriculum present different challenges in terms of 'bridging the gap' between children's and scientific ideas and so require different teaching strategies (Leach and Scott 2002). This includes the use of analogies, introducing scientific models and discussing vocabulary. For the teacher, this means ensuring that they and the children 'stay on the same wavelength' and they maintain a shared 'intermental space', so that new ideas can be introduced and developed in ways that are meaningful to the children is of central importance.

Cognitive science views of learning (cognitive psychology and neuroscience)

Models of learning from cognitive psychology have become very influential in English education policy documents such as the Early Career Framework (DfE 2019). Learning is seen in terms of the formation of memory. A popular model is summarised by American cognitive psychologist Dan Willingham (2017). In this model, information from the person's environment (e.g. pictures, spoken words) is held in their 'working memory' for processing. Importantly, it is only what we pay attention to that enters the working memory. We also draw existing memories into our working memory. The processing is what we experience as awareness and 'thought'. Some of what happens in working memory is then transferred to long-term memory – it is 'stored' – and some is lost. The evidence that supports this theoretical model comes from experimental observations of human behaviour. For example, experiments can explore how much information a person can hold and work on at any one time, how well memories can be recalled over time. As with all science, it takes an imaginative human to construct a model that makes sense of empirical data; this model of memory is attributed to Baddeley (2003) and has been updated with more recent studies (Baddeley et al. 2020).

A key feature of this model is that it is what we pay attention to that enters the working memory. The role of attention is a fascinating area of cognitive psychology – if you haven't seen it already look up videos of The Invisible Gorilla experiment. It is clear that we are not entirely passive recipients of the world, but that we can actively choose what we see, hear and touch. Although we do unconsciously process some information from the environment and create 'implicit memories' (think about how a smell can be associated with a feeling), building the kind of knowledge that is the focus of much learning in school requires active attention to develop 'explicit memories'. Scientists are exploring factors affecting children's attention in schools. For example, reducing classroom noise seems to have beneficial effects on improving attention control, particularly for noise sensitive children, who might otherwise be labelled as being less focused or as not caring about their work (Massonnié et al. 2020). As primary science classrooms can be lively, busy environments filled with many resources, we might think carefully about how different children experience this.

Another important feature of this simple model of memory is that the working memory has a limited capacity and can be 'overloaded'. Advocates of this model argue that 'cognitive overload' is less likely if learners have already committed key facts to long-term memory that can be retrieved into the working memory as a single 'chunk' that doesn't take up much of the capacity (Willingham 2021). Psychological studies have found that 'retrieval practice' – bringing information to mind from memory – strengthens the formation of long-term memories (e.g. Roediger and Karpicke 2006). In the classroom, retrieval practice could take the form of a test, maybe a short answer quiz, or labelling a diagram, but could also be writing down everything you can remember (sometimes called a 'brain dump').

Whereas cognitive psychologists create abstract models that explain experimentally observable behaviours, cognitive neuroscientists are interested in describing how the physical structures of neurons, the brain and nervous systems are related to behaviours and experiences. On her useful webpages, neuroscientist Efrat Furst offers visual representations of learning as neurons (brain cells) connecting together. She explains that 'The main way that the brain acquires skills, abilities, and knowledge, is through changing the strength of the connections between neurons, mostly based on experience.' and 'Knowledge is built into the structure of the brain' (Furst n.d.). Patterns of connections between neurons that are repeatedly activated are 'consolidated' as a meaningful set of links that could be labelled a concept. Baddeley et al. (2020) explain the theory that a concept consists of a hub with many spokes that connect to many other parts of the brain. They give the example of the concept of a specific cat 'Lulu' (the hub) holding together information about her shape, colour, sound, how her fur feels and how she moves and acts (the spokes). A further level of consolidation can happen when these concepts are integrated into existing networks of connections or 'schemas'. Furst suggests that this integration gives us the experience of 'understanding', seeing this as different from the disconnected memory of a fact. A schema is a more general structure of information, with less detail, so we might have a general schema for 'cats' that gives us a *frame* for our knowledge. Schemas that give information about what sequences of events generally follow each other could be described as *scripts* (Baddeley et al. 2020), for example what happens when you plant a seed.

In his (freely downloadable) e-book, *MARGE: A Whole Brain Approach to Learning*, cognitive neuroscientist Art Shimamura (2018) says that 'our vast storehouse of knowledge is distributed widely in broad regions of the cerebral cortex as a network of interconnected information' (p. 22). He describes three stages in conceptual learning. The first stage, activating prior knowledge, is a kind of simultaneous lighting up of neurons and networks of neurons across the brain – and he sees this as constituting 'working memory'. The next stage is a 'binding' of that information, and the third stage is of consolidation which involves reactivating it and relating new information into existing knowledge networks stored in the cerebral cortex (p. 22).

This description of knowledge as interconnected networks in the brain is a very different image than memory as a box in the brain that we put facts into. Images such as Figure 1.1 from the Human Connectome project enable us to see the pathways of connections across the brain. Some parts of the brain are more specialised than others to carry out a particular function such as processing sensory information, but what is striking is how the brain operates as an integrated whole in which perception, cognition and emotions are 'entangled' as a complex system (Pessoa 2022).

So a constructivist view of learning is supported by neuroscience which sees learning in individual people (and other animals) as the process of making and remaking of connections between neurons (brain cells). These connections are the traces of action and of thought as humans get on with living in their environment. Cognitive psychologists see these traces as the basis of memory. The way our brains continuously change as we live and learn is called 'neuroplasticity'.

As we know from our own attempts to learn things, it isn't always easy, and we forget things. Memory is clearly not like a video recording of life that we can replay. Memory is selective and organised; it has to be or we would be overwhelmed and never be able to find useful information in time. Forgetting is essential! Our brains have evolved to be adaptable to a changing environment. We only remember what our brains have decided is important for us to remember. And sadly, we don't have direct control of that! Cues that something is important enough to remember are that it is emotionally significant, it is repeated or it is meaningful to us.

Willingham (2021) describes memory as the 'residue of thought'. This gives a sense of the need for attention and effort in creating long-term memories. Much of everyday thinking and action (switching on a light because it has become dark, feeling a T-shirt stretch as we get dressed,

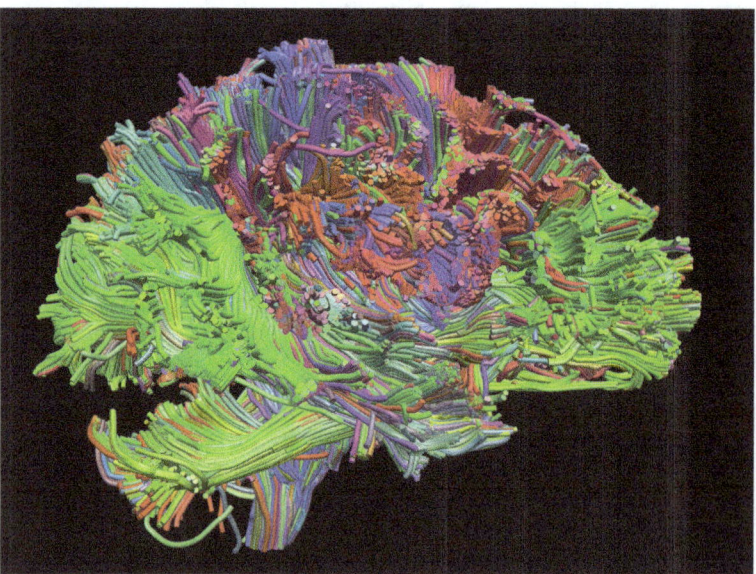

Figure 1.1 Pathways of connections across a human brain.

Credit: Healthy adult human brain viewed from the side, tractography. Henrietta Howells, NatBrainLab. Source: Wellcome Collection.

noticing that we feel breathless after running fast) is repeated naturally as part of living, so this learning does not feel effortful. It is meaningful because it is part of what we do. In contrast, much school learning is of ideas that we would not encounter in our everyday lives, e.g. that a lamp lights when an electric circuit is completed, a pull is a force that be measured with a Newton meter, that our hearts pump oxygenated blood to our muscles. The Russian psychologist Lev Vygotsky (1978) made the distinction between 'everyday knowledge' and 'scientific knowledge'. By 'scientific knowledge' Vygotsky meant all the kinds of formalised knowledge that we are taught in school, not just in science lessons. For this school knowledge to be built and consolidated as an explicit long-term memory, we need to make it significant and meaningful and we need to 'rehearse' it – to engage with it repeatedly. A renewed focus on teaching and learning strategies that help learners to consolidate knowledge has provided a useful counterpoint to just 'covering the curriculum'.

The simple model of memory tells us little about the role of emotion or of how social interactions matter to learning. However, there are insights to glean from the wider field of 'the learning sciences'. From his work with brain-damaged patients, Damasio (2006) found that without emotions, decision making was impossible. He argues that we should see the brain and body as a whole entity with parts that interact to produce a social, conscious person. Some scientists are starting to look at brain changes when people are interacting. Children's brain waves synchronise when 'thinking together'. Ido Davidesco and colleagues (2019) found that pupils' brainwaves are more in sync with each other when they are more engaged in a lesson and when there are closer relationships between teacher and pupils and between pupils. People's 'reward' brain networks are activated when they 'share attention' with another person – in other words when more than one person is paying attention to the same thing (Schilbach et al. 2010). Perhaps this is why some of us find it easier to stay engaged in a real classroom than online. Even so, cognitive science still can't tell us everything about the complex role of the teacher and of other people in learning. There is much to be learned from the tacit knowledge and professional expertise of experienced teachers. We can also draw on other kinds of education research, such as research into classroom talk, and that is the focus of the next section.

Exploring dialogic talk and learning in science

Alexander (2008, 2020) uses the term *dialogic* to express a 'genuinely reciprocal' process of communication between teacher and pupil in which ideas are developed cumulatively over sustained sequences of interactions. Using dialogic talk can support children in both understanding the scientific view and having their own viewpoints valued. Dialogic talk in which children's viewpoints are considered can be understood by contrasting it with authoritative talk in which children's ideas are only accepted if they are in line with the scientific message (Mortimer and Scott 2003, p. 33): 'either the teacher hears what the student has to say from the student's point of view, or the teacher hears what the student has to say only from the science point of view'.

Imagine if all a teacher's interactions with children were like this:

Teacher: Can you tell me something a plant needs to stay alive?
Anna: Water.
Teacher: Water, that's right. What else does it need?
Max: Food.
Teacher: Food, not really no. Plants don't eat food, they make their own. What else do they need to stay alive?
Sam They need air.
Teacher: Air. Right.

This kind of interaction might be useful for a brisk recap of information, but it is not about supporting new learning and deep understanding. It also conveys the hidden message that the teacher has all the answers. It is made up of 'IRE triads'; the teacher **initiates** with a question, the child **responds**, and the teacher **evaluates** their answer.

Instead of evaluating a child's response to a question: 'Yes that's right' and moving on, teachers can use children's ideas as starting points for further discussion: *What makes you say that? Can you give me an example? What do you mean by…? Would anyone else like to add to that?* This helps to develop an extended discussion in which children's ideas are explored and then different contributions are linked together to build up ideas. This process of building and connecting ideas is called 'elaboration' by linguists and also by cognitive psychologists.

Learning has emotional and social dimensions as well as the cognitive elements. If the classroom provides a safe environment in which children can express their views without fear of ridicule or of them being ignored, then the teacher is more likely to be successful in eliciting their ideas and in finding out whether understanding is shared. If children are secure, they take responsibility for checking their own understanding by asking the teacher questions: 'Do you mean that…?', or they contribute: 'Oh yes, that's like…'. Children can help to explain new ideas to each other, 'You know, it's like when…', by accessing their shared culture in a way that teachers cannot. If the class accepts that changing your ideas is part of learning, this reduces fear of 'getting it wrong' and, at the same time, this also supports the idea that scientific knowledge is tentative and open to change. In this book we provide ideas for approaches to teaching that can help teachers to develop a culture in which questioning is valued and ideas are to be explored and developed together. The teacher plays the lead role in establishing this culture, by their example and by the ways in which they interact with children. You will find these 'open-ended' and 'person-centred' openings to dialogue suggested for each topic in Sections 2, 3 and 4.

This emphasis on dialogic talk and valuing children's ideas does not mean that the scientific ideas should not be introduced or discussed, but that this should happen in relation to the children's ideas. Mortimer and Scott (2003) suggest that teaching may involve cycles of talk in which there is a focus on exploring the children's ideas, then developing their ideas by relating them to the scientific ideas, followed by more authoritative summaries of the scientific point of view, then cycling back to a focus on the children's ideas. (See case studies 1 and 2 for examples of dialogic talk for different purposes.)

The teacher encouraged the children to respond to each other's suggestions – creating an environment in which different ideas can be considered, rather than expecting everyone to agree. There is a balance to be struck here of valuing everyone's contributions while simultaneously marking all ideas as start points that could be changed. The underlying message that needs to come across is 'We all have something to contribute, and we all have something to learn'.

A feature of Case study 2 that makes it dialogic is the way that children initiate lines of discussion. Clearly the relationships within the class mean they feel comfortable in expressing their ideas. The children also listen to each other's ideas and build on them. The teacher is not always asking questions, but often takes the role of choosing who will speak from the different children who have something of their own to say – much like chairing a meeting. However, she does steer the discussion in particular directions and emphasises ideas that are in line with the ones she wants the children to learn by selecting, repeating and rephrasing them. It could be described as a 'scaffolded dialogue' (Alexander 2008, 2020) – it is not open-ended, it has a clear objective, but the children's ideas and the data are used together to get there.

CASE STUDY 1 LIVING OR NON-LIVING? EXPLORING CHILDREN'S IDEAS THROUGH DIALOGIC TALK

In this case study, we illustrate how the way a teacher began a topic helped to establish a class culture of open discussion and sharing of ideas. The class teacher's comments are shown in italics.

I wanted to find out what the children (9–10 years old, class size 37) knew about the characteristics of living things and set our topic on plants in this broader context. The children sat on the floor in a circle around a varied collection of objects, including some living plants. Initially, we classified the collection into living and non-living, and discussed some of the characteristics of living things.

The opening question was an 'invitation to participate' that had two functions. First it handed over control of the direction of the conversation to the children, and second it signalled to them their ideas were going to be explored, not tested.

Teacher: We're going to look at these things and think about whether they're living… whether they're non-living or anything else you've got to say about them to do with that. …So does anyone want to start us off? Who's got something to say? Max?

Child 1: Well Miss, if it was living, every living thing right, it has to have something to eat or to drink to live. Say like a table for instance, is non-living because it doesn't eat, it doesn't drink.

Teacher: So what about a plant then? (*Max has used the words eat and drink, which we usually associate with animals rather than plants.*)

Child 1: Well down in the soil, it's got that and they eat it through the roots.

Teacher: I see. Does anyone else want to add anything about that?

Child 2: Sometimes you can give them food, if they haven't got enough in the soil you can give them some food. (*This indicated to me there could be a widely held idea within the class that plants get their food through their roots.*)

Teacher: I see, you can actually buy something called plant food can't you? … (*Acknowledging that there was evidence to support this idea.*) Paul?

Child 3: Well another thing about how plants live, is when we breathe out oxygen, they get it, when we breathe in…carbon dioxide, they get it.

Teacher: Is that the right way round? (*A number of children had appeared to be concerned about Paul's idea and I assumed I knew why.*)

Child 4: No! No!

Teacher: Shh. I'm really glad you mentioned those two gases. (*Valuing his contribution.*) Just listen again to what you said. Donna, do you want to pick up on that? Not at the moment, we'll come back to you. Tom, do you?

Child 5: Plants take in the carbon dioxide and make it into oxygen.

Teacher: They certainly take in carbon dioxide and what they do with it, we'll think about more as we go through the term. (*Tom's response had indicated an area that would need intervention and I signalled this to them.*).

Edited extract from McMahon (2010)

The children could make distinctions between living and non-living and could identify a number of characteristics of living things. It also enabled me to identify the common alternative idea that plants get their food from the soil (rather than by photosynthesis). Some of the children had been introduced to the idea that plants use carbon dioxide and expel oxygen, but they seemed to see it as the opposite of breathing rather than being about plants making food. Although not every child had been able to express their ideas, I had begun to build up a picture of the range of ideas held by the class.

CASE STUDY 2 DO SEEDS NEED LIGHT TO GERMINATE? INTERPRETING RESULTS THROUGH DIALOGIC TALK

Discussing results of scientific enquiries with children can be challenging for teachers as they need to work with the actual results they observed, the associated 'correct' scientific explanations and the children's existing ideas all at the same time. The intention is that this extract exemplifies some aspects of dialogic talk in science and provides a start point for reflecting on practice. This transcript has been annotated by the class teacher and her comments are shown in italics.

Dishes containing ten cress seeds on moist filter paper had been placed under transparent, translucent and opaque covers. The results showed small differences between the number of seeds that germinated in each dish. We first discussed whether we thought these differences were meaningful and decided they might just be because of the odd 'dud' seed. Then I reminded the class of the prediction we had made beforehand.

Teacher: Right just have a look at that for a moment. And think back to what we were trying to find out. Did we think it mattered how much light they had? …We did didn't we?

Child 1: Yes.

Teacher: What did we predict would happen, perhaps especially to the opaque one? Ellen?

Child 2: We predicted it wouldn't grow.

Teacher: We predicted that those wouldn't grow. Because we thought, well they haven't got any light so they won't grow, they won't germinate; they won't begin to grow…Look at those results. Is that what we found? (*Here I needed to draw the children's attention back to the data, helping them to interpret it and use it to challenge their constructs.*)

Child 3: No.

Teacher: No…That's not what we found at all.

Child 4: Gasps.

Teacher: Kate?

Child 4: It might not have been a fair test, Miss. (*I was interested to hear Kate criticise the test we had carried out as a possible interpretation that would mean she wouldn't have to change her ideas.*)

The children then suggested and discussed various possible problems with the test design, for example that one container may have been close to the window.

Teacher: Mmm, it might not have been quite as accurate as we might have hoped, so that could be one explanation. Suppose it was accurate. Suppose it was a fair test. What would our results tell us? Sophie?

Child 5: That plants don't really need light that much so…

Teacher: That's what our experiment's telling us isn't it? That they don't need light that much to get started on growing, to germinate. (*Here, I have decided on an interpretation of the experiment that I consider to be the correct one. It might have been better if I had continued to treat it as tentative.*)

Child 6: They need water really.

Teacher: Just water?

Child 7: And food really. (*This was a missed opportunity to open a discussion on where seeds get their food.*)

Teacher: What do plants use the light for? (*This was a critical question in getting the children to apply their developing understanding of photosynthesis to explain what they had observed.*)

Child 8:	*Gasp.*
Teacher:	Pete?
Child 8:	To make food.
Teacher:	To make food. Is there any reason, why seeds, when they begin germinating, might not need to make food? (long pause). What do you think Carla?
Child 9:	Well, I think there's some food in there, like…
Teacher:	In where?
Child 9:	Like the seed like saves, like got a bit of food, already made like water and everything.
Teacher:	Sort of trapped inside the case?
Child 9:	Yes.

After a few more comments from the children that showed their acceptance of this idea, Tracey, a child with a statement of special educational needs for learning difficulties, made a vital connection between real life and our experimental set up:

Teacher:	Tracey, what do you want to say?
Child 10:	When you plant seeds in the ground they can't get any light.
Teacher:	And you're saying when, if they're planted in soil, they couldn't get any light could they? (pause) Oh, that's a thought. So, maybe, they don't need light to start growing, because, if you bury a seed underground, which you often do when you plant it, it doesn't get light. Good point. Polly, you've been waiting patiently.
Child 11:	In the, haven't got leaves right…you can't get light, so you can't get food.
Teacher:	Aahh, so it's because the leaves aren't really there yet doing their job, the seed has to have the food ready instead. That's a really good thought, I like that.
Child 12:	There's no need to make food yet, because the food's in the seed.

Edited extract from McMahon (2010)

In this discussion, attention is drawn to evidence that conflicts with the children's previous ideas and through the discussion an alternative idea is introduced and, after some debate, accepted. It shows how the constructivist principle of building on prior learning and making new connections might look in action. The science enquiry process in combination with dialogic talk has supported children in building new ideas. There is evidence of application of previous learning – that plants make their own food using sunlight – in this new context of seed germination. Perhaps this helps children to consolidate their conceptual understanding into a larger, more complex schema about plant growth.

Talk is essential for developing abstract concepts such as 'a solid', or 'force' or 'habitat', but must be related to practical experiences for these concepts to become meaningful. When we give explanations in science lessons, we are 'constructing entities' and 'putting meaning into matter' Ogborn et al. (1996). Educational neuroscientists Tolmie and Dündar-Coecke (2020, p. 195) explain that in later childhood 'language-based concepts become dominant and remain so, and these are often only partially accurate compared to more implicit perceptual representations and later emerging abstract models'.

There is still work to be done to understand better how through teaching we can use language to help children to build bridges between their perceptual (sensory) experiences and the abstract symbolic representations of science to develop what we believe, perhaps intuitively feel, is deep understanding.

Science capital

So far, our discussion of learning science has focused on knowledge of science concepts and processes. This isn't enough. We want children to acquire knowledge about science, but also to participate in it with confidence. This might mean becoming a scientist in the future, but it can also mean thinking scientifically in everyday life, enjoying science content on television and other media, being engaged with scientific issues that affect communities and the planet. Unfortunately, at the end of their primary education, most children see science as interesting, important and relevant, but still 'not for me' (Archer et al. 2015). Only about 15 per cent of children aspire to being a scientist. Those that do see science as being for them tend to have high levels of 'science capital' (DeWitt et al. 2016). The idea of 'Science capital' has roots in the concept of cultural capital developed by sociologist Pierre Bourdieu. Bourdieu argued that what helps people to get on in life is not just their wealth and their economic capital, but their social and cultural resources too: the people you know and the opportunities to participate in events such as concerts and art exhibitions. Science education can help to build science capital.

Your science capital includes all the science-related knowledge, attitudes, experiences and resources you build up in your life. You can imagine that having close family members who are scientists or who use science in their work would increase familiarity with science and make it something that 'people like me do'. When children are taken to a science museum, or their parents talk about a new scientific finding over dinner, this also builds science capital. Rewiring a plug or repairing a car alongside your parent might build your sense of self-efficacy in physics and engineering. Girls studying physical sciences beyond GCSE are still exceptional (Archer et al. 2017) and Black researchers in STEM subjects are significantly underrepresented (Forrester 2020). We might see science as not for us if we don't see ourselves represented among scientists. Teaching with science capital in mind involves taking a sociocultural and inclusive perspective on learning in science. Darling-Hammond et al. (2019) encapsulate this beautifully when they say that as well as considering what learners know, we must consider who they are.

Building science capital is a tool for social justice (Archer et al. 2017) and for inclusion. Teachers and schools play a key role in helping more young people see science as 'for me'. Teachers can seek to build science capital for all young people and not just assume that some groups will naturally have more. We can build opportunities for all pupils to identify with scientists through the examples of scientists we choose, and we can bring scientists into the classroom to demystify and humanise their roles (look up STEM Ambassadors). We can create opportunities for out-of-school science learning at local science centres and nature reserves. In each chapter of this book, we offer a section on 'breaking down barriers' that provides ideas and examples that are relevant to that topic.

Pedagogy – Engage, Build, Consolidate

In this section we bring together the theories of learning discussed above to consider what this means for teachers. How can we use the ideas to guide how we teach science to children in primary school?

Paul Howard-Jones and colleagues (2020) made a careful selection of the science of learning they saw as relevant for educators and linked it with social constructivist (Vygotskian) theory. They framed it around three headings: Engage, Build, Consolidate (EBC). In doing so they are very clear that the model does not tell teachers what to do, it helps us to make informed professional decisions. They also stress that all three elements can be taking place at the same time. The full version and useful videos can be found at www.scienceoflearning-ebc.org. In this book, we have created our own version of the EBC framework to help integrate and organise the ideas about teaching and learning different science topics that we present in each chapter in the book. Here we first introduce the Howard-Jones model and then explain how our version is built on it.

In the EBC model, **Engage** means that pupils are being 'caught and held in a learning opportunity' (Howard-Jones et al. 2020, p. 449). It reminds us that throughout the learning process, not just at the start, that brain processes for reasoning and memory are intertwined with those for emotional processes. Every brain is unique; which means that children differ in what engages their attention. They also differ in how well they can control and sustain their attention. Engagement is increased when 'reward networks' in the brain are stimulated with praise and tokens (such as stickers), but also by novelty and by having choices. However, there is a trade-off here, if the novelty is not related to the learning, it can be a distraction; there is a need for professional judgment. Shared attention, being engaged in the same thing as others, also increases engagement. On the negative side, fear and anxiety can reduce capacity for engagement. The classroom culture matters. It can help engagement if teachers and children understand a bit about neuroplasticity, that our brains change, and that, given effort and support, everyone can learn more. This is sometimes called having a 'growth mindset' (Dweck 2006).

The first key idea for **Build** is that we can only build on prior knowledge. Young children need more support with making connections that link new ideas to old ones than older children or adults do. 'Once a student is engaged with a learning opportunity, a channel of communication opens up, that can lead to learning', but 'much depends on the quality of that communication' (Howard-Jones n.d., spoken on Build video, www.scienceoflearning-ebc.org). So as with 'Engage', other people are important in the process of building knowledge; it is socially constructed. Talk plays an important role in mediating this bridge-building.

We all communicate our emotions, such as how we feel about science topics, often consciously, but also unconsciously, through our voices, faces and bodies. Paul Howard-Jones suggests that 'mirror neuron systems', mean that pupils unconsciously 'mirror' (at a neuronal level) how teachers feel. We have probably all experienced being inspired to learn by a teacher whose fascination with an idea comes across. (Even though we are not actually in the room with you for you to pick up cues from our faces and voices, we hope our enthusiasm for the science topics in this book is infectious!)

The initial build phase is a temporary construction in working memory networks, vulnerable to being forgotten. We need to **Consolidate** newly learned knowledge. Consolidation can help is helped by 'rehearsing', bringing it to mind and practicing it so it is automatic. Once the knowledge has been consolidated – stored in long-term memory – it is more easily retrieved and frees up working memory capacity for new learning. Consolidation is also about expressing and connecting *different representations of a concept* – so that we have multiple representations of it created through different modes such as writing, drawing, talking, acting, modelling using a variety of materials and using our bodies. Looking specifically at learning in science, 'The neuroscience account suggests that a good understanding of science requires the building of bridges…between perceptual (in the widest sense), conceptual and abstract capacities' (Tolmie and Dündar-Coecke 2020, p. 215). Having knowledge stored in different ways makes it easier to recall and to use. Applying and using new knowledge also consolidates it (Bell and Darlington 2020). Teachers have less control over this final point, but a good night's sleep also consolidates the day's learning. During 'slow wave' phases of sleep, there seem to be physical changes that distribute memories from a part of the brain called the hippocampus to a range of areas across the cortex of the brain.

Other acronyms are available! Shimamura (2018) introduces the acronym MARGE (Motivate, Attend, Relate, Generate, Evaluate) to capture his thoughts about the implications of neuroscience as principles for teaching and learning. A brief summary of this ideas is given here and it usefully recaps and draws together the discussion above. Unless we are **motivated** in some way, we are not going to **attend**. We then need to **relate** new knowledge to existing knowledge so that it becomes categorised and linked as part of our knowledge structure (or 'schemas). We **generate** stronger and new connections by repeated use and reactivation of what has been learned. Shimamura also says that we should **evaluate** how well we have learned something – this reflection on our own learning is sometimes called metacognition.

The EBC model takes a Vygotskian constructivist approach by taking into account the social and emotional processes involved in learning. Following this lead, we have developed our own version of EBC for primary science to structure the parts of each chapter in Sections 2, 3 and 4. We have interwoven this cognitive neuroscience account of learning with what we know from educational research in general, and science education research in particular, and taken sociocultural perspectives into account too.

> **ENGAGE BUILD CONSOLIDATE FOR PRIMARY SCIENCE**
>
> **Engage**
>
> *Situating the topic*
>
> Plan engaging contexts, consider cross-curricular contexts and outdoor learning, think about motivation to engage and hold children's attention, such as surprises related to the topic.
>
> *Breaking down barriers*
>
> Be oriented to social justice and inclusion, e.g. take antiracist, antisexist, non-binary approaches. Use diverse examples of scientists for the topic. Be aware of disabilities and neurodiversity. Consider children's different starting points and the science capital the local community might bring to the topic.
>
> *Activating Children's ideas*
>
> What might pupils bring to the topic? Use strategies for eliciting children's existing ideas. Find out about their experiences and interests in relation to the topic.
>
> **Build**
>
> *Constructing new knowledge*
>
> What topic-specific strategies could build children's understanding? How might these be adapted for different learners?
>
> *Working scientifically*
>
> Some kinds of science enquiry are particularly pertinent for some topics. What practical work might be relevant and purposeful for this topic?
>
> *Monitoring and feedback*
>
> Identify suitable strategies for formative assessment and feedback.
>
> **Consolidate**
>
> *Retrieving*
>
> What strategies could be used for retrieving and rehearsing new knowledge?
>
> *Applying*
>
> How might new knowledge be built into complex schemas by extending and elaborating it? Are there opportunities for applying understanding in this topic to action on environmental sustainability?
>
> *Reviewing*
>
> How can we support pupil metacognition and also make summative assessment judgments?

Engage

Situating the topic

Perhaps the most important part of any teaching is getting the topic and each lesson underway in a positive, engaging way. Piagetian principles (Slavin 2005) that inform constructivist and 'child-centred' education include the recognition of the crucial role of children's self-initiated, active involvement in learning activities. In its purest form, to be 'child-centred' means to encourage children to discover themselves through spontaneous interaction with the environment. However, teachers are also required to teach a curriculum, so they are faced with the challenge of engaging children with topics that do not arise 'spontaneously'. Skilful teachers will capture the attention and the curiosity of their pupils and motivate them to learn.

A process of introduction, setting the scene, of putting the topic into a meaningful context and of engaging the children's interest is needed. It is a regular part of primary classroom practice in many subjects and is likely to involve the whole class. This orientation involves a provocation for learning that the teacher introduces; reading a story, exploring a collection or discussing a local event or it might be a response to something that the children have initiated. There are opportunities for talk as children share their perspectives on a topic or relate it to their interests. For example, in a topic called 'Clothes we wear' (planned to address understanding of properties of materials), children could watch a short video clip of children doing an activity such as riding a bike and be asked what activities they enjoy and what clothes they would wear to do it. Children could discuss the clothes they wear to school and think about why different clothes are worn for different purposes. One challenge here for the teacher is to be mindful of the objectives they have for the scientific learning and choose their questions carefully, so that the discussions don't stray too far – children are experts at 'side-tracking' any discussion.

Breaking down barriers

Consider children's different starting points and the science capital the local community might bring to the topic. The whole class can benefit from the breadth of ideas and questions that different children might bring. Think about how children might see themselves in relation to that topic and actively challenge stereotypes. For example, given the frequent stereotyping of children's bedrooms (rockets and stars for boys, flowers for girls), careful selection of images for the classroom wall and slide presentations would help to draw children in, rather than alienate them from the outset. Children like to feel part of things, that they have something to contribute and that the topic is meaningful for them. Planning a thoughtful orientation with time for the children to respond by talking together can help to establish a shared commitment to the topic for the class.

Might there be people in the community with relevant expertise who could be invited to talk about what they do? Perhaps a parent would come in to talk about managing a textile factory, or about the pros and cons of different kinds of nappies. Again, you can look for opportunities to challenge common stereotypes. (Who invented disposable nappies and why? Are they a good thing?)

Choose your examples in a way that avoids stereotypes and actively introduces a diverse range of people in a diverse range of roles. In each chapter of this book, we offer examples of relevant scientists you can draw on. The webpages of the science4everyone project and Primary Science Teaching Trust's 'A scientist just like me' provide examples of scientists and people in science-related roles. On the 'A scientist just like me' pages, in addition to explaining their job each scientist notes personal details such as any disabilities, their gender, ethnic ancestry and sexual orientation. The site also provides useful checklists to help challenge our own biases and build the 'science capital' of all children.

Think about the neurodiversity of your class; some noisy, busy activities might be overwhelming for some children, and you may need to make adjustments. In this section of the following chapters, we consider disabilities that you might need to take into account to provide access to the topic, such as hearing disability in the topic of sound, and take a positive approach to what such differences can contribute to the learning of the class.

Activating children's ideas

Elicitation is the powerful process of finding out children's existing ideas. In 1968 an eminent psychologist David Ausubel wrote: 'The most important single factor influencing learning is what the learner already knows. Ascertain this and teach him accordingly (Ausubel 1968, p. vi).

This famous quote has influenced science educators and researchers ever since. For the twenty-first-century teacher, this means gaining an insight into the child's current understanding of the concept(s), so as to adapt their teaching. Essentially, this is a process of assessment (more of this below), which is seen as an integral part of constructivist learning. For the child, it is a process of becoming aware of their own ideas, of making them tangible, of 'activating' them. This is the start of developing and possibly changing their ideas by making new connections. Visualising learning as a process of making connections between neurons helps us to see that this stage is essential. We have seen above how thought and talk are closely associated. Through talking and (importantly) listening, children may begin to be aware that others have somewhat different ideas or that they cannot explain something to their own satisfaction. Recording these ideas may be part of the process of clarifying them and may be useful for both teacher and children to reflect on later. Different topic areas lend themselves to different ways of finding out and recording children's existing ideas, and these are known in science education as 'elicitation strategies'. In Section 5 you will find them discussed in detail.

Eliciting children's ideas is important at the start of a topic or unit of work as it can then inform medium-term planning for the class as a whole and identify groups or individuals who may need additional support or extension. However, it is not only for the start of the topic: it is important that teachers continue to provide children with opportunities to express their developing knowledge, and the elicitation strategies can be used at any point as part of monitoring for formative assessment. They can also be used at the end of a topic so the children can think about what they have learned. In this way, the elicitation is linked with review and 'metacognition'. Reviewing can take place at any point in a teaching sequence; it is a good idea to build in frequent opportunities for children to reflect on their ideas. In this book we support the use of elicitation strategies to help teachers gain insights into children's minds as an integral and ongoing part of their practice, rather than a one-off event at the start of a topic.

By seeing the activation of ideas as a collaborative rather than solely individual activity, a variety of ideas and views are made available on the social plane of the classroom for children to consider (McMahon 2012). The process of elicitation can be seen as creating a shared pool of different ideas and experiences providing a rich starting point for everyone to learn from. Owning a range of ideas as a class might enable those ideas to be examined more critically – it is not a person being examined, it is the idea.

In each chapter we explore relevant elicitation strategies, and exemplify them. Many of the strategies can usefully be applied in a range of conceptual areas but, by exploring the benefits of each elicitation strategy for certain purposes, we hope that teachers will be able to make informed choices about which to use when.

Build

Constructing new knowledge

Having elicited children's ideas, the teacher can then decide how to help move the children's understanding forwards. Of course, different children in the class will have different starting points, and meeting the needs of the whole class can be quite challenging. Some may need to extend and develop existing ideas, others may have alternative ideas that need to be challenged and new ideas introduced. Sometimes children's alternative ideas can be very resistant to change, as they keep hold of ideas that make sense to them, and a range of different teaching strategies may be needed to help the children learn the scientific version. This intervention is an active process for the teacher, requiring careful analysis of the children's ideas and selection of appropriate kinds of activities.

Working scientifically

Cognitive neuroscience suggests that experience through a range of different 'modalities', or senses, can help to build a rich scientific concept because neurons in different parts of the brain are activated and connections made between them. Practical work offers opportunities for children to touch, to smell, to hear and (with the right safety precautions) even to taste as well as to see. If we want children to connect these sensory experiences to build meaningful concepts, they need to be 'minds-on' as well as 'hands on'. In a social constructivist approach, an important intervention is to encourage children to test their ideas through the processes of scientific enquiry to extend, develop or replace them. This is not suggesting that children can 'discover' what has taken thousands of years of experimentation and thinking. However, they *can* create more local knowledge (which is the grippiest trainer, which part of the school garden is best for growing courgettes?). The role of the teacher is crucial in helping to identify productive lines of enquiry and in making sure that children understand the relationship between their own ideas and any activities. To do this the teacher needs not only to know what the child's ideas are, but also to have an understanding of the thinking behind them. A child may say that a toy car eventually stops rolling along the floor because it has 'run out of energy', and then through exploring how different surfaces affect how the car travels, develop their understanding of the role of friction in slowing the car down. Building new ideas involves effortful processes – controlling attention and manipulating information in 'working memory'.

Taking a socio-cultural view, the process of building and rebuilding ideas could be seen as a collaborative gathering of relevant experience and sources of evidence and a communal evaluation of the possibilities. It mirrors the view of scientists, not as brilliant loners, but as a community with a collective responsibility to criticise each other's interpretations of data, to look for exceptions to rules and to find the best possible explanations.

Practical work may not always be in the form of a full investigation (see Table 1.1 for a summary of alternatives). Teachers can plan activities with a purpose in mind. For example, first-hand observation of their teeth might be combined with the teacher raising a question about why food needs to be broken into smaller bits. Children might go on to research different kinds of teeth (Do birds have teeth? Are snake fangs teeth? Has everyone still got their baby teeth?).

Practical work can be engaging and fun, but concerns have been raised that it does not always support learning in the way that teachers might expect (Bianchi et al. 2021, Ofsted 2021). Children's attention may not always be on what we see as the most important or 'salient' feature and we may need to use talk to help direct children's attention. For example, demonstrating a bicarbonate of soda 'volcano' might be dramatic and may seem to encourage shared attention, but what are the children learning from it? If it is being used to provide examples of solids, liquids and gases, is that what the children remember about it? In response to these concerns, there has recently been a renewed emphasis on *'purposeful practicals'*: making sure that practical activity is well planned with clear aims and that teachers know how it fits into a sequence of learning activities.

Other forms of intervention do not directly involve scientific enquiries. Ideas may be based on colloquial use of language such as a sign on a shop door saying 'No animals allowed here'. Discussion about what people mean by the term animal would be helpful in this case. Ideas may be based on limited experience, for example, 'our food goes into our tummies and then into our arms and legs' in which case evidence such as models and drawings of what is inside our bodies

Table 1.1 Types of scientific enquiry

Type of enquiry	Explanation	Examples
Observing	Observe, sometimes over a period of time (observation includes all senses), possibly using cameras/digital/data logging equipment to record the observations or to take measurements.	Study of the changes that occur to a habitat over a period of time, observing what happens when an ice cube is left on the windowsill.
Classifying, identifying and grouping	Examine the similarities and differences between objects, organisms and phenomena. Name the item, put it in a pre-existing category or create groups and categories. This may be part of another enquiry or an end in itself. Classifying and identifying can be the starting point for generating hypotheses and making creative links between aspects of phenomena.	Deciding what different objects are made from. Noting characteristics of animals that live in desert environments could lead to ideas about how they survive. Noticing that some objects let light pass through, and others do not.
Comparisons and fair testing (controlled investigations)	Examine the properties or behaviours of two or more similar things in a systematic way. Answer a question by carrying out an enquiry by altering one variable (factor) and observing or measuring the effect while keeping other variables (factors) the same. This is appropriate when it is possible (and ethical) to control the different variables and when the purpose of the enquiry is to explore relationships between the variables.	*Do two pet dogs eat the same type and amount of food? Why might there be a difference?* *Is it true that the hotter the water, the faster the sugar dissolves?*
Pattern-seeking	Answer a question by conducting a survey or a keep a record of lots of examples and look for patterns in the data collected. This is particularly appropriate when variables cannot be controlled, such as when investigating living things. The outcomes are often descriptive, and may describe correlations, but provide weaker evidence for establishing a cause-and-effect relationship.	*Are there fewer different kinds of plants living under trees than in the hedgerows?* *Do people with the longest arms also have the widest handspans?*
Problem solving	Make something or design a system to solve a problem. This approach has overlaps with design and technology; sometimes by applying our understanding in a problem-solving context, the limits of the understanding are pushed, and the process might stimulate further exploration	Design a switch to go into an electrical circuit. Designing a 'magnetic fishing game' could develop children's understanding of which materials are magnetic and which are not, and about the differing strengths of magnets.
Research using secondary sources	Find a secondary source of information to answer the question: a book, a person or a website. This involves making a judgement about the reliability of the source and possibly looking for different versions and explanations. Older children can find out about some of the historical stories associated with scientific discovery	*Mr. Lucas said that a spider isn't an animal – how can we check?* *Why did the dinosaurs die out?* *Is the space station bigger than a comet?* *When and how did we discover the Earth isn't flat and that it orbits the Sun?* *Why do people think Darwin is an important scientist?*

and alternative ideas about what happens to food could be introduced. Challenges to existing ideas might come from various sources: other children, books, videos, visits, visitors or the teacher – *'The way I see it is that…Does that make any sense to you?'*. The use of models and analogies can be very helpful in discussing ideas that are not immediately accessible to children.

Monitoring and feedback

A great feature of teaching science is that some feedback to the learners comes directly from the outcomes of enquiry. For example, children might be surprised to find that a magnet doesn't pick up a copper coin or when they find out from their research that an octopus has three hearts. Neuroscientist Micheal Thomas explains that human brains are 'wired' for noticing when things are not as we expected (have a look at his webpages How the Brain Works). We can imagine how being alert to differences in our environment would be an advantage in evolution of the brain:

> predictions optimise the brain to learn from when its predictions are wrong. Surprise is a powerful teacher. Curiosity and exploration are about playing with the world, poking it, seeing if it responds in the way you expect, and learning when it doesn't.
>
> (Thomas n.d.)

One of the reasons that teaching can be tiring is that teachers are constantly alert during lessons, noticing what children are doing and making assessments 'on the fly' (Harrison et al. 2018). It is quite easy for that to slip into monitoring of behaviour rather than of science learning, especially in a busy practical lesson, and it helps teachers focus to their own attention if they have thought in advance about what they are going to be looking out for. Just like children, our attention is limited, and we need to focus on what matters. To help with this the Teacher Assessment in Primary Science (TAPS) project has developed 'focused assessment' activities freely available online that suggest key points to look out for and give examples of what these might look for in practice (McMahon 2018).

Neuroscientist Stanislas Dehaene (2020) set out his four pillars of learning: attention, active engagement, consolidation (these may seem very familiar now) and error feedback. He carefully points out that error feedback does not mean punishing mistakes and that grades are often demotivating. Instead he emphasises regular self-testing. For example children could be given a set of five cards with key vocabulary for a science topic on them and children could look at each in turn, doing their best to explain each word, and sorting the cards as then go into words they can define with confidence and those they are not sure about. The TAPS project provides examples of pupil self-assessment and approaches to peer feedback in primary science and some of these will be given in the following chapters.

Of course much of the feedback to pupils in school comes from their teacher, and to provide useful feedback, teachers need to make insightful judgments about their pupils' understanding and skills. Again the TAPS project is a great source of strategies for doing this 'formative assessment'. More about different kinds of assessment is explained in a later section.

Consolidate

Retrieve

For learning to be retained in long-term memory it must be actively retrieved and rehearsed over time to consolidate it (Howard-Jones et al. 2020). Cognitive psychology has found that the strategy called 'retrieval practice' strengthens the long-term memory of knowledge. Retrieval practice involves recalling information from memory; psychology experiments have shown that retrieval is more successful than other revision strategies such as reading the same information again (e.g. Karpicke et al. 2014). It can feel hard – perhaps many of us have experienced this in our revision for exams – it is less effort to highlight some key words instead of closing the book and creating a mind map. Retrieval should involve effort, but not be stressful – there is an optimum level of 'desirable difficulty'. It has been widely adopted in primary classrooms in the form of low stakes quizzes but could involve using a variety of strategies to recall information from memory, for example using flash cards, practice tests, or mind-mapping. However, in spite of this being a very robust finding in the laboratory, there is much less evidence that this effect is as strong in real classrooms (Perry et al. 2021). We need to adopt thoughtful approaches to setting up retrieval practice drawing on our wider professional knowledge of children's learning.

The current popularity of retrieval practice is also due to an emphasis on the long-term retention of knowledge in English education policy. Knowing some things so well that recalling them requires very little effort (known as 'automaticity') is clearly sometimes very useful, such as knowing your times tables in maths. However, we are concerned that it could overemphasise recall of facts over understanding. We want children to be consolidating their understanding of concepts by elaborating them with detail and examples and then we want them to be organising these rich concepts in complex schema that connect with prior learning. (We have high expectations!) The authors have been developing strategies to do this in the 'Rich Retrieval' project.

A metaphor for the value of rehearsal is how pathways are worn across a grass field or park simply by people walking them again and again. Those pathways are often convenient shortcuts (known as 'desire lines') rather than the route the park designers would want us to take, and the metaphor is helpful here as we want to set up mental habits of going the right way! Retrieving knowledge could be recalling the same thing again and again – what we might call 'rote learning'. Although there might be satisfaction in getting better at recalling a particular chunk of knowledge or performing a skill, it could also become boring for many children.

The retrieval of a memory is not the same as opening a file on a computer – rather than opening an existing copy, the memory is 'reconstructed'; the many connections between neurons are activated again. And because memory is reconstructive, when a memory is retrieved it can be changed by making new connections. So, as teachers we may decide to provoke this during the process of retrieval so that new connections are made. This process could be called elaboration.

However, there is evidence to suggest strongly held original ideas are not easily 'rewired' and that instead we need to learn to suppress the 'wrong' ideas and activate the 'correct' scientific view. You might have heard children doing this: 'a whale is a fish, oh, no – actually it's a mammal'; 'a tomato is a vegetable – no wait, it's actually a fruit as it has seeds'. The 'Stop and think' project (Bell et al. 2021) developed a computer programme to help children to get better at doing this inhibiting their old ideas.

Shimamura recommends a range of teaching and learning strategies: Categorise, Compare, Contrast, Talk (tell someone, ask how and why questions) and creating stories, metaphors and analogies. We can use these to support a rich form of retrieval practice. For example, we might want children to learn about different parts of a flower (petal, sepal, stamen, stigma). We can set up a quick retrieval practice by putting on the board the same image they encountered when the words were first introduced and asking the children to recall them. If we wanted to go beyond retrieval and extend their ideas, we might put up images of two different flowers and invite the children to compare and contrast them, encouraging them to use their science vocabulary as they do so (McMahon 2022). In this example children would be both rehearsing and extending their knowledge: a stamen can look a bit different in different flowers, we know it is the stamen because it's got pollen on it. In this way the idea of 'a stamen' becomes elaborated. This broader idea of what a stamen is also helps to make it more transferable to different contexts, to identify the stamen on different plants, which is a more useful concept. This more generalised idea of what a stamen is (the male bit of a flower that makes pollen) makes it easier for children to *apply* their knowledge (Figure 1.2).

Compare and Contrast

yellow poppy

apple blossom

Figure 1.2 An example of Rich Retrieval: Comparing and contrasting flowers.

Apply

Children need to use new ideas in different contexts to take ownership of them and to be secure in their understanding of them. Also, they need to see the value of the new ideas, or they are likely to revert to previously useful ways of thinking. Applying learning in new contexts can be really challenging (cognitive psychologists call it the problem of transference), but it's also is a key aim of science education. We want children to be confident that they can make use of their science knowledge in their lives beyond school. Bell and Darlington (2020) argue that it is important to see application as a distinct aspect of consolidating learning.

Cross-curricular work may be a rich source of contexts for application. Designing and making provides many opportunities to apply scientific ideas. Children can be presented with problems to solve using their new understanding, such as working out how to separate out rubbish for recycling using their knowledge of the properties of materials or how to create a shadow-puppet show. Sometimes ideas developed in one science topic can be applied in another – a child might draw on their understanding from a topic on light to suggest using transparent, translucent and opaque materials to cover germinating seedlings to test the effect of different amounts of light on how they germinate. A class culture that values children's ideas and sees them as relevant can also help them to make connections between ideas rather than compartmentalise different aspects of their learning. In response to the climate crisis, in this book we are considering how scientific knowledge might be applied in the context of understanding local and global challenges and taking positive action.

Taking a Vygotskian view of learning, Mortimer and Scott (2003) suggest that there are three stages of 'appropriation'. In stage 1, children see new ideas as belonging to others as the teacher opens up the topic, explores the pupils' views and introduces the scientific version. In stage 2, as the teacher guides them to work with the new ideas and supports their internalisation of it, the children see the idea as half belonging to others and half belonging to them. Finally, in stage 3, the teacher guides children to apply the scientific view and 'hands-over' responsibility for its use: the children see the idea as fully their own. These three stages map very well onto the Engage Build Consolidate model we are presenting here.

In each chapter we suggest opportunities for applying understanding in that topic. For example, we might think about making connections between learning and environmental sustainability (with links to UN Sustainable Development Goals).

Review

Reviewing is sometimes seen as what is done at the end of an activity but can be a much more continuous process. A better way of seeing review might be as part of the ongoing dialogue with and between children about their ideas. This thinking about thinking, or metacognition, is an important theme of other approaches to learning in science such as CASE (Cognitive Acceleration in Science Education, more details in Section 3). In science children can both think about how their ideas might be different now from ones they held previously, and how the change in their ideas came about. 'I used to think this and now I think this because…' Teachers might also talk about what they have learned. This is an important time for teachers to help children make the link between ideas and evidence and how scientific knowledge is continually changing. Part of progression in learning science is moving from personal knowledge to shared knowledge (Harlen and Qualter 2018). The process of reviewing ideas collectively enables the class to decide which ideas are particularly significant and give them the special status of shared knowledge. However, time for individuals to reflect on their personal learning is also important.

In a summary based on a review of research evidence Muijs and Bokhove (2020) metacognition is seen as a higher-order process that supports self-regulated learning such as maintaining attention and motivation. So, we could say that it involves what learners do with the feedback they receive; do they say to themselves, 'Yep, I'm rubbish at that', or do can they see not only what could be developed but have an idea of how they might do that. And are they motivated (engaged) to keep working at it? This is a good place to note again that Engage, Build and Consolidate do not happen in a neat sequence, but are intertwined.

Teachers also need to review pupils' learning, making assessment judgements so they can reflect on what teaching strategies did and didn't work so well and what learning activities need to be planned next. Teachers also have to make summative assessment judgments to report and record pupil learning at the end of topic, and it is under this heading 'review' that we offer support on this for the science topic in each chapter.

In Sections 2, 3 and 4 of this book, we will use this 'EBC' model – Engage, Build Consolidate – for Primary science to help structure how we share and exemplifying different teaching approaches as relevant to each science topic.

CONSTRUCTIVISM – A CRITICAL EXAMINATION

Undoubtedly, theories that draw on 'constructivism' have hugely influenced science education in the UK and around the world. Almost as soon as science education began to be influenced by these ideas that emerged from psychology cognitive learning theory, there have been debates about its relevance and usefulness. It has been argued (Matthews 1998) that constructivism necessarily involves considerations of philosophy because the consideration of how new and valid knowledge is generated is an epistemological one. Furthermore, there are many varieties of constructivism – educational, sociological, philosophical, each associated with different perspectives and stances – but science educators have not resolved some deep questions about the validity of claims made. We can't go into the nuanced and complex arguments in this book but do wish to alert the reader that the 'pedagogical constructivism' that we explore here has its critics and indeed ought to be challenged. The central questions that Matthews and many others since have posed is this: How can we reconcile the notion of enabling and permitting children to explore their own ideas and come to their own conclusions (because we believe knowledge is constructed by the individual) when those conclusions may be erroneous or very different to the established body of scientific knowledge (which exists independent of the individual)? Is it not true that at some point, teachers will have to tell children the right answers? Is to pretend otherwise to put teachers in an impossible situation? These questions arise because there is arguably an erroneous connection between two fields of study – epistemology and psychology – that understand constructivism in differing ways. Matthews (1998) believes educators largely ignore the deeper issues and mistakenly continue to promote 'constructivist teaching'. The debate still rages in academic circles, but we cannot ignore the fact that educators still find constructivism to be a powerful guide to pedagogy.

The recent emphasis on memory-based views of learning from cognitive psychology has led to the reemergence of a critique of some constructivist-based approaches to teaching. Kirschner et al. (2006) argue that problem solving approaches and 'inquiry-based instruction' places a huge burden on working memory leading to 'cognitive overload' and a lack of learning. What we do not advocate in this book is what might be described as 'minimal instruction' or 'discovery learning' where the teacher's main role is to stand back and watch children learn. Constructivist pedagogy values 'hands-on experience' but that does not mean that scientific concepts emerge neatly and inevitably from those experiences; there is a difference between first-hand experience of phenomena and the human explanations for it. Often the human explanations involve an act of imagination. For example, children might be able to see that sugar dissolves faster in warm water than cold water, but the reason for this does not emerge from the practical enquiry. The current human interpretations and explanations can only be found through social and cultural interactions – with people, books, the internet and so on. This is because the ideas are not in the 'stuff', the ideas are held by people. This is consistent with the social constructivist view proposed by Jerry Bruner:

> The Vygotskian project [is] to find the manner in which aspirant members of a culture learn from their tutors, the vicars of their culture, how to understand the world. That world is a symbolic world in the sense that it consists of conceptually organised, rule bound belief systems about what exists, about how to get to goals, about what is to be valued. There is no way, none, in which a human being could possibly master that world without the aid and assistance of others for, in fact, that world is others.
>
> (Bruner 1985, p. 32)

We do recognise that a teacher has many roles during teaching, and we discuss these throughout. We have already highlighted the importance of talk. It is during discussion, questioning and dialogue that teachers should challenge children's thinking, present relevant evidence to them and promote critical thinking. Again, this is consistent with the social constructivist view, expressed succinctly by Rosalind Driver and colleagues:

> The view that scientific knowledge is socially constructed, validated, and communicated is central to this article. We have presented a perspective on science learning as a process of enculturation rather than discovery, arguing that empirical study of the natural world will not reveal scientific knowledge because scientific knowledge is discursive in nature.
>
> (Driver et al. 1994, p. 11)

> However, there are other challenges to this social constructivist viewpoint, such as that from new materialist, post human perspectives that don't accept a simple division between the human mind and the material world. From this perspective, knowledge is in a continual state of 'becoming' in the changing interaction between the material and the human and children's 'knowing is enacted at once through talk and materials' as they engage in creative scientific enquiry (Digby 2023, p. 127). These theories are not easy to understand, but it is good to have a sense that these matters are not easily resolved and academics continue to debate them.

Assessment and feedback

Assessment is an integral part of learning and teaching and will be discussed and exemplified throughout this book. Neuroscientist Stanislas Dehaene sees feedback as one of four pillars of learning; he explains that brains have inherent systems for comparing our predictions with feedback and using this to modify our internal models of the world. Much of this happens naturally as we live – we push on a door using a force we expect to open it and find it is stiff, so we push harder, and so next time we come to open a similar door we are better prepared. In education this natural learning from feedback happens all the time, but we also formalise it in our assessment processes. School assessment operates in the space between individual learning and the social expectations of what should be learned. There has been considerable research, discussion and debate about assessment in the education world for many years, with practice heavily influenced by accountability measures. In this book, we propose that consideration of the purpose of assessment will help the practitioner navigate this complex area. In the design and carrying out of assessments we should always bear in mind these questions: 'Why are we assessing?', 'What are we going to do with the information gained', 'What will the impact of assessment be on the learner?'

Assessment comes in many forms: tests, quizzes, discussion, observations, practical tasks, group work, presentations and so on. It can be carried out during everyday classroom activity (teacher assessment) or by conducting externally prepared testing (such as national tests or exams). Teacher assessment could have summative or formative purposes. For example, a quiz could be used at the end of a unit of work to 'sum up' the knowledge a child has retained from a month of science learning. The same quiz could be used at the start of a unit to elicit the knowledge that exists across the class on a new topic and inform a teacher's subsequent plans and approaches to further classwork (formative use or Assessment for Learning (AfL)). We can also see assessment as learning. Another purpose for that same quiz could be 'retrieval practice' for consolidating children's knowledge.

We can view the teacher assessment as a process that begins with the collection of data or evidence. As a teacher interacts with her pupils, she will gather information about what they say, what they can do, how much help they need, where they are struggling, what they can explain with ease. These data are usually stored either in the head of the teacher or elsewhere – in the child's book, in a notebook, in electronic form as text, photos, video or sound clips. Of course, not everything a child says, does, draws or writes will be stored or captured. In most cases, this will rely upon teachers' professional judgement. We will discuss throughout the book some of the strategies that teachers use to catch significant moments. The next phase of the process is to examine the data for useful information. Again, professional judgement is required, although it also may involve the judgement of colleagues and of the children themselves. In all probability, the analysis will be used to inform further learning and teaching and therefore perform a formative function. Harlen (2012) recommended that the rich formative assessment data collected by teachers in ongoing classroom work should also be used to serve summative purposes (more of this in Section 5).

Teaching science: theory and practice

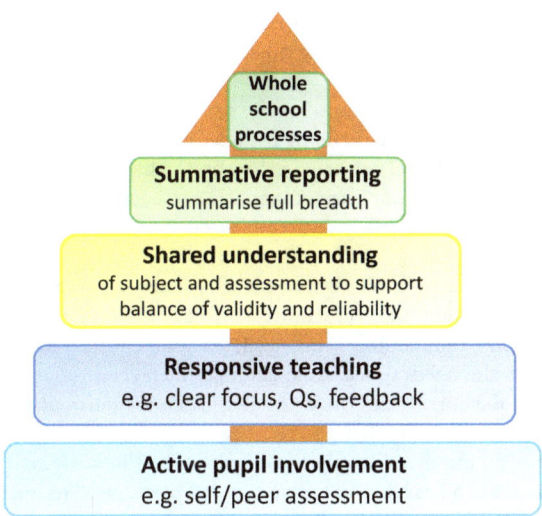

Figure 1.3 Teacher Assessment in Primary Science (TAPS).

The authors of this book have been conducting a major Teacher Assessment in Primary Science (TAPS) project based at Bath Spa University and funded by the Primary Science Teaching Trust (PSTT). One of the outcomes of this project is a pyramid-shaped framework to support teachers in implementing a valid, reliable and manageable assessment system that values teacher assessment. The 'formative to summative' model proposes that, with a shared understanding of progression, outcomes from classroom activities can be used both formatively to support learning and to inform later summative judgements (Earle 2021). The model aims for pupils to be active in their learning (e.g. being clear about what they are learning and using self/peer assessment) and for teachers to be responsive (e.g. adapting the activities to respond to the needs of the learners). It is summarised in Figure 1.3 and discussed further in chapter 5.

Figure 1.3 shows that teachers *and pupils* have important roles in assessment. For example, pupils are responsible for revealing their own thinking and advancing their learning by acting on feedback. This notion is consistent with constructivist theory that claims that individuals construct their own meaning (von Glaserfeld 1995) and neuroconstructivist views of how the brain works (Tolmie and Dündar-Coecke 2020). Teachers' responsibilities include the need to plan opportunities for children to reveal what they know and can do and to use assessment to adapt the pace, challenge and content of the lesson.

Planning sequences of lessons

The teacher (in most cases) has a curriculum to follow and targets to meet. However prescribed curricula still offer children and teachers room for manoeuvre, and teachers can be experts in transforming the prescribed through negotiation with their class to creating a relevant and motivating curriculum (McMahon et al. 2016). Teachers are professionals with judgement and creativity. It is in the space between 'prescribed' curriculum (what children *ought* to learn, as defined by the adults in charge) and the 'wished for' curriculum (what children would like to learn) that we see as the opportunity for a 'creative' curriculum. So, when planning a sequence of lessons, (sometimes called 'medium term planning') is an important moment in which teachers stop and think about what really matters; why is this content worth learning for these children? At this point they can think about what contexts might make it meaningful and relevant to their class and how to make the curriculum accessible and inclusive for the individuals in it.

However, an understandable desire to choose activities which look 'fun', can lead to a collection of experiences that lack clear learning outcomes and don't build on each other in a coherent way. According to Ofsted:

> A high-quality science curriculum is organised to ensure all pupils learn extensive and connected knowledge of substantive concepts. These concepts are developed over many years, during which pupils learn content that is sequenced in a logical order.
>
> (Ofsted 2023)

So, it is important for teachers to think about what science has come before and what will come afterwards. And it is not only the 'substantive concepts' (such knowledge of habitats or electric circuits) that needs to be thoughtfully sequenced, we want children to progress in how they work scientifically, and this also needs thoughtful planning, often across science topics. As most primary teachers teach across the curriculum, they can also plan cross-curricular opportunities to build on other learning, for example by applying measuring skills learned in maths.

Medium-term planning may identify focus points fixed in advance, such as planned visits or motivating endpoints like an exhibition for parents. It is also a good moment to check and consider what resources are available to support the topic, as well as materials, these could be human too! Siraj-Blatchford et al. (2002) also acknowledge that a teacher will engage in 'pedagogical framing' that is all the 'behind-the-scenes' work including provision of materials, arrangement of space, time and resources. This too will make a significant contribution to the success of the subsequent lessons.

Schools sometimes buy in schemes that can help with this, and there are also online resources designed by expert science educators such as the freely available PLAN matrices for the English National curriculum. We recommend that when using resources designed by someone else that teachers take the time to make sense of them for themselves and to adapt them for your own class. Children will respond better if they feel that you have taken ownership of it and it will be more satisfying. In this book we intend to help teachers develop a repertoire of possible pedagogical interventions to choose from and to support them in finding their own creative responses to children's needs.

So, medium-term lesson plans need to be seen as a framework that sets out key learning objectives and possible pathways and activities that might support children's learning, but these need to be changed, developed, amended, removed or added to in response to the children. Beginning a topic by engaging children with orientation activities and elicitation of children's existing ideas establishes a context and starting point before going on to build and then consolidate new learning. Although Howard-Jones et al. (2020) note that every episode of learning, however short or long, will involve all three elements of 'Engage, build and consolidate', Bell and Darlington (2020, p. 518) suggest that there will be shifts in emphasis over time with engagement being strongest at the start, building in the middle and consolidation and application being more prominent near the end of an episode of learning.

Opportunities for focused assessment should be identified at the medium-term planning stage. For example, the topic may present opportunities to develop and assess certain aspects or types of scientific enquiry. Being aware in advance of what resources are available or need to be prepared is also important.

Focused assessment as a strategy for making a detailed assessment of one or two aspects of scientific enquiry at a time, within the context of a whole investigation (McMahon 2018). This means that assessing the full range of children's science enquiry skills and understanding of science processes becomes more manageable with a whole class. Specific areas for development can be identified and subsequent teaching can take this into account – the assessment is formative.

Teachers in the Improving Science Together project (Davies and McMahon 2004) found that carrying out these focused assessments helped them to develop their own understanding of progression in scientific enquiry and that they can also contribute to an ongoing summative record of children's attainment in scientific enquiry. The TAPS project has produced plans and examples of focused assessments, and these are available on the Primary Science Teaching Trust (PSTT) website. Key questions are listed on the plans to support discussion with the children and assessment indicators suggest the kind of responses the children may have to the activity to help compare progress with national expectations.

Such focused assessment should ideally occur about two-thirds of the way through a topic – far enough that the children have had the opportunity to develop their understanding and skills, but not right at the end of the topic so that there is still time to act on the assessment information. The elements of scientific enquiry to focus on are chosen according to the planned emphasis of the unit and activity. During the lesson children may well be involved in aspects of scientific inquiry that are not the focus (e.g. if the focus is on interpreting data), the children may also have discussed how to carry out the enquiry and used their measuring skills to collect data, but the learning objectives and recording of assessment are focused on certain aspects of the investigation. Teachers using this approach are planning so that over the course of a year each element of scientific enquiry is the focus for an assessment. If these focused assessments are used to form part of a summative record of the children's attainment, then they should be considered alongside other teacher assessment information such as (informal) observations during everyday teaching.

Planning lessons

A concern with focus is also necessary when planning lessons 'from scratch'. A lesson plan needs to identify a particular learning objective or objectives. This will be linked to the medium-term plan but will also depend on ongoing assessment of the children's understanding and skills. The objective will help inform the teacher's decisions about how the lesson will be structured. Science lessons may have a distinct beginning, middle and end, but the lesson structure and timing can be varied and need not follow a prescribed format.

It is a good idea for science lessons to have a clear beginning that engages the children's interest and attention, maybe by looking at an unfamiliar object or image, or posing a question. Links can be made to previous learning. This could take the form of a short retrieval activity with the dual purpose of consolidating previous learning and activating it ready to make new connections with it. The teacher might provide the children with feedback on the last lesson and discuss the new learning objectives. Often there may be one learning objective that has a conceptual content and one that is more concerned with process skills. Including a learning objective concerned with scientific attitudes would help children to understand what kinds of thinking and behaviour help them to 'be scientists'. Some examples of learning objectives are set out below:

- 'At the end of today's lesson, I will be asking you to tell me what a seed needs to germinate.'
- 'When we are doing practical work today, I will be looking for children who notice something about the plant (that no one else has observed).'
- 'I am now looking for children who show they are curious by asking questions about this collection.'

Watson et al. (2000) stress the importance of ensuring that children understand the lesson's purpose and revisiting it. However, this should be done in such a way as to retain the spirit of enquiry and be open to unforeseen possibilities.

The middle section of a lesson can be hugely varied: children may be working independently or in groups for most of the time, or there may be short bursts of activity and group discussion interspersed with frequent whole-class discussions. The children may all be doing similar activities, or they may be doing very different kinds of work. The teacher may rotate their time around every group or plan to spend more time with certain children. The work may take place in the classroom or might involve working outdoors.

Having a distinct 'ending' to a lesson ensures that children are given time to reflect on what they have learned and helps their ideas take shape. Sharing thoughts and experiences contributes to the collaborative culture and is a real opportunity for children to learn from each other. The teacher can help to signal particularly significant ideas and support the children in making links with their existing ideas. This is also another key moment for consolidation by inviting the children to recap their learning.

Adapting lessons to meet the needs of different children in the class is a challenge. Finding out children's existing ideas means that activities can be planned to move children forward, and these may need to be different for different children. But not all adaptive teaching has to be based on activities. Children can be grouped together so that they challenge each other's ideas. Teachers may plan to spend more time with groups or individuals, talking about aspects of the work. Much adaptive teaching happens 'on the spot' as teachers respond to children's actions and comments during a lesson.

It is important to note that children who are low attainers in other areas of the curriculum, for example in English, may be high attainers in science. A child may need support with recording their ideas or in accessing information, while still thriving on a high level of conceptual challenge. In such a situation, teaching could be adapted through using analogies to explain concepts in different ways (see Section 4 for examples). A child with high mathematical attainment could be challenged to apply this through investigative work involving sophisticated data-handling, but we must not make assumptions about their understanding of the scientific concepts. Some children may need more structure, or scaffolding, for carrying out a scientific enquiry, while others may benefit from the opportunity to become more independent and to take more decisions themselves.

There are inevitable tensions between the theory and the practice of teaching and between what is ideal and what can be achieved. While we believe each child will have an individual understanding of the world and therefore particular learning needs, we also recognise that teachers have to teach large groups of children with limited time and resources. We have been mindful of this while writing Sections 2, 3 and 4, where we offer advice on how approaches suggested in each chapter might be put into practice.

All lesson-planning should involve a risk assessment. This simply means that thought needs to be given to any possible sources of risk and that action needs to be taken to minimise any danger. This may involve discussing safety issues with children, or it may mean checking that certain materials are suitable to use in a primary classroom. We have identified any specific areas of risk associated with the topics in each chapter. Detailed guidance is provided in the publication *Be Safe! Health and Safety in Primary School Science and Technology* (4th Edition available from the Association of Science Education 2011), and a copy of this should be kept in all schools.

The processes of science

The National Curriculum in England (NCE) (DfE 2013) requires that children 'develop understanding of the nature, processes and methods of science through different types of science enquiries that help them to answer scientific questions about the world around them' (p. 3). This suggests children should be learning how to 'do science' and also learn why scientists do things in a certain way. The NCE coins the phrase 'Working Scientifically' (WS) that encompasses the nature, processes and methods of science to be encountered. The NCE is clear that 'working scientifically' should not be taught as a separate strand but should be embedded within the content of biology, chemistry and physics. Here we see the NCE attempt to integrate our three elements of scientific knowledge – epistemic, content and process discussed above. The statutory document goes on to say that there should be a focus on the 'key features of scientific enquiry' (DfE 2013), so that children are taught to use a 'variety of approaches to answer relevant scientific questions' by collecting analysis and presenting data gathered from scientific enquiries.

So, what are the 'key features' of scientific enquiry? Doing science involves practicing a range of skills. These terms reflect the nature of science as a complex activity that is carried out through a combination of thinking and doing. Some process skills are *thinking skills* – hypothesising, interpreting and evaluating, while others are physical or motor skills, such as using measuring or magnifying equipment. Some of these involve manual dexterity – holding, pouring, cutting, and also have a conceptual component. For example, to use a hand lens, a thermometer or a newton meter requires a combination of physical manipulative skills and an understanding of what the tool does.

The processes of science are common to constructing biological, chemical and physical knowledge – all involve hypothesising, making observations and interpreting data. However, there are ways of applying those processes that are specific to particular disciplines. Studying the feeding behaviour of a python might involve observation in the natural habitat during which the scientist aims to avoid disturbing the natural environment. Developing a new plastic might require systematic control of different variables, for example, temperature or the ratios of various chemical additives, in a laboratory environment. Data collection methods depend on how much it is possible or desirable to control variables, so, for example, in biological sciences it is more common to use random sampling to provide a form of controlled testing. All enquiries take a systematic, rigorous approach, but the methods and strategies are quite different and particular to the field of study.

Scientific processes are often defined as distinct – exploring, questioning, predicting, hypothesising, planning, testing, observing, measuring, recording, interpreting, evaluating, concluding and communicating – and can be seen as processes that make up a whole enquiry. These processes often flow from one to the next, and the outcomes of one enquiry can feed into the next enquiry. However, these processes often become intertwined – in short, there is no neat sequence that is *the* 'scientific method'. Exploration can be thought of as a process within a scientific enquiry, but for young children, manipulating objects and materials and using different senses to find out about them is an enquiry in itself. Older children will make observations, generate hypotheses to explain observed phenomena and then seek evidence to support or refute these hypotheses. Process skills contribute both to the evidence base and the stimulus for generating new hypotheses. Being scientific therefore leads to conceptual development. Treating the processes as distinct may lead children to a simplistic view of science as a set of standard procedures that have to be gone through, that produce an idea at the other end, rather than a complex relationship between creative thinking and production of evidence. We take the view that in understanding the holistic nature of things, it is often helpful to think about the various aspects that make it up, and so we sometimes discuss the processes as separate, while understanding that they are actually parts of a whole process (McMahon and Davies 2003).

Attitudes towards science will fundamentally affect engagement with it. Curiosity with a questioning attitude is a springboard of science, so the primary curriculum has a clear role in encouraging this through the way in which science is taught throughout primary school. Beginning an exploration into uncharted territory requires courage as well as curiosity. Other scientific attitudes – attention to detail, accuracy and willingness to accept evidence – are also important.

Different ways to work scientifically

In Sections 2, 3 and 4 of this book we show how different areas of content knowledge emphasise different processes of science. So, rather than treating the 'processes of science' as homogeneous and generally applicable, we have identified how teachers can emphasise different approaches to 'doing science' when they teach different topics.

The NCE (DfE 2013) lists the types of scientific enquiry as:

- observing over time;
- pattern-seeking;
- identifying, classifying and grouping;
- comparative and fair testing (controlled investigations);
- researching using secondary sources

In Table 1.1 we have explained these and offer some examples. Note that the NCE rarely uses the word 'experiment'. Primary science experts tend to refer to 'investigations' to avoid the connotation associated with 'experiment' as a prescribed set of textbook instructions to follow, experienced by many of us in our own 'old-fashioned' science education. We prefer to highlight science enquiry as a spur to open-ended creative problem-solving and critical thinking.

For children to carry out a 'full enquiry' they would go through the process of raising questions or predicting and hypothesising, or both, deciding how to answer the question, perhaps through a survey or fair test, collecting data through observations or measurements, and interpreting their results to draw conclusions and suggest explanations. Children can do this independently when the subject matter is within their conceptual understanding and when they have experienced the enquiry process before. It is a challenging undertaking, and children may find it difficult to keep focused on the original question and take a systematic approach. For this reason, teachers often provide 'scaffolding' in the form of some kind of framework, for example 'planning boards' (Goldsworthy and Feasey 1998). Another teaching strategy is to break the investigation into stages, with support through discussion at each step. Alternatively, the teacher might take some of the decisions, while leaving children to make other decisions. It is important, however, that over time children do have experience of taking control of all the aspects of an enquiry, and that sometimes they should control the whole enquiry. It is worth noting here that this does not necessarily mean that every step has to be 'written up'. Not only can this be very boring for children if it takes the same format every time, but it also takes a considerable amount of precious science time. Varying which part of the enquiry process is recorded and creative thinking about how this is done are important in maintaining children's enthusiasm.

We have used the enquiry categories shown in Table 1.1 within this book to help explore how to teach the processes of science. In each chapter we have identified aspects of scientific enquiry that are most relevant to that topic area. Although this categorisation is helpful, it is not meant to be prescriptive. For example, although we have emphasised observation in the chapter on plants, it may also be appropriate to answer a question on plants through a pattern-finding approach or a fair test. By explaining these different approaches in context, we hope that they will be made more meaningful to the reader and will offer guidance on how children can be supported in developing them. Some areas of the curriculum offer opportunities that others do not, and by noting these we hope teachers will be able to provide a rich experience of science for children.

Planning for purposeful practical work

Practical work is an essential part of science education as science is about understanding the material world, however, research shows that practical activities in primary school sometimes lack clear purpose and might not effectively contribute to learning (Bianchi et al. 2021, Ofsted 2021). Teachers should be clear whether the aim of practical work is to help children understand a concept (substantive knowledge) or to develop their skills in and understanding of science enquiry ('working scientifically' or 'disciplinary knowledge') or some combination of both.

However, practical work that is like following a recipe is unlikely to develop children's understanding of concepts or of working scientifically. Children will need to draw on relevant prior conceptual knowledge to make appropriate decisions, such as identifying possible factors that might affect the outcome of a test. Also, if teachers have done all the designing of the experiment already then there are no opportunities for children to make their own decisions and evaluate the strengths and weaknesses of their own plans. On the other hand, leaving all the decisions to children, especially those with a limited experience of working scientifically, is likely to lead to a chaotic classroom, frustrated children and any learning that takes place may not be what the teacher had hoped for. There is a happy medium to be found between being over-prescriptive and total freedom by planning for purposeful practical work.

So, what are the purposes of practical work? In Table 1.2 we have drawn on the work of other authors (Abrahams and Reiss 2012, Abrahams and Millar 2008) who have addressed this question along with our own primary school focused professional experience.

Just as with the conceptual content, a well-sequenced curriculum planning can help children to gradually build up the specific skills and processes of science enquiry. Working scientifically is complex and multifaceted, however; different kinds of phenomena and different kinds of questions

Table 1.2 Purposes of practical work

Purpose: To help pupils to	Example
Become familiar with objects and phenomena	Handle materials such as glass, wood and metal.
	Feel two magnets repelling and attracting each other.
	Explore a meadow to see what lives there.
Learn a fact	Observe that salt dissolves in water and sand doesn't.
	Use a mirror to identify your own teeth as canine, incisors and molars.
Learn a concept	Notice that some materials block light better than others.
	A comparative test shows that some materials keep heat in a baked potato better than others.
	From observation over time of caterpillars becoming moths, realise that not all animals look like their offspring.
Learn a relationship	From an investigation, conclude that the lower the angle of the torch, the longer the shadow.
	From observation of a teacher demonstration, realise that the longer the chime bar, the lower the pitch of the note.
Get insight into a model or theory	By building a simple circuit, accept that electricity only flows when a there is a complete circuit of conductors.
	From observing sugar dissolving and tasting the solution, agree that the bits of sugar are so small we can't see them anymore.
Learn a skill	Be shown how to hold a magnifying glass and use it to look at rocks.
	Practice connecting a wire to a bulb to make a circuit.
	Practice using a paintbrush to pick up a beetle without damaging it.
Carry out a procedure	Generate five questions provoked by a collection of leaves.
	Use a planning sheet to change just one variable at a time in a fair test.
	Draw on previous learning to design a table for results of comparing paper airplanes.
Use a measuring instrument	Be shown how and apply how to read a scale on a measuring jug. Choose the right sensitivity of Newton meter from a selection provided by using trial and error.
Understand a process	Discuss why it is good to repeat trials when comparing how many paper clips a magnet picks up.
	Focus on writing a good conclusion to an enquiry that summarises all the evidence on which materials make the best earmuffs.
Understand what doing science feels like	Not 'cheating' when our design of parachute doesn't get the result we predicted. Being patient when a plant takes a week to germinate.
	Celebrating when the bulb lights up!

need different approaches to researching them. This book is designed around the view, helpfully summarised by (Ofsted 2023) that 'the best curriculums embed disciplinary knowledge within the most appropriate substantive content'. But importantly in all of this planning, we need to keep sight of the overarching aim of science education that encounters with a wide range of objects and phenomena should cultivate curiosity and wonder about the natural world.

Teachers sometimes feel a tension between wanting children to carry out their own investigations and wanting them to find out certain information, (for example, about the relationship between layers of insulation and how quickly an ice cube melts), so that their understanding of particular topics is developed (Driver 1983). Decisions about how much the focus of an enquiry should be directed by the teacher and how much by the interests of the child are not easy. There are times when teachers can see how an investigation might challenge or extend the ideas of a whole class in a certain direction and they may frame the enquiry more closely. On other occasions they may help an individual child or small group to test their own hypotheses to help them see limitations in their ideas. At other times, opportunities can be given for children to follow their own lines of enquiry within a topic without a predefined direction. There may also be occasions when children carry out practical activities that are not complete enquiries but have other purposes such as demonstrating a particular phenomenon or practicing a measuring skill.

As a note of caution, much modern science involves work across the traditional subject disciplines. For example, understanding the possible impact of overhead power cables on health has involved doctors specialising in childhood leukaemia, epidemiologists (scientists who study the incidence and distribution of diseases) and statisticians, as well as physicists with expertise in electromagnetic fields. We have made sure that we identify links within and beyond the science curriculum in each chapter.

Summary

In this section we have reflected on the aims of primary science – to support children in developing a sense of 'awe and wonder' about the world and in gaining 'scientific literacy'. We considered how these aims are informed by views about the nature of science. The ways in which we approach teaching science also depend on ideas about how children learn. Social-constructivist theories and brain-based views of learning both stress the importance of understanding the existing ideas a child has because these will affect how they make sense of any new experiences. The child is seen as actively making sense of the world rather than as a passive receiver of knowledge. The role of dialogic talk in learning in science was introduced and exemplified through some short case studies. Socio-cultural theory helps us to understand that the meanings children construct about the world are rooted in their experience within a culture and how language shapes our thinking as well as hands-on, physical encounters with objects and phenomena. Drawing on the way the Howard-Jones et al. (2020) have organised insights from the science of learning into three categories; Engage Build, Consolidate, we developed a version of this for primary science. We will use that EBC structure in Sections 2, 3 and 4 of this book where we offer guidance on how to approach the teaching of science topics. We have identified the key importance of assessment in learning then offered advice on putting the theory into practice. We have also explored what is meant by 'practical' science and 'enquiry', emphasising the need for purposeful practical work, that maintains children's curiosity about the natural world.

Discussion questions

1. What were your own experiences of science at school?
2. What messages about the nature of science did you come away with from your own education?
3. What examples of children's alternative ideas have you come across?

Further reading

Harlen, W. and Qualter, A. (2018) *The Teaching of Science in Primary Schools* (7th ed.). London: David Fulton.

This book provides an accessible discussion of learning and teaching in science, taking a social-constructivist perspective. It takes different aspects of the teaching of science such as 'teachers' and children's questions, ways of helping the development of process skills, and considers them in depth, drawing on relevant research.

Davies, D., Howe, A., Collier, C., Digby, R., Earle S. and McMahon, K. (2019) *Teaching Science and Design and Technology in the Early Years (3–7)* (3rd ed.). London: David Fulton.

A companion to the book you are now reading, this title is for teachers of children aged 3–7 and shows how science-rich activities contribute to their learning. It advises practitioners how to build on children's early experiences and ideas about science, first through play and then through more structured teaching.

Rogers, C. and Thomas, M.S.C. (2023) *Educational Neuroscience: the basics*. Abingdon and New York: Routledge.

This is book is a friendly, very readable introduction to scientists' current understanding of the brain and learning that goes beyond the messages from cognitive psychology that are so evident in English policy to explain neuroscience to teachers in a light-hearted way.

Alexander, R. J. (2020) A *Dialogic Teaching Companion*. London: Routledge

This book summarises the research and theory behind Robin Alexander's version of dialogic teaching and provides guidance for developing it in the classroom.

References

Abrahams, I. & Millar, R. (2008) Does practical work really work? A study of the effectiveness of practical work as a teaching and learning method in school science. *International Journal of Science Education*, 30(14), 1945–1969.

Abrahams, I. & Reiss, M. J. (2012) Practical work: its effectiveness in primary and secondary schools in England, *Journal of Research in Science Teaching*, 49(8), 1035–1055.

Alexander, R. J. (2008) *Towards Dialogic Teaching: Rethinking Classroom Talk* (4th ed.), Cambridge: Dialogos.

Alexander, R. J. (2020) *A Dialogic Teaching Companion*, London: Routledge.

Archer, L., Dawson E., DeWitt, J., Seakins, A. & Wong, B. (2015). 'Science capital': a conceptual, methodological, and empirical argument for extending Bourdieusian notions of capital beyond the arts, *Journal of Research in Science Teaching*, 52(7), 922–948.

Archer, L., Moote, J., Francis, B., DeWitt, J., & Yeomans, L. (2017) The 'exceptional' physics girl: a sociological analysis of multimethod data from young women aged 10–16 to explore gendered patterns of post-16 participation, *American Educational Research Journal*, 54(1), 88–126. doi:10.3102/0002831216678379.

Association for Science Education (ASE) (2011) *Be Safe!: Health and Safety in School Science and Technology for Teachers of 3- to 12-year olds* (4th ed.), Hatfield: ASE.

Ausubel, D. P. (1968) *Educational Psychology: A Cognitive View*, New York: Holt, Rinehart and Winston.

Baddeley, A. (2003) Working memory: looking back and looking forward, *Nature Reviews Neuroscience*, 4(10), 829–839. https://doi.org/10.1177/0963721420925518.

Baddeley, A., Eysenck, M. W. & Anderson, M. C. (2020) *Memory* (3rd ed.), London & New York: Routledge.

Bell, D. & Darlington, H. (2020) Educational neuroscience: so what does it mean in the classroom?. in M. Thomas, D. Mareschal & I. Dumontheil (Eds), *Educational Neuroscience Development Across the Lifespan*, New York and Abingdon: Routledge.

Bell, D., Mareschal, D. & The Unlocke team (2021) Unlocke-ing learning in maths and science: the role of cognitive inhibition in developing counter-intuitive concepts, *Journal of Emergent Science* 20, 19–26.

Bianchi, L., Whittaker, C. & Poole, A. (2021) *The 10 Key Issues with Children's Learning in Primary Science in England*, The University of Manchester and the Ogden Trust. 3634_Childrens_Learning_in_Primary_Science_Report_2020_v8.pdf (scienceacrossthecity.co.uk).

Bruner, J. (1985) Vygotsky: A historical and conceptual perspective, in J. Wertsh (Ed), *Culture, Communication and Cognition, Vygotskian Perspectives* (21–34), Cambridge, England: Cambridge University Press.

Bruner, J. (1996). *The Culture of Education*. Cambridge, MA: Harvard University Press.

Damasio, A. R. (2006) *Descartes' Error*, Random House.

Darling-Hammond, L., Oakes, J., Wojcikiewicz, S., Hyler, M. E., Guha, R., Podolsky, A., … & Harrell A. (2019). *Preparing Teachers for Deeper Learning*. Cambridge, MA: Harvard Education Press.

Davidesco, I., Laurent, E., & Valk, H. (2019) Brain-to-brain synchrony between students and teachers predicts learning outcomes. *bioRxiv*; 2019 DOI: 10.1101/644047.

Davies, D. & McMahon, K. (2004) A smooth trajectory: developing continuity and progression between primary and secondary science education through a jointly planned projectiles project, *International Journal of Science Education*, 26(8), 1009–1021.

Dehaene, S. (2020) *How We Learn: The New Science of Education and the Brain*. Penguin.

Department for Education (DfE) (2013) *Science – Programmes of Study for Key Stages 1–2*. London: DfE. Science programmes of study: key stages 1 and 2 (publishing.service.gov.uk).

Department for Education (2019) *Early Career Framework*, https://www.gov.uk/government/publications/early-career-framework

DeWitt, J., Archer, L. & Mau, A. (2016). Dimensions of science capital: exploring its potential for understanding students' science participation. *International Journal of Science Education*, 38(16): 2431–2449.

Driver, R. (1983) *The Pupil as Scientist?*, Milton Keynes: Open University Press.

Driver, R., Asoko, H., Leach, J., Mortimer, E. & Scott, P. (1994). Constructing scientific knowledge in the classroom, *Educational Researcher*, 23(7), 5–12. https://www.jstor.org/stable/1176933

Driver, R., Guesne, E. & Tiberghien, A. (eds.) (1985) *Children's Ideas in Science*. Milton Keynes: Open University Press.

Dweck, C. S. (2006). *Mindset: The New Psychology of Success*. Random House.

Earle, S. (2021) Formative decision-making in response to primary science classroom assessment: What to do next?, *Frontiers in Education*, (5) 584200.

Forrester, N. (2020) Diversity in science: next steps for research group leaders. *Nature*, 585, S65–S67. www.nature.com/articles/d41586-020-02681-y

Furst, E. (n.d.) *How the Brain Works*, Efrat Furst. https://sites.google.com/view/efratfurst/home?

von Glaserfeld, E. (1995) *Radical Constructivism: A Way of Knowing and Learning*, London: RoutledgeFalmer.

Goldsworthy, A. & Feasey, R. (1998) *Making Sense of Primary Science Investigations* (2nd ed.), Hatfield. ASE.

Harlen, W. (2012) *Developing Policy, Principles and Practice in Primary School Science Assessment*, London: Nuffield Foundation.

Harlen, W. (ed.) with Bell, D., Deves, R., Dyasi, H., Fernandez de las Garza, G., Lena, P., Millar, R.… Yu, W. (2015) *Working with Big Ideas of Science Education*. Treieste: Science Education Programme of IAP. www.ase.org.uk/resources/big-ideas/

Harlen, W. & Qualter, A. (2018). *The Teaching of Science in Primary Schools* (7th ed). London: Routledge.

Harrison, C., Constantinou, C. P., Correia, C. F., Grangeat, M., Hähkiöniemi, M., Livitzis, M.… & Viiri, J. (2018). Assessment On-the-Fly: Promoting and Collecting Evidence of Learning

Through Dialogue, in Dolin, J. & Evans, R. (eds) *Transforming Assessment. Contributions from Science Education Research*, vol 4. Springer, Cham. https://doi.org/10.1007/978-3-319-63248-3_4

Howard-Jones, P., Ioannou, K., Bailey, R., Prior, J., Jay, T., & Yau, S. (2020) Ch 17 Towards a Science of Teaching and Learning for Teacher Education, in M. Thomas, D. Mareschal & I. Dumontheil (eds), *Educational Neuroscience Development Across the Lifespan*, New York and Abingdon: Routledge.

Karpicke, J. D., Blunt, J. R., Smith, M. A. & Karpicke, S. S. (2014) Retrieval-based learning: the need for guided retrieval in elementary school children, *Journal of Applied Research in Memory and Cognition*, 3(3), 198–206.

Kirschner, P. A., Sweller, J. & Clark, R. E. (2006) Why minimal guidance during instruction does not work: an analysis of the failure of constructivist, discovery, problem-based, experiential, and inquiry-based teaching, *Educational Psychologist*, 41:2, 75–86.

Leach, J. & Scott, P. (2002) Designing and evaluating science teaching sequences: an approach drawing upon the concept of learning demand and a social constructivist perspective on learning, *Studies in Science Education*, 38, 115–142.

Matthews, M. R. (ed.) (1998) *Constructivism and Science Education: A Philosophical Examination*, Dordrecht: Kluwer Academic Publishers.

Massonnié, J., Frasseto, P., Mareschal, D. & Kirkham, N.Z. (2020) Scientific collaboration with educators: practical insights from an in-class noise-reduction intervention, *Mind, Brain, and Education*, 14(3) DOI: 10.1111/mbe.12240.

McMahon K. (2010) *Interactive Whole Class Teaching in Key Stage Two Classrooms* (PhD thesis), Bath Spa University.

McMahon, K. (2012) Case studies of interactive whole-class teaching in primary science: communicative approach and pedagogic purposes, *International Journal of Science Education*, 34(11), 1687–1708, DOI: 10.1080/09500693.2012.702360.

McMahon, K. (2018) Assessment of working scientifically – the TAPS Focused Assessment approach, *Primary Science*, (151) 15–16.

McMahon, K. (2022) Doing retrieval practice better, *School Science Review in Practice*, 103, 30–31.

McMahon, K. & Davies, D. (2003) Assessment for inquiry: supporting teaching and learning in primary science, *Science Education International*, 14(4), 29–39.

McMahon, K., Howe, A., Davies, D., Collier, C. & Earle, S. (2016) Creative pedagogies in early years science: thematic planning and sustained scientific dialogues, in Lavonen, J., Juuti, K., Lampiselkä, J., Uitto, A. & Hahl, K. (eds), *Electronic Proceedings of the ESERA 2015 Conference. Science Education Research: Engaging Learners for a Sustainable Future, Part 15* (co-ed. Glauert, E. and Stylianidou, F.), (pp. 2626–2638), Helsinki, Finland: University of Helsinki.

Millar, R. & Osborne, J. (eds) (1998) *Beyond 2000: Science Education for the Future*, London: King's College.

Mortimer, E. & Scott, P. (2003) *Meaning Making in Secondary Science Classrooms*, Maidenhead: Open University Press.

Muijs, D. & Bokhove, C. (2020) *Metacognition and Self-regulation: Evidence Review*, London: Education Endowment Foundation. https://educationendowmentfoundation.org.uk/education-evidence/evidence-reviews/metacognition-and-self-regulation

Ofsted (2021) *Research review series: science*, https://www.gov.uk/government/publications/research-review-series-science/research-review-series-science

Ofsted (2023) *Subject report series: science*, https://www.gov.uk/government/publications/subject-report-series-science

Ogborn, J. Kress, G., Martins, I. & McGillicuddy, K. (1996) *Explaining Science in the Classroom*, Buckingham and Philadelphia: Open University Press.

Ollerenshaw, C. & Ritchie, R. (1997) *Primary Science: Making It Work* (2nd ed.), London: David Fulton.

Osborne, J. (2015) Practical work in science: misunderstood and badly used? *School Science Review*, 96(357) 16–24.

Perry, T., Lea, R., Jørgensen, C. R., Cordingley, P., Shapiro, K. & Youdell, D. (2021). *Cognitive Science in the Classroom*, London: Education Endowment Foundation (EEF). https://educationendowmentfoundation.org.uk/evidence-summaries/evidencereviews/cognitive-science-approaches-in-the-classroom/

Pessoa, L. (2022) *The Entangled Brain: How Perception, Cognition, and Emotion Are Woven Together*, MIT Press.

Piaget, J. (1929) *The Child's Conception of the World*, New York: Harcourt Brace.

Richardson, M., Isaacs, T., Barnes, I., Swensson, C., Wilkinson, D. & Golding, J. (2020) Trends in international mathematics and science study 2019: national report for England, Department for Education. https://www.gov.uk/government/publications/trends-in-international-mathematics-and-science-study-2019-england

Roediger, H. L. & Karpicke, J. D. (2006). Test-enhanced learning: taking memory tests improves long-term retention. *Psychological Science*, 17(3), 249–255. https://doi.org/10.1111/j.1467-9280.2006.01693.x

Rogoff, B. (1990) *Apprenticeship in Thinking: Cognitive Development in Social Context*. New York: Oxford University Press.

Saskatchewan Ministry of Education (2011) Science (Elementary school) – Saskatchewan – Curricula. 2. Competency-based education – Saskatchewan. Saskatchewan. Ministry of Education. https://curriculum.gov.sk.ca

Schilbach, L., Wilms, M., Eickhoff, S. B., Romanzetti, S., Tepest, R., Bente, G.… Vogeley, K. (2010) Minds made for sharing: initiating joint attention recruits reward-related neurocircuitry. *Journal Cognitive Neuroscience*, 22(12):2702–2715. doi: 10.1162/jocn.2009.21401. PMID: 19929761.

Science Processes and Concept Exploration Project – various authors 1989–1998. https://www.stem.org.uk/resources/collection/3324/space-research-reports

Shimamura, A. (2018) *MARGE: A whole brain approach to learning*. https://shimamurapubs.files.wordpress.com/2018/09/marge_shimamura.pdf

Siraj-Blatchford, I., Sylva, K., Muttock, S., Gilden, R. & Bell, D. (2002). *Researching Effective Pedagogy in the Early Years*. Department of Education and Skills. Research Report RR 356. Norwich: DfES, p. 24.

Slavin, R. E. (2005). *Educational Psychology: Theory and Practice*, Needham Heights, Mass.: Allyn and Bacon.

Thomas, M. (n.d.) How the brain works. Living in the future borrowing from the past, University of London Centre for Educational Neuroscience (CEN). http://howthebrainworks.science/how_the_brain_works_/living_in_the_future_borrowing_from_the_past/#:~:text=Second%2C%20predictions%20optimise%20the%20brain,learning%20when%20it%20doesn't

Tolmie and Dündar-Coecke (2020) Lifespan Conceptual development in science: brain and behaviour, in M. Thomas, D. Mareschal & I. Dumontheil (Eds), *Educational Neuroscience Development Across the Lifespan*, New York and Abingdon: Routledge.

Vygotsky, L. (1978) *Mind in Society: The Development of Higher Psychological Processes*, London: Harvard University Press.

Watson, R., Wood-Robinson, V. & Goldsworthy, A. (2000) *AKSIS Investigations Targeted Learning*, Hatfield: ASE Publications.

Welsh Government & Education Wales (2021) *The Curriculum for Wales, Science and Technology*. https://hwb.gov.wales/curriculum-for-wales/science-and-technology/

Willingham, D. (2021) *Why Don't Students Like School?* (2nd Ed), Wiley Jossey-Bass. New Jersey.

Willingham, D. T. (2017) A mental model of the learner: teaching the basic science of educational psychology to future teachers. *Mind, Brain, and Education*, 11: 166–175. https://doi.org/10.1111/mbe.12155.

SECTION 2

Teaching biology topics

Introduction – the big ideas

Biology often seems the most accessible of the areas of science; the study of humans is immediately relevant, and most children are quick to engage with topics about animals. Studying plants has a long history in the primary classroom and has been given a high profile in the national curriculum in England (NCE) (DfE 2013). Concern for the world's natural environment, how to protect disappearing habitats, prevent extinctions and restore biodiversity are some of the most serious and pressing issues humanity currently faces, and this is highlighted by the seventeen sustainable development goals (UN General Assembly 2015) which underpin the 2030 agenda for sustainable development adopted by all members of the United Nations. Even quite young children are aware of the impact climate change is having upon the world around them and are knowledgeable about the work of environmental activists such as David Attenborough and Greta Thunberg. Children understand that there are issues of public importance to be considered as well as the role they have to play in protecting their planet from further destruction. A good grounding in biological concepts will help us understand our own health and wellbeing and that of the world we inhabit.

The conceptual concepts of biology can be surprisingly demanding and with the huge diversity of living things that we encounter, teachers need to continue to develop and consolidate their breadth of knowledge of specific plants and animals alongside the children.

It is possible to imagine a view of learning biology in which disconnected 'facts' – labelling parts of a flower, listing the characteristics of living things, correctly classifying a lizard as a reptile – mean that children have a fragmented collection of ideas. It would be far better for them to build a coherent picture of how the natural world works, connected by a depth of conceptual understanding and insights into how such knowledge comes. Science educators call these the 'big ideas' of science (Harlen 2010). Children will not fully comprehend these big ideas in primary school, but if they are exposed to a good range of experiences and develop relevant knowledge through skilful teaching, we can lay solid foundations for later conceptual development.

An understanding of energy is a big idea that goes across the domains of physics and chemistry as well as biology. In biology it is important to understand that the total amount of energy is always the same, but it can be transferred and exist in different forms, such as the chemical energy of food in food chains, which becomes movement, sound and heat. A related key concept is that living things (organisms) require a supply of energy and materials on which they depend and compete for with other organisms. Understanding that green plants use energy from the Sun to generate complex molecules that animals then use as food, is essential to grasp the significance of environmental issues such as why cutting down a rainforest matters.

There is an incredible diversity of living things, including plants and animals, and broadening the range of living things that children know about is an important part of primary science. Science has long established that a healthy and stable ecosystem is one that supports a diverse range of organisms, even though we sometimes still don't fully understand the complex relationships between them. We also know that we should be very concerned about the continued loss of species diversity on land and in our oceans. During their time in primary school, we should strive to introduce children to an increasingly wide range of organisms within ecosystems such as ponds, woodlands and rainforest, starting with those closest to home. By Year 6, children will be more than ready to learn about the exotic and extraordinary life that abounds across our planet. We can hope that they will also gain a sense of fascination, awe and wonder of the natural world that will sustain them throughout their life.

The interdependence of different living things is another big idea that can be developed in many different contexts, for example by planning and preparing a meal using potatoes grown in a bucket or growing and eating fruit and vegetables produced in the school garden, learning about food chains and webs or how an oak tree supports a whole range of bird and insect life. Different organisms may depend on each other, but in any ecosystem, there is also competition for the limited energy resources and materials that are needed to live and reproduce.

Although it may not be visible to children, all living things at some stage in their life cycle are sensitive to their environment and all will carry out the life processes of respiration, reproduction, feeding, excretion, growth and movement. Our own human bodies provide a relevant context in which to learn more about why we need to breathe and have beating hearts, and children are fascinated by learning about how we can move and what happens to the food inside our bodies. Learning about how our bodies work is one dimension of health, and understanding the effects of diet, exercise and drugs on the body contributes to taking control of these.

Science is never separate from people, and the ideas of science are relevant to people's everyday decision making. This can be emphasised by planning for personal, social, health and economic education (PSHE) alongside science, ensuring that moral and ethical dimensions are considered. Children should be encouraged to think how personal decisions and also collective decisions by society, such as imposing limits on fossil fuel emissions or implementing COVID vaccination programmes, can impact on our health and the environment. The Practical Action website contains some excellent science, technology, engineering and maths (STEM) resources designed around real-life climate change challenges; such as designing a model of a hand washing device to prevent the spread of disease for primary school pupils in Kenya or making a model of a floating garden to support farmers in Bangladesh.

Evolution is seen by many as one of the most important ideas in biology and understanding it involves connecting other biological concepts. For example, sexual reproduction and inheritance leads to variation within species. The demands of ecosystems over long periods of time can lead to natural selection where individuals with particular inherited characteristics have a better survival rate and this trait is passed genetically to their offspring. If this process doesn't result in a species being well adapted to its habitat, perhaps during a period of rapid climate change, then it will become extinct. Fossils provide us with an intriguing glimpse into the biology of the past, and the study of dinosaurs can be an exciting way to engage children with this topic.

Substantive biology content and its embedded disciplinary knowledge concepts in the primary NCE are emphasised within the programme of study for every primary year group. These will now be explored in more detail in the following chapters.

References

Department for Education (2013) *The National Curriculum in England: Key Stages 1 and 2 Framework Document.* https://www.gov.uk/government/publications/national-curriculum-in-england-primary-curriculum

Harlen, W. (ed.) with Bell, D., Devés, R., Dyasi, H., Fernández de la Garza, G., Léna, P., Millar… Yu, W. (2015) *Working with Big Ideas of Science Education*, Trieste: Science Education Programme of IAP. www.ase.org.uk/bigideas.

UN General Assembly (2015) *Transforming our world: the 2030 Agenda for Sustainable Development*, 21 October 2015, A/RES/70/1, https://www.refworld.org/docid/57b6e3e44.html

CHAPTER 2.1

Living things and their habitats

Purpose of this chapter

After reading this chapter you will:

- have an appreciation of how the study of living things in their environment, including evolution, will progress from early childhood until the beginning of secondary education;
- have knowledge of key concepts and how children's understanding of these develop;
- know how to teach about living things in their environment, including how the topic relates to citizenship and education for sustainable development;
- understand how to make meaningful connections to children's own experiences and communities to support the development of their science capital;
- understand the importance of developing children's awareness of global environmental issues as well as the role they can take to help mitigate against climate change;
- understand how to make connections and reinforce learning about living things and their habitats through purposeful retrieval practice activities.

Introduction

This chapter considers the phrase 'think local; act global' in the context of primary school science. The initial focus of this chapter will be the use of local settings and frequent outdoor explorations to develop understanding of living things within the children's own immediate environment. We will suggest a range of sensory activities to engage children's interest in the natural world and suggest appropriate steps to move from explorations to systematic investigations of plants, animals, habitats and ecosystems. We will then consider how a scientific understanding of the interdependence of living things within a local ecosystem can lead to a wider understanding of global issues such as conservation, climate change and sustainable development with purposeful connections to the sustainable development goals (UN General Assembly 2015). This understanding of how living things are adapted to their environment is developed in learning about evolution and inheritance.

Planning for progression

Children often find 'living things and their habitats' (National Curriculum for England (NCE) 2013) an interesting and rewarding area of science, not least because it should involve lots of practical outdoor learning, which has a positive impact upon children's enjoyment of lessons and their engagement with learning (Waite et al. 2016). The key concepts of this area of science are concerned with the diversity and quantity of living things in particular places, the ways in which living things interact with each other and how animals and plants are adapted to survive and thrive in their environment. As children come to understand that animals are intimately connected to the places where they live, they will begin to appreciate that ecosystems need to be left undisturbed, protected or managed.

In the Early Years Foundation Stage (EYFS), children should freely explore outdoor natural environments using multi-sensory approaches and be supported in developing their observational skills and scientific vocabulary when comparing and contrasting natural materials (DfE 2020). Good Early Years settings encourage children to play and explore outside regularly. This may take the form of 'Earthwalks' or 'welly-walks', where children might discover the sights, sounds, smells and textures of a field or wood, or of digging and planting a small garden:

> In one reception class, children planted seeds in trays and nurtured them until they were big enough to plant out. Unfortunately, many of the plants were either eaten by slugs or wilted over the weekend. New seeds were planted and watered more carefully. The teacher discussed with them what to do about the slugs. The children noticed some plants had not been eaten, so it was decided to grow more of these.

Beeley (2012) describes the importance of letting children guide their teachers through their world with the adult acting as a facilitator to support and develop emerging ideas and skills rather than having these forced upon them. Early Years practitioners will also make good use of incidental events, such as finding spiders lurking in the outdoor sandpit or snails slithering up the window, to develop young children's knowledge and understanding of living things.

In the early primary years (Key Stage 1 or KS1), children will find out about different kinds of plants and animals in the local environment and how these are affected by seasonal change. They will identify similarities and differences between local habitats and how these provide for the needs of the animals and plants that are found there exploring their dependent relationships. Children will learn about how animals rely on plants and other animals for their food sources and use simple food chains to express these. They should also be taught to care for the environment.

In the later primary years (Key Stage 2 or KS2), this work is developed to consider more formal classification schemes and how different plants and animals are found and are adapted to their environments and how this adaptation may lead to evolution. Children will construct and interpret different food chains understanding the role of producers, predators and prey within these. They are also taught about beneficial and harmful microorganisms. Through this programme of study children should consider how to protect the environment. In secondary education (Key Stage 3 or KS3), the curriculum develops the concept of interdependence, including how this relates to crop pollination by insects, that food webs are composed of several food chains, and how toxic materials can accumulate in food chains. Ideas about DNA and genes are introduced to explain inheritance and evolution. It is worth noting, however, that children of primary age may well be encountering ideas about DNA beyond school.

At KS1 and KS2, teachers should take advantage of the opportunities for cross-curricular application of skills and knowledge. We shall see below that studying an ecosystem requires skills that may be developed in mathematics or geography contexts. Surveying, mapping and finding out about the rocks, soils and weather all contribute to an understanding of the habitats that living things populate.

The key concepts taught at KS1 and KS2 are identified in Table 2.1.1, along with some notes to inform the teacher's understanding.

Table 2.1.1 Living things and their habitats' key concepts

Key concepts	Teachers' background knowledge
Life processes are common to all living things	Although young children have trouble seeing plants and fungi as 'alive' in the same way as animals, they are classified as living things because they carry out all of the following processes (MRS GREN or MRS NERG can be useful mnemonics to remember them by): **Movement** They do not get up and walk, but plants will move their leaves, stems or flowers (e.g. sunflowers) to find the light or support (e.g. beans). Animals may have voluntary (e.g. walking, raising a limb) and involuntary (e.g. heart beating, muscles moving food through the digestive system) movements. Although plants cannot move away from where they are planted, they do move their leaves, stems or flowers to find light (e.g. sunflowers) or support (e.g. beans). **Respiration** Within cells, energy is released from food (or the sugars which have been produced through photosynthesis in plants) in the presence of oxygen. **Sensitivity** Plants can sense light, gravity and water. Some can sense if they have been damaged. Animals use senses such as touch, sight, smell, hearing and taste to respond to environmental triggers around them (e.g. moving a hand away quickly if it touches something too hot). They also react to hormonal changes within the body (e.g. the production of adrenaline which speeds up reflexes and increases heart rate). **Growth** Cells can get larger and also divide, so living organisms get bigger. **Reproduction** All populations create new organisms otherwise they wouldn't survive. Plants can do this either sexually (flowers and seeds, etc.) or asexually cloning from one parent plant (e.g. runners or cuttings). **Excretion** This is the process of getting rid of the waste products of metabolic processes (e.g. gases, liquids and solids). **Nutrition** Living things rely on nutrients and energy from food sources to maintain their life processes and to stay alive. Plants use food they make themselves (see next chapter) to get energy.
Living things can be classified into different kingdoms	The five kingdom system is a common classification system for organisms and comprises the following: Animals; Plants; Fungi (e.g. mushrooms, yeast); Protoctista (e.g. the single celled amoeba, and multicellular algae such as seaweed) and Monera (cells without a proper nucleus, e.g. bacteria). Although primary children focus on plants and animals and more detail is given on these in the next chapters, it is helpful for teachers to recognise that not all the living things children will encounter will fit into these two kingdoms. Viruses are generally considered not to be living things, but this is debated. Scientists in the US and Canada often use a six kingdom system, dividing Monera into Eubacteria and Archaebacteria. This is a good example of how scientific 'facts' change and are disputed.

(Continued)

Table 2.1.1 (Continued)	
Key concepts	**Teachers' background knowledge**
Biodiversity: that there are many different kinds of plants and animals	There are an estimated 8.7 million different species on our planet. About 1.2 million are known and more than half of these are insects. It is exciting to think that there are plenty of species out there to be discovered by today's primary children. There is also diversity within species – just look at the variation found in different breeds of dogs and cats. Species are incredibly important because they are irreplaceable. This is a fundamental piece of knowledge needed to comprehend the fragility of some ecosystems. Biodiverse ecosystems are important to preserve for a variety of reasons. Rainforests, for example, harbour species that may be useful to us but are as yet unknown. Diverse populations tend to be better at surviving changes, such as the introduction of a disease or pest, and they also tend to be more beautiful places.
Ecosystem	An ecosystem is a community of plants and animals and the environment that supplies them with water, air and other elements they need for life. Ecosystems can be studied on very different scales, from a slice of mouldy bread, to a single tree, (both microhabitats) to a forest, to the Pacific Ocean.
Interdependence	Each living thing depends on others to survive. Species are unable to survive without others (e.g. bean plants cannot grow without special bacteria). This interdependence includes food (one eats another), provision of shelter (e.g. hermit crabs use the shells of other species), dispersal of seeds and the control of competitors. Competition can come from other individuals from the same species (the population) or from other species.
Energy transfers through a food chain	Food chains indicate feeding relationships, as energy transfer, between organisms from producers (green plants) to consumers (animals). Arrows indicate the passing of food (chemical energy) from one living thing to another and therefore the direction is important. The chain generally begins with a green plant, e.g.: stinging nettle → tortoiseshell butterfly caterpillar → sparrow → sparrowhawk or with dead organic matter (detritus), e.g.: leaf litter → earthworm → blackbird → fox Older children will be able to understand the more complex representation of a food web. Food chains need not always include whole animals, e.g.: grass → cow (milk) → human A common mistake in making food chains is to use the arrow to mean 'eats' (e.g. cow → grass), which is wrong because the energy transfer is from grass to cow.
Sustainability	Sustainability has a special meaning in environmental contexts. One way to describe it is to think of a bank balance that lists all the resources the planet has. Most resources are finite. The list would include soil, water, air, fossil fuel and all our different species. If we are to behave in a sustainable way, then the bank balance should be just as healthy when we leave this planet to our children as it was when we inherited it from our ancestors. Unfortunately, current generations are likely to leave less soil, clean water, fossil fuels and species for future generations – our level of consumption is not sustainable – it cannot go on like this forever. Governments around the world agree that we need to concentrate our efforts on saving the planet from destruction. Building upon international agreements and legal treaties, such as Rio Earth Summit's Agenda 21 (1992) and the Paris Agreement (2015), the United Nation (UN) General Assembly 2030 Agenda for Sustainable Development (2015) was adopted by all member states and agreed on an urgent call for global action focused on seventeen sustainable development goals. Sustainable Development Goal 4, quality education (UN General Assembly 2015), includes a commitment that children should be educated on sustainable development and global citizenship and be equipped with the knowledge and skills to promote a more sustainable world.

(Continued)

Table 2.1.1 (Continued)

Key concepts	Teachers' background knowledge
Materials are cycled in an ecosystem	When plants or animals die or are eaten then the materials that made up their bodies remain in the ecosystem, and some are used to make other plants and animals. If plants and animals are poisoned, then these chemicals may pass to the next animal in the food chain.
Micro-organisms are living organisms that can be beneficial or harmful	Micro-organisms, such as bacteria and some fungi, cannot be seen individually with the naked eye, yet are present almost everywhere in their millions and billions. We may be able to see groups or 'colonies' of them. Many microorganisms are completely harmless and some are beneficial, such as those that help break dead organisms down into useful materials. Some are not helpful, such as the mould that appears in a damp bathroom. Some are harmful, such as those that cause disease and food poisoning.
Adaptation	Animals and plants are adapted to survive and thrive in specific environments. Children can look for adaptation in the behaviour or physical features of organisms. For example, animals that live in cold climates are generally large and have a small surface area to volume ratio to ensure minimal heat loss (e.g. polar bear). They have thick layers of fat or fur for insulation. They have a white coat in winter for camouflage and may hibernate during the coldest months. A dandelion can survive in a meadow grazed by animals (or a lawn) because it has a short stem and grows close to the ground. It quickly grows a flower on a long stem, which then moves in the wind to release parachuted seeds. The seeds germinate quickly to colonise new pastures.
The differences between living things can be explained by evolution	Different species exist because over time, earlier life forms have been selected. We assume that some small variations that come from mixing in sexual reproduction or from mutations, gave that organism an advantage in a particular habitat and made it more likely to reproduce and pass on its characteristics.

Teachers' self-assessment questions

1. Explain how a cat exhibits all the characteristics of living things.
2. Now explain how a sunflower exhibits all the characteristics of living things.
3. Identify the producer and consumers in this food chain:

    stinging nettle → red admiral butterfly → bat
4. In which kingdom would you classify yeast?
5. If a child told you that giraffes have long necks because they stretch up to get the leaves from tall trees, how would you respond?
6. Why is it important that children should learn about ecosystems and sustainability?
7. Which of the sustainable development goals could link to the topic of living things and their habitats and how could you explore these connections with children within a meaningful context?

Engage

Situating the topic

The most obvious way to start work on living things in their environment is to go outside. Outdoor education, especially through the forest school movement, is becoming more popular in primary school settings, however, there is still concern that children do not have enough time exploring their natural environment and that they do not realise the impact that humans have upon it (Constable 2019). This is particularly worrying considering that there is a need for them to be equipped with the skills and understanding about how to promote and work towards developing a more sustainable world (UN General Assembly 2015). There is a strong tradition of outdoor activity in Scandinavian countries, even in their winter months, so we in the UK, should not use the weather as an excuse for staying indoors; as long as children have the right clothing and footwear then they can explore outside in all seasons.

A walk outside can provide a novel, sensory experience that engages and interests children and which makes purposeful connections between their understanding of living things and their needs. Even if the school lacks a pleasant environment, there may be some possibilities for starting points. One urban school with a small concrete playground noticed how gulls congregated on the rooftops during playtime. The children observed that the gulls came to feed on the scraps of snacks left by the children. This led to work finding out if gulls were welcome visitors and then thinking about how to discourage them in places where their droppings were causing health concerns; an illustration of how we might need to debate whether animal 'pests' need to be managed. Schools with more limited spaces for wildlife (or even those with plenty of space) could ask the children to solve this real-life problem through designing and making insect hotels; creating small nature areas or growing produce in a variety of different containers placed in different places around the school. Pupils could then survey these and carry out enquiries to determine which made the most effective habitats. Activities which encourage children to share attention through working together and which are relevant to children's real-life experiences are more likely to engage them in their learning.

The aim of any initial outdoor activity should be to 'orientate' children to the idea that walls, fields, trees, hedges and ponds can be habitats for a diverse range of plants and animals. It should also contribute to their awe and wonder at the bounty and beauty of living things, as they begin to appreciate the complexity and abundance of life.

The range of activities we call 'Earthwalks' can be used to encourage children to explore natural environments using all their senses (see Box 2.1.1 Earthwalks activities in the Build section). They also perform the function of engaging children with a place at a kinaesthetic and emotional level which we think is a prerequisite for thinking about ecosystems as places to enjoy and look after.

Breaking down barriers

Scientists are often 'blamed' for the demise of our planet because it is they who discover new ways to use our finite resources. However, it is also scientists who draw our attention to the consequences of our actions, and their research offers us choices about our future. In many cases, scientists can be the 'goodies' rather than the 'baddies'. One starting point for environmental science might be to learn a little about the lives of scientists who have made, and are continuing to make, a contribution. Whilst most children will have heard of the great Sir David Attenborough, it is also important to share a range of role models from more diverse backgrounds so that all pupils are introduced to scientists who look and behave just like them. Children's perceptions of whether science is a career for them are formed early during their primary education and resistant to change as they progress through secondary education (Archer et al. 2013) so we, as teachers, have a responsibility to develop the science capital of the children in our class, particularly those from under-represented groups (Nag Chowdhuri, King and Archer 2021). The Primary Science Teaching Trust's 'A Scientist Just Like Me' website contains freely accessible resources focusing on a wide range of modern-day scientists working with animals, plants, the environment and climate (as well as all other topics within the science curriculum). School visits and communications from active environmental scientists can also be easily facilitated through the excellent, free STEM ambassadors programme where volunteers from a vast database are matched to particular topics and interests of the class, however niche these may be. Other inspirational role models can be found within the children's more immediate communities; perhaps through arranging a guided visit to a family's allotment or a city farm.

Three examples of inspirational scientists are listed below although as we have just explored in the section above, there are a wealth of others, both famous and otherwise, to draw upon.

Greta Thunberg (born 2003) is a Swedish environmental activist who, as a young child, became so concerned about the impact of climate change that she founded the School Strikes for Climate Change. She recognises that whilst having Asperger's can make her a little different from other people, this can in fact be regarded, as a superpower as it has contributed to her commitment to the cause of raising awareness of climate change. In 2019, she was awarded *Time* magazine's 'Person of the Year' and included in the *Forbes* list of 'The World's 100 Most Powerful Women'. She has also been nominated for the Nobel Peace Prize and been the subject of children's books such as *Greta and the Giants* (Tucker 2019), *Just Like Me* (Gooding 2020) and *Greta Thunberg* (Sanchez Vegara 2020). Learning about the ways she is continuing to make her voice heard by those in power across the world could inspire other children to realise that they are never too young to start making a difference.

Professor Wangari Maathai (1940–2011) received a Nobel Peace Prize in 2004. This is particularly notable as she is the first African woman to be awarded the prize. She received her prize 'for her contribution to sustainable development, democracy and peace'. She was a highly qualified scientist, a commissioner for the Earth Charter Initiative and a politician who, in 1976, initiated a massive tree-planting campaign through Kenyan women's groups to conserve the environment and improve their quality of life. Her campaign began when she planted trees in her own backyard and realised how these could provide a family with shade, fuel, food and income. Despite being frequently told that she should be at home looking after her husband, being harassed at public meetings and physically attacked by opponents, Professor Maathai became internationally famous for her work. Her example may inspire children to do their own planting or to learn about how plants can be used to reclaim and stabilise soil.

Dr Jane Goodall (born 1934) is world famous for her observations of chimpanzee behaviour. She made careful study of the lives, loves, 'wars' and peace of chimps in Tanzania and was the first to observe chimps as toolmakers. She also revolutionised the way such science was carried out by considering the chimps' emotions and personalities when interpreting their actions. As well as writing scientific papers, she has written children's books including *Pangolina* (2021) and *The Eagle and the Wren* (2014) and been the subject of those written about her life (Sanchez Vegara 2018). She set up the Jane Goodall Institute that works towards 'creating healthy ecosystems, promoting sustainable livelihoods and nurturing new generations of committed, active citizens around the world'. This and more can be found on her website.

The work of these scientists and others like them can be used to illustrate the positive contributions that science can make to sustainable development. It also shows us that scientists sometimes need to communicate their message to a wide audience, present convincing arguments and be more than a little persistent. Through combining science, citizenship and communication skills, science can be taught in a way that reflects the work of 'real scientists'.

Activating children's ideas

Living and non-living

You might elicit children's understanding of what makes something living by asking them to sort a collection into 'living' and 'non-living'. To explore some common alternative ideas, such as those identified in the Science Processes and Concept Exploration (SPACE) project research

(Osborne, Wadsworth and Black 1992), the collection could include: an earthworm, a potted plant, an apple, a toy car that moves, a doll or a lit candle (supervised). The following teacher prompts could be used to stimulate discussion:

Tell me about why you have grouped those things together.
What makes this different from the others?
How did you decide that this was living?

Children sometimes classify things that move as alive and so might consider the toy car or candle to be alive. Children may decide their own additional categories such as 'used to be living' and the apple might provoke debate. This could be a useful prompt for discussing how we need to consider the whole life cycle of living things. Adding a fossil ammonite to the collection could generate discussion about extinction. Children can then be invited to make their own list of the features of living things. Through dialogic talk, children can start to reason with and test each other's ideas whilst the teacher identifies their more resistant alternative frameworks, which will need further practical exploration and teacher input. The role of dialogic talk is explored further in chapter 1.

Seasonal change

What do you think the school woodland area is like at night?
How might it be different in the summer?
Do plants and animals live here all the time?

Children may have a stereotypical view of ecosystems (for example, the Arctic is always cold and the desert is always hot) or of seasons (for example, it is always sunny in summer but never in winter). Seasonal changes may be overlooked apart from the very obvious such as leaves falling in autumn and new plants growing in spring. A popular idea among children is that all plants die during the winter (Nuffield Primary Science 1995). Children should have plenty of opportunity to observe and explore their local environment throughout each season. In September, different parts of the outdoor area could be allocated to groups of children who then become responsible for recording and communicating the way it changes throughout the rest of the school year. They could take ownership of how they will record and communicate their observations and measurements, for example, through a mixture of photography, film, art, databases, poetry etc. They should also be encouraged to predict how their area will change in three months, six months, nine months etc. and then compare their predictions with their observations.

Food chains

What do you think this animal (example) eats?
Is this animal (example) eaten by anything?

Children's food chains are likely to reveal alternative ideas such as confusion with life cycles (egg → chick → hen). When questioned about the numbers of living things involved at each level of a food chain, children may think consumers (animals) rather than producers (plants) constitute the largest population. This may be true in some cases – for example, beetles on an oak tree – but in all cases, plants will make up the largest amount of 'biomass' or living matter (Leach et al. 1996). Children can also struggle to understand the impact that population changes have within an ecosystem. They may realise that a decrease in predator numbers will lead to an increase in prey but fail to consider that the amount of predators is also affected by the availability of animals which they prey upon (Allen 2020). The Qualifications and Curriculum Authority (QCA) (2004) reported that when drawing food chains, children should 'pay attention to the arrow direction', i.e. indicating food and energy transfer from producer to consumers. Children may not have a clear understanding that plants make their own food through photosynthesis (Driver et al. 1985, Barman et al. 2006).

Some children may believe that all ecosystems are controlled or created by people – of course many of those that children know about have been. Children in Key Stage 1 may think that all living things depend on human care (Leach et al. 1996). Again, this is an understandable alternative idea given most children's experiences of animals.

Microorganisms and biodegradation

If we left a leaf/apple core on the soil, what would happen to it?
What do you think happens to plants'/animals' bodies when they die?
What would happen to this plastic bag if we left it buried in the soil?
Why do things rot in the ground?
What does 'recycle' mean?

Children may not have any conception of rotting or decay. They may therefore explain the 'disappearance' of leaves and animal bodies by saying 'something ate it' or 'it blew away'. Others may have some idea about things rotting but have no idea what causes the process. Although many children in upper KS2 have started to understand that the bacterial microbes which are responsible for causing human infections are living things, they often fail to realise that environmental microbes are living organisms (Allen 2020) or their role in decay (Driver et al. 1985). When children were asked to think about why a chicken sandwich left in a warm place in the classroom had gone smelly, 40 per cent thought it had been contaminated by the warm temperature itself, 70 per cent of children mentioned something about 'bugs' or 'germs'. Others thought it had been ill when alive, the ink on the wrapping had contaminated it or it had been deliberately poisoned (Grace 2000).

Adaptation

A key step is to help children understand that particular living things live in certain habitats, preferably by looking at them first hand. You could ask:

- *Where do plants and animals live?*
- *Why do they live there?*
- *What kinds of plants and animals would live in these places: the air, water, land, underground?*
- *Can you think of animals that could live here (e.g. school grounds) and those that could not? Why not?*
- *How is…adapted to live in the sea/soil/cold climate?*

Children might think that animals make a conscious choice to live in a certain habitat – 'the worm lives under the soil because it's dark and the worm likes it like that' (Nuffield Primary Science 1995, p. 27), rather than that the worm is adapted to live in such a habitat. Children's thinking might turn the concept of adaptation around and say something like 'the bear grows a warm coat so it can live in a cold place'. Of course, polar bears cannot decide whether to have a warm coat or not. It is more correct to say 'only bears with thick warm coats can survive in cold climates'. Another common alternative framework children may hold is that within their lifespan, individual animals are able to adapt to unfavourable changes in their immediate environment (Allen 2020) believing that if a habitat is destroyed then the living things can just go and find somewhere else to live. This might be the case with a few species, but the majority do not have the ability to do so.

Build

Constructing new knowledge and working scientifically

The needs of life

In 'life processes', children will have learned about some of the MRS GREN (see Table 2.1.1) processes common to all life, and within this strand there is an opportunity to learn about the needs of life: air (oxygen), water, food and a place to live (habitat) where they can be safe.

To understand the needs of life, the best approach is likely to involve encounters with real animals – whether as pets, working animals or in a zoo, and the people who look after them. Ask parents and other members of the children's wider community whether they would be willing to bring in pets or discuss the work they do with animals. Some animals, particularly invertebrates such as giant African land snails, can be safely kept in schools. The Consortium of Local Education Authorities for the Provision of Science Services (CLEAPSS) offers advice on this. It may be possible to set up a hide in or near the classroom so children can do some birdwatching. A bird table could be set up outside the classroom near a window that is blanked out apart from a small viewing hole. Morning is usually the best time to catch birds feeding. The birds will need to get used to the table so do not expect immediate results. Some research into the foods and habitats that local species prefer will help children develop their understanding of the birds' needs and may help them attract more species. Clips from nature programmes such as *Springwatch* or David Attenborough's *Wild Isles* can be used to inspire children to make their own mini documentaries about a local species of their choice. A sense of awe and wonder can arise from children interacting with natural materials using magnifying aids such as the Easi-Scope microscope and home learning tasks requiring children to go on a family walk and document/bring back something from nature that they find interesting can encourage closer observation with natural environments. A range of ways for children to explore their local areas are suggested in the following Earthwalks activities.

BOX 2.1.1   EARTHWALKS ACTIVITIES

Earthwalks is a general term we give to a range of sensory activities that can be used to encourage children (and others) to explore their environment. The Earthwalks activities can be adapted and used in any setting, in the built and green environments: they are as useful for exploring walls and buildings as they are a woodland. The aim is to encourage children to become involved in a place, to get to know what is there, the sights and sounds, the smells and textures, and to view it closely from different perspectives. From these initial, broad explorations, questions may arise that could be followed up with investigations to find out more. These sensory activities can be easily adapted to suit children of all ages. Be aware of general health and safety precautions for working outside which can be found in the ASE's (2011) Be Safe! guidance. Some of our favourite activities are as follows:

Squirrels hide their nuts

As you set out on a walk, give each child two acorns (or any small biodegradable object). Ask them to hide them and not tell anyone else where they are. On the way back from the walk ask the children to find them again. Who are the lucky squirrels? What would happen to the acorns that have been lost?

Hug a tree

Find some trees. Work in pairs. One child has their eyes closed or wears a blindfold (place a paper towel inside the blindfold to prevent any risk of contracting conjunctivitis). Child 2 leads their partner to a tree, invites them to touch, feel, smell the tree, get to know it well, its girth, texture, etc. The child is then led away from the tree and twirls around a few times. The blindfold is removed, and the child tries to find 'their' tree. How do they know it? Now swap roles. Remind children to visit their tree again another time, if possible.

Skywalkers

This activity encourages children to look skywards. Give each child a safety or flexible mirror. Remind children they should never look at the Sun. Get the children to walk in a crocodile with one hand on the shoulder of the person in front and the mirror under their chin, so that they can see whatever is above them. Lead the children along slowly, get them to look in their mirrors. Stop under a branch. Invite the children to observe one of the reflected leaves closely; get to know it. Then ask them to look upwards into the tree. Can they see 'their' leaf? This technique can also be used to look at carvings on church ceilings, etc. Alternatively, if it is dry, take a lie down and survey the sky above.

Opposites

This activity uses touch. Pairs of 'opposites' (e.g. rough–smooth, warm–cold, hard–soft) are printed on card and couples given two words and an egg box. They are not to tell anyone what their pair of words is. The children then collect six things in their egg box: three things that are in keeping with one word and three for the other word. The children then show their objects to another pair of children and let them handle them. Can they guess what the descriptive words are? Now the other pair has their turn.

Pick and mix

This is another activity designed to encourage children to look closely at an object. Each child chooses a similar small object (e.g. a stone, conker, leaf) and examines it carefully. They then put their objects into a bag. Later that day the children see if they can remember their object well enough to find it again amongst all the similar but different objects.

Matching colours

Collect colour charts or strips from a DIY store. Invite children to find little stones, leaves, etc. which match the colours on the card. The range of colours and tones can be varied according to age and environment studied. The has links with art and colour mixing.

Nature palette

Stick a small piece of double-sided sticky tape on a card shaped like an artist's palette. Ask children to find tiny pieces of petal, grass, leaf, etc. to create a picture. Share their pictures with each other. Again, this activity encourages children to observe different colours and materials in their surroundings. Children can also attach natural items of interest to belts or bracelets made from sticky tape, and double-sided tape can be added to a treasure stick for children to decorate with larger natural materials.

Andy Goldsworthy inspired designs

Following a study of artist Andy Goldsworthy's outdoor artwork, children produce and photograph their own environmental sculptures and pictures.

Sound symphony

Ask children to sit or stand separately and be quiet and still for one minute. Invite children to record on paper, in pictures or symbols, the sounds they can hear. Ask children to identify sounds they like, sounds they dislike and whether some sounds seem out of place. Discuss findings.

Nature mini-safari

Children work in pairs. Each pair has 1 metre of string and several matchsticks. Children stake out points of interest along their string trail with matchsticks and study the ground so they become experts and know this small patch of the world better than anyone else. Then invite an adult or another child to be taken on a mini-safari with an expert guide.

Shake-down

Put a white sheet under and around a bush, give it a little shake and see what comes tumbling down! A pooter can be used to collect small invertebrates for a closer look.

Perfume potion

In a small container, select leaves and other fragrant items that give a pleasant odour (you may need to crush leaves). Children could then design packaging and advertising for their perfume which they could 'pitch' to the class in a Dragon's Den style presentation.

Photo-quiz

Each member of the group takes a photo of part of the environment from an unusual angle, and then shows others the photo. They have to work out where the photo was taken and what the picture is of.

Scavenger hunt

Give groups a list of things to collect/photograph. Criteria for a scavenger hunt could include: once living, a compound leaf, something spiky, evidence of a consumer (e.g. photo of eaten leaf/animal hole, etc.).

Leaf matching

Collect leaves with children or share pre collected leaves. Can they use the leaf identification chart to find out which leaf they have found? Encourage the use of senses for observation. Look carefully at the veins, shapes and arrangement.

The variety of life in different habitats

After children have spent time in the local area getting to know it through the Earthwalks activities described above (Box 2.1.1), the next task of an environmental scientist is to survey the ecosystem to be researched. Children can do this in a range of ways for a variety of purposes. Table 2.1.2 below describes a variety of survey types. The final type, managerial, shows how science can become a starting point for the promotion of values and attitudes relevant to education for sustainable development.

The kinds of initial surveys described in Table 2.1.2 could lead children to be able to ask questions about the ecosystems studied:

- Do you find more small insects on the top or the underside of leaves?
- Is there any difference in the length and width of leaves on the top, middle and bottom of a shrub?
- Will we find different kinds of animals if we take a sample of water from the top, middle or bottom of our school pond?
- If we make small patches of bare earth in different locations, e.g. under a tree or near a wall, will there be a difference in the type of plants which first grow there?

Table 2.1.2 Ideas for ecosystem surveys

Type of survey	Activities	Outcomes
Descriptive	Make an annotated sketch of the ecosystem including details such as plants, animals, water, soil, walls. Repeat for each season.	A collection of sketches that can be made into a book for children to compare.
	Make a drawing or painting on a footprint-shaped piece of paper to show what is on the ground beneath your feet.	A display of footprints across the classroom wall.
	Write a paragraph about 'a day in the life of a tree' including details about the air, water, rain, sunshine, animals and plants that it encounters. Note the 'good' and 'bad' aspects of the environment.	A collection of 'The secret lives of trees'. A list of likes and dislikes about the environment from the perspective of the children and imagined views of animals and plants.
Spatial	Use simple mapping techniques to make a plan and cross-section of the ecosystem on which the positions of different types of plants and animals found can be plotted. Mapping techniques include measuring dimensions (including depth of ponds, height of trees, depth of soil) and finding north.	A scale plan and cross-section of the ecosystem. A wall display of the plan or cross-section, e.g. 'our pond' showing above and below ground and water level.
Physical	Use simple scales or measuring devices, including data-loggers/computer apps, to record the factors and gradients of the physical environment such as temperature, wind, light and sound levels. Notes could be made of the materials found, e.g. wood, stone, soil.	A list of non-living parts of the ecosystem. Notes about how wet or dry the soil was in different areas. Graphs or contour maps showing key measurements.
Numerical	Use sampling techniques to estimate the populations of different species. For example, use a metre-square quadrant or a hoop placed on the ground randomly and count the grasses, daisies, spiders and ants within. Repeat and multiply up to find the estimated population. Estimate the numbers of birds visiting the area during one day by making observations each hour. Sweep different parts of a pond and identify the living things found.	A 'pyramid' of numbers showing the different populations of plants and animals. A food chain showing the relationships between plants and animals found in the habitat.
Temporal	Study a single plant and how it changes over time.	A 'tree diary' from autumn to summer.
	Study an ecosystem over time, making a record of its appearance, the weather, plants and animals to be seen.	A set of photographs and captions showing changes in the environment and populations during a school year.
Managerial	Find out from adults how the ecosystem is cared for and managed. Find out what information exists about the ecosystem and what information would be useful to help maintain and improve the biodiversity of the ecosystem.	A fact-file presentation dossier that can be presented to the school governors or parent–teacher association about a local environment and what needs to be done to improve it.

Table 2.1.3 Teaching survey skills

Tool/technique	Teaching point
Hand lens, magnifying glass, two-way magnifiers	Ensure the object is well lit. Keep it still and move the lens between eye and object to focus.
Line transept	Take a standard length (e.g. 1 metre) of string and plot each plant or animal touching the string.
Quadrant	Drop the square or hoop after taking a random number of steps in a random direction. Count the populations of plants and animals within the area.
Pooters, brushes	Show children how to collect small animals without harming them using a small paintbrush or pooter to suck the animal into the collecting jar. Reassure them it is not possible to suck the animal up into their mouth!
Collecting bottles	Ensure animals are not left for long in 'bug jars' and that they are replaced where they were found.
Nets	Sweep through water in the same way each time and for the same length of time. Avoid stirring up silt. Show how to tip the animals into a white shallow tray to observe the contents.

Children might also need to be taught how to use some survey tools or how to apply some techniques such as those outlined in Table 2.1.3.

These are pattern-seeking enquiries that are best answered by analysing the findings of a survey rather than carrying out a 'fair test'-type investigation. Tablets can be taken into the 'field', and carefully selected apps will help children with plant and animal identification. Furthermore, the location of measurements can be accurately recorded on some tablet apps so that, for example, a profile of the physical environment can be produced, or the distribution of a population mapped. As they work to find answers to such questions, children should be encouraged to suggest reasons for their findings using scientific knowledge where possible, for example, 'There are fewer animals in the middle of the pond because there is less food.' They should also draw conclusions recognising limitations in evidence, for example 'On the whole, there were fewer insects on the tops of leaves, but they may have flown off when we came near.' The raising and answering of such questions will provide opportunities to develop children's understanding.

Dataloggers/apps can be used to record environmental measurements such as light, sound or temperature (see Section Planning for progression), and similarly they can also support studies of ecosystems. Just leaving a logger outside, possibly in the school's conservation area, over a 24-hour period provides a wealth of fascinating data. How does the temperature change, and is it in step with light readings? Does the sound level remain constant, or do you notice a change at dawn? Children can be encouraged to tell the story of day and night-time activity through the readings taken. A woodland walk can be accurately mapped using a tracker app and the level of light intensity recorded by a datalogger. Then back in the classroom it is possible to produce a visual record of your position, sensor data and images from a digital camera, using Google Earth and Google Maps.

Food chains and webs

Children will grasp the idea of a simple chain where one organism is eaten by another as it suggests the energy flow in the right direction. As we have seen above, there are several alternative ideas that children may hold beyond this concept. The first task is to ensure children understand every food chain begins with plants (producers). This can be done through reference to the diet of any familiar animal (humans, for example, by looking at the contents of a lunchbox), and tracing back the source of all food. However, it is important to be conscious of food poverty issues children may be facing so best done through studying the 'teacher's prepared lunchbox'. Food chains with two, three and four or more organisms can then be developed, ensuring the concept of food (and therefore energy) transfer from one level to the next is understood. A web can be constructed by assigning each child an animal to represent, or a population, in an ecosystem. A pond ecosystem could have populations of pond weed (algae), water fleas (that feed on algae) and stickleback (that feed on water fleas) to begin with. Each population is joined to its predator by a length of wool. As other plants (duckweed, reeds) and animals (insect larvae, pond skaters, fish, ducks) are added, lengths of wool will criss-cross to show plants and animals providing food to populations higher up the trophic levels. While the details of exactly 'what eats what' may not be remembered, the enacted embodiment of being part of a web may remain. A further development of the activity is to introduce a catastrophic event – perhaps all the pondweed is killed by pollution – which takes out one whole part of the web. The effect on the subsequent feeding levels will be drastic!

Microorganisms

There are some activities that can be conducted safely in the classroom to demonstrate to children the presence of 'invisible' organisms. To focus only on microorganisms that turn food 'bad' will give the impression that microbial activity is always unwanted. A key learning outcome in relation to ecology will be to understand that the micro-organisms involved in decay and rotting can be an important part of any ecosystem in that they recycle material by returning useful material to the soil. One way to do this is to bury a range of items (e.g. apple core, stone, leaf, stick, paper, plastic bottle) in the soil at the edge of the school field and return to the spot at weekly intervals to take a photo. The children will see that some items are 'biodegradable' and some are not. In exploring ideas about why some objects 'disappear' children may think an animal has eaten it or it has 'washed away'. To test this theory, similar items can be placed in jars with a little soil and sealed (they must not be reopened). Biodegradable materials will start to decompose within a few weeks. This works well with packaging: compare biodegradable starch packaging with polystyrene chips. The polystyrene will remain for years. This kind of activity will also help children realise that whatever we put into an ecosystem is likely to stay there: when we throw a plastic bottle 'away' it will still exist for years to come.

Adaptation and evolution

Children's work in this area can begin by looking at some animals and plants in detail. First-hand observation should reveal plenty about the organism. These details could be recorded by an annotated drawing, creating a labelled plasticine model or by writing in a fact file with relevant headings such as number of teeth, number of limbs, size, colour, body covering. The way in which these features allow the animal or plant to survive can then be considered. *Does the body covering or colour protect the animal from a particular predator? Are the teeth adapted to eat a particular food? Are the eyes adapted to be useful in particular conditions?* Other information such as lifespan, life cycle and natural habitat can be supplemented by reference to secondary sources. These fact files could be compiled by the class into a reference book and supplemented with all the features of a non-fiction text including table of contents, index and glossary. Alternatively, small groups of children could produce a Michaela Strachan-style recording to present in assembly or share with parents through the school learning platform.

One way to encourage children to think about adaptation is by giving a list of environmental features that an animal would have to cope with and by asking children to 'design' such an animal. For example, if the animal preys on small invertebrates, lives in burrows in soil and is preyed upon by foxes, then what adaptations would it have to survive? The animal might be nocturnal, have large eyes and a sensitive nose to detect prey, strong front feet for digging and sharp teeth to eat and defend itself. These could also include more imaginative hostile environments such as a newly discovered planet or the bottom of an older sibling's school PE bag!

Children will find some animals inherently interesting and appealing. With other animals, such as bats and spiders, teachers may have to work harder to show that these animals too have needs and are valuable parts of an ecosystem. One approach to achieve a shift in attitude is to elicit children's beliefs about certain animals and ask them to research the truth behind them. A list of possible beliefs about bats is shown in our Battitudes table (Table 2.1.4). Younger children may wish to explore the lives of animals through role-play. For example, the teacher could construct with the class a story through which children can contrast their own behaviours and activities with those of nocturnal birds and animals.

Through studying the ways animals and plants are adapted to their environment and how these differences can be used to identify species, precise and accurate use of vocabulary can be encouraged. Children's initial responses about the variety of life before them can be refined by providing them with suitable identification keys so that 'lots of bits floating about in the pond' is more accurately expressed as 'water boatmen coming up to the surface then diving down' or 'the midge larvae are moving by wiggling their bodies from side to side'.

As evolution was included in the NCE for the first time in 2014, Russell and McGuigan (2013) developed a new study building on the SPACE project to explore children's understanding of adaptation and evolution as well as effective teaching strategies. Understanding that although offspring may be similar to the parent, there are small differences, is a foundation for understanding evolution, and they found that children's literature, such as the book *Monkey Puzzle* (2016) by Julia Donaldson and Alex Scheffler in which a young monkey is being helped by a caterpillar to find his mother, or Jules Pottles' (2019) *The Molliebird* which explores the topic of natural selection, was a good way into talking about this. Inventing and modelling imaginary parents and offspring was another creative introduction to the concept.

The title of one article 'Why are there still apes if apes have changed into people?' (Russell and McGuigan 2015) captures a key question that can be addressed by considering Darwin's 'tree of life' and the notion of common ancestors. Teachers' language needs some thought too; saying that, for example a caterpillar 'is *designed* to hold onto a leaf upside down' may inadvertently reinforce the idea that living things have been made to suit their habitat rather than having evolved through natural selection. Children can be very concerned about species that are threatened with extinction making connections between evolution and the impact of environmental change. It is also important to explore how they can start to play an active role in mitigating against this through their daily habits, consumer choices and their engagement in wider debate and communication.

Table 2.1.4 Battitudes		
Battitude	**True or false?**	**Details**
Bats are blind	False	Bats do have eyes but find their way mainly by using echoes (sonar).
Bats get caught in people's hair	False	Bats are very agile flyers and are very sensitive.
If a bat bites you, you will get rabies	False	Recent studies have shown bat populations in the UK do not have rabies. It is extremely unlikely that a bat will bite.
Bats need to be protected	True	All 18 UK bat species are rare and protected.
Bats drink blood	True…but	No UK species drink blood.
Bats are flying mice	False	Bats are more closely related to primates than rodents.

Monitoring and feedback

After children have been orientated to the topic, perhaps by doing some of the Earthwalks activities outlined in Box 2.1.1, you will want to find out their level of understanding and identify how teaching can build on the children's starting points. Finding out about their interests as well as their knowledge and conceptual understanding is part of this. However, these activities could be used to assess children's understanding at any point in a teaching sequence. Active, formative assessment should be integral to the learning and teaching cycle with responsive teaching providing clear guidance, support, challenge and time for all children to make further progress (Earle et al. 2018). To ensure validity, assessment for learning strategies need to be accessible for all children and enable them to evidence their developing science understanding and skills rather than just how well they can read and write. This can be achieved through a variety of multimodal approaches such as creating a set of top trump playing cards with key facts about animals and plants found in a particular ecosystem; recording a radio advert informing the school community about one of the sustainable development goals (UN General Assembly 2015) and how to take action towards meeting it; acting out a year in the life of the flora and fauna of the school playground or producing a short documentary about how a particular species of animal is adapted to survive in its habitat. Other assessment for learning approaches include observing and facilitating children's group discussions, perhaps using a concept cartoon to elicit their understanding of the impact that a decrease in foxes would have on a population of rabbits both in the short and long term; sorting photos/models of animals into different classification groups or deciding which of three invertebrate animals is the odd one out and why. Both the TAPS and PLAN resources are designed to support ongoing formative assessment throughout a topic which in turn can be used to inform more summative judgements. The free Explorify website also has a wide range of excellent short activities which can be used to assess and develop children's ongoing understanding about living things and their habitats.

Consolidate

Retrieving and applying

Children should have regular opportunities to consolidate new and existing learning through effortful and purposeful low stakes retrieval activities. Regular rehearsal and application of knowledge and skills to new contexts strengthens connections and their retention in long-term memory and can be more effective when spaced over time (McMahon et al. 2021). There are many different forms retrieval practice can take and using a variety of approaches to keep children engaged and motivated is important, otherwise there is a risk that they will switch off when faced with yet another short 'quiz'. Retrieval activities linked to the topic of living things and their habitats could include using a graphic organiser to compare and contrast animals from different classification groups; identifying and correcting the deliberate mistakes in a newspaper article about the evolution of the giraffe or working in small groups to produce physical food chains and topic webs with string and photos of organisms.

Children should be taught to care for and protect the environment as part of science, yet this requirement hides a far more complex range of issues. Such learning could be completely passive (knowing what to do to) or fully active (actually caring and protecting). Imagine a scenario where a class discovers that a local ecosystem (perhaps a neglected school conservation area) is not biodiverse, that a habitat, for example, a pond, is polluted and in need of management. It is important to make connections to real life situations which evidence the negative and inequitable impact that climate change is having on living organisms both in children's immediate environment as well as more globally.

Pupils should explore the meaningful long-term changes they can make both as individuals and members of a wider community to mitigate against this. Engaging with and learning to critically analyse research-based claims will support the development of lifelong scientific literacy skills enabling children to become active citizens and critical consumers of science who make informed contributions to environmental discussions and decisions throughout their lives. For example, children could research the impact of the palm oil sector upon the populations of endangered species such as the orangutan, pygmy elephants and Sumatran rhinos as well as the farming communities which rely on this stream of income. They could explore alternative sustainable products and fair trade, communicating their findings through a short documentary video to show other year groups during assembly or in a leaflet or poster to be shared with parents and the wider school community.

As children become more environmentally aware, they will need to refer to some guiding principles to inform action. The concept of sustainable development and the actions we all need to take to achieve sustainable development are very clearly laid out in the sustainable development goals (UN General Assembly 2015). We think science in primary schools has a responsibility to address these and can do so by teaching science in a way that helps children to understand some of the key concepts needed to appreciate the beauty and complexity of living things in their environment. To be active, children will need skills beyond science to make the case for action and to decide what action to take. To act on scientifically gathered information and achieve the 2030 sustainable development goals (UN General Assembly 2015), children will need skills and knowledge developed through citizenship. Taking action to protect or develop habitats connects science to real and motivating contexts. Strachan and Davey's (2022) book, Saving the Planet One Science Lesson at a Time, relates each of the sustainable development goals (UN General Assembly 2015) to purposeful science enquiry activities and includes creative challenges based on engaging contexts. The chapters linked to goals 13, 14 and 15 (climate action, life below water and life on land) are particularly worth exploring when teaching the topic of living things and their habitats.

Reviewing

The Teacher Assessment in Primary Science (TAPS) website is a good source of assessment materials which all have a clear, narrow focus on assessing children's specific disciplinary skills in a valid, reliable and manageable way. There is a wealth of one page focused assessment plans linked to the topic of living things and their habitats across all primary age groups, which includes the Year 2 'Nature Spotters' focused assessment that helps teachers make judgements about how children are using identification guides 'in the field' and the Year 6 'Fossil Habitats' focused assessment, which looks at how children evaluate sources of evidence for life in prehistoric times. Clear exemplification materials of how children are meeting the assessment criteria can also be found on the TAPS website. The PLAN primary materials are another good resource which can be used to plan and assess both children's substantive and disciplinary knowledge progression across all Year groups. Their website contains several free sample materials for each topic including excellent knowledge and vocabulary progression matrices and exemplification materials.

Prompt metacognition by asking children what they found most difficult to learn in their topic and how they managed this. What did they find most surprising? Hearing birdsong or the gurgle of a stream, witnessing the visually restful colours of autumn, smelling the strong garlic odour in a spring wood; all promote our feeling of wellbeing. Invite children to reflect on how they *feel* about plants, animals and their habitats. Do they think their attitudes to living things and their habitats have changed since the start of the topic? Could they see themselves doing a job related to living things in the future?

Classroom management

Working outside is rewarding and it is also unpredictable. Teachers have a duty to consider the risks of any activity, to take action to minimise risk and to know what to do if children's health or safety is compromised. The Association for Science Education's (ASE) (2011) publication *Be Safe!* is the definitive guide to health and safety. Things for teachers to consider when working outside include

Table 2.1.5 Risk assessment: working outside

Hazard	Action to reduce risk
Sharp items/syringes in leaf litter/undergrowth	Teacher to check general condition of the site. Use disposable gloves for collecting from the ground. In the event of a cut, inform parents as soon as possible.
Falling into pond	Children to be taught about appropriate behaviour. Adult to control access to pond. Consult doctor immediately in the event of children swallowing pond water.
Allergic reaction to found material/animal (most likely to manifest itself as hives/nettle rash or breathing difficulties)	Ensure data on children's known allergies is collected and checked and prescribed medication is available. Children at risk could use gloves and keep specimens in plastic bags.
Cuts caused by garden tools	Show children how to use tools properly. Clean tools afterwards. In the event of a cut, inform parents as soon as possible.
Tick bites	Insist that children wear long trousers and closed toe shoes in areas likely to have ticks. In the event of a bite, inform parents as soon as possible. It is advisable to remove the tick with tweezers or a tick puller. Lyme disease is a potential further risk. A GP should be consulted and told about the bite if the child begins to feel unwell in the coming days.

the adult-to-child ratio. If you are in doubt, visit the site to make a risk assessment and seek advice from your headteacher. All adults should be briefed about the possible risks and how to control them. Children too should be briefed about potential hazards and how to mitigate them. Some of these hazards are listed in Table 2.1.5.

It is obviously difficult to study at first-hand anything other than the local environment, but it is possible to use webcams to look further afield so that, in real-time, an elephant can be seen coming down to the water hole in Africa; an ostrich observed sheltering under the shade of a bush or house sparrow chicks watched in their nesting box. Clips from programmes such as *Springwatch* and nature clips featuring Ranger Hamza or David Attenborough can also be used to inspire and engage children's learning of both familiar and less familiar habitats. All in all, there is something rather magical about bringing these experiences to the classroom. It is now very easy for children to be part of national and international 'citizen science' projects such as community nature monitoring schemes which can be accessed through the natural history museum website.

The environment and the law

Many of Britain's wild plants and animals are legally protected, and although it is unlikely that teachers will transgress these laws, they do need to be aware of them. The law most relevant to living things in their environment is the Wildlife and Countryside Act (1981). Parts of the Wildlife and Countryside Act and some other laws dealing with species protection are described briefly here.

Teachers should be aware of the legal aspects of collecting plants and animals. It is *not* normally an offence to pick the 'Four Fs' – fruit, foliage, fungi or flowers – assuming that none of them are protected, specifically if they are growing wild and are for personal use and not for sale. This is not part of any Act, but a part of common law. It covers such customs as blackberry picking and taking ivy and holly at Christmas. To exercise this right, you must be somewhere you have a legal right to be, such as on a public footpath or in a public park. Of course, if enough children exercise this right at the same time and in the same place, it could cause a lot of damage to habitats and species. It is therefore worth considering some approaches to collection, such as the 'nature palette' activity (Box 2.1.1) that encourages children to gather only a tiny sample. In some places, such as parks or commons, local by-laws may prevent such activities altogether. The Wildlife and Countryside Act (1981) identifies measures for the protection of wild plants. It prohibits the unauthorised intentional uprooting of any wild plant species and forbids any picking, uprooting or destruction of listed plants. It provides certain defences, for example, provision to cover incidental actions that are an unavoidable result of an otherwise lawful activity, so the chances that a teacher would fall foul of this law are minimal.

Some of the animals protected by law are listed here and should not be disturbed or collected:

- adders;
- bats;
- some beetles, for example the stag beetle;
- some butterflies;
- some crickets, for example the mole cricket;
- common lizards;
- grass snakes;
- great-crested newts (also a European protected species);
- slow worms (in that they must not be sold, killed or injured);
- smooth snakes (also a European protected species).

It is also against the law to take birds, their eggs or other protected wild animals from the wild; to intentionally kill or injure birds or other protected wild animals or to destroy or possess birds' eggs. The places these animals use for shelter and protection (for example, a bird's nest when it is in use or being built, or a bat roost) are also protected. If children do collect invertebrates (minibeasts) from the wild or the school conservation area, ensure that they are returned as soon as possible to the same spot. Do not take animals from the wild to keep for long periods in the classroom: they can quickly die from overheating.

Summary

In this chapter we have discussed how the science of living things in their habitats relates to other concepts within the science curriculum and beyond it. We have shown how children can study local environments in a way that helps them appreciate the diversity and beauty of the natural world. These experiences can then be developed into systematic investigations of ecosystems that can be the basis for informed involvement in active citizenship. As children learn about the environment, they will begin to learn skills and knowledge that are relevant to education for sustainable development.

Discussion questions

1. How will an understanding of habitats help children understand the concept of sustainable development?
2. What animals and plants are children likely to have knowledge of, and which common groups of living things may children not know much about? Might this vary for different groups of children?
3. What connections can be made to children's prior learning in other topics both within science as well as other curricular areas?
4. Is it best to begin with the local environment before embarking on a study of a rainforest? Why?

5. Is a scientific understanding alone enough for children to become citizens engaged with environmental issues? How else can they be supported to develop the skills needed to become active citizens?
6. How might a socio-cultural view of learning science shape approaches to teaching this topic?

Further reading

Strachan, A. & Davey, J. (2022) *Saving the Planet One Science Lesson at a Time*, Hatfield: Millgate House.

Tucker, Z. (2019) *Greta and the Giants: Inspired by Greta Thunberg's Stand to Save the World*, London: France Lincoln Children's Books.

References

Archer, Ker L., Dewitt, J., Osborne, J. F., Dillon, J. S., Wong, B. & Willis, B. (2013). *Aspires Report: Young People's Science and Career Aspirations, Age 10–14*, London: Kings College London.

Allen, M. (2020) *Misconceptions in Primary Science* (3rd ed.), London: McGraw-Hill Education.

Association for Science Education (ASE) (2011) *Be Safe!: Health and Safety in School Science and Technology for Techers of 3- to 12-year-olds* (4th ed.), Hatfield: ASE.

Barman, C. R., Stein, M., McNair, S. & Barman, N.S. (2006) Students' ideas about plants and plant growth, *The American Biology Teacher*, 68(2), 73–79.

Beeley, K. (2012) *Science in the Early Years: Understanding the World Through Play-Based Learning*, London: Bloomsbury.

Constable, K. (2019) *The Outdoor Classroom in Practice, Ages 3–7* (2nd ed.), Abingdon: Routledge.

Department for Education (2013) *The national Curriculum in England: Key Stages 1 and 2 Framework Document*. https://www.gov.uk/government/publications/national-curriculum-in-england-primary-curriculum

Department for Education (2020). *Development Matters: Non-statutory Curriculum Guidance for the Early Years Foundation Stage.* https://assets.publishing.service.gov.uk/government/uploads/system/uploads/attachment_data/file/1007446/6.7534_DfE_Development_Matters_Report_and_illustrations_web__2_.pdf

Donaldson, J. & Scheffler, A. (2016) *Monkey Puzzle*, Basingstoke: Macmillan Children's Books.

Driver, R., Guesne, E. & Tiberghien, A. (eds) (1985) *Children's Ideas in Science*, Milton Keynes: Open University Press.

Earle, S., Qureshi, A., Rodger, P. & Sampey, C. (2018) Supporting assessment across the school, in Serret, N. & Earle, S. (eds), *ASE Guide to Primary Science Education* (4th ed.), Hatfield: The Association for Science Education.

Goodall, J. (2014) *The Eagle & the Wren*, Hong Kong: Minedition.

Gooding, L. (2020) *Just Like Me*, London: Studio Press.

Goodall, J. (2021) *Pangolin*, Hong Kong: Minedition.

Grace, M. (2000) *Ecosystems in SciCentre: Developing Primary Teachers' Science Knowledge - A Bank of Self-Study Materials*, Leicester: SciCentre.

Harlen, W. (ed.) with Bell, D., Deves, R., Dyasi, H. Fernandez de las Garza, G., Lena, P. ...Yu, W. (2015) *Working with Big Ideas of Science Education*, Treieste: Science Education Programme of IAP. www.ase.org.uk/resources/big-ideas/

Leach, R., Driver, R., Scott, P. & Wood-Robinson, V. (1996) Children's ideas about ecology 3: ideas found in children 5–16 about the interdependency of organisms, *International Journal of Science Education*, 18(2), 129–142.

McMahon, K., Lee, A., Etchells, P., Howarth, L., Humphreys, K., McKay, D. ... Salter, L. (2021): *The Learning Sciences and the Core Content Framework for Initial Teacher Training*, BathSPAdata. Online resource. https://doi.org/10.17870/bathspa.14258333.v1

Nag Chowdhuri, M., King, H. & Archer, L. (2021) *The Primary Science Capital Teaching Approach: Teacher Handbook*, London: University College London.

Nuffield Primary Science (1995) *Living Things in Their Environment: Teachers' Guide*, London: Collins Educational.

Osborne, J., Wadsworth, P. & Black, P. (1992) *SPACE Project Research Report: Processes of Life*, Liverpool: Liverpool University Press.

Pottle, J. (2019) *The Molliebird*, Bristol: Primary Science Teaching Trust.

Qualifications and Curriculum Authority (QCA) (2004) *National Curriculum (NC) Tests 2004: Implications for Teaching and Learning from the 2004 Tests, KS2 Science*, Norwich: QCA.

Russell, T. & McGuigan L. (2013) *Understanding Evolution and Inheritance at KS1 and KS2: Final Report*. www.nuffieldfoundation.org/sites/default/files/files/Final%20report%20-%20Understanding%20evoluation%20and%20inheritance%20-%20July%202015.pdf

Russell, T. & McGuigan, L. (2015) What are there still apes if apes have changed into people? *Primary Science, 139*, 22–25.

Sanchez Vegara, M. (2018) *Jane Goodall*, London: France Lincoln Children's Books.

Sanchez Vegara, M. (2020) *Greta Thunberg*, London: France Lincoln Children's Books.

Strachan, A. & Davey, J. (2022) *Saving the Planet One Science Lesson at a Time*, Hatfield: Millgate House.

Tucker, Z. (2019) *Greta and the Giants: Inspired by Greta Thunberg's Stand to Save the World*, London: France Lincoln Children's Books.

United Nations General Assembly (2015) *Transforming Our World: The 2030 Agenda for Sustainable Development*, A/RES/70/1, https://www.refworld.org/docid/57b6e3e44.html

United Nations General Assembly (2016) *The Paris Agreement*. Resolution A/RES/70/1. https://unfccc.int/sites/default/files/resource/parisagreement_publication.pdf

Waite, S., Passy, R., Gilchrist, M., Hunt, A. & Blackwell, I. (2016) *Natural Connections Demonstration Project, 2012–2016: Final Report*. Natural England Commissioned Reports, Number 215. York: Natural England. https://publications.naturalengland.org.uk/publication/6636651036540928

CHAPTER

2.2
Plants

Purpose of this chapter

After reading this chapter you will:

- know key concepts and understand relevant subject knowledge when teaching about plants;
- know a range of appropriate activities to teach about plants through an enquiry-based approach;
- know about research into children's ideas about plants and strategies for eliciting children's understanding of plants;
- understand how to make meaningful connections to children's own experiences and communities to support the development of their science capital;
- understand the importance of developing children's awareness of global environmental issues as well as the role they can take to help mitigate against climate change;
- understand how to make connections and reinforce learning about plants through purposeful retrieval practice activities.

Introduction

All our lives depend on them. Understanding and appreciating the life of plants is fundamental to the survival of our species and to sustainable development of the planet. This is an area of science that is relatively easy to resource, it lends itself to a range of scientific enquiries and it has great potential for developing children's creative and aesthetic responses to the world around them. This chapter will show how the study of plants in schools can, and should, be much more than growing cress and learning the reproductive cycle of a typical plant. Ways in which careful observation can be taught will be discussed, including the use of digital technology and more traditional aids. The chapter will also show how the diversity of plants can provide a range of opportunities for the exploration and investigation of life processes with contexts that have proven motivating to children such as food, gardening and art.

It is impossible to imagine our existence without plants, as most of our fundamental needs are connected to them: oxygen, food, fuels, building materials, medicines. Many of our favourite luxuries from coffee to cola, cotton to cocoa, have all been provided by the green kingdom.

Plants are a vital part of every ecosystem, providing the food energy that every other species depends upon. If we are to understand anything about the big issues of sustainable development, preservation of biodiversity, famine and poverty, then we need a basic understanding of plant life cycles and their habitats. Good cooks are often also plant experts – they can name a wide range of plant species, identify varieties from subtle differences in appearance, recognise herbs from their leaf shape and know when fruit is ripe and fresh by its colour or its smell.

Activities such as gardening, visiting historic parks or botanic gardens, cooking with locally sourced fruit and vegetables and autumn walks are very much part of our culture. On a sunny Sunday, thousands of us make the pilgrimage to the garden centre with the intention of beautifying our tiny patch of the earth. The Eden Project in Cornwall has been a staggering success built on plant life. There is something deeply satisfying and intrinsically pleasing about growing plants, cooking them, eating them, smelling them or simply looking at them.

If we start soon enough, we can help children understand the importance of plants, know some details of their life and death, and instil in them an appreciation of the diversity and beauty of this particular group of living things.

Planning for progression

In the Early Years, children will have had all sorts of encounters and experiences with living things in the classroom and environment. They will have used all their senses to explore plants and begun to appreciate that they are all around us and can be put into groups and named – perhaps 'flowers', 'trees', 'grass', 'plants' (by which they may mean anything that does not fit into their other groups). They may well have grown plants from seeds or bulbs knowing that soil and water are important and started to notice the changes plants go through over time.

In the early primary years (Y1–Y3), the study of plants is a distinct strand of the National Curriculum for England (NCE) (2013) programmes of study. Plants also appear explicitly and implicitly in other strands including 'living things and their habitats'. As children progress, they will need further experiences of a variety of types of plants to develop their concept of plants to include: grasses, trees, shrubs, 'flowers' and aquatic plants. They will certainly need to have the opportunity to grow plants from seed and to observe the growth in detail. They will also need to study plants in the local environment, for example, a garden, field, conservation area, hedgerow or wood. They will need to begin to see plants as part of the 'living things' group, different to animals in some ways, similar in others.

Although photosynthesis is not named in the primary NCE and children are not expected to know the details of the chemical reactions until Key Stage 3 (KS3), children should be coming to a clear understanding that plants make their own food by the end of Key Stage 2 (KS2), and teachers will need to understand how this happens. The key ideas about plants are outlined in Table 2.2.1. At KS2, some understanding of the concept of sexual reproduction in flowering plants as well as the mechanism for it is also developed, although the details at cell level (such as fertilisation as a fusion of gametes) is left to KS3.

During KS3, children will learn about photosynthesis and summarise it as a word equation. They will also be taught that nitrogen is a requirement for plant growth, the role of root hairs in absorbing water and minerals from the soil and that plants carry out aerobic respiration. If teachers want to adapt activities for higher attaining children at KS2, it is better to concentrate on broadening the children's understanding of plant diversity rather than introducing these new concepts. The key concepts teachers need to understand are summarised in Table 2.2.1.

Plants

Table 2.2.1 Key concepts for teachers: plant biology	
Key concepts	**Teachers' background knowledge**
Flowering plants have leaves, flowers, stems and roots	Plants come in every conceivable shape and size. Their sheer variety makes them fascinating and sometimes amazing. Observing their form and habit carefully is vital if we are to identify them. Leaves, designed to catch as much light as possible, can be little or large, smooth or rough, veined, ribbed, hairy, spotty, striped, fleshy, prickly, needle-like, jagged, split or holed. They can be every colour of green, red, yellow, purple, even black. Leaves are held on stems that are equally diverse – round or square, hollow or solid, horizontal, twisting or vertical, edible or poisonous. They can be positioned on these in opposite (two leaves growing on opposite sides of the same leaf node), whorled (at least three leaves growing from the same leaf node) or alternative (only one leaf on leaf nodes spread out along both sides of the stem) leaf arrangements. Roots can be delicate, thick and swollen or like branches of a tree.
	Plants store food as starch, and it is this fact we take advantage of when thinking of 'vegetables' to eat. Vegetable is not a scientifically useful word – it can refer to leaves (cabbage, bok choy), stems (celery, rhubarb), roots (carrot, parsnip, yam, cassava), flowers (broccoli, cauliflower) or fruit (marrow, pumpkin, okra).
Plants need light and water to grow	Plants needs a good deal of light once germinated, otherwise they will put all their resources into growing up and up, thus becoming leggy, yellow (as resources are diverted from producing chlorophyll) and eventually falling over. If growing plants in class, careful consideration needs to be given to where they are left, as many places will be too dark to sustain healthy growth. Plants need oxygen, so too much water will drown them or encourage mould to grow. Too little water and the plant's cells will lose sap and go flaccid – the plant will look limp and fall over. As we need vitamins and minerals to supplement our diet, so too plants need minerals, which they get from chemicals dissolved in water in the soil.
Seeds grow into flowering plants	Germination of seeds requires an appropriate temperature, moisture level and oxygen, but not usually light. When conditions are right, the seed will begin to absorb water, swell and burst its coat or testa. From the testa, one or two seed leaves will emerge. These are not true leaves but stores of energy in the form of starch. The radicle (root) heads for the soil and the plumule (shoot) goes in the opposite direction. The plant will rely on the stored food until it can produce its first leaves to begin photosynthesising food. If all goes well, roots will draw up water, leaves will develop on the shoot and the plant can grow.
	Once seeds are produced, they are spread afar to avoid overcrowding and competing with the parent plant for resources. Seed dispersal is a fun aspect of plant biology to study in the primary school as plants have evolved a variety of methods:
	Wind dispersal – the sycamore, ash and maple drop their winged 'keys' from a height, while the dandelion seeds are launched in feathery parachutes on a gust of wind. Poppies have long wobbly stems topped with 'pepper pots' that shake.
	Water dispersal – many water plants and shore dwellers (e.g. the coconut palm) have floating fruits that are carried by water currents to new desirable destinations.
	Hitchhikers – the 'sticky' cleavers and hooked burdock achieve dispersal of their seeds by hooking to the coat (or clothing) of a passing animal.
	Edible fruits – juicy fruits entice animals to eat them. The seeds pass through the digestive tract unharmed and are deposited in a new location. Nuts lend themselves to being stored, buried and forgotten.
	Exploding fruits – as some fruits dry, they suddenly explode open when ripe, expelling their seeds. The gorse, broom, wisteria and busy lizzie (impatiens, also a herbal cure for impatience!) are examples. Once the seeds find themselves in a suitable spot, they may lie dormant for some time.

(Continued)

Table 2.2.1 (Continued)

Key concepts	Teachers' background knowledge
New material for plants' growth is produced in leaves (by photosynthesis)	Plants make their own food through the process of photosynthesis. Leaves contain chlorophyll, a green pigment vital for photosynthesis as it enables the energy from sunlight to be stored and used to convert simple raw materials into new plant matter. This food is then transported around the plant so new roots, stems and flowers can be made. Photosynthesis literally means 'assembly by light'. In simple terms, carbon and oxygen from carbon dioxide gas, and hydrogen from water are combined to make a sugar molecule of carbon, hydrogen and oxygen (carbo-hydr-ate) ('-ate' refers to oxygen). This can be represented simply as: $$6CO_2 + 6H_2O \xrightarrow{\text{(energy)}} C_6H_{12}O_6 + 6O_2$$ There is excess oxygen in the reaction so some of it is given off as O_2 (oxygen gas) which enriches our atmosphere.
Roots have specific functions	Roots have two main functions – to anchor the plant, and to take up water and dissolved minerals to be transported through the stem to other parts of the plant.
The role of flowers and fruit in the life cycle of flowering plants includes pollination, seed formation, seed dispersal and germination	Plants can reproduce sexually or asexually (without sex). The flower is the structure in which sexual reproduction takes place. 'Perfect' flowers have both male and female reproductive organs while 'imperfect' flowers have only male reproductive organs (stamens) or only female reproductive organs (ovary, style and stigma). Some plants have both male and female flowers, while others have males on one plant and females on another. Complete flowers have a stamen (anther and filament), a carpel (containing the ovary, stigma and style), petals and sepals. Sepals are the leaf-like structures at the base of some flowers. Sometimes flowers are 'incomplete', meaning they lack one of these parts. Be aware of this when selecting flowers to use for a lesson, although it is good to provide a range of more diverse examples for children to compare and contrast. Sexual reproduction involves the mixing of genes from female and male organs through the combining of sex cells or gametes (KS3 concept). At KS2, children will learn about pollen (male) and the ovum (plural ova) (female). The flower's anther makes pollen, and the ova are contained within the ovary, usually found at the base of a flower in the stigma. Plants have devised a wonderful variety of ways to get these two cells together through a process called pollination. Pollen does the travelling; therefore, it is usually as light and small as dust – and can make some of us sneeze. Pollen is carried by the wind (in the case of grasses) or by bees and other insects. The pollen is caught by the feathery or sticky stigma found at the centre of most flowers. Once on a stigma, the pollen grain grows a tube that finds its way through the stigma and style to the female ovum. The male sex cell, containing half the information to make a new, unique individual, will unite with the female half of the genetic information to produce a seed. This is called fertilisation. The ovary then swells and changes to become the fruit. A pea pod is the fruit and the 'pea' is the seed. The peas may look identical, but they will each grow into a unique individual with characteristics combined from their parents. The mother will be the same but the fathers could be different. Gregor Mendel discovered heredity and sex in peas; his ground-breaking work conducted, somewhat ironically, in a monastery garden. It is easy to become pedantic about whether what we call a fruit is actually a fruit. For the purpose of primary teaching, it is useful to categorise anything that contains a seed or seeds as a fruit. This is complicated by seedless fruits (e.g. bananas, cucumbers and some grapes); seedless because humans have selected what would be naturally useless varieties. Tomatoes, pumpkins, peppers and green beans are all fruits.
Life processes are common to all living things	Although young children have trouble seeing plants as 'alive' in the same way as animals, they are classified as living things because they carry out all the following processes. MRS GREN or MRS NERG can be useful mnemonics to remember them by:

(Continued)

Key concepts	Teachers' background knowledge
	Movement They do not get up and walk, but plants will move their leaves, stems or flowers (e.g. sunflowers) to find the light or a support (e.g. beans). **Respiration** Within their cells, energy is released from food in the presence of oxygen. In plants they make this food themselves. **Sensitivity** Plants can sense light, gravity and water. Some can sense if they have been damaged. **Growth** Cells can get bigger and divide, so the plant gets bigger – usually growing for the whole of its life. **Reproduction** Making new organisms – plants can do this either sexually (flowers and seeds, etc.) or without sex (e.g. runners or cuttings) (see section on reproduction above). **Excretion** Getting rid of waste materials – oxygen is a waste product of photosynthesis. **Nutrition** Plants use food they make themselves (see section on photosynthesis above) to get energy to do all the above. Perhaps **MRS GREN** is a green-fingered gardener!
Living things can be grouped according to observable similarities and differences	'Green plants' as they are referred to in the NCE, or properly speaking 'Plantae', are one of the two main kingdoms of living things studied in primary school (Animalia being the other). Scientists disagree about many things, and the definition of a plant is no exception. One way to identify a member of this kingdom is to study it at cell level. A plant cell will have a cell wall made of cellulose, a sap-filled space within the cell and some tiny grains called chloroplasts that contain the green pigment chlorophyll, which is vital for photosynthesis. If all these features are present, then you probably have a plant. This knowledge about cells is, however, reserved for the KS3 curriculum. It is usually obvious to children that something green with leaves, a stem, roots and flowers is a plant, although as explored later, children are likely to hold alternative ideas about what is and what is not a living plant. To complicate matters, not all the four main groups of plants have features that children usually associate with plants. **Mosses** are plants that, apart from being very green, have no flowers, stems or leaves. They keep low to the ground as they are non-vascular, which means they cannot transport water and nutrients through their bodies. They reproduce by making spores, rather than seeds. **Ferns** are a group of plants that can transport liquids in vessels so have developed roots, leaves and stems, but they are non-flowering. They reproduce by making spores on structures usually found under their leaves. **Conifers** reproduce by making 'naked' seeds in cones (coniferous = cone-bearing). There are always exceptions in biology – the yew and the beautiful ginkgo tree from this group make seeds in soft 'berries'. Flowering plants are at the top of the evolutionary tree, so to speak. These are the plants that most children and adults will recognise as plants. Seaweed, slime, mushrooms and mould are the tricky things to classify. Seaweed and pond slime are called algae, which does not help say whether they are plants or not. If you want to study them in school, treat them as plants as they are green. Mushroom and moulds are fungi, which have their own kingdom. Fungi cannot photosynthesise – they feed off dead or living things. Lichens (studied in detail by Beatrix Potter) are a curious group and are actually two organisms – algae and a fungi – living in perfect harmony.

Teachers' self-assessment questions

1. Name at least five different plants that you might find on a school playing field.
2. Often it is flowering plants that spring to mind, what other kinds of plants are there?
3. How does water get into leaves?
4. What do seeds need to germinate? Are these the same conditions that are needed for healthy plant growth? Why?
5. Why might some flowers be brightly coloured and other flowers green?
6. Name five different ways in which seeds are dispersed.
7. How would you respond if a child said that plants get their food from the soil? What would you do if another child said they get it from a bottle of 'plant food'?
8. Which parts of a flower are involved in pollination?

Engage

Situating the topic

We have identified a number of ways in which plants are very relevant to adult lives – farming, cooking, gardening, appreciating nature – but how can we connect them to children's experiences and interests? To orientate children to such topics, several starting points can be suggested:

- looking at a collection of plants, for example a bag of 'vegetables' from the local greengrocer;
- a trip to a local park, woodland, allotment or garden centre;
- a visit from a gardener or farmer;
- a visit to the supermarket or international food market;
- a classroom display that focuses on the uses of plants such as food, medicine and textiles.

The above suggestions can lead to some interesting cross-curricular projects, but we can also find a strong justification to place learning in science in a cross-curricular context by looking at school initiatives associated with the health and wellbeing of children (e.g. the National Healthy Schools Programme (healthyschools.org)) and of our planet (e.g. the Eco-schools project) as well as the responsibility we have as a country towards achieving the sustainable development goals (UN General Assembly 2015). Specific science-based questions can lead to some issues of global importance. Teachers might use some of the following questions to promote a class discussion:

> What does 'Eat 5-a-day' mean?
> What counts as a fruit or 'vegetable'? Why?
> Where does the school get our fruit from?
> Can we grow our own? Is that a healthier option?
> What other benefits might there be from growing food in school? What problems would we have to overcome?
> Where would we get the water and soil? What should we do with the waste?

As this kind of enquiry unfolds, so skills and knowledge from many areas of the curriculum and themes such as economic awareness and sustainable development become central to the curriculum. Perhaps the most meaningful way to learn about plants is to grow them. Setting up and maintaining a garden, allotment or conservation areas has huge potential for learning across the curriculum from reception to Year 6. Organisations such as Learning Through Landscapes, Eco-schools and Countryside Classroom can offer plenty of advice.

The Ripple Effect's (previously known as the Send a Cow farming partnership) website provides instructions for making bag or keyhole gardens. The latter is a circular raised structure that is often used in Africa when soil is poor or infertile. It can even be constructed straight onto concrete. Local or recycled materials such as plastic bottles filled with sand can be used to create the walls. The garden can be used to grow vegetables, fruit and herbs. Lesson resources are available to link in with global issues, such as sustainability, poverty, life in Africa, social justice, education and the environment. The Practical Action schools' website also contains some great STEM teaching resources based around solving real life problems such as creating a floating garden for Bangladeshi farmers and designing and building a model to move tomatoes down a Nepalese mountain. Through this kind of experiential learning, children can begin to learn about the importance of plants in their own lives and those of others around the world.

A wholly integrated approach to cross-curricular work may not be possible in every school, but the creation of links between subjects usually is. Design and Technology (D&T) provides opportunities for the knowledge and skills gained during science lessons to be applied in the real context of making a product. For example, children could have the opportunity to apply knowledge about fruits to making a fruit salad in food technology, which in turn would lead to a kinaesthetic way of learning more about the structure of fruits. The first lesson could be a sensory exploration of fruit and vegetables with children choosing how to record their findings, for example, using digital technology, models, drama, poetry or drawings and notes. The lesson might conclude with the compilation of a display of photographs of the foods and children brainstorming all that can be made with fruit and vegetables. Later lessons would then be planned for the designing and making of a fruit salad.

The art curriculum also offers potential for connections. After observing and exploring the diversity of colours and patterns in plants, flowers and leaves, art-exploration activities that incorporate colour-mixing and matching could follow. Many artists have used plants as inspiration for their work. The style of work of Georgia O'Keefe (1887–1946), in which she painted large-scale depictions of flowers seen close up and cropped, has potential for the primary classroom: work that is developed from observational drawing and sketches into large-scale paintings and pastel images could make a striking display. The work of painters Van Gogh and Monet, the environmental sculptor Andy Goldsworthy, textile designers Kaffe Fasset and Cath Kidston, or botanical artist and author Beatrix Potter all offer inspiration for further creativity.

Breaking down barriers

As with any science teaching, when teaching about plants it is important to recognise and support the development of all children's science capital through focusing and building upon the unique contributions that they and their communities can bring to the topic (Nag Chowdhuri, King and Archer 2021). Visiting a family member's allotment, inviting volunteers to teach the class how to prepare a family plant-based recipe from their home country or going to a local international food market on a scavenger hunt for more exotic fruits and 'vegetables' from a range of countries represented by the children in the class are just a few ways how you could make science more relatable and relevant to your pupils. Ultimately, it is important to spend time eliciting and valuing the unique scientific skills and life experiences that the children and their families from your class bring as often pupils fail to understand how science connects to their own lives, particularly when they come from more diverse backgrounds (Nag Chowdhuri, King and Archer 2021).

In addition to the wealth of science connections which you will find within your own school communities, the STEM ambassadors programme is a great free way to arrange both face-to-face and online visits from a wide range of scientists whose work relies on plants. The Primary Science Teaching Trust's 'A Scientist Just Like Me' website also contains resources detailing the work of several contemporary scientists from diverse backgrounds who work with plants.

Three scientists who could inspire learning about plants are listed below, although as previously discussed, meaningful and relevant connections can be made to many more based upon the interests and the communities of the children in your classroom.

Mary Seacole (1805–1881) was a Jamaican born 'doctress' and herbalist who came to England in the 1850s and was an unsung hero of the Crimean war. Despite being initially turned down as a volunteer, she independently travelled to Crimea where she treated hundreds of sick and injured soldiers using traditional Caribbean herbal treatments such as aloe vera to treat cuts in the skin, ginger for sickness and diarrhoea, and lemongrass to bring down a fever. Mary Seacole received the Jamaican Order of Merit in 1991 and was voted the greatest Black Briton in a 2004 internet poll. Learning about her work could inspire children to consider the uses of plants in medicines and treatments with a link to keeping healthy. For example, pupils could grow their own aloe vera plants from cuttings and then work together on a cross curricular project to develop and market them as natural after sun treatments.

Danny Clarke is a British garden designer and television presenter otherwise known as The Black Gardener. He co-directs Grow2Know, an organisation inspired by the Grenfell Tower community who transformed a neglected and barren site into the Grenfell Garden of Peace, a positive space of hope. Grow2Know aims to use horticulture to inspire, heal and educate making gardening more accessible and inclusive for all. Children could be challenged to produce their own designs to transform part of their school grounds, or a local area, into a greener, more inviting space. The scale of such a project could range from creating small planting areas to working with the local council and wider school community to plant larger community spaces.

Dr Tanisha Williams is an American plant ecologist and botanist who founded Black Botanists Week, an annual summer event which highlights the work of Black botanists and aims to provide greater diverse representation within the field of botany. Dr Tanisha Williams is passionate about conserving biodiversity and has studied how the flowering of Pelargonium, a South African plant genus, has changed over the last century. Her work could motivate children in carrying out research of a plant of their choice or they could be inspired by an event or scientist promoted through Black Botanists Week.

Activating children's ideas

As suggested above, an ideal way to begin a topic would be to use a collection of plants. This collection can also be used to elicit children's ideas through questioning or sorting activities. The collection should be carefully selected to include some specimens that would be likely to cause questions to be raised. Rymell (1999) asked children 'What defines a plant?' Their responses revealed a range of definitions based on different experiences:

> *It's quite small, not high up.*
> *That's [dandelion] a weed not a plant. It grows in the ground.*
> *It's like a plant; it needs watering.*
> *A plant is … a flower that grows in the garden.*
> *A fungus is not a plant … because it has a trunk like a tree* [i.e. suggesting trees are not plants].

An elicitation collection would therefore include plants such as those children might know as 'weeds' (e.g. dandelions), plants not in flower, a tree (or at least a picture of one), grass, a cactus, a tiny seedling, even an air-plant. The inclusion of a mushroom, a fruit and a cut flower in a collection would further challenge children's ideas. Adults or children could note comments in a floor book or concept map. You may find that, to some children, 'plant' may mean 'small or medium-sized, green-leafed thing', which excludes trees, grasses and anything too far removed from a pot plant. 'Plant' may include or exclude 'flower'. 'Flower' and 'weed' may be mutually exclusive groups. Fruits and vegetables may be separate groups, perhaps not connected to plants. Fruits could include only obvious contenders, such as apples, oranges and grapes. Plants may not be seen as living because they do not move in ways obvious to a child. Although sunflowers turn their heads through 180 degrees during a day and some climbing plants can grow up to a metre a day in the summer, these changes will not be discernible to a child who cannot remember if they have had lunch. A plant's lack of apparent growth, 'feeding' and 'breathing' will all contribute to a child setting them outside a concept of 'living thing' and children may also hold the misconception that plants don't reproduce due to a limited understanding of their life cycles.

Although first-hand exploration is always preferable, there will not be the opportunity to do this for all species you wish to study, especially those found in more extreme habitats, any which are potentially harmful and when conducting studies over a long period of time. In such cases, digital technologies such as live webcams, time lapse photography and videos, as well as good quality textbooks, can provide a valuable insight into the life processes of more obscure plants. There is a wealth of short David Attenborough video clips exploring variation, life cycles and adaptations which can be freely accessed through the BBC website. In the plant kingdom there are wonderful examples of how plants cope with a range of conditions: cacti storing water in their stems which are protected by leaves adapted into spines; onions exuding chemicals when damaged to ward off attackers; dandelions producing tall flower bearing stems to give their parachuted seeds a chance of a good launch into the wind. Russell and Watt's (1990) SPACE research on growth found that KS1 children usually identified only three conditions for growth: water, Sun and soil. Very few children mentioned all three. Soil was typically viewed only for support, rather than a source of water and dissolved minerals. At KS2 children mentioned water, soil and Sun (distinguished between sunlight and heat in some cases). Few children at KS1 or KS2 mentioned air or gas as a requirement for growth.

Russell and Watt (1990) also found that children held a number of alternative ideas about how and when growth occurred. Growth was often seen as an 'unfolding' of material in a seed, rather than understanding that plants generate new material from water and carbon dioxide. Twenty-five per cent of KS2 children thought growth occurs in plants during the night rather than understanding it as a continual process. This is understandable, as children will witness that plants have 'magically' grown overnight.

Concept cartoons can be an excellent way to elicit children's ideas about the conditions needed for germination of seeds or those needed for plant growth, and to unpick misconceptions which often can form from conflating the two processes.

Build

Constructing new knowledge and working scientifically

Scientific enquiry may well emerge from an elicitation activity. In one school, a group elicitation session with a Year 6 class revealed a whole range of ideas and vocabulary associated with the topic of plants from being able to list just water and light as the needs of plants to citing 'photosynthesis' and 'oxygen' as key vocabulary. Further exploration showed that one child had some understanding of the process of photosynthesis while the rest of the group were happy just to use the word. One group said of a plant, 'it's a living thing' and 'the flowers grow from seeds, need Sun and water and absorb the Sun'. Such comments suggest the teacher could explore the children's use of the word 'flower' to mean plant, whether the 'Sun' is understood as providing light energy and whether the function of leaves and flowers is understood. During the elicitation, the children in this case also raised some questions that they wanted to answer:

> *What would happen if we broke the veins of a leaf? How long would a plant live without food?*
> *Could you put a plant back if you uprooted it?*

These questions then lead to some fascinating and worthwhile scientific enquiries but need to be developed further to move them from simple exploration to other guided investigations. For example, *What would happen if we broke the veins of a leaf?* could remain a simple exploration, could be developed into a pattern-seeking enquiry to find *Do all leaves have visible veins?*, or could be developed into an enquiry to test a prediction such as *A leaf will die if its veins are broken, but the plant would survive. How long would a plant live without food?* could be developed into a reference search *Do plants need food?* or a fair test enquiry: *Do some plants last longer than others without soil/light/water?*

A second way of initiating enquiry is through observation. Picture the scene: a vase of daffodils on each table, children drawing with crayons or pastels as the spring sunshine streams through the Portakabin window. Teachers will be familiar with 'observational drawing' as a way of getting children to look more closely. Drawing leads to learning – the process of in-depth observation and careful recording is a fundamental way of knowing and has a long tradition in botany and biology. The children's author Beatrix Potter (1866–1943) was a skilled artist and created a large portfolio of botanic drawings before turning to the telling of tales. The knowledge she gained from drawing can be seen in her children's books where Jeremy Fisher and friends can be seen sitting on very accurately portrayed mushrooms. Skills need to be taught including observation and recording through drawing.

OBSERVATIONAL DRAWING, STEP BY STEP

Setting up the task

- Is the lighting and background suitable? Bright light and an uncluttered background are ideal for scientific observation. Has the Sun stopped streaming in? Does light need to be shed on the subject? Is the child inadvertently blocking light from the object?

- Do the children know how to use magnifying aids? Do they know that you must move the object (or the lens) until the image comes into focus?

- Are appropriate drawing media and tools available? This depends on the type of drawing required. If colours are to be matched, can the paints or pastels be mixed or blended? If fine detail is required are pencils sharp or small brushes available?

Making observations

- Has each child had the opportunity to handle or be close to the objects? The learning experience will be a richer one if the child could look at, feel and smell the flower too. It may serve to focus attention on the specimen, rather than the vase.

- Have the children's observations been focused by discussion? What do they notice? The texture of the leaf, the colours, the cross-section of the stem or number of structures within the flower? How do they describe the feel of the sap exuding from the cut stem?

Recording

- What are the children to focus on? Drawing all the flowers in a vase may be less purposeful than honing in on specific features. A hand-held card frame – rather like a camera viewfinder – might help here. You might direct them to look particularly at: a visual element such as colour; texture; form; pattern (e.g. by sketching 'swatches' of pattern and colour, specimens could be compared); structure, such as leaves, anthers, petals (e.g. by enlarged line drawing of these dissected parts); variation and diversity (e.g. by six sketches of different leaf shapes).

> **Considering evidence**
>
> - Will there be time to share observations, to celebrate the work and to discuss what has been learned?
> - Ask the children to say one thing they noticed that perhaps no one else noticed. Make a record of questions about the plants that have been raised. Are the stems of other plants hollow? Do other plants have six anthers? A KWHL (what I know, what I want to know, how I will find out and what I learned) chart could be regularly updated on a science working wall as children carry out further investigations to answer their questions.

To complement drawing activities, children could also make digital images on the same themes to develop a 'picture library' of the plants in a collection or in the local environment. The resulting images can be sorted, collated and manipulated to show similarities, differences and patterns in plant structures. Figure 2.2.1 shows, for example, images that show leaf veining and patterns.

Figure 2.2.1 Photographs showing the diversity of leaves.

Digital cameras, magnifying apps and portable digital microscopes can all be used to view, record and then share enlarged close up images of both individual plant parts, as well as taking photos of the whole organism. Images can be captured to produce a PowerPoint slide show, a non-fiction book or a quiz for others to recognise and label enlarged photos of different parts of a plant. When displayed on a class screen, small plants (try daisy flowers) become wonderful things. The surface of a leaf, pollen on stamens and root hairs all become remarkable structures when magnified 10 or 60 times. Magnified images can also be a great way to inspire children's own artwork through a variety of media.

Living things can be grouped according to observable similarities and differences

If you feel your class does not have a clear idea that plants are living things that carry out the same processes as animals, then it would be worth spending time making that point through a sorting activity. Provide children with a range of items that includes some non-living things (e.g. stones, classroom objects), plants and animals (or representations of animals, ensuring the children understand the picture or toy is meant to stand for the real thing). When they have sorted the collection, discuss the common processes of living things and how plants and animals are similar.

If children are clear about plants being alive then move on to simple classification within the plant kingdom. Provide specimens for children to discuss and group according to similarities (e.g. tomatoes, Brussels sprouts, peas, beans, lettuce, cabbages, carrots).

Encourage children to say why they have grouped the plants together. Ask them to construct an identification key to help other children identify the plants. Figure 2.2.2 shows children sorting fruit and in Figure 2.2.3, an example of how they recorded this.

The NCE places more emphasis on children being able to identify and name common wild and garden plants. This could become dull rote learning, but it can also be taken as an opportunity for encouraging careful observation of similarities and differences – is the yellow flower growing on the playing field a dandelion, buttercup or a celandine? Children can be encouraged to look at details in their everyday world that they may not have noticed before. A look at the way Carl

Figure 2.2.2 Children sorting fruit.

Plants

Figure 2.2.3 Children's recording of a sorting activity.

Linnaeus carefully documented different kinds of leaves in his sketchbooks transforms how we see leaves and recognise them as different.

Using common names (daisy, blackberry, beech, speedwell, rosebay willowherb) is appropriate, but the Latin names can be demystified by thinking about their meaning – rosa canina – is the wild 'dog rose', cinquefoil, has five (cinque) leaves (as foliage) making cross-curricular links to language work. Children could make up their own names for plants that encapsulate their key features.

Investigating the effect of light, air, water and temperature on growth

Growing cress does not feature in the suggestions for scientific enquiries in Table 2.2.2. While it is undoubtedly an easy and cheap way of allowing children to grow plants, most children have had such an experience by the time they reach KS1. Many other seeds will germinate within seven days (try broccoli or begonias) and can be used to illustrate variety and diversity. Rice is one of the most important crops in the world; it can be germinated from brown cooking rice and grown in a 'paddy field' (from *padi*, meaning rice in the Malay language) in a bucket.

Seed germination offers scope for the gathering of good numerical data for older children to work with. If seeds are sown in groups of ten in a petri dish or similar (see the very useful Science and Plants for Schools (SAPS) website for detailed guidance on this and other investigations), the data generated can lead to calculations and graphs exploring the rate of germination and growth rates of roots and shoots. Another great SAPS idea is to sow seeds in small pots that have lids on, a hole punched in the side or coloured cellophane over the top. The seeds will use their store of energy to grow in search of light. If there is no light, they will grow upwards quickly in an effort to find it. This has the effect of making the shoots look spindly and yellow (etiolated). If light is coming in from one side, the shoots bend to that source. Shoots that grow in light will be strong with green 'seed leaves' as the stored energy is used to make chlorophyll to enable the plant to make its own food. This technique also allows the variables of light colour and light direction to be explored.

Flowering plants have leaves, flowers, stems and roots which have roles in growth and nutrition

At KS1, children are required to know the names of the external parts of a plant. Children will be familiar with leaf, flower and probably stem, but roots will need to be investigated as, of course, they are not usually visible. Some opportunities for children to uproot and examine the root systems of plants such as grass, dandelions and potted plants can be provided to address this. At KS2, the emphasis shifts to considering the functions of plant structures. A classic primary demonstration is to put a stick of celery or a carnation flower stem in coloured water that can then be seen drawn up through the plant. In one class, a child raised the fantastic question of whether it would still work if you turned the celery upside down. Does it? This activity demonstrates one function of the stem, but does little to develop an understanding of the role of roots in the process of taking water from soil to leaves. A similar investigation can be done using a rooted plant (e.g. radish or cress seedling) compared with another without water. Put the roots of one seedling in a small tub of coloured water and another in a similar tub without water. Leave over playtime. *Can the 'dry' seedling be revived? Have the roots taken in any of the coloured water?* This will also demonstrate the concept of a plant being supported by water in the plant (turgidity), as the 'dry' seedling will be very floppy. Roots also have the function of anchoring the plant. This could be shown by a model-making activity using art straws or pipe cleaners to make stable tree models anchored by their roots in a sand or soil tray.

The flower's role in the life cycle of flowering plants includes pollination, seed formation, seed dispersal and germination

To ensure children understand the part seeds play in the life cycle of plants, it is advisable to involve them in opportunities to grow plants from seeds they have collected themselves, which will then set seeds in a reasonable time. One of the best plants for this is the sunflower, which produces hundreds of seeds from the 'composite' flower-heads, which in fact consist of hundreds of florets, or little flowers. One problem with sunflowers is that the growing season is spread across the summer holidays, although this might be an opportunity to plan transition work between two teachers. Some seeds, such as mustard or peas, will germinate early in the year and produce seeds that can be dried and are ready to sow again before the summer break. SAPS recommend rapid cycling brassicas to see the full life cycle of flowering plants.

At KS2, children should begin to learn from secondary sources the processes of pollination and fertilisation. They should have the opportunity to examine a range of flowers to understand the similarities and differences between flower 'designs'. Role-play is a fun way to learn about pollination – tennis balls can represent pollen grains that can be transferred between flowers and from anthers to stigmas by willing pollinators (bees or butterflies).

New material for plants growth is produced in leaves

Children need to begin to understand the function of leaves as the 'food factories' of the plant. These factories need a supply of raw materials: carbon dioxide from the air, water and light. A bottle of fizzy mineral water is a useful visual aid to demonstrate this concept. It contains all those ingredients a plant needs to make its own food: water, carbon dioxide and dissolved minerals. Table 2.2.2 shows how a number of other scientific enquiries are possible.

Monitoring and feedback

As well as eliciting and making connections to children's prior learning and experiences at the start of any science topic, as explored above, it is important to ensure that active, formative assessment approaches continue to be embedded and acted upon throughout sequences of lessons so that all children can be supported and challenged to make good progress with their learning

Table 2.2.2 Scientific enquiries: plants

Key concepts	Suggested enquiries	Possible multi-media outcome
Where plants grow	Observations of growing plants. A local survey: what kinds and numbers of plants, grasses and trees can be found on the school premises? How do we use the plants? Green plants need light: is this true? Ask the class how we could test this statement and support them in planning their own investigations. A plant survey of two contrasting sites or schools within the local area. A twinning project with a school in another part of the world, perhaps from the home country of a child with EAL. The two schools could swap data and photos via email, videos or online meetings.	Labelled drawings, photographs and films showing the parts of plants and what plants need to grow. A diary or journal: *My Plant Diary*. A big book of the class investigations. A brochure/film about the flora found within the school grounds and/or wider community.
Recognise similarities and differences between plants (variation and diversity)	Observe and draw contrasting plants (e.g. tree vs. pot plant or conifer vs. deciduous tree). Observe and draw/photograph a range of leaves, stems and roots.	A 'coffee-table' book entitled *Our Green Kingdom* to show the variety of plants in the locality.
Flowers produce seeds	Fruits investigation. Collecting seeds from flowering plants and fruits grown both locally and from other countries. How many seeds? How are they arranged? How are they dispersed? How do they germinate? Use reference sources to discover the life cycles and cultivation of crops such as rice, bananas and potatoes.	An information sheet, poster or display about the variety of fruits and seeds produced in different locations. Drama about the life cycle of a flowering plant.
Recognise plants make and provide us with food	Visit an allotment/local farm and survey the food plants growing. Do we eat the roots, stems or leaves? Grow, harvest and cook a selection of fruits and vegetables for a class meal.	Photographic diary of the journey of food from the allotment to our plates. Documentary/interview with the allotment owner or farmer about the growing conditions/planting times of different plants. Quiz/Top Trump cards based on which parts of the plants we eat. Shared lunch.
Recognise plants need light, water, warmth	Observe celery sticks in dyed water. Compare a plant growing well and one failing to thrive. Raise questions such as *Do you think the more you water a plant the bigger it will grow?* Encourage children to generate their own additional questions to investigate. Observe patches of grass in light and masked (dark) areas. Test children's ideas about what will happen.	Produce a leaflet or web page about looking after plants. Group presentation of *Our Plant Investigation*. Plant Investigation. Drama activity/song/poem about the conditions needed for optimum plant growth.

(Continued)

Table 2.2.2 (Continued)

Key concepts	Suggested enquiries	Possible multi-media outcome
Plants can be identified and classified	Sort and classify plants through discussion (specimens ideally but if not, photographs). Identify plants with a key and use this to create their own branching tree diagram.	Keys and branching tree diagrams to distinguish common plant species.
How plants are suited to their environment	Plan and carry out a survey to find out how dandelions growing in two locations differ. Investigate the best house plants to keep in school. Use primary and secondary sources to investigate how plants overcome challenges to thrive (e.g. getting water, getting light, protection from primary consumers).	Scientific report to be published in the school's Journal of Science.
How animals and plants are interdependent	Use primary and secondary sources to investigate the populations in a local habitat and discuss how changes in populations will affect other organisms (e.g. grass, rabbits and foxes). Study the affect climate change has had upon populations in local and global habitats.	Create complex food webs. Filmed documentaries and presentations.

about plants. Pupils should be provided with clear feedback about their developing progress as well as guidance about how to achieve their next steps, and it is important that they are given the time and opportunity to address these which often means adapting subsequent lessons within the medium term plan. Any formative (or summative) assessment should enable children to demonstrate their understanding and skills of the specific concept being assessed and not be hindered by difficulties they may have in reading or writing. Activities using a range of multimodal approaches can not only engage children but also provide them with an accessible method for evidencing their learning. For example, pupils could present a short drama to demonstrate their understanding of insect pollination, record a Chris Packham style documentary to explain how a particular plant has adapted to its habitat or draw annotated diagrams to describe the role of a plant's leaves, stem, roots and flowers.

The Teacher Assessment in Primary Science (TAPS) website provides a wide range of free, focused assessment tasks linked to the topic of plants for different year groups. For example, Year 3 children taking on the role of environmental scientists as they make close observations of flowering plants or Year 2 botanists exploring the conditions needed for plant growth. Whilst TAPS lesson plans outline whole investigations about plants, the focus for assessment is a specific working scientifically strand which makes the process more manageable for both the teacher and the children. It is recommended (PSTT 2019) that these assessment tasks are used approximately two-thirds of the way through a topic so that there is still time to identify key areas of learning to target in subsequent teaching. This information can also feed into teachers' continuing summative judgements. The PLAN website also contains some free sample exemplification materials as well as excellent knowledge and vocabulary matrices linked to plant topics for each year group which can be used to support formative assessment of children's substantive and disciplinary knowledge.

Consolidate

Retrieving and applying

Providing regular, effortful opportunities for children to rehearse, extend and elaborate new knowledge strengthens its consolidation in memory and enables it to be more readily retrieved in the future (Weinstein et al. 2019). Whilst low stakes quizzes can be a popular form of retrieval practice, there are many other approaches which also support children to make meaningful connections between their learning and which help develop the understanding and skills underpinning substantive knowledge. For instance, children could work in pairs to compare and contrast the key features of two different flowering plants and then join another couple to share findings and ideas about why any parts may be atypical or missing. This activity could be extended to identifying parts of both flowering and non-flowering plants found in different habitats (e.g. focusing on the difference and similarities of the leaves, stem and flowers of a cactus, fern and a sycamore tree). To rehearse learning about the life cycle of a flowering plant, each group of children could be given a different photo of a seed head (e.g. dandelion, thistle, coconut) so that all forms of dispersal are covered and asked to tell the story of what happens to the last seed either through a quick drama or drawing.

The free Explorify website is well worth signing up for as it provides a wealth of short activities which can also support children's retrieval practice, for example, choosing which of three autumn leaves could be the odd one out and providing reasons why. Another way to help children consolidate their learning about plants is to make meaningful connections with other areas of their experiences and learning. For instance, children could be shown photos of the Ukrainian flag, a field of sunflowers and a bumble bee and asked what connections could be made between any of the images. In this case, they might draw upon their understanding of how Ukraine is the largest exporter of sunflower oil and the impact that the war has had upon this or how the survival of bumblebees is essential for the reproduction of many flowering plants. Whatever form of regular retrieval practice is carried out, it is important that time is allocated for meaningful feedback so that any arising misconceptions are addressed and the correct knowledge and understanding is reinforced.

As explored in other sections of this chapter and book, children need to explore the impact climate change is having and the steps they can take to help preserve both their immediate environment and the wider world around them. Exploring the role plants play in absorbing carbon dioxide and the habitats they provide for wildlife will help children to understand how important it is to protect them as well as the negative impact that over farming and deforestation has upon important species throughout the world. Pupils' research and critical thinking skills can be developed through active engagement with conservation issues affecting their local communities but also through exploring the worldwide impact that climate change has on crops and plant life and how this affects all citizens. When teaching about plants, meaningful links should be made to the sustainable development goals (UN General Assembly 2015) with clear guidance about the action that children can, and should, take towards achieving these. Strachan and Davey's (2022) book, *Saving the Planet One Science Lesson at a Time*, explores how each of the goals connects to children's own experiences. For example, the chapter on goal 11 (sustainable cities and communities) considers how flowering plants can be grown on the balconies of inner-city flats to attract pollinators and encourages children to consider how more green spaces can be introduced in towns and cities.

Reviewing

Teachers need to make summative judgments of children's learning in a topic. Useful resources to support this for the theme of plants can be found at the TAPS project website. Here, there is exemplification of what meeting a learning objective would look like in practice. In one example children's observational drawings of the growth of a bean from seed show that they can make observations over time and also recognise that plants are living things that grow. In another example, older children did drawings showing that they were able to link the differences between seeds to the different ways they are dispersed.

Children could be invited to reflect on what scientific skills and attitudes they developed through this work (perhaps patience and attention to detail might feature). They could be encouraged to think of plant-related jobs or hobbies that they might have in the future – helping to connect the science knowledge they have learned with themselves.

Classroom management

It will be apparent from the above discussions that timing and preparation of resources will be an important consideration when working with plants. The spring and summer terms will be the best time to study plants, as they will germinate more readily and receive more light if they are growing on the classroom window sill. If there is not enough classroom space to keep trays of seedlings, then a good solution is to sow seeds in soil or water-soaked cotton wool inside small plastic bags. The bags can then be stuck to a window with waterproof tape. If the bags are sealed, they cannot be spilled and will not need watering, as a little 'water cycle' will be created in the bag. This technique has the added advantage of ensuring the plants get maximum light. If you wanted to engender in your class a caring attitude to plants, children could carry the bags around with them, safety-pinned to their sweatshirts!

The start of a new topic is often the time when children's interests are captured. With preparation, children could have access at that point to seeds, germinated seeds, seedlings and mature plants rather than waiting a week or two for tiny seeds to germinate. A good deal of practical work on this topic is likely to be organised as group work. One way to ensure this is effective is to provide sufficient material for children to handle. Within a class of children, it is very likely some parents will be gardeners and will be happy to donate material for study. Cut flowers are often used as specimens – but the greengrocer will also be able to provide leaves, roots and stems. It is a good idea to contact shops a couple of weeks before plants are needed, as greengrocers, florists and supermarket staff are often willing to collect and donate produce which is past its sell by date but still excellent for studying and often a large variety of free plants can be acquired this way. School grounds may also be a good source of material. Even if only grass and weeds, a certain amount of investigation can be done, investigating dandelion growth, for example. One strategy to focus children on research using a mixture of primary and secondary sources is to divide the class into groups and to assign them different aspects of the same topic to investigate.

Theme	Examples of aspects for each group
Diversity of plants	Tall, tiny, prickly, edible, poisonous
The parts of a plant	Stem, root, leaf, flower
Plants we eat	Fruits, stems, leaves, roots
Plant reproduction	Pollination, fertilisation, fruits, seed dispersal, germination
Growing plants	Vegetables, fruits, flowers, weed control

You may need to support groups to subdivide their tasks further: for example, each child may research one example, or one child might write an explanation while another draws a diagram. A significant plenary then needs to be planned to allow each group to offer feedback on what they have discovered. This is also a time when the teacher could make note of the contributions children make to the research. The final stage may be a class presentation, display or book publication that draws together the information (see Table 2.2.2 for more ideas on this).

Good identification guides make the spotting and naming of plants into a game. Spotter sheets which are particularly accessible for primary children can be found through the Tree Tools for Schools website, and free tree packs for school planting can also be ordered here.

Time lapse video is one of the most powerful ways to illustrate that plants move and grow and can be produced using digital videos cameras or digital microscopes. Alternatively, there are lots of ready-made videos that teachers can access through an internet search such as the BBC's collection of plant time lapse clips or the Plants in Motion website which provides a very good array of material (e.g. a passion flower opening, plant stems growing 'away' from gravity and towards light).

Health and safety

Most plants are very safe to handle, particularly if you make use of food plants such as beans, peas, mustard, rice and radishes. Bought seeds are likely to have been treated with pesticides, so ensure children do not put them in their mouth, even if they look like food, and that they wash their hands after handling them. Health-food shops will sell untreated seeds and sprouts such as mung beans and rice. When working outside, it is important to warn children against eating any berries or other plant produce, and to ensure that they always wash their hands thoroughly before eating. The following common plants or parts of plants are poisonous and should be avoided during outdoor learning:

- holly
- privet
- red kidney beans (before cooking)
- rhubarb leaves
- tomato leaves
- potato leaves
- yew
- mountain ash seeds.

Be Safe! (ASE 2011) provides a more comprehensive list of poisonous species. If you think a child has swallowed any poisonous plant material, keep a sample of the material and seek medical advice immediately.

Summary

In this chapter we have seen that the green kingdom is very significant to our lives and, if taught in an appropriate way, we could initiate a child's lifelong interest in growing and enjoying plants. Even though plants share the same life processes with animals, children are likely to have several alternative ideas about plant life and do not necessarily appreciate the range and diversity of organisms that make up the kingdom. We have shown how children's ideas can be starting points for scientific observations and enquiries to enable a better understanding of life processes, plant structures and their functions. Finally, we have offered advice on how to use resources and organise teaching in appropriate ways.

Discussion questions

1. How could the cross-curricular topic of food address some key concepts and knowledge of plants?
2. How could a teacher in an inner-city school make plants seem relevant to children?
3. Is it better to ask children to make an observational drawing or take lots of photographs of different specimens?
4. Which of the sustainable development goals are particularly relevant when teaching about plants? How can meaningful links be made between these and the children's own experiences?

Further reading

We strongly recommend that you visit the website: Homepage - Science & Plants for Schools (saps.org.uk)

If you are feeling wobbly about your own plant identification, then the WildID fold out guides available at www.field-studies-council.org would be very helpful. (They are great for children too.)

Hoath, L. & Spring, H. (2018) Teaching in the outdoor setting in Serret and Earle (Eds) *ASE Guide to Primary Science Education* (4th Ed.), Association for Science Education.

References

Association for Science Education (ASE) (2011) *Be Safe!: Health and Safety in School Science and Technology for Techers of 3- to 12-year-olds* (4th ed.), Hatfield: ASE.

Department for Education (2013) *The National Curriculum in England: Key Stages 1 and 2 Framework Document.* https://www.gov.uk/government/publications/national-curriculum-in-england-primary-curriculum

Nag Chowdhuri, M., King, H. & Archer, L. (2021) *The Primary Science Capital Teaching Approach: Teacher Handbook*, London: University College London.

Primary Science Teaching Trust (2019) *TAPS Focused Assessment Teacher Assessment in Primary Science (TAPS): Support for Working Scientifically.* TAPS - Primary Science Teaching Trust (pstt.org.uk).

Russell, T. & Watt, D. (1990) *SPACE Projects Research Reports Growth*, Liverpool: Liverpool University Press. https://www.stem.org.uk/resources/collection/3059/nuffield-primary-science

Rymell, R. (1999) 'What defines a plant?', *Primary Science Review*, (57), 23–25.

Strachan, A. & Davey, J. (2022) *Saving the Planet One Science Lesson at a Time*, Hatfield: Millgate House.

UN General Assembly (2015) *Transforming Our World: The 2030 Agenda for Sustainable Development*, 21 October 2015, A/RES/70/1, https://www.refworld.org/docid/57b6e3e44.html

Weinstein, Y. & Sumeracki, M. with Caviglioli, O. (2019) *Understanding How We Learn*, Abingdon: Routledge.

CHAPTER 2.3

Animals including humans

Purpose of this chapter

After reading this chapter you will:

- know a range of strategies for eliciting children's ideas about humans, including annotated drawing, and how to build on their ideas using visual models and secondary sources;
- have considered how PSHE and citizenship provide a context for learning about humans and other animals
- know about scientific enquiries that are used to investigate humans, with a particular emphasis on pattern-seeking, and how these enquiries can be developed with primary-aged children.

Introduction

The relevance of the theme of humans and other animals to everyday life is immediately obvious, and children are fascinated by it. One could argue that it is more important for children to learn about themselves and how to ensure their physical, mental and emotional wellbeing than anything else in the school curriculum. During their lifetimes, children will be faced with many important and life-changing choices about diet, exercise, drugs and sexual relationships. Understanding our bodies can help us in making decisions about what to eat and drink, how and when to use medicines and the kinds and amounts of exercise to take. This theme could also raise questions about sex and gender, and sexuality that will need sensitive handling by teachers.

The importance of wellbeing has been recognised in the government's updated schools' guidance (DfE 2021): Promoting children and young people's mental health and wellbeing which draws upon evidence linking children's good mental health and education engagement with their academic achievement. As discussed later in this chapter, we can't draw conclusions about the causality from such correlations alone, but we would claim that a good science education supports them all.

The scientific study of humans and other animals raises ethical and values-based questions: Should all animals be treated with equal respect? Should we use animals as subjects for 'fair testing'? As adults we are bombarded with information on health in the media and need both biological knowledge and an understanding of research methods used in this field to evaluate and judge the different, often conflicting, sources. This topic has several key concepts running through it leading to some 'big ideas' about the structure and function of different parts of animals and how these parts work together as systems to support life. Different animals have evolved different solutions to the problems of feeding, protecting themselves against predators and disease, and reproducing. Part of the fascination of this topic is exploring the diversity of animal life and making comparisons between humans and other animals. We can ask questions about the way that animals, including humans, are constructed: *What do we look like inside and how do the parts work?* Relating the structure of parts of organisms to their function is a useful approach to understanding animals. Understanding the way that various organs and organ systems work and interact to keep us alive is the basis of this area of study. In primary science, children develop their understanding of what is happening inside our bodies.

Related to this, but with a different emphasis, is a consideration of health. What it means for humans to be healthy is based on social ideas and varies across different cultural and historical contexts. Does it mean just survival, or does it refer to some ideal model of physical and mental fitness? Looking at how ideals of body shape have changed in Western society in the past 100 years provides an example of how this is culturally defined. The challenges to health are also different for different groups of people: sedentary lifestyles leading to lack of exercise might affect one group of people, poverty may restrict access to certain foods for another group. There are workplace-related challenges to health such as back pain resulting from sitting at a computer all day, but there are also global challenges of malnutrition and diabetes related to obesity. Questions about what we can do to keep healthy have both a social and a biological dimension.

The biological dimension includes an understanding of what it means to be ill, including a scientific understanding of disease and the role of micro-organisms, but improving health often requires changing social structures too. This has been particularly evident during the recent global COVID-19 pandemic which has raised people's awareness of the impact of newly emerging viruses and the importance of developing worldwide vaccination programmes to mitigate against their potentially life-threatening symptoms not just for themselves, but to help protect more vulnerable members of the wider community. This means that when teaching about health, we need to link the science and the personal and social issues.

Another key area of interest is growth and reproduction. There are different solutions to this need to reproduce in the animal kingdom and studying different life cycles, such as those of butterflies and birds, as well as that of humans, is of interest as part of celebrating the diversity of species and understanding relationships between various organisms within ecosystems. There is an overlap here with the themes explored earlier in the chapter 'Living things and their habitats'.

Reproduction is also about inheritable information, about how similarities and differences between living things can be understood, perhaps in terms of DNA and genetics and how these characteristics are passed between generations. This leads to ideas about evolution and natural selection that are fundamental to how we understand life. These issues are very much in the public domain through discussions about reproductive technologies such as in-vitro fertilisation, cloning and debates about the extent to which our genes or the environment determine our identity and behaviour. Again, the science is clearly embedded in social contexts. So if a class of children is investigating variation in their hand spans, perhaps they could be challenged to think about why they might be different. This could lead to some fascinating philosophical discussions and some deep thinking!

Children will raise interesting questions when learning about animals including humans, many of which will need to be addressed through research using secondary sources due to the ethical and impractical implications of accessing internal body organs and systems within a primary classroom! When carrying out any research, it is important to check that websites, books and other available resources are safe and age appropriate for the children to access. Children should also be taught to check the reliability of sources and provided with strategies to keep themselves safe when using the internet for any home research. Research using secondary sources can still be engaging with a range of analogies and models drawn upon to make more abstract concepts meaningful and relatable to children, and some examples of these will be explored further in this chapter. However, there are still many opportunities to explore other types of enquiry too including observation using the different senses and pattern seeking enquiries such as, does the person with the longest arms have the slowest reaction times?

Planning for progression

In the Early Years Foundation Stage (EYFS), children become aware of their own needs and bodies, using their senses, developing physical skills and developing language to name and describe parts of their bodies and actions. They develop awareness of other humans and of other living things and see that they have similar needs to their own. Good practice in personal hygiene and habits is promoted in EYFS settings.

The Statutory Framework for the Early Years Foundation Stage (DfE 2023) has these goals for children:

- Managing self: Manage their own basic hygiene and personal needs, including dressing, going to the toilet and understanding the importance of healthy food choices.

- The natural world: Explore the natural world around them, making observations and drawing pictures of animals and plants; know some similarities and differences between the natural world around them and contrasting environments, drawing on their experiences and what has been read in class.

In the Early Years of primary school (Key Stage 1 (KS1)), children build on this by learning about their different senses, naming parts of their bodies and developing ideas that different parts of the body do different things. Teachers can encourage children to extend this beyond humans by providing a rich curriculum with experiences of a range of different animals. Children learn about how to keep healthy by thinking about what goes inside them – food, water, medicines – and how they use their bodies. This is further developed later in Key Stage 2 (KS2) when children learn more about what happens inside our bodies; identifying internal organs and their functions, mainly focusing on humans, but also relating their understanding to other animals. Ideas about why some choices are healthier than others are explored by learning about the effect, often invisible, that various actions, such as exercise or smoking, have on the human body.

This area of the curriculum is often one in which primary teachers feel relatively confident about their subject knowledge. One of the dangers of this is that children could be taught content that is more appropriate for secondary schools, such as details of the structure of the heart or the inner ear that may not be very meaningful to most primary-aged children. Of course, if children are interested, there is nothing wrong with helping them to explore these ideas further, but primary teachers should avoid asking children to label complex diagrams, such as a cross-section of the eye, that are difficult to interpret, just because they remember these from their own science education.

It is helpful to pick out the key concepts that children will revisit at different stages of education, both to understand what level of conceptual understanding might be expected for most children, and also to consider how to provide an extra challenge for children whose ideas could be extended further. Table 2.3.1 provides an overview of the key concepts for teachers relating to animals including humans in primary education. For convenience, this has been split into four themes relating to the 'big ideas': classifying animals, parts and functions of the body, staying alive and healthy, and growth and reproduction.

In the first years of secondary education (Key Stage 3), children go on to learn about the structure of cells and to explain how the body functions at the cellular level. For example, they would learn about how different types of cells combine to form different tissues, then organs. An example of this would be learning about red and white blood cells contributing to the tissue called blood. They study the processes of digestion in more detail, such as the names of the various enzymes involved in breaking down different kinds of food, and they identify various parts of the digestive tract such as the duodenum (small intestine). The children would also be expected to learn about the role of the lungs in more detail and the process of gaseous exchange at the lungs where oxygen is taken in and carbon dioxide expelled. This is taken further into a

Table 2.3.1 Key concepts for teachers: animals, including humans

Key concepts	Teachers' background knowledge
Classifying animals	
Animals can be classified into groups based on their observable features and evolutionary links	The accepted classification system used by biologists is to group animals according to a combination of observable features from the simpler forms to the more complex. Evidence about how they are grouped in terms of evolution is also taken into account. All animals, including humans, are grouped in a single kingdom: Animalia.
	The phylum 'Chordates' – meaning having a form of 'spinal cord' – includes the following groups of animals that are vertebrates (with 'backbones'):
	Fish – live in water and have gills. Most fish are cold blooded – that means that their temperature varies with the environment unlike warm blooded animals that work to maintain a constant temperature.
	Amphibians – frogs, toads, newts. These animals have a stage in their lifecycle when the animals have gills and breathe underwater (tadpoles); they are cold blooded.
	Reptiles – lizards, snakes, turtles. Reptiles lay eggs in soft shells and are scaly; they are cold blooded.
	Birds – characterised by being egg-laying and having feathers and wings. Birds are warm blooded.
	Mammals – includes humans, whales, dolphins, horses. Mammals are warm blooded, have hair and generally give birth to live young (egg laying monotremes such as platypus are the exception). Females have mammary glands to suckle their young.
	Invertebrates are animals without a backbone or bony skeleton; this group includes the following:
	Arthropods – insects, arachnids (spiders), crustaceans, myriapods (millipedes and centipedes). Arthropods have a hard exoskeleton, jointed legs and segmented bodies.
	Annelids – segmented worms with soft bodies (e.g. earthworms).
	Molluscs – usually have a broad, muscular foot and may have a shell. This group includes gastropods (e.g. snails, slugs, limpets etc), bivalves (e.g. clams, oysters) and cephalopods (e.g. octopuses, nautiluses and squid).
Parts and functions of the body	
Different parts of animals have different functions	Complex animals are made up of systems, (e.g. the circulatory system) formed of various organs (e.g. the heart, arteries) which are made of tissues (e.g. muscle) which are made of various kinds of cells (e.g. heart muscle cells).
Skeleton and muscles act together to protect bodies and for movement.	
The digestive system breaks down food into pieces small enough to be absorbed into the blood and transported all around the body where it is used for energy, growth and repair. Teeth can be damaged if not properly cared for.	In humans the main systems and their functions are:
	Nervous system – brain and spinal cord, nerves, senses. Information from the senses is sought and travels to the brain and spinal cord along nerves. The brain is a complex network of nerve cells whose function results in thinking, feeling, controlling movement and some hormones. The details of brain function are not well understood, and it is a huge field of current research.
The heart, lungs and circulatory system take oxygen to all the parts of the body and remove the waste product, carbon dioxide.	Digestive system – mouth, teeth, stomach, pancreas, liver, intestines, anus. These are concerned with absorbing nutrients from food and water into the body. The digestive tract from mouth to anus can be

(*Continued*)

Animals including humans

Table 2.3.1 (Continued)	
Key concepts	**Teachers' background knowledge**
Active muscles need more energy so the heart pumps faster to supply oxygen.	thought of as being 'outside' the body, and its purpose is to break food down into molecules small enough to pass through the walls of the intestine and into the bloodstream. The digestive system first breaks down food mechanically in the mouth, and different teeth have particular roles in doing this: incisors for cutting, canines for gripping and tearing, molars for chewing and grinding. The outer coating of teeth is called enamel and can be damaged by acid that is created in the mouth by bacteria that feed on remnants of sugary and starchy foods stuck on and around the teeth. This mixture of food, bacteria and the acid they produce is called plaque. The acid will eventually dissolve part of a tooth to cause a hole or cavity. It is therefore important to remove plaque regularly by brushing the teeth and best to avoid eating too many foods that have a high sugar content. Saliva helps prevent tooth decay by neutralising the acid. Keeping the teeth clean and free from plaque also protects our gums. If left, plaque can harden into 'tartar'. This coating will make cleaning the teeth difficult as it can harbour more plaque, which attacks the gums and causes them to bleed (gingivitis). This is the beginning of gum disease that can lead to tooth loss. At various points in the digestive tract, chemicals known as enzymes are released, and these help break down particular kinds of food. Any undigested food is what forms the faeces (aka 'poo'). Of course, what comes out at the end of the digestive tract is also fascinating to children. The book *Poo* by Nicola Davies (2014) is a delightful and informative children's book on this popular subject. Circulatory system – heart, blood vessels (arteries, veins and capillaries), blood (red blood cells, white blood cells, platelets and plasma). This is a transport system for taking nutrients from food and oxygen to cells as well as removing waste products. The heart acts as a pump to move the blood through the vessels around the whole body and back. It also plays a key role in defence against damage by carrying blood-clotting agents and against diseases that may be attacked by white blood cells and antibodies. Respiratory system – lungs, mouth, nose. Breathing and respiration are often confused. We breathe in air through our mouths and noses that goes into the lungs. There are tiny blood vessels close to the lungs which enables oxygen from the air to pass into the blood, latching on to the red blood cells, and carbon dioxide dissolved in the blood to enter the air in the lungs to be breathed out. The purpose of this is to support a process called respiration that happens in all living cells. In respiration oxygen is used to release the energy in food (carbohydrates) and carbon dioxide is produced as a waste product. This is sometimes represented by the equation: $C_6H_{12}O_{16} + O_2 \rightarrow 6CO_2 + 6H_2O + energy$ Excretory system – kidneys, liver, bladder, urethra. The function of this system is to remove certain unwanted or waste products such as urea (a waste product from breaking down proteins) from the body. This includes regulating the amount of water in the body. The urethra opens at the end of the penis in males and just above the vaginal opening in females.

(Continued)

Table 2.3.1 (Continued)	
Key concepts	**Teachers' background knowledge**
	Skeletal system – bones, muscles, tendons. The skull and ribs protect the vital organs of the body. The skeleton provides a framework to support the body, and something for muscles to pull on to produce movement. When a muscle gets a signal to act, it contracts and gets shorter; pulling on the bone it is attached to. Muscles cannot lengthen themselves, so they need another muscle to contract in the opposite direction to stretch them out again, and muscles are thus organised in pairs.
	Reproductive system – in males this is the testes and penis; in females the ovaries, uterus and vagina. Reproduction is explained in the text on sensitive issues below.
Staying alive and healthy	
Humans and other animals need food for energy, growth and repair.	Humans need a variety of different foods in their diets. Carbohydrates (bread, rice, potatoes, pasta, sugar) are the main source of energy, proteins (in pulses such as beans, and in meat, fish, milk) are the main building material of the body and are mainly used for growth and repair. Fats (oils, butter) are also a source of energy, but certain fats are needed in small quantities for specific purposes such as insulating nerve cells. Vitamins and minerals found in a range of vegetables and fruit have a number of specific functions, for example, vitamin C has a role in strengthening skin, and the mineral iron plays an important role in the transport of oxygen in red blood cells. Fruit and vegetables also provide fibre (actually plant cell walls) that is necessary to move food along the digestive tract. Water is essential as a medium in which all the chemical processes of the body take place and is one of the main constituents (approximately 60 per cent) of the human body.
	Exercise maintains and builds muscle strength, including the heart muscle and muscles around the lungs, and maintains the range of movement of various joints. If more energy is taken into the body (in the form of food) than is used, then the excess is stored as fat, and this can have consequences for the health of the circulatory system.
Humans and animals may have other needs, including sleep and emotional needs.	Lack of sleep leads to poor mental functioning and general irritability. Rest is also a need and is an important requirement for the consolidation of new learning.
Drugs are chemicals (other than food) we put into our bodies that affect how they work. They may be helpful or harmful, and this may depend on how much is taken and when.	If the emotional needs of humans are not met, this may also have physical outcomes as well as emotional ones. It might be an interesting area of discussion to explore what the emotional needs of other animals might be – what kind of care does a dog need compared with a tropical fish?
	Although we use the terms drugs to mean illegal drugs in everyday conversation, medicines are drugs, though not all drugs are medicines. Different drugs act at different sites in the body, for example, alcohol affects how messages are transmitted between brain cells. Some drugs, including some used as medicines, affect the nervous system and may reduce feeling pain, slow down mental activity or lead to hallucinations.

(*Continued*)

Animals including humans

Table 2.3.1 Key concepts for teachers: animals, including humans (Continued)

Key concepts	Teachers' background knowledge
	Smoking cigarettes has a stimulant effect, increasing alertness, but the nicotine in tobacco (which is often found in vaping products) is also addictive, so that smokers may need to continue to smoke to feel 'normal'. Regular smoking leads to a build-up of tar on the lungs, reducing the area available for oxygen and carbon dioxide to be exchanged. Carbon monoxide in the smoke passes into the blood and prevents red blood cells from carrying oxygen as efficiently. It also increases the build-up of fat in arteries, which increases the risk of a heart attack.
	The effect of alcohol, as with many drugs, depends on the 'dose' – on how much is taken. It has a number of effects – it causes blood vessels to expand, leading to flushed cheeks. It also causes excessive passing of urine, leading to dehydration. Brain function is affected; at low intakes this leads to a feeling of disinhibition that is often experienced as being pleasant, but as the levels of alcohol in the blood get higher, mental function is increasingly affected and can lead to risk-taking behaviour as well as impairment of coordination affecting speech and movement, and judgement. High levels of alcohol intake also lead to liver damage. Dependency on alcohol is a serious condition which can have significant consequences for the individual and their families.
Microorganisms can be beneficial or harmful.	As well as their role in decomposition of matter, microorganisms are also relevant to health as some are the causes of disease or illness. Good personal hygiene such as handwashing is important in reducing the transmission of microorganisms (often called 'germs' in this context) between people. We need to store food in such a way that harmful microorganisms do not grow, so we refrigerate or freeze foods at temperatures below which they can reproduce. We preserve foods in sugar or salt or vinegar – all chemical environments in which the cells of microorganisms cannot survive. Processes such as bottling and canning (tinning) keep out the oxygen that microorganisms need to live. However, some microorganisms have a positive role in health. 'Bio-yoghurts' are marketed as having benefits because the digestive system contains some microorganisms that are helpful to the processes of digestion which these yoghurts may increase.
Growth and reproduction	
Humans and other animals all reproduce, but they have different life cycles.	Different animals have different means of reproduction and have different life cycles. For some simple animals, reproduction means replicating themselves through cell division. Insects (e.g. butterflies) have life cycles in which the animal takes distinctly different forms, i.e. a caterpillar (larva), a pupa, a butterfly (imago). As with insects, amphibian life cycles are particularly interesting to children as they involve metamorphosis. For the frog this cycle is: frogspawn–tadpole–frog. Birds and reptiles lay eggs. Birds, reptiles and many, but not all, fish lay different kinds of eggs from which smaller, immature versions of the adult hatch. The leathery eggs of reptiles and hard shells of birds are laid on land. Mammals give birth to live young.

(*Continued*)

Table 2.3.1 (Continued)	
Key concepts	**Teachers' background knowledge**
The human life stages can be seen as: birth, childhood, adolescence, adulthood (parenthood), old age and death.	An essential feature of human reproduction is that it is sexual – half the genetic material comes from the male and half from the female so the resulting offspring has inherited genetic material from both parents. The cells with half the genetic information are called gametes. In the testes of the male, cells divide in a special way to split the genetic information on chromosomes and produce sperm cells. A similar process happens in the ovaries of the female producing the egg cells or ova. Bringing the two together is achieved by sexual intercourse when sperm from the man's penis travels up into the uterus. At the midpoint of the woman's menstrual cycle, an egg cell will be released from one of the ovaries then travel down a fallopian tube (oviduct) to the uterus where one sperm cell may fuse with it, fertilising the egg cell. For a wonderful account of how this is achieved see Babette Cole's (1995) book, *Mummy Laid an Egg!* The fertilised egg now has the full set of genetic information that is a unique combination of each parent.
In sexual reproduction, genetic information from both parents is inherited by the offspring. DNA is the chemical that carries this information.	Sexual reproduction is the basis for much natural variation within a species. This cell divides repeatedly, forming more and more cells, all with the same genetic information and, in a process that is only partially understood, different cells become different parts of the developing foetus. This all takes place in the uterus (womb) of the mother until the birth of the baby.
	The DNA molecule can 'unzip' and make a copy of itself – this is the basis for reproduction and how information encoded in our genes is passed from generation to generation.

consideration of respiration as the process by which oxygen is involved in releasing energy from food. They are taught more about various types of joints of the skeleton and how muscles act in antagonistic pairs.

The curriculum builds on that of KS2 as children encounter more information about the effects of smoking on the lungs along with the health implications for abuse of alcohol, solvents and other drugs. Other PSHE-linked work includes learning about the changes that occur during adolescence, about the human menstrual cycle and the development of the foetus in the uterus.

Teachers' self-assessment questions

1. Describe some similarities and differences between a fish and an amphibian.
2. What is the main purpose of the human digestive system?
3. How do the respiratory, cardiovascular, digestive and skeletal systems all work together so that we can run?
4. What affect does alcohol have on human beings?
5. Can you give examples of microorganisms that are helpful and some which are harmful to humans?
6. Why isn't a baby girl identical to her mother?

Animals including humans

Engage

Situating the topic

There are some obvious areas of overlap between this area of science and PSHE and citizenship, such as learning about personal health and hygiene, drugs, sex and relationship education, and making informed personal choices about these issues. Science can also make a contribution to other areas of PSHE and citizenship including:

- Communication skills and debating: for example, *Should crisps be allowed as break-time snacks?*
- Social/moral issues: for example, *Should we care for farm animals as much as pets?*
- Loss and bereavement: for example, understanding illness.
- Making choices: for example, *Why should we keep safe from the Sun?*
- Meeting and working with people: for example, school nurse or dentist.

Clearly we *could* link science with PSHE and citizenship, but there are also reasons why we *should*. Scientific knowledge and understanding about health needs to be understood in the context of ideas about relationships and personal development. For example, smoking could be taught just in terms of its harmful effects on the body, but it is better if children understand the reasons why people might take up smoking, and how peer pressure might influence people's choices. This seems to be more effective in promoting health than a more didactic approach or using scare tactics, as it supports people in taking control of their own health, as far as is possible given their social circumstances. Making these cross-curricular links also provides an opportunity to learn about risk-taking and about how to weigh evidence and make judgements that are the basis for personal choices. It can both strengthen science learning, by providing a real and motivating context, and support some of the aims of PSHE and citizenship, such as developing personal insights and understanding of relationships with others.

Understanding how science can contribute to decision making, at a social level as well as at an individual level, makes an important contribution to developing a better public understanding of the nature of science. This was certainly evident during the COVID-19 pandemic when advice from the scientific advisory group for emergencies (SAGE) underpinned public health measures such as shielding, isolating and vaccination programmes, and the science behind these was shared during daily public briefings. Science does not provide cut and dried solutions to problems, but evidence that needs to be interpreted and judged. Some adults have responded to the lack of certainty provided by science by rejecting it altogether or making decisions based upon unsubstantiated pseudo-science, such as refusing to have their child vaccinated against MMR because of a report which suggested a tenuous, and since disproven, link between the inoculation and autism. Teachers should encourage a critical, but not cynical, view of science.

A whole-school approach to PSHE and citizenship could provide valuable contexts for learning science. For example, recent national concerns about lack of exercise in children could be the basis for investigative work: children could devise a survey into how much exercise children at the school have and make recommendations based on the evidence and their knowledge and understanding.

Some form of orientation at the start of the topic will engage children's interest and help them to access their existing ideas. For example, to encourage children to think about what happens to food when you eat it, provide them with a tangible experience of eating a piece of bread and drinking some water, and ask them to feel, observe and think about what is happening. They might discuss their ideas in pairs and give feedback to the whole group. If you were about to begin some work on the heart and circulatory system, rather than assuming children will remember what exercise feels like, ask them to do some. Younger children could be encouraged to notice changes to their breathing and perhaps that they feel hot or may be a bit flushed. Older children could observe their breathing and feel their heartbeat before, during and after exercise. You could make good use of a PE lesson to do this.

Other starting points could be making a comparison between humans and other animals and also plants. Comparing life cycles, or different ways of eating or moving, would also be interesting ways of approaching the topic. A resource bank of photographs and video clips of various living things would be useful in arousing curiosity and generating questions:

> *How do different animals move?*
> *Why can't humans breathe underwater?*
> *Do dolphins lay eggs?*
> *What do ducks eat?*
> *Where do cows sleep?*
> *Do humans have the same number of bones as a gorilla?*

You might want to start this off with some questions before inviting groups or pairs of children to come up with more of their own. Perhaps a display of questions children have raised would make an interesting visual starting point to a topic.

Breaking down barriers

When teaching about animals including humans, there are many opportunities to invite expert visitors from within the children's own communities and families to talk about the practical application of science within their work and to also share important advice for keeping healthy (e.g. nurses, dentists, pharmacists, health visitors). One advantage about drawing upon expertise within the local community, is that where appropriate, children can often walk to their workplace to have a more immersive experience, such as visiting the local farmer's market to select produce representing each of the major food groups. As well as exploring important links within children's immediate environment, connecting to the work of other inspirational, modern scientists, including those from diverse backgrounds, can also help support children's developing science capital. The Primary Science Teaching Trust's Just Like Me website contains free resources detailing the work of a range of contemporary scientists working with animals and in medicine, and the STEM Ambassador programme is a good way to connect teachers with representatives across any science discipline or field of interest.

Three examples of scientists who could inspire learning within the topic of animals including humans are listed below:

> **Ntombizodwa Makuyana** is an immunologist researching lung and viral infections, such as COVID, at the Babraham Institute in Cambridge and is one of the scientists highlighted in the Primary Science Trust's Just Like Me website. Her work could be drawn upon when exploring respiration or microorganisms, or to develop children's learning by making meaningful connections between the two.
> **Nicola Davies** is an English zoologist and author of more than 50 beautifully illustrated children's books, and was also an original presenter of *The Really Wild Show*, a CBBC wildlife show. She writes fiction, non-fiction and poetry with a focus ranging from the microscopic in *Tiny: The Invisible World of Microbes* to the massive in *Big Blue Whale* and has written a range of engaging animal books for all primary age groups. Other children's favourites include *Extreme Animals: The Toughest Creatures on Earth*, *Bat Loves the Night* and *Deadly: The Truth About the Most Dangerous Creatures on Earth*.
> **Dr Edward Jenner** (1749-1823) developed the vaccination process of introducing a milder virus (cowpox) under the skin to provide immunity against a more deadly one

(smallpox), which eventually led to the eradication of this contagious disease in 1980 through a worldwide vaccination programme. The ASE's cross curricular set of upper KS2 resources, 'Why You'll Never Catch Smallpox', explore Jenner's work, the ethics behind his research and the impact of vaccination today, and is especially topical for children who have lived through the COVID-19 pandemic. The resources also include an activity which compares and critiques the ethics and scientific processes of Jenner's smallpox research with more modern day medical trials.

Teachers need to make sure they are being inclusive when thinking about reproduction, sex and what a family means. The animal kingdom has been used to justify stereotyped human gender roles as 'natural'; females as passive and males as active (Cooke 2022). So present a diversity of animals that challenge this: lionesses are great hunters, male emperor penguins incubate eggs, and male seahorses give birth. The dominant female meerkat in a group is very aggressive. Clown fish (like Nemo) are hermaphrodite – they change sex so there is always one dominant female in the group.

Activating children's ideas

For ease of reference we have separated the topic into the four sections that mirror how they are likely to be split in school planning: classifying animals, parts and functions of the body, staying alive and healthy, and growth and reproduction. Elicitation is important at the beginning of a new topic so that plans can be made in the light of children's existing ideas, but ongoing formative assessment is also essential so that plans are adapted and changed to take account of children's learning. These suggestions could be used at various points in a teaching sequence to find out what ideas children are developing or to explore a different aspect of the topic with them. For more ideas and examples, visit the Teacher Assessment in Primary science (TAPS) website.

Classifying animals

Through discussion, children could be asked to think of different sorts of animals. They may tend to talk about mammals, and not include other animals such as spiders or birds. It is very common for people not to include humans in the category of animals – this is often reinforced in everyday conversation. Think about signs on shops that say 'No animals allowed except guide dogs'. They may have a range of knowledge of various animals, or it may be quite limited. Are they able to give examples of different kinds of birds? Can they describe different sorts of beetles they have seen? Be aware that there may be colloquial or regional names for some creatures, for example, woodlice are also known as cheese logs, pill-bugs, coffin-cutters, bibble-bugs and chucky pigs! Older children could be asked to sort photographs of a range of animals into groups, explaining the criteria they have used. Among various possibilities, they might classify them according to observable features, such as fur or legs, or according to where they live. It might be interesting to keep to hand some photographs of animals that are less easy to classify, for example, starfish and dolphin, and ask them where they might fit into their system.

Parts and functions of the body

A simple elicitation strategy when working with young children would be to play a game of 'Simon says … touch your elbow' – observing which children can identify and name which external body parts and noting any areas for development. Children could be invited to lead as 'Simon' providing a further insight into their confidence in naming parts of the body and making it easier for the teacher to make notes.

This topic is very accessible through the elicitation strategy of annotated drawing. Children can be given an outline of a human body and invited to draw on it: *What's inside me?* This could be open-ended and general, such as the location and naming of any different parts the children want to show, or made more specific – for example, children could be asked to show their ideas about what happens to food and drink inside your body, or about what the heart does. The annotation could be labelling of names of body parts, or could be extended to include ideas about what the part does. An exciting variation on this is to make it human scale by drawing around a child to give a full-size outline of a body. A group can then work collaboratively to draw and annotate it with their shared ideas. This strategy can be used to develop children's ideas as well as elicit them, as children share knowledge and understanding, and providing secondary sources of information to use could extend this further.

Children's responses to this elicitation were analysed by the SPACE project (Osborne et al. 1992). This research found that young children focus on parts they can see or feel or hear, so external parts feature and there may be representations of a stomach, or a heart and perhaps some bones. These bones may not yet show ideas about joints but be randomly scattered through the body and might be a stereotypical cartoon dog-bone shape. A common alternative idea is not to see blood as moving around the body contained in vessels, but that the body is a big bag of blood – an idea that makes sense of what happens if you cut yourself. Children's ideas about digestion also make sense in terms of what we experience when we eat and how we talk about food. There is often some awareness of food going down tubes, but these may be shown as ending in the middle of the body, rather than being seen as a continual pathway from mouth to anus. Food and drink may be seen as separate, and may be shown as having a tube each from the mouth rather than all going down the same oesophagus. Again, it is possible to see how this idea develops from the experience of going to the toilet. Older children's drawings may show organs (heart, brain, muscles, stomach) as separate rather than interrelated systems, and they might be encouraged to think about this with questions such as *Is that part linked to any other parts?* This helps them to see the body as an integrated system so when they think about running, the role of the brain, heart and lungs are considered as well as the legs.

Older children may have ideas about the heart 'beating' and may know about blood travelling in veins. Veins are observable and are talked about while the term arteries is not in common conversation, and so children are often not aware of the distinction that veins carry blood towards the heart and that arteries carry blood away from the heart. They tend to have very vague ideas about breathing and what happens to the air they breathe in. If they are aware of muscles, they tend to see them as only being in arms and legs, and not as being needed for every movement.

Staying alive and healthy

One possible elicitation activity would be to ask children to sort different foods into groups. Examples of real foods (or their packaging) are better than words or pictures as far as possible. It is important that the kind of food eaten by all the children in the class is represented. Children could sort the foods in as many different ways as they can think of. They might begin with categories such as 'I like/I don't like', but teacher questioning could explore this further – *What is the same about those foods that you like?* – to draw out common elements. It is important to remember that this is open-ended exploration of the ideas the children have about food, and to resist trying to impose classifications, such as carbohydrates, until you have a good understanding of children's starting points and of whether this would be helpful.

Various aspects of health could be explored through a true/false quiz about healthy lifestyles. However, the answers may not be clear cut. Adding a column for any comments might be helpful in promoting tentative responses. For example, in response to the question *Is eating a bag of crisps bad for you?*, you might explore children's ideas about how many bags should be eaten and how often, and what it is about crisps that might be an issue (the relatively high fat and salt content). Ideas about a balanced diet are quite subtle, and teachers need to be careful to promote positive ideas about food, rather than make it a source of guilt and concern that might support eating disorders.

Questioning is a very important elicitation strategy and can be used as a starting point for whole-class or group discussion. To give individuals time to organise their own ideas, it is a good idea to identify key questions and give thinking time for these rather than expecting instant answers. Asking pairs of children to discuss their ideas is a useful strategy for this and helps to keep all the children engaged. Recording children's ideas means that you can reflect on them and their implications for teaching. Having a record also means that children's ideas can be revisited and reviewed. You might scribe children's comments onto a flip chart, piece of sugar paper or interactive whiteboard, possibly including the child's name, or children might be asked to keep a record of their own ideas.

The following suggestions for key questions are based on the SPACE project research (Osborne et al. 1992):

> *Can you point to some parts of your body and name them?*
> *Can you think of any parts inside your body?*
> *What do you think those parts are for?*
> *What parts of the body are needed for moving/eating/breathing?*
> *How can you move different parts of your body?*
> *Can you feel any of your bones? Where are they?*
> *What kinds of food do you like to eat?*
> *What do you think happens to food and drink inside your body?*
> *What do you think is happening inside you when you move your arm?*
> *How do you feel when you are healthy?*
> *What can you do to keep yourself healthy?*
> *Why do you think people start smoking?*
> *What senses do you use when you eat your dinner/have a bath/go for a walk?*

Using 'person-centred questions' phrased as *Why do you think …?* helps to communicate that it is the child's ideas you are interested in, rather than a 'right answer' (Harlen and Qualter 2018). The question *What keeps us healthy?* could be used as the starting point for an individual or group concept map for older children. A concept map is appropriate here because of the different interrelated ideas. For example, exercise could be linked to a healthy heart, to strong bones and to the need for eating foods for growth and energy.

In the SPACE project research (Osborne et al. 1992), when children were asked what they could do to keep healthy, they often focused on food. They had ideas about fruit and vegetables as healthy but had less understanding about balanced diets. They sometimes noted that exercise was important, often giving examples of adult forms of exercise, or doing specific exercises rather than running, playing and walking in everyday life. It might be a good idea to explore with children their ideas about what exercise is.

Research by Barnardo's (2004) into children's ideas about lunchtime food showed how what we eat is a powerful part of expressing our identity. A lunch of burger and chips was associated with a boy who was a bit cool, a bit of a laugh, whereas children in their research thought a lunch of sandwiches and fruit would belong to a 'sporty girl who lives in a big house in London'. So, making choices about eating is not just about having knowledge about a healthy diet, but about the images and social meanings attached to food. However, when planning lessons about healthy eating, it is important to be sensitive and aware of the impact that the cost of living crisis may be having on many families' meal choices and to also ensure that food is not wasted during any activities.

Annotated drawing is useful too in exploring children's ideas about drugs, for example, 'Someone has dropped a bag of drugs. Draw what might be inside it'. This activity provides an insight into children's experience and opens up questions of how to define drugs. Medicines, alcohol, tobacco and alcohol are drugs, though we tend to use the term as shorthand for illegal drugs.

Growth and reproduction

Questions and discussions are also a useful elicitation strategy in this theme. Questions could include:

> *What do you think makes you grow?*
> *How have you changed since you were born?*
> *What changes might happen to you as you grow older?*

Children's ideas about changes that will happen at puberty can be explored in a similar way to other organ systems by drawing on an outline of the body. It is useful to provide two outlines so children can show changes for boys and girls. As with all records of elicitation, this can be revisited later and amended so that the children can reflect on what they have learned.

Other fascinating insights into children's ideas can be found by asking them to draw a picture of what they think is happening inside an egg from a hen or butterfly. SPACE research (Russell and Watt 1990) analysed children's responses to this in detail and found a variety of alternative frameworks: some children drew a miniature version of the adult, some a complete animal 'in limbo' just waiting to hatch whilst other wonderful drawings showed that some children imagine different component parts such as legs, feet, body and wings waiting to be assembled. Other children have a view closer to the scientific understanding of a gradual development from an undifferentiated mass to the formation of different parts. Exactly how this takes place is not fully understood and is one of the great sources of awe and wonder and questions in contemporary science.

Susan Carey's (1985) research into young children's ideas about human reproduction revealed stages in the development of their understanding. The first stage of understanding is that there was a time when they did not exist, then thinking of babies as 'manufactured'. This is followed by an awareness of the need for a mother and father and ideas about the baby growing in the mother's tummy. Then they move to ideas about a 'seed' and an 'egg', and by the end of primary education, children may be aware of the reproductive role of sexual intercourse.

Build

Constructing new knowledge

Using secondary sources and models

Alongside the first-hand observations and enquiries, which will contribute to developing children's understanding, teachers may want to introduce children to conceptual knowledge and understanding in different ways. One of the challenges of this topic is to help children to understand what they cannot directly see – what is happening inside living bodies. Using visual material such as pictures, video and three-dimensional models can help to develop explanations. Another strategy is to use models and analogies to help children relate new ideas and more abstract concepts to existing knowledge and experiences, making them more concrete and accessible (DfE 2019a) although it is important to ensure that their points of difference do not introduce any misconceptions. The use of secondary sources of information is not only helpful as a teaching and learning tool but provides an opportunity to evaluate them as sources of evidence, supporting some of the big aims of this topic – to take a critical approach to information. Information texts in English lessons can be made more motivating by linking them with research into questions raised in science lessons. Developing meaningful contexts for learning through links with PSHE can be supported by the use of stories and poems. Teaching about drugs and sex raises issues about how to approach these sensitive subjects and these will be considered in the section on class management.

Animals can be classified into groups

Visits to children's city farms, wildlife centres, such as those run by the Wildfowl Trust, or zoos, provide children with rich experiences of the variety of life and how different animals are cared for. They also raise issues for discussion: *Is it right that animals should be kept for us to look at or should they all be in the wild?* Try not to neglect the rich diversity of wildlife in the UK which children may often be unaware of but which programmes such as *The Watches* (Springwatch, Autumnwatch and Winterwatch) and *Wild Isles* highlight so well. Purposeful connections should be made to children's prior learning about habitats and seasonal changes to help them build more complex, meaningful schemas of science knowledge.

Children could carry out research into different animals using secondary sources and the results can be presented in various ways. For example, each group or pair of children could focus their attention on one animal and compile a fact file, perhaps presenting this to the rest of the class in the form of a recorded documentary video or a PowerPoint presentation. A class information book could be constructed by making collections of photographs of the range of ears, feet, body coverings and eyes that different animals have, and discussions could explore the variety of these making links to how they function and to the environment they live in. For example, the kind of mouth could be related to what the animal eats. Again, there are strong links here with the study of habitats.

Parts and functions of the body

Kress et al. (2001) describe how a teacher used hand gestures and drawings together with verbal explanations and reference to children's own bodies to help explain how the heart and circulatory systems works. This 'multimodal' approach to explaining about the functions of different parts of the body seems to be generally useful. However, choosing illustrations and three-dimensional models with an appropriate level of detail can be quite difficult as many include so much information it is difficult to make sense of it. It is possible to buy or make 'body aprons' – tabards worn by a child with organs, such as the heart, made of felt and labels that can be stuck on using Velcro. They have the advantage over paper versions of relating the position of organs to the real human body and of being more three-dimensional. This provides a kinaesthetic dimension as the child can feel the position of the various body parts. Davies (2013) reports on a project that used a huge diagram or body map laid out in a school hall to enable children to take a 'giant tour' of the human body.

Teeth are the first stage in the process of digestion. The 'big idea' of digestion is that food is broken down into small enough parts that it can cross the wall of the intestine, be taken up by capillaries and so move into the bloodstream to be taken around the body. This happens at a molecular level with different enzymes breaking down different types of food, which is addressed at secondary school, but the process begins with a mechanical breaking down of food in the mouth by the teeth. Engaging demonstrations can be an effective way to support children's understanding and retention of more abstract concepts such as the model of digestion described in the box.

MODELLING DIGESTION

In the mouth (bowl), incisors (scissors) snip food (1 banana, 1 cracker and a tablespoon of oats) into smaller pieces. Molars (potato masher) grind the food. Saliva (squirt of water) contains enzymes which start to break down the starches in the food.

The food travels down the oesophagus to the stomach (sealable plastic bag): Acid (squirt of orange juice) is added which starts to break down the proteins in the food. The stomach acts like a washing machine to churn the food (mix sealed bag with hands).

> The food passes into the small intestines (transfer using a funnel into a cut off leg from an old pair of tights). Here water and small, digested particles get reabsorbed into the bloodstream (squeeze so liquid passes through pores in the tights to a tray underneath).
>
> Undigested food passes to the large intestines (paper cup with a small hole cut in the bottom) where more water is absorbed (pat gently with a paper towel). This gets transferred out of the body in the form of faeces (use a second paper cup to push the contents through the hole in the second.

Tooth decay occurs when bacteria (in plaque) break down sugars forming acids that dissolve the enamel and attack the gums. Brushing teeth reduces tooth decay because it helps stop the plaque layer from building up. Disclosing tablets can be bought from the chemist. When they are chewed, they will turn plaque a bright red – it can be a striking demonstration of how much plaque remains even after teeth have been brushed, although it may be better to provide these for children to carry out as a home activity to avoid highlighting poor dental hygiene in individuals in front of the rest of the class.

Models can also be drawn upon to make research using secondary sources more engaging and memorable. One example of this is children collecting a representation of each component of blood once they have researched its role and any other key facts using age-appropriate websites and books which the teacher has already reviewed to ensure they provide the information they seek. Weak orange squash would represent plasma (which is straw coloured rather than red); small, red jelly sweets for red blood cells, small white marshmallows for white blood cells and rice would represent platelets.

Other strategies to support children's learning through secondary research include KWL grids: the grid has three columns with the headings 'What I know' (K), 'What I want to know' (W) and 'What I have learned' (L) (Wray and Lewis 1997). The first two columns are completed to set up the enquiry, for example into teeth, and then sources of information are used to try to extend the knowledge and answer questions. Any new information is recorded in the last column. An additional column, 'How I plan to find out' (H) can also be added to encourage children to consider and plan appropriate research strategies. Older children can refer to several different sources of information and can compare them. They can also discuss the reliability of internet sources – should we trust a website that is also promoting a product?

Having existing questions to answer that the children have raised themselves is motivating and helps children with restructuring information from texts, rather than just copying it. Inviting a guest 'expert' provides another good secondary source for information, and again, having some questions prepared in advance makes the best use of these opportunities.

Staying alive and healthy

It is important to make sure that different foods are not presented as good or bad, or as healthy or unhealthy in themselves, but that a diet can be healthy or less so. To some extent, what makes a diet healthy depends on the age of the person and their lifestyle. So what is healthy for an active, growing child may not be the same as for a more sedentary adult. The updated Eatwell Guide (Public Health England 2016) is a good visual means of exploring this message. In one classroom, two trainee teachers brought in their lunch boxes – one full with chocolate, cakes and crisps, and the other with a pork pie, chicken drumstick and cheese sandwiches. The class were highly amused by this and readily suggested their lunches were not balanced. A collaborative group activity to develop this idea would be to have a set of 'lunch boxes' made from laminated card with pictures of foods stuck on with Velcro. Groups could be given 'mixed up lunches' and asked to share out the foods so that each person had a balanced lunch. Older children could examine food labels and make comparisons about the amount of energy or salt they contain or even use the nutritional information in a game of 'top trumps'. The fat in packets of crisps can be compared by emptying the packet onto a piece of graph paper, covering the crisps with greaseproof paper and using a rolling pin to crush them. The children can then work out the area of the greasy patch on the squared paper and see which have the most fat.

Growth and reproduction

Although mentioned in the non-statutory section of the science National Curriculum for England (NCE) (DfE 2013), animal organisations such as the British Hen Welfare Trust do not support the hatching of chicks in schools for ethical reasons. However, this topic can be explored using virtual chick hatching video resources or by visiting a local farm or animal sanctuary where children can experience the hatching process in a more natural environment. Virtual resources such as time lapse videos of the transformation of butterflies and moths as they emerge from cocoons, can also provide fascinating insights into the life cycles of these mysterious insects. Inviting a parent with a new baby into the classroom and watching how it is bathed stimulates questions and discussion among young children. They could be asked to bring in photographs of themselves as babies and toddlers and to think about how they have changed, although teachers need to be certain that this won't be challenging for any individual circumstances (e.g. looked after children). Children could be invited to make zig-zag books (folded paper strips) of annotated drawings that track the changes in their lives: *How have you changed since you were born? How do you think you will change as you grow up?* This provides cross-curricular links with history as it involves developing a sense of time and change over time.

It is not only non-fiction that provides useful sources of information. Effective use can be made of stories about caring for animals, growth and change, birth, death and illness, both as sources of information and to help to explore the feelings associated with these issues. Babette Cole has written some wonderful picture books that take a light-hearted but informative look at some of these subjects, such as *Dr Dog* (1996) and *Hair in Funny Places* (2001). Many natural links can be made between relationships and sex education (SRE) and science curricula. Whilst the science NCE (DfE 2013) includes a statutory responsibility to teach children about the main external body parts, the human life cycle (including puberty) and reproduction in plants and animals, it is also recommended that all primary schools have a sex education programme which prepares pupils for the changes they experience during adolescence (DfE 2019b) and that this must be shared with parents. There is a statutory responsibility to teach about positive relationships so it is important that these should represent the diverse range of families who can provide nurturing environments within all school communities including single, LGBT, adoptive or foster parents. Again, there are many excellent children's books and resources which teachers can use to support inclusive RSE teaching including *And Tango Makes Three* (Richardson and Parnell 2007) and *Julian Is a Mermaid* (Love 2019).

Working scientifically

In topics on humans there are opportunities to develop particular elements of scientific enquiry. Pattern-seeking and researching using secondary sources are two of the categories of scientific enquiry (DfE 2013) explored in this chapter. Pattern-seeking involves observation, measurement and sampling, and there are links with data-handling skills in mathematics when constructing and interpreting graphs. These will be discussed here. The use of secondary sources of information to answer questions has been considered above but might include providing a model for children to interact with, perhaps of the heart, or pupils creating these themselves, based on their own research.

In primary classrooms first-hand observation is a key aspect of scientific enquiry to develop in this topic area. Looking carefully at skin, ears, eyes, how our joints move, listening to a heartbeat and breathing with a stethoscope, and studying the different shapes of our teeth using a mirror provides valuable sources of evidence for discussion. This observation can be developed into more focused explorations into our senses:

Which smells do different people like and dislike?
Can we identify different surfaces better with our hands or our feet? How far away can we hear a pin drop?
How do we feel after running on the spot?

Observation of different animal bones is fascinating. Children can make detailed observational drawings, making links with art. The artist Georgia O'Keefe has done some striking paintings based on animal skulls that the children could look at and respond to. Asking questions can support the exploration further:

Why do bones have holes in them?
Are they heavy?
What shapes are the ends?

These observations can be developed with measurements:

How big is my handspan?
Are my legs longer than my arms?
How many star jumps/bunny hops can I do in half a minute? How fast is my heart beating?
How much puff do I have in my lungs?

When children are challenged to come up with different ways of comparing 'puff', they have some ingenious ideas, some involving balloons, others tape measures, so these are useful resources to have to hand. You can also buy lung-capacity bags to blow into – the visual impact of the large volume of air in our lungs is impressive. Measuring skills may need to be taught explicitly (Goldsworthy and Holmes 1999). Time spent, for example, in learning to use a stop clock reduces frustrations and will increase the accuracy of children's results.

Pattern-seeking enquiry

In this topic some forms of scientific enquiry are less applicable. In particular, 'fair testing' by controlling variables, i.e. changing only one factor and keeping the rest the same, is often not possible for two reasons: ethical considerations and the variation and complexity of natural systems. Ethical considerations limit the extent to which variables can be controlled. For example, half of the class could have fizzy drinks with every meal and the other half water, and after half a term you could count how many fillings each group had. That, of course, would not be ethically acceptable if your hypothesis was that half of the class would suffer from tooth decay as a result of the investigation!

It is difficult to control variables in research into humans as the natural variation is so great. For example, if a medical researcher was testing a new treatment, they could not force the subjects to have an identical lifestyle or to have an identical attitude to the treatment – both of which might affect the outcome. They might select participants to reduce the variation, for example, by having the same age band and gender. Another strategy is to have a sufficiently large sample so that all the individual differences become less important. Alternatively, they might have a 'control' group, a group with a similar range of variation who are not given the treatment; the overall results are then compared.

Another strategy for investigating natural systems, and one that is more accessible to primary classrooms, is to carry out a survey and to look for patterns and correlations. A scientist might look for any lifestyle or genetic features that seem to be associated with high or low blood pressure. Of course, if there are multiple causes this becomes difficult to make sense of. A danger is that correlation is linked with causation when it may not be that clear cut. So, if there was a correlation between biting your nails and high blood pressure, it does not mean that nail-biting causes high blood pressure rather than an alternative explanation, such as stress leading to both nail-biting and high blood pressure. Children could predict whether the tallest people will also have the longest arms and test their ideas by lining up in order of age and taking a photograph, then lying on the floor (in the same order) with arms stretched up in the air and taking another photograph. This needs sensitive handling, as do all comparisons of body size and shape, yet is an opportunity to talk and think about diversity in a positive way.

Investigations also provide a good opportunity to develop mathematics – in particular children's data-handling skills – appropriate graphs can be drawn and examined together. Younger children can do this physically, for example, by putting a block in the stack next to a picture of their favourite food, or visually, by cutting a strip of paper to match the length of their foot and comparing it with those of others in the group. Through constructing graphs, children will understand the relationship between the data and the graph.

One tricky part of constructing graphs comes when deciding how to represent data in graphs. Children can also be introduced to computer programmes such as databases or spreadsheets and can use these to store data and present it as graphs. Using ICT in this way is a valuable skill and can speed up graph construction to allow more time for considering patterns in data. However, sometimes they seem to suggest that any data can be represented using any kind of graph, leading to mathematically inappropriate choices that cause problems when trying to interpret the data. The decision depends on the nature of the variable:

Categoric variables

Eye colour is a categoric variable, which means it has no numerical value, and there are whole numbers of cases (children with that eye colour), so the data can be represented in a 'pictogram' (Figure 2.3.1). Since every case has an eye colour, these are also proportions of the whole, so we can use a pie chart, although an understanding of angles is needed to construct one by hand (Figure 2.3.2). Pie charts and pictograms can help us see at a glance which are the most and least common or popular values, although pictograms are easier to construct and show actual numbers of cases more clearly.

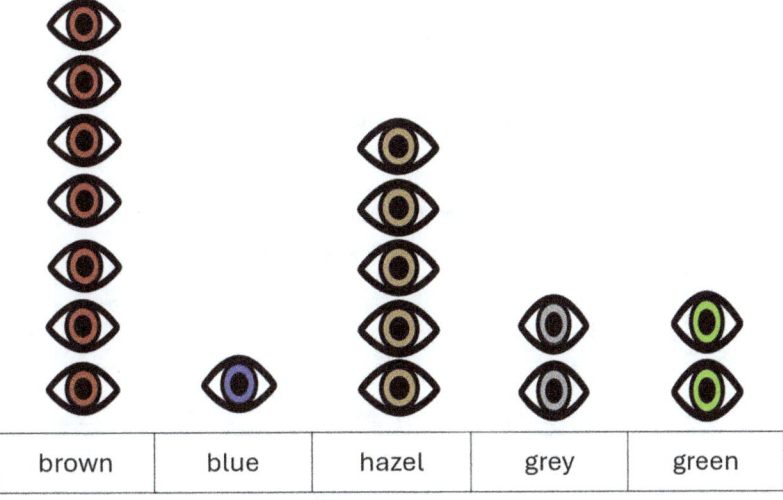

Figure 2.3.1 A pictogram of eye colour in class 2.

Teaching biology topics

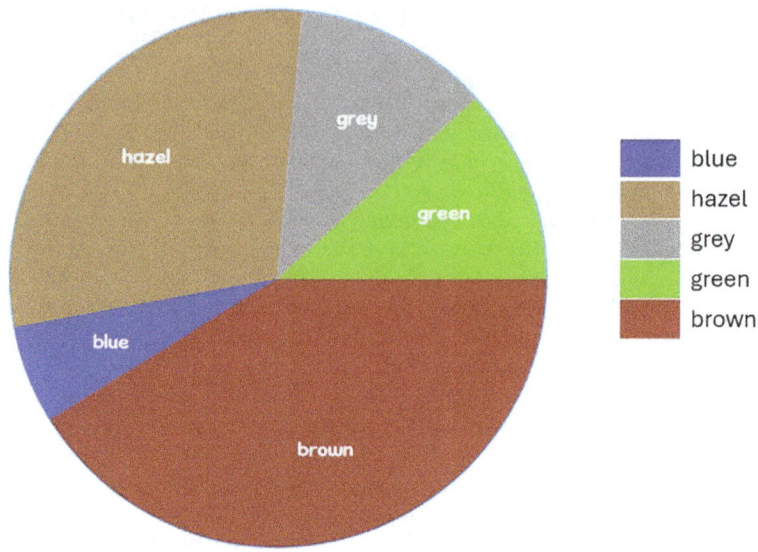

Figure 2.3.2 Pie chart of eye colour in class 3.

Discrete variables

Discrete variables, such as the number of brothers and sisters you have, are whole numbers; the numbers in between are meaningless (e.g. you can't have 3.5 siblings!). This kind of data can be represented in a bar chart (Figure 2.3.3). There should be gaps between the bars because the spaces between them have no mathematical meaning. Bar charts help with making comparisons.

Continuous variables

Height is a continuous variable. If we want frequencies of various heights, we need to use a histogram that divides the variable into class intervals (e.g. 5 cm). A histogram looks very like a bar chart, but the bars touch, showing that the variable is continuous (Figure 2.3.4). The histogram shows patterns in the data, such as the distribution, spread and centre of variation.

If we want to show change in a variable over time (e.g. heart rate after exercise), the best option is a line graph (Figure 2.3.5). Line graphs can reveal trends in the data.

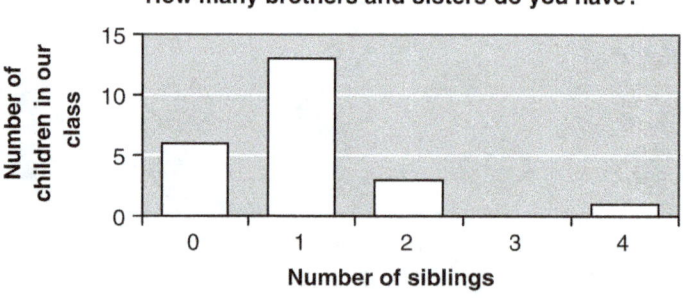

Figure 2.3.3 Bar chart showing the number of siblings for children in class 4.

Animals including humans

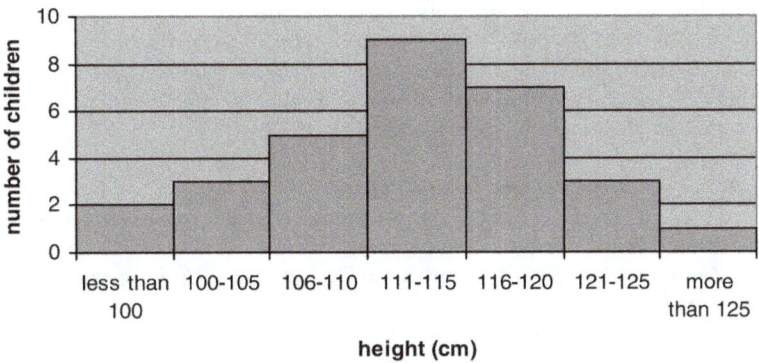

Figure 2.3.4 A histogram to show the height of children in class 5.

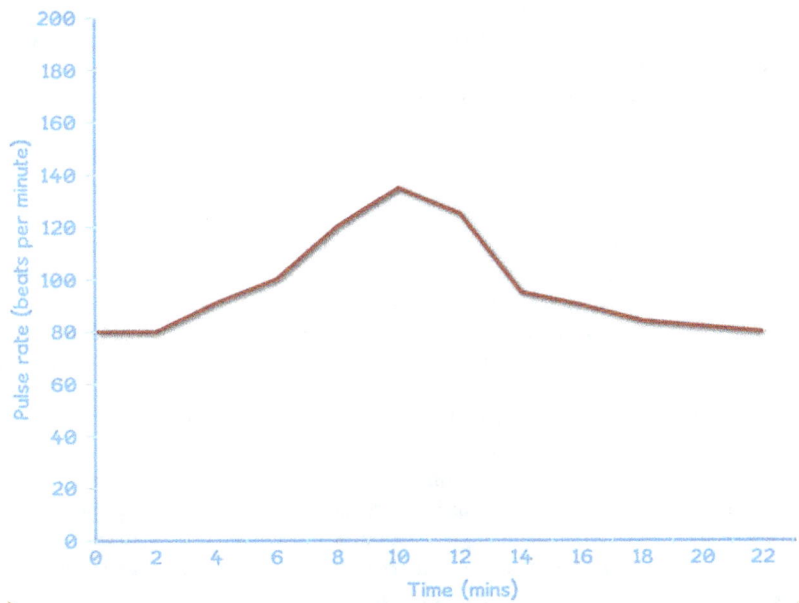

Figure 2.3.5 A line graph showing my pulse rate before, during and after exercise.

If we want to plot two continuous variables against each other (e.g. height and handspan), the most appropriate chart is a scattergram which shows strength of association between variables.

Asking question such as:

Who was the tallest?
How many children had a handspan between 6 and 8 cm?
What is the most common eye colour in our class?

can help children understand how to interpret data presented in this way. This provides a good introduction to pattern-seeking enquiry. Data collected for a whole class could be gathered on a database. More complex questions to encourage searching for patterns might include: *Are people with the biggest arm span also the tallest? Can people with longer legs jump further?*

The outcomes of surveys are not always easy to interpret. This need not involve complex statistics, but children can look at their results and think about them. Questions that might be useful in promoting this thinking could be along the lines of:

> *When the … increases, what happens to the …?*
> *Some people say that children's hearts beat faster than adults'. Is this what our survey shows?*
> *We predicted that … Is that what our survey shows?*
> *How big are the differences between … and …? Do you think they matter? Can you suggest an explanation for this?*
> *Could there be anything else that would explain our results?*

Older children should be encouraged to make generalisations about results if appropriate, for example, 'The longer the legs, the longer the arms.' A further step is to qualify these generalisations if they need to represent their results more accurately: for example, 'In most cases, the taller the person, the further they jumped, but some short people can jump a long way.' These are not trivial skills: they help prepare children for making sense of data and statements presented to them in later life so are an important part of developing scientific literacy. The publications *Science Enquiry Games* (Goldsworthy and Ponchaud 2007) and *Science Enquiry Games 4–7 Years* (Blacklock, Eccles, Goldsworthy and Shields 2010) offer some engaging ways to develop this understanding.

Monitoring and feedback

It is important to ensure that formative assessment strategies are embedded throughout all science lessons with purposeful and timely feedback provided to enable pupils to address any arising misconceptions and to achieve their next steps. Elicitation strategies were explored earlier in this chapter but can support formative assessment at any stage of the children's learning, not just at the start of a topic and are worth revisiting to determine how children's thinking has changed and developed over time. To ensure that clear guidance can be given to children about their progress and how to achieve their next steps, any formative assessment approach needs to be focused on a key aspect of their science learning and enable them to evidence this in a way that is accessible for all. One way to do this is through a multimodal approach such as working together in a group to produce a model of the digestive system in plasticine with labels explaining the function of each key component or acting out the lifecycle of animals from different classification groups. Sharing or creating a clear success criteria beforehand could support children's self or peer assessment and targeted questioning could also be used for any individuals who the teacher has identified as needing a further check in.

The Teacher Assessment in Primary Science (TAPS) website contains a range of plans for each primary year group assessing specific working scientifically skills within the plan, do and review enquiry cycle, related to topics about animals including humans. These range from an assessment of Year 1 zoologists' classification and naming skills when sorting common animals to Year 5/6 children's conclusions and evaluation of methods when carrying out a pattern seeking enquiry to determine whether there is a correlation between the distance/speed of an agreed athletic activity (e.g. height of a jump) and a bodily feature (e.g. size of feet). The TAPS plans are designed to be carried out approximately two-thirds of the way through a topic so that the assessment information they provide can be shared with the children and used meaningfully to inform and adapt subsequent teaching within the rest of the topic. These formative assessments can also be drawn upon when completing summative judgements at the end of the topic. Other good resources to support assessment of children's substantive and disciplinary knowledge can be accessed on the PLAN website.

Consolidate

Retrieving and applying

To consolidate and extend learning, children should have regular opportunities to rehearse and elaborate upon it using effortful retrieval strategies (Weinstein et al. 2019). Whilst one way of doing this is through a low stakes quiz, this approach can be overused in lessons throughout the curriculum so it is important to ensure that learners experience a range of engaging retrieval activities, which they are motivated to complete and which support them in strengthening connections to learning across different science topics as well as in other curricular areas. Marshall (2001) developed some models and analogies to use with children to develop their ideas about the body. In groups the children considered the similarities and differences between the model and what it represented: ketchup for blood, a camera for an eye, a tape recorder for ears, a balloon for lungs, and a bicycle pump for a heart. Comparing and contrasting activities such as this can provide a stimulus for discussion, opportunities for the teacher to contribute new ideas and engaging ways for children to retrieve and build upon their prior learning.

Other forms of retrieval practice could be for children to reason why they agree or disagree with a set of statements about keeping healthy or to sort facts about animal classification groups into true/false/don't know categories. Short drama activities such as taking on the role of a blood cell transporting gases and nutrients around the body or working in a group to model a part of the digestive system using their bodies can also be creative and engaging ways to extend learning.

Reviewing

The third sustainable development goal (UN General Assembly 2015) focuses on everyone having good health and wellbeing throughout their lives so purposeful links should be made to this when teaching about healthy lifestyles, including good diet and exercise choices. Children could be encouraged to reflect on what choices they are able to make now and in the future and what needs to be done to make this a realistic global expectation for all.

The Primary Science Teaching Trust Teacher Assessment of Primary Science (TAPs) project website has a range of free downloadable resources to help teachers make judgments about children's learning and animals including humans. In one example, children make careful drawings of the inside of a fish, having first predicted what they expected to see, showing observation skills and also knowledge of the key characteristics of fish

Classroom management

There are two main management issues in this topic. One is to do with the teaching of 'sensitive issues', and the other concerns the particular information about health and safety that needs attention when teaching about animals.

Teaching about sensitive issues

'Sensitive issues' refer here to teaching about sex and illegal drugs. They are sensitive because there are moral and value positions attached to these areas that might also be linked to religious beliefs and customs. There is legislation around children's involvement in sex, alcohol, smoking and other drugs. Schools will have agreed policies on teaching about sex and relationships, and are likely to have clear guidance on what is considered appropriate teaching on drugs. Teachers need to develop these policies and then work within their boundaries. Parents have the right to withdraw their children from all or some of their sex education, except for statutory relationships education (DfE

2019) and content included in the science NCE (DfE 2013). One of the implications of this is that it is important that parents be kept informed about what is happening and when.

Teachers are sometimes anxious about teaching sensitive subjects, and there are strategies that can be used to create a learning environment that feels safe for everyone:

- Set ground rules, for example no one has to answer a personal question.
- Specify names to be used for body parts.
- Use distancing techniques, for example role-play, stories, puppets, board games, video.
- Use boxes for anonymous questions, where children can write independently.

However, thoughtful discussion – in groups and circle time – is important too. Visitors, such as the school nurse, can provide useful sources of information, but it is a good idea to discuss the content carefully first, as there may be differences between their views and those of the school. A particular concern teachers may have about discussing sensitive issues is how to respond to 'difficult' questions or comments from children. If questions are too personal, teachers can remind children of the ground rules. Sometimes it is appropriate to either suggest that a child talks to their parents, or to alert the parents to an issue. If a comment or question is judged to be too explicit, then it should be acknowledged and the teacher should offer to talk about it later on an individual basis. Knowledge that seems too explicit for the child's age may be a cause of concern, and if this is the case, teachers have a duty to follow their school's normal safeguarding procedures and report this to the Designated Safeguarding Lead (DSL) who will decide on any action that is needed. This topic may open up opportunities for children to disclose abuse, so it is important that teachers are prepared for this. When talking to children, never promise to keep something private, because if a child discloses abuse, then this must be reported.

Children may also want to talk about sex, gender, sexuality and identity. At the time of writing this, guidance for primary schools on how to respond to children and how to involve their parents is debated. Many of us are learning that sex is more complex and less binary than we may have been taught. There is uncertainty about the place of science in these discussions, but something the authors of this book are sure about is that science should never be used to justify unkindness or exclusion. We accept and celebrate all the variation of humans.

Health and safety issues

If children are using the internet as a source of information about their bodies, then it is vital they are protected from accessing inappropriate images such as pornographic material. Most schools have controls and filters installed, but teachers, and children too need to be aware that if an image gets through they need to quickly move away and report it immediately. Having conversations about it helps ensure that children can protect themselves in their independent use of the internet.

If children are exploring their senses by tasting foods it is very important that all the surfaces and utensils are clean and that food has been stored correctly so there is no cross-contamination between the children. You need to be aware of any food allergies and dietary needs, and children should not be made to taste anything they do not want to. Children need to wash their hands and dry them before tasting, and preferably after too. If mouthpieces of some kind are being used, such as to measure lung capacity, then disinfect shared mouthpieces. Any teeth that the children are going to handle should also be sterilised.

Animal materials from butchers are safe to handle and cut up, again washing hands in soap and water after touching them, but children may not be happy about seeing or touching dead animal parts, and attention would need to be given to religious and ethical beliefs about animals and food. Bones can be prepared to use in the classroom by simmering them with calcium carbonate (washing soda), scrubbing them well, and then rinsing them and putting them in undiluted household bleach for a day to sterilise them. Dead mammals and birds are likely to be infected and should not be used, so if a child does bring one in, wrap it in newspaper and a plastic bag and dispose of it as kitchen waste. Explaining why this needs to be done is a teaching opportunity! There is detailed guidance in *Be Safe!* (ASE 2011) on keeping live animals in school and dealing with animal material.

Summary

In this chapter we have recommended that learning about humans and other animals can be linked with PSHE and citizenship because it provides real contexts for scientific learning that are relevant to the children. We focused on the elicitation strategies of sorting, annotated drawing and questioning, providing examples of how these might be used in various contexts in this topic. Humans and other animals as a topic, lends itself to developing scientific enquiry skills of observation and pattern-finding, and effective use of links with ICT and maths can support this. Finally, we identified other teaching strategies that are useful in developing and consolidating children's conceptual understanding, including using visual models and secondary sources of information, and provided guidance on teaching the sensitive issues of sex and relationships and drugs. Children applying their knowledge and understanding in one curriculum area to another consolidates learning and helps break down the compartmentalisation of science as a way of knowing that is separate from everyday understanding.

Discussion questions

1. What benefits and issues might there be in keeping animals at school?
2. What science knowledge and understanding do children need to make choices about the food they eat?
3. How could schools make a positive contribution to the health of pupils and teachers?
4. How can primary education acknowledge that not all people see themselves as being female or male and heterosexual, explore gender identity and take an inclusive view of sexuality?

Further reading

Arbuthnot, G. (2013) *What makes you you?*, A&C Black Childrens & Educational. (This book provides an accessible guide to evolution and genetics

Cooke, L. (2022) *Bitch: On the Female of the Species*, Basic books. (Read this for an engaging and thought-provoking look at how animals and evolution have shaped our current ideas about sex being female.)

Symonds, R. illustrations by Armstrong, G. (2023) *Paper World: Human Body*, Templar Publishing. (ASE Book of the Year 2023).

References

Association for Science Education (ASE) (2011) *Be Safe!: Health and Safety in School Science and Technology for Techers of 3- to 12-year-olds* (4th ed.) Hatfield: ASE.

Barnardo's (2004) *Burger Boy and Sporty Girl*, Ilford: Barnardo's.

Blacklock, K., Eccles, D., Goldsworthy, A. with Shields, T. (2010) *Science Enquiry Games 4–7 Years*, Hatfield: Millgate House.

Carey, S. (1985) *Conceptual Change in Childhood*, Cambridge, MA: MIT Press.

Cole, B. (1995) *Mummy Laid an Egg!*, London: Penguin Random House Children's UK.

Cole, B. (1996) *Dr Dog*, London: Penguin Random House Children's UK.

Cole, B. (2001) *Hair in Funny Places*, London: Penguin Random House Children's UK.

Cooke, L. (2022) *Bitch: On the Female of the Species*, Basic Books.

Davies, D. (2013) Taking a 'giant tour' to explore the human body, *Primary Science*, 127, 26–28.

Davies, N. (2005) *Poo: A Natural History of the Unmentionable (Animal Science)*, London: Walker Books.

Davies, N. (2014) *Deadly!: The Truth About the Most Dangerous Creatures on Earth*, London: Walker Books.

Davies, N. (2015a) *Bat Loves the Night*, London: Walker Books.

Davies, N. (2015b) *Big Blue Whale*, London: Walker Books.

Davies, N. (2015c) *Tiny: The Invisible World of Microbes*, London: Walker Books.

Department for Education (2013) *The National Curriculum in England: Key Stages 1 and 2 Framework Document*. https://www.gov.uk/government/publications/national-curriculum-in-england-primary-curriculum

Department for Education (2019a) *ITT Core Content Framework*, London: Crown.

Department for Education (2019b) *Relationships Education, Relationships and Sex Education (RSE) and Health Education*. https://www.gov.uk/government/publications/relationships-education-relationships-and-sex-education-rse-and-health-education

Department for Education (2021) *Promoting Children and Young People's Mental Health and Wellbeing: A Whole School or College Approach*, London: Crown.

Department for Education (2023) *Statutory Framework for Early Years Foundation Stage*, London: Crown.

Goldsworthy, A. & Holmes, M. (1999) *Teach it! Do it! Let's Get to It!*, Hatfield: ASE.

Goldsworthy, A. with Ponchaud, B. (2007) *Science Enquiry Games*, Hatfield: Millgate House.

Harlen, W. with Qualter, A. (2018) *The Teaching of Science in Primary Schools* (7th ed.), Abingdon: Routledge.

Kress, G., Jewitt, C., Ogborn, J. & Tsatsarelis, C. (2001) *Multimodal Teaching and Learning: The Rhetorics of the Science Classroom*, London: Continuum.

Love, J. (2019) *Julian Is a Mermaid*, London: Walker.

Marshall, F. (2001) *Models and Analogies*, ideas presented during an Improving Science Together Project meeting.

Osborne, J. Wadsworth, P. & Black, P. (1992) *SPACE Project Research Report Processes of Life*, Liverpool: Liverpool University Press. https://www.stem.org.uk/resources/elibrary/resource/29210/space-project-research-report-processes-life

Public Health England. (2016) *Eatwell Guide*, London: Crown.

Richardson, J. & Parnell, P. (2007) *And Tango Makes Three*, London: Simon and Schuster.

Russell, T. & Watt, D. (1990) *SPACE Project Research Report Growth*, Liverpool: Liverpool University Press. https://www.stem.org.uk/resources/elibrary/resource/27929/space-project-research-report-growth

UN General Assembly (2015) *Transforming Our World: The 2030 Agenda for Sustainable Development*, 21 October 2015, A/RES/70/1. https://www.refworld.org/docid/57b6e3e44.html

Weinstein, Y. & Sumeracki, M with Caviglioli, O. (2019) *Understanding How We Learn*, Abingdon: Routledge.

Wray, D. & Lewis, M. (1997) *Extending Literacy: Children Reading and Writing Non-Fiction*, London: Routledge.

SECTION 3
Teaching chemistry topics

Introduction

The science of matter – part of which we call chemistry – at primary level falls into two broad areas: the study of materials and their properties, and changing of materials. An understanding of these topics is fundamental to science because it helps us understand so many aspects of our natural and manufactured worlds. Ideas about planet Earth, rocks, soil, the weather, food, clothes and life itself all make more sense if we know something about chemistry.

One of the biggest 'big ideas' of science is the particulate nature of matter: that all materials are made from tiny particles or atoms that bond to each other in various ways (Harlen et al. 2015). This idea, which has taken scientists over 2,000 years of thinking and experimenting to develop, helps to describe the structure and composition of materials, which in turn determines their properties; explaining for example why diamond is hard and the graphite in pencils is soft. It also helps us understand phenomena such as conduction, evaporation, melting and dissolving. In the first chapter of this section – Everyday materials and their properties – we identify different approaches that enable us to teach about the properties of materials in response to current theories of learning in science.

Another of science's big ideas that is connected to understanding materials is that the composition of the Earth and its atmosphere and the processes occurring within them shape the Earth's surface and its climate (Harlen et al. 2015). The importance of understanding this big idea cannot be overstated as it is needed if we are to fully comprehend global climate change. In the news we hear about global warming, the need to find renewable energy sources and how habitats are changing. Yet the scientific explanation for climate change may not be something we fully grasp, and without this comprehension we may wonder why there is a push to reduce our use of fossil fuels, why driving our car is affecting the climate or why we should be striving to live more sustainably. An understanding of how materials change is fundamental to understanding these crucial environmental concerns and the role of humanity in changing our planet. This will be explored further in the changing of materials chapter.

References

Harlen, W. (ed.) with Bell, D., Devés, R., Dyasi, H., Fernández de la Garza, G., Léna, P., Millar, R., Reiss, M., Rowell, P., and Yu, W. (2015) *Working with Big Ideas of Science Education*, Trieste: Science Education Programme of IAP. www.ase.org.uk/bigideas.

CHAPTER

3.1

Everyday materials and their properties

Purpose of this chapter

After reading this chapter you should have:

- an understanding of how the study of the properties of materials will progress from early childhood to the beginning of secondary education;
- a knowledge of key concepts and strategies for developing children's understanding of these concepts;
- an understanding of how to design engaging, meaningful learning experiences to develop children's science capital;
- an appreciation of an approach to science education that begins with exploring children's existing ideas to develop or challenge their understanding;
- knowledge of how to monitor and assess children's learning in science;
- an understanding of how to provide opportunities for children to retrieve and apply their knowledge in purposeful contexts, with links to education for sustainability;
- an understanding of how thinking skills can be developed through the teaching of science.

Introduction

We are at all times of the day interacting with a world that is made of matter. Through our everyday experiences we have learned much about the properties of common materials. For instance, we know which material is more likely to make a warm coat, an effective sunshade or an absorbent mop. We will know that picking up a metal spoon that has been left in a saucepan is to invite a nasty burn. However, it is less likely that we have stopped to consider the reason why – in the last example because metals tend to be good conductors of heat energy. It is unlikely we have considered that the properties of the metal are a result of the structure and arrangements of its atoms, but it is our knowledge of its properties, albeit at an intuitive level, that affects our actions. Similarly, children will have made many observations about the material world and devised explanations to make sense of their interactions.

We begin this chapter by considering the everyday life experiences of children at an early age, then map out how progress is structured for primary-age children by the National Curriculum for England (NCE). It's difficult to imagine themes which include practical, hands-on experience that do not link to the topic of materials, and some of these are considered as we discuss engaging, cross-curricular contexts to introduce this topic, making connections to children's experiences and building their science capital. We consider ways to develop children's substantive and disciplinary knowledge, with a particular working scientifically focus on observation, sorting and classifying, and comparative/fair testing. Ways to assess children's ongoing learning about materials are discussed, including consideration for the role of the child in monitoring their own learning. We explore approaches to purposeful application of children's knowledge in the context of cross-curricular community projects, with links to sustainability. Research about thinking skills and how these can be developed through the teaching of rocks is presented later in the chapter.

Planning for progression

From the moment of birth children experience, and soon begin to interact with, the materials that compose the world around them. Splashing in the bath, tracing the way in which water disappears down the plughole, dropping toys and listening to the satisfying noises they make when they hit the floor, or 'finger-painting' with food on their high-chair tray all provide playful means of finding out about the natural and made world in which they live. Howe (2004, p. 1) explains that 'providing children with natural materials will do more to foster curiosity than providing a toy or resource that evidently has a specific purpose usually predetermined by the adult mind'.

> In the Early Years Foundation Stage (EYFS), developing children's understanding of the world involves exploring natural materials and collections of materials with a range of properties. Children are encouraged to look closely at similarities and differences, and to talk about what they see using a wide vocabulary (DfE 2020). Children are encouraged to observe and interact with natural processes, including changing states of matter.
>
> (DfE 2021)

Adults teach these skills and knowledge in the context of practical activity. For example, children could learn about the characteristics of solids and liquids by involving them in melting chocolate or boiling eggs. Activities that allow children to explore and play with a range of materials, together with careful questioning by adults, will help them appreciate some of the properties of the materials and develop their vocabulary. Play with sand, water, clay, dough, 'feely bags', papers, glues, fabrics, toys, wood and metal objects and finger-painting provide opportunities for this kind of exploration.

Questioning will focus on how the material looks or feels – *Is it hard, soft, rough, smooth, transparent, bendy, stretchy, shiny? Why has it been used in this particular way?* In one Nursery class a casual question: *Why is your teddy made from fur fabric?* led to several weeks of fun and a number of the children becoming engrossed in speculating and discovering why Wellington boots are good for rainy days, pencils are made from wood, glass is good for windows and towels are good for drying oneself. Earle (2022) highlights the important role of the adult in developing children's scientific language and vocabulary through open questioning, including crucial 'wait time', sustained dialogue and modelling. The Primary Science Teaching Trust's website has some excellent, freely accessible resources for developing science in the EYFS. This includes provision maps, with key science vocabulary, based on a range of topics, books and nursery rhymes.

By the time they reach KS1, children in English primary schools will be working on specific materials topics within the National Curriculum Science programmes of study (DfE 2013). For example, in Year 1 (Everyday materials) pupils need to identify everyday materials, describe the simple physical properties of these materials and use these physical properties to compare and group materials. They need to be able to distinguish between an object and the material from which it is made. In Year 2 (Uses of everyday materials) pupils identify the suitability of materials for particular uses, developing their knowledge from the EYFS by conducting comparative tests, and recognising that some materials are used for more than one thing or different materials are used for the same thing.

At lower KS2 in Year 3 (Rocks) pupils compare and group together different kinds of rocks, describe how fossils are formed and recognise that soils are made from rocks and organic matter. This represents progression from KS1 because the differences between rocks that enable them to be grouped are more difficult to observe.

In upper KS2, Year 5 (Properties and changes of materials) they compare and group together materials on the basis of properties such as hardness, solubility, transparency, conductivity (electrical and thermal) and the response of materials to magnets. They provide reasons for the uses of materials based on evidence from comparative and fair tests. Pupils are expected to build on understanding of properties of materials developed in earlier year groups by building a more systematic approach to their work and by exploring and comparing a broad range of materials.

The key concepts to be taught at KS1 and KS2 are identified in Table 3.1.1, along with some notes to inform the teacher's understanding. A useful progression in vocabulary document can be found in the resources section of the PLAN website.

It is only in the KS3 curriculum that pupils are formally introduced to the way in which the particle theory of matter can be used to explain the properties of solids, liquids and gases. However, many primary teachers find it difficult to teach the concepts of the states of matter without some reference to the particle model. In addition, in KS3 pupils learn about the rock cycle and the formation of igneous, sedimentary and metamorphic rocks. Their work at identifying rocks in Year 3 will have begun to develop this understanding by making them consider the arrangement of grains in different types of rocks.

Table 3.1.1 Key concepts to be taught at KS1 and KS2

Key concepts	Teachers' background knowledge
Materials can be classified according to their origin, type, properties or uses	The term material has a very specific scientific use. It refers to the form of matter from which substances are made. Usually this matter is in solid form but it can also be in the form of a liquid or gas. These are known as states of matter.
	Materials can be classified according to their origin, type, properties or uses. However they are classified, nearly all of them originate from the resources of the Earth (the exception being meteorites). In some cases, the materials are natural and can be used with little or no modification, whilst in other cases the natural (or raw) material needs to be manufactured or processed in some way before being used to make something else.
	Natural materials include: ■ those from the biological environment: wood, vegetable fibres, animal fibres and products; ■ those from the physical world: rocks, soil, air, water.
	Soil is made up of the weathered remains of bedrock and contains the mineral nutrients needed for plant growth mixed with humus – the decaying remains of dead organisms. Soil also contains water from rainfall and air from the atmosphere. Other geological raw materials are the result of processes that have been operating in and on the crust of the Earth for millions of years. They include permeable rocks such as chalk and sandstone and non-permeable or 'hard' rock such as marble or granite. Limestone, sand, gravel and clay, as well as fossil fuels such as coal and oil, are extracted from the Earth's crust and used for a variety of purposes.
	Rocks fall into one of three groups (igneous, metamorphic or sedimentary) depending on the processes that formed them. Igneous rocks are formed by the melting and subsequent cooling of geological materials, and are characterised by randomly-orientated, angular, interlocking grains. Metamorphic rocks are formed by heat and pressure acting on an existing rock so that over a long period of time the rock recrystallises with grains often in a banded or layered orientation. Sedimentary rocks result from material at the Earth's surface being broken down, transported, deposited and then compacted and cemented into rock, so that grains are often rounded and non-interlocking.

(*Continued*)

Key concepts	Teachers' background knowledge
	In some sedimentary rocks, such as shelly limestones, a high proportion of the material making up the rock consists of fossils. Fossils are the remains of plants and animals which died in environments that led to their preservation. Characteristically the plants and animals that become fossilised are rapidly buried by sediments after death so they are protected from scavengers and the elements. Usually it is only hard parts such as shells and skeletons that are preserved. Over geological time, the original plant and animal material is often replaced by minerals crystallising out from the solutions that percolate through the host rock. This process preserves the fossil for longer. *Manufactured materials* are made from raw materials which have been processed in a variety of ways and include: ■ metals from ores: for example, iron, copper, lead, tin, zinc and aluminium; ■ alloys: steel (carbon and iron), brass (copper and zinc); ■ ceramics and glass: bricks, tiles, earthenware, pottery, china, glassware; ■ polymers: natural fibrous materials such as hair, skin or rubber, and synthetic materials such as plastics made from products of the oil industry; ■ composites: combinations of materials such as chipboard, fibreglass or reinforced concrete.
Materials have properties and characteristics	Each material has its own characteristics and these are important when we try to distinguish between them, or choose materials for particular purposes. The uses to which we put materials depend upon their particular properties. These properties can be measured as the materials react to a variety of influences and include: ■ mechanical properties such as hardness, strength, elasticity, toughness, stiffness; ■ thermal properties such as conductivity (how well a material will conduct heat); ■ electrical properties such as conductivity (how well a material will conduct electric current); ■ chemical properties such as reactivity and solubility; ■ optical properties such as transparency, reflectivity, refractivity; ■ magnetic properties.
Properties of materials determine how we use them	Materials used for making objects and structures are chosen because they exhibit particular properties, for example, glass because it is transparent and has heat insulation properties. Other factors need to be taken into account: cost, aesthetic qualities and availability might be considered. Materials that are becoming scarce, such as oil or hardwood timber, have increased the need for alternatives to be developed. A distinction can be drawn between the property of the material and the property of the object. A property of the material is related to the intrinsic qualities of the material. A property of an object is dependent not only on the material but also on its size and shape. For example a metal rod can be either stiff or flexible depending on its thickness. Although strictly speaking stiffness is a property of the object, at primary level it is taught as a material property.

Teacher's self-assessment questions

1. Can you identify at least one property for each of the following types: mechanical, electrical, chemical, optical, thermal and magnetic? Are you able to provide a definition for each property and explain why you grouped it as you did?

2. Can you name three examples of natural and manufactured materials, and explain what distinguishes one set from the other?

3. What properties of rocks can be used to sort them into different groups?

Engage

Situating the topic

In our model of teaching outlined in section 1, the first stage – engage – is aimed at introducing a topic, developing engagement and motivation through familiarising children with the objects to be explored and allowing them to make connections to their prior learning, experiences and personal interests. It also provides time for playful exploration of new or unusual items and gives children the opportunity to think about questions they would like to ask. One starting point is the use of a collection of objects to introduce different concept areas of science. A small display of objects from the collection chosen accompanied by a question board will encourage children to begin thinking about a new topic, what they know and what they would like to know, discussing it and raising questions that can be 'posted' on the question board. Young children can have their comments and questions scribed for them.

The choice of objects can be planned to maximise not only learning about materials but also other areas of the curriculum. Some examples of how the choice of objects can be linked to a theme are given below. Thought was given to selecting objects that give children experience of a range of properties (toys), states of matter (bath-time) and the origin of materials (seaside), as well as meaningful links to other topics. Children can contribute to these collections, either through shared experiences such as trips and outdoor learning, or by providing suggestions based on their interests and experiences. In this way, connections can be made to their own lives, making science learning more relevant and meaningful, building their 'science capital' and the idea that science is for them (Archer et al. 2015).

Toy collection: include mechanical and soft toys, although be careful the scientific definition of 'soft' is understood (a material that is easily marked or indented), and consider providing puppets. Shadow puppets are particularly good as links can be made to optical properties of materials (translucent, transparent and opaque). A collection that includes toys that move by being pushed or pulled provides an opportunity to make links with the topic of forces. There is the potential to make links with the history curriculum if toys from the past are included in the collection.

Bath-time collection: include liquids such as shampoo, shower gels, bubble bath, warm water; solids such as a bar of soap, a shampoo bar, towel, pumice stone; and gases formed from perfumes and aftershaves. Links can be made to the topic of 'staying healthy' (the importance of washing and cleanliness) and to environmental issues associated with single-use plastics.

Collections of 'rubbish': packaging made from a variety of materials enables pupils to make links between the properties of those materials and recycling/composting, thus contributing to our teaching of sustainability.

Seaside collection: include a range of natural (e.g. sand, seashells, water, dried seaweed, rocks – including ones with fossils) and manufactured objects (e.g. parasol, sun-cream, inflatable beach toys, Lycra swimwear).

Teaching with collections lends itself well to peer evaluation. Children can review each other's work and provide helpful feedback based on co-constructed success criteria.

Stories and picture books can be a useful 'way in' for children, helping to provide a context for learning science concepts, and an engaging shared experience. They can help to make science more relevant to children and provide a 'risk-free' context for making predictions and testing ideas (McCullagh et al. 2010). Traditional tales and rhymes provide a great, accessible starting point for investigating materials. Goldilocks gives a context for exploring the properties of household objects, whilst the Three Little Pigs invites enquiry into the properties of different building materials. Comparative tests might include finding the most absorbent mop for Cinderella, the most protective material for Humpty Dumpty or the most waterproof fabric for Red Riding Hood's cape.

Picture books, such as *Princess Smartypants* (Cole 1986), can be used as a stimulus for science enquiry by encouraging children to 'solve' problems presented in the story. They could make and test the strength of bags for the Queen Mother's shopping by adding potatoes until the bags break. To enable comparisons to be made, potatoes could be laid out on the ground, pictures of potatoes could be used in simple pictograms or children could use bar charts to record their findings. This might spark discussions about fair tests, the best way to present results and encourage evaluative thinking about the 'best' design and material for a bag. Conversations may include the impact of plastics on the environment and ways to reduce our usage. Bags can be buried and dug up in six months' time to see which have degraded. Encouraging children to ask their own questions is a powerful way to inspire genuine enquiry and exploration.

A small selection of picture books with particular links to materials and the planet include *Clean Up!* (Bryon and Adeola, 2020), *Somebody Swallowed Stanley* (Roberts and Peck 2019), *The Street Beneath My Feet* (Guillain and Zommer, 2017), and *A Planet Full of Plastic* (Layton 2019). Books such as *One Plastic Bag: Isatou Ceesay and the Recycling Women of the Gambia* (Paul 2015) might inspire children to consider action that they could take in their own communities to reduce waste.

Breaking down barriers

Inviting members of the community to explain or demonstrate part of their work which uses or relies upon specific materials can help children to make connections to their own lives and experiences. A parent who works in a trade such as carpentry or construction could demonstrate part of their work and perhaps even help to support a practical workshop. For example, children could learn how to mix cement and build a wall around a flower bed in the playground. A nurse or hygienist could talk about the use of materials to keep medical equipment sterile, or children could visit the school canteen to hear about how food is safely transported to the kitchen. Visits and visitors can help to increase engagement and motivation through novelty and shared interests. If children have a particular passion for skateboarding, for example, a skateboard designer or engineer could come into school to talk about the materials used to build a skateboard, or a surfer could show how boards are shaped. These could lead to larger projects where children design and make their own skim or balance boards. In addition to the local community, making links to inspirational contemporary scientists in lessons, such as materials scientist Dr Pearl Agyakwa (see 'A scientist just like me' resources from the PSTT), can help to build children's science capital.

Activating children's ideas

Everyday usage of the word 'materials' usually refers specifically to fabric, and this is probably the understanding of the term that young children will bring to school. The SPACE project (Russell et al. 1991) found that, when asked to identify and sort objects according to what they are made of, young children in the EYFS and KS1 are inclined to describe them by referring to a particular property – often what the material feels like. Some children confuse smoothness with softness and suggest that smooth materials feel soft. A few children describe observations made with senses other than touch: for example, some describe what noises the materials make or what the materials look like in terms of colour, shape or size. Many children describe the material in terms of how it is used. At KS2 they are more able to identify the material from which objects are made, such as metal, plastic, wood, soil, stone or polystyrene, and the uses to which objects could be put, for example, food, building materials, and things to write on are common responses. Some children describe how objects are perceived to have observable properties in common: hard, soft, shiny, bendy or that they feel the same.

Natural objects are identified by children as not having been subjected to any manufacturing process; however, the term 'manufactured' is notable by its absence from their classifications. Commonly at upper KS2, pupils classify on observational criteria that results in them adopting active, manipulative approaches. Empirical tests such as scratching, cutting or filing to determine 'hardness' involve more detailed consideration of how testing can be fair.

Children's ideas about what constitutes a rock are based around characteristics such as roughness, hardness, size and heaviness; the inference being that rocks are rough, hard, large and heavy. A good deal of confusion exists about the differences between rocks, stones and pebbles, so that for example a smooth sample of sandstone may be rejected as an example of a rock because it is not jagged. Furthermore, 'Children lack a conceptual framework within which to consider and compare the attributes of rock' (Russell et al. 1993, p. 142).

When asked to relate properties of materials to their uses, KS1 children generate around one suggestion per material and upper KS2 children twice that number. Functional properties are by far the most commonly identified, e.g.: 'Wood is good 'cos it's strong, if it's out in the rain it won't rot for a long time.' Less frequent responses concern manufacturing, aesthetic and (rarely) economic properties.

Seldom do descriptions of materials include labels such as 'solid' or 'liquid'. When asked to draw some solids, the preference is for 'hard' objects such as stones to be chosen, and some children choose solids they associate with 'strength', such as weights. Drawings of liquids often include washing-up detergent, indicating that they are perhaps thinking of the word 'liquid' on the label rather than of the properties of the detergent.

Build

Constructing new knowledge

Properties of materials and their uses

Using games such as those in Box 3.1.1, children will not only learn to identify and name many common materials, but will also realise that each material has its own characteristics and that the uses we can make of materials depend upon their particular properties. The Explorify website provides free online games that can be displayed on the interactive whiteboard and can be used as a class to develop discussion and thinking skills. At KS1 pupils can carry out simple comparative tests on pairs of materials. Later in KS2 pupils can, with support, develop a variety of fair tests to investigate a broader range of properties of a wider selection of materials. Some of the more important properties of materials that could be investigated include transparency, density, hardness, strength, elasticity, stiffness and flexibility, compressibility, thermal and electrical conductivity and magnetic properties. Such comparative/fair tests might include:

- a simple circuit used to test for conductivity;
- using a magnet to find out which materials are attracted;
- a torch to test which materials allow light to pass through;
- a scratch test to see which material can be marked by another;
- a 'pull test' to see which materials will stretch or are elastic;
- a 'bend test' to see which materials are flexible or stiff;
- a 'squeeze test' to find out which materials can be compressed.

The setting up of all these tests will contribute to the development of the skills of fair testing. Finding out the elasticity of various thicknesses of rubber band, the hardness of different rocks, the absorbency of paper towels or the permeability of different materials can be accomplished in various ways, and can provide scope for children to think about how best to test for properties and how to carry out their tests to arrive at valid and reliable results. For example, the hardness of rocks could be determined either by a scratch test with reference to a metal nail (the rock is either harder or softer than the nail) or by scratching one rock with another so that an order of hardness is the outcome. Testing each rock with the same nail and applying the same pressure are two of the ways that tests can be made fairer (Table 3.1.2).

Teaching chemistry topics

BOX 3.1.1 SORTING AND CLASSIFYING GAMES

These games can be adapted for children of various ages and stages of development from the EYFS to the end of KS2. They are designed to develop the skills and language of sorting and classifying.

Sorting into groups

Give out a group of objects and ask children to sort them. For Nursery and KS1, keep the number of objects small, no more than ten. There is no need to tell them what to sort for – they will have their own interesting (and often unexpected) ideas. This gives you an insight into their thinking, not whether they can sort according to your criteria!

You may need to demonstrate. Stick to two groups initially, e.g. Is … red, is not … red. Young children usually choose colour, shape and size as a starting point. You may need to introduce the concept of 'bigger than', 'smaller than'.

Coloured PE hoops can be used for the sorting and overlapped for items which fit both groups, thus introducing Venn diagrams.

Guess the criterion

With the children in a circle, look at the collection of objects. Talk about what's there and the characteristics of one or two objects, particularly any unfamiliar ones. Begin to sort into two groups, and ask the children to guess the criterion you are using. Then ask one child to sort them while other children try to guess the criterion s/he has used. This can be repeated many times with different criteria.

It is a good idea to start with a small collection and divide it into two groups, gradually increasing the size of the collection and number of groups over a period of time. Children can work in small groups, each with a collection to sort. With very young children ask them to 'whisper' their criterion to you: this ensures they don't change it when the right answer is given!

Guess which object

Choose one object from the collection, but do not reveal which it is. Children ask questions based on various criteria to try to discover which object it is (e.g. is it made from wood?). If the answer is no, remove all wooden objects and further questions centre on those that are left. Only allow yes or no answers. Choose a child to select the object while others try to find out which one has been selected.

Give us a clue

Select an object from a collection but do not reveal the choice. Provide clues one at a time until children identify the object.

Mystery object

Put one object from the collection into a closed box or bag without giving the children a chance to see which it is. Pass the box round the children and give them the opportunity to feel, shake and listen before asking one question about its hidden contents. Children can describe what they feel. Continue until the object is identified. A small group each with a box ensures the children's interest is maintained.

Spot the criterion

Split the class into groups and give each group a small collection and a coloured pencil. Ask each group to sort their collection in three different ways and to record these ways on a sheet of paper. They then sort using a fourth criterion, leave the objects so arranged but without recording the criterion. Each group moves to the next collection and tries to guess the final criterion used by the previous group. They then record in a different colour their own three ideas for sorting and leave the objects sorted in a fourth way.

This can be continued as long as is thought appropriate. It allows you to find out a great deal about how the children are thinking, and each group's responses can be easily identified. This activity could be used at the start and end of a topic and help the teacher to assess changes in the children's thinking.

Adding to a collection

Select an object and choose a criterion but do not reveal it. Children take it in turns to add one more object which is accepted or rejected depending on whether it fits the chosen criterion. Children have to identify the criterion being used.

Domino game

This game can be used to identify similarities or differences (differences are easier to begin with). Each child holds an object from a collection. One child is asked to place their object on the floor; the others are then asked if their object is different in any way from the object on the floor. One child is asked to place their object alongside the first and the criterion is recorded. Children are then asked for an object which is different from the second object on the floor. The process continues until all objects are on the floor. The game can be made more difficult by insisting that criteria can only be used once (e.g. shape, size, texture, material).

Finding similarities

Children work with a partner, examine at least three collections and select one object from each which they think has something in common. They share with the whole class their items and the similarity between them.

Odd one out

Children explain which of three objects is the odd one out and why. This is a risk-free way to elicit children's knowledge and understanding as there are many possible responses.

Making a key

Children work in groups, each with a small collection of 5–10 objects and a large sheet of paper. They are asked to develop an identification key using yes/no questions. Groups move round and try each others' identification keys.

Label-it

On Post-its, write single words that would describe a property or attribute of the object (e.g. shiny, hard, red). Stick the labels on appropriate objects. Can we move the labels to different objects in the room? Can we add more words?

Word bank

Using the word bank made above, sort the words in a variety of ways (e.g., nouns, adjectives), those that can be both (e.g. glass), alphabetically, etc.

Grids and Carroll diagrams

Chalk a matrix (e.g. 2x2) on the floor. Put three real objects down the side. Use the word bank again as headings of the table. Use ticks or crosses to record the properties of the objects (see below).

	Shiny	Red	Clear
Cup	x		
Box		x	
Tin	x	x	

This can be developed by using a Carroll diagram that shows two criteria and the alternative 'not' category.

	Transparent	Not transparent
Flexible		
Not flexible		

Objects can then be placed in the appropriate sector of the diagram.

Debates that develop from group discussion can provide the motivation for exploring further. In a Year 2 class in a Somerset primary school the teacher actively sought to develop dialogue and debate regarding which material would make the best thermal insulator. Pupils initially discussed their predictions in pairs by building on their prior knowledge, then moved on to discuss their ideas with other pupils in groups of three. After an extended debate regarding the merit of each prediction, eventually one was chosen. Pupils were encouraged to not only select a prediction but to explain the reason for their choice. The prediction they made framed the test they then went on to conduct on the thermal properties of a range of materials. After completing their fair test, pupils can apply the results to answer questions such as which material should be used for making black-out blinds or, in this example, which material should be used to keep a drink cool on a warm day.

Working scientifically

As discussed in section 1, teaching the enquiry skills and disciplinary knowledge that can be used to generate or test scientific knowledge should be focused and relevant to the topic area being taught. The focus in this chapter is on the process skills of observing, sorting, classifying and predicting that we have already identified as essential in developing an understanding of materials. These types of enquiry are included within the categories of exploration, identification and classification developed by the AKSIS project (Goldsworthy et al. 2000). It is suggested that, particularly for the EYFS and Year 1, the emphasis should be on exploration, handling materials to look for physical properties, similarities and differences, and ways in which they can be used and changed. The NCE (DfE 2013) in KS1 also emphasises observing closely, identifying and classifying, and using observations to answer questions.

Sorting has traditionally been an activity developed with younger children and – particularly with use of Venn diagrams and Carroll diagrams for sorting – has clear links with the mathematics curriculum. However, the development of the skills of observation and classifying through sorting activities should be ongoing throughout primary education if we are to ensure that these skills become increasingly sophisticated and that properties identified include more scientific ones such as malleability, strength and transparency.

Venn diagrams are often an appropriate way to sort collections of objects by property, particularly when the collection includes objects made from more than one material. For example, a toy car with a metal body and rubber wheels could be sorted in the intersecting group when distinguishing between hard and soft materials.

Other ways of sorting data that can be taught through collections include Carroll diagrams (see Box 3.1.1 for examples) and branching databases. When pupils develop branching databases encourage them to use properties of materials if this is the conceptual demand of the lesson. So, for instance, sorting the rubbish collection could begin with the question *Is the material flexible?* All materials that are flexible go along one branch; the rigid materials are sorted along the other branch. Next those materials that are flexible might be sorted further by the question *Is the material biodegradable?* and so on.

Software packages such as *Flexitree 3* can help create a binary tree or branching database that can then be used by other children to identify a sample of material. Using a branching database is rather like playing '20 Questions'. The programme stores a series of questions, each of which must be answered yes or no, in relation to an object or material under consideration. Finally, only one of the items in the database matches your answers and the object is identified. If the item is not in the database, it can be added along with further questions and answers. Playing such a game will encourage children to generate questions such as *Is it flexible? Is it transparent? Does it conduct electricity?* Of course, similar games can be played without using IT although having the opportunity to input questions for others to use at a later date, and displaying them on an interactive white board for all to see can be motivating factors.

Sorting games based upon collections of objects can be used in a variety of ways to develop both the skills and an understanding of the properties of materials, helping children to become aware of the variety of materials that form the world around them and fulfilling the requirements of the NCE. We have collected, over time, ideas for a number of sorting games used by teachers and trainee teachers in the classroom to add motivation and fun. These are described in Box 3.1.1. These games need to be planned with care and have recognition given to the development of the associated scientific vocabulary. Classroom management should be considered. While a whole-class introduction is worthwhile, small groups working to handle and sort their collection allows for greater participation.

Raising questions is an important scientific skill and one highlighted in the NCE Working Scientifically strand. 'During years 1 and 2 pupils should be taught to ask simple questions and recognise that they can be answered in different ways' (DfE 2013). Some of the games outlined in Box 3.1.1 provide opportunities for children to practise raising questions. Other sorts of questions can also be raised during a sorting and classifying activity or game. Questions can be categorised according to how they might be answered:

- *What does it look like? What does it feel like?* (Answer by observation)
- *Which object will float or sink? Which material allows light through?* (Answer by exploration)
- *Which material is hardest? Which is most flexible?* (Answer by comparison)
- *How is it made? Where does it come from?* (Answer by research through secondary sources)

Children are fond of asking questions that are not easily answered. It may be worth pointing out that science does not have an answer to some questions (e.g. *Which is the prettiest object?*) or that there may be an answer, but the teacher doesn't know! Rather than seeing this as a problem, this could be an opportunity to value children's contributions by finding out together, planning these topics into future lessons or emphasising that genuine questions are worth asking even if they cannot be answered. Lynne Bianchi's book *Smart Pickings* (2016) is a great way to scaffold enquiry by encouraging children to think about what they want to find out and the best way to answer these

Table 3.1.2 Suggestions for comparative and fair test-type investigations

Material property	Context	Possible investigation
Waterproofness	Which materials are suitable for an umbrella or raincoat?	Dropping water onto samples, observing if water soaks into the material, sits on the surface or passes through to an absorbent layer beneath.
Transparency	Which material is suitable for a sunshade?	Using a light meter or sensor to determine which sample allows least light through.
Absorption	Which material is best for mopping up spills?	Decide what the 'best' paper kitchen roll means. Examine the paper samples closely to determine the factors or variables involved (e.g. pattern, thickness, layers).
Tensile strength	Which cord or thread is best for tying a parcel?	Use a Newton meter or a range of weights to conduct a 'pull' test.
Hardness	Which material is best for a floor-covering in a kitchen? Which rocks or building materials will be most resistant to weathering?	Develop a 'rub' test or scratch test to determine hardness. Consider other tests relevant to the context (e.g. reaction to vinegar to mimic acid rain). Discuss how to combine the results from different tests.

questions. It also presents a variety of ways to share findings of investigations and introduces a range of inspirational scientists.

Children will need practice in raising and phrasing questions that can be investigated through comparison. For example, a child could initially ask 'Which fabric is best for making a sun hat?' This would need to be modified to 'Which fabric lets the least light through?' if the intention was to carry out a comparative or fair test.

'Materials' provides many opportunities from Year 3 onwards for fair testing (controlled investigations). It is important that such investigations take place in an appropriate context to ensure science is seen as having relevance to everyday life – examples are given in Table 3.1.2. Children can learn much about the composition of materials and about their classification by handling them, but first and foremost safety concerns need considering. To ensure they carry out their investigations safely, the ASE guide *Be Safe!* (ASE 2011) should be referred to for a comprehensive list of 'chemicals' that are suitable and unsuitable for primary school investigations. This publication also includes guidance on safe methods of testing; for example, when adding weights to samples of polythene to determine tensile strength a cardboard box should be placed underneath the rig to catch weights when they fall and avoid damage to children's feet.

Monitoring and feedback

Taking note of what children say and the questions they ask is the beginning of the elicitation process that enables teachers to make a formative assessment of where children are in their present understanding. Using the collections introduced above, key questions might include:

> *Can you use your senses* (except taste in most cases!) *to find out about the materials? Can you group the materials?*
> *Can you identify materials such as metals and plastics?*
> *Can you explore the collection and ask questions?* (For example, *Does it float or sink? Is it magnetic? Will electricity pass through it?*)

Teachers can observe children as they sort and group objects, asking them to explain their categories and noticing how they deal with materials which will not easily fit into one group. They can encourage children to generate their own groupings or to decide upon headings for materials which have already been sorted. Listening to and observing children engaged in these activities will provide teachers with a huge amount of information about their understanding of both substantive and disciplinary science knowledge. A dialogic approach (see section 1) will enable teachers to challenge children's thinking or to provide additional support, as needed.

Visible thinking tools, such as 'see, think, wonder' charts, where children are encouraged to observe a scientific phenomenon, image or object and to note down what they see, what their thoughts are and questions that they have, enable the teacher to understand children's current knowledge. They can highlight any alternative frameworks or misconceptions, as well as providing useful information about children's interests and questions for future planning. Similar tools include KWHL charts (know, would like to know, how I will find out and learned), mind maps and other graphic organisers. To ensure that science knowledge is being assessed, rather than writing ability, children can be encouraged to draw, explain, act, sing, model or present their thoughts. These tools can be used anywhere in a sequence of lessons to formatively or summatively assess substantive science learning. If children are asked to revisit these over the course of several lessons, they will be able to reflect on their new learning and address some of their own misconceptions.

Opportunities to assess the working scientifically elements of the curriculum need to be carefully planned and purposefully assessed, so that children do not experience cognitive overload when attempting to demonstrate all of these at the same time. Children can design a comparative/fair test to answer their own question, giving the activity meaning and purpose. One example might be to determine the most absorbent nappy, paper towel, tissue or toilet roll. The focus of the assessment could be to plan comparative tests to answer questions, including recognising and controlling variables. Children can present their investigation to the class, explaining the question they are hoping to answer, the dependent/independent and control variables, and how the investigation will be carried out. Assessment can be carried out through observation, discussion and questioning, and both peers and adults can provide constructive feedback.

Consolidate

Retrieve

Providing opportunities for children to retrieve and apply their knowledge in new contexts can support them to make connections, making this learning more useful and accessible (Howard-Jones 2018). It will also allow them to receive timely feedback on their responses. To ensure that these support the consolidation of new concepts, retrieval activities should be effortful but achievable, spaced over time and carried out in low-stakes environments. Examples include matching activities, quizzes, drawing diagrams and multiple choice questions. It is important that children receive immediate feedback on responses, either by finding these out for themselves or by the teacher presenting them. This learning can be even more effective if the tasks are varied and children are encouraged to make links to other areas of learning and experiences. Children might be asked to make connections between a bamboo plant, a wicker chair and a t-shirt. They could recreate the 'life story' a glass bottle through drama.

Apply

Connections can be made to other areas of the science curriculum, highlighting the interconnected nature of knowledge. For example, explicit links to forces can be made when investigating the shoes with the best grip on a variety of different surfaces. Plants and animals can be discussed when considering where materials, such as bamboo and wool, come from. Children can be encouraged to retrieve their knowledge about electricity when thinking about the conductive properties of different metals.

Connections to other subject areas and 'real life' contexts can make the application of learning in school more evident. In addition to the links discussed previously, mathematical skills can be developed when learning about the properties of materials. For example, keeping accurate measurements of volume and of temperature as water cools is necessary if pupils are investigating the thermal conductivity of a range of materials by testing how well each insulates a mug of warm coffee. Tables will be necessary to record observations and a graph used to show how temperature changes over time. As with so much science in primary school, the development of mathematical and scientific skills will go hand in hand.

Consideration for the use of plastics lends itself well to discussions and debates. For example, children can take on different roles in debates around the use of single-use plastics. Roles might include a medical professional arguing *for* their use to keep medical equipment sterile, a shopkeeper considering the role of plastics in keeping food fresher for longer, and activists emphasising their negative impact on humans, animals and the planet. Older children might consider the concept of 'greenwashing', or exaggerated claims made by companies to appear more environmentally conscious, as well as the increased costs associated with 'going green'. This could lead to children writing persuasive letters to local businesses to influence policy, or to producing short documentaries or pamphlets.

Taking a more global view, with links to geography and the UN's sustainable development goals (UN General Assembly 2015), children could consider the source of materials, the costs associated with producing them and the transportation considerations. This links well to discussion around 'fast fashion' and the environmental impact of different materials, such as bamboo vs cotton. Secondary sources can be used to find out about where our waste ends up and to learn about initiatives to reduce our environmental impact. For example, The Ocean Cleanup charity collects plastics from rivers and oceans around the world, and in Kenya, Gjenge Makers turns waste plastics and sand into construction materials. Children can design their own systems to collect waste based on these findings, or can implement systems to reduce, reuse and recycle materials in the classroom and wider school or community.

Cross-curricular projects are a great way to support children in meaningful application of science, particularly if this involves an authentic audience or community link. Children can use their knowledge to design and make wind-powered toys for children in reception class, with video instructions for how to use them. They can design and make products to sell at the school fair, with consideration for materials chosen based on the suitability of their properties and their impact on the planet. This would include researching, sourcing and pricing materials, testing their suitability, making products, marketing, selling and calculating profit. In these examples, cross-curricular links with science include D&T, art, English, computing and mathematics.

Review

Focused activities which assess particular elements of the science curriculum can be found on the PSTT's web page *Teacher Assessment in Primary Science* (TAPS). These plans are organised by topic and include links to both the disciplinary working scientifically knowledge and the substantive curriculum content. For example, a materials hunt in Year 2 requires children to search for materials around the school to find objects made of specific materials and to record their ideas in a table. This allows the teacher to assess how the children gather and record data to help in answering questions and to identify everyday materials. Through discussion, children can make links between the properties of the materials and their uses. The plans provide useful adaptations, questions to support discussion and assessment indicators. In this example, children are meeting expectations if they can record their observations of a range of objects made from different materials and, in discussion, make links between properties of materials and their uses.

Teachers could invite children to reflect on which parts of the topic they enjoyed the most, or to say which bits they think were the most important to learn about and give reasons for that. This metacognition is intended to help children see the science they are learning as 'for me'. It also helps children to step outside the immediacy of their feelings and take stock of how they are managing their learning. The next section explores metacognition further in the context of learning about a particular group of natural materials – rocks.

Rocks and CASE

The following structured approach to teaching rock identification demonstrates how to support children to develop a conceptual framework through encouraging them to play an active role in their learning, including opportunities for metacognitive thinking, ongoing feedback and application of new learning.

Hawley (2002) describes how the teaching of rock identification to KS2 children has relied upon descriptive–inductive approaches characterised by children comparing a series of rock samples to secondary sources such as photographs. Such an approach results in children having a fixed image of a particular rock so that, for example, those children that can identify a white granite are frequently unable to identify a sample of pink granite. Also, this approach does little to develop children's understanding of a conceptual framework against which they can compare and test an unfamiliar rock, a finding echoed in the SPACE research referred to above (Russell et al. 1993). Without this conceptual framework children will struggle to make meaningful interpretations of rocks. However, by using a structured approach to identify and classify rocks into generic groups, children will begin to understand the geological processes that have led to the rocks' formation. The Earth Science Education Unit (ESEU) have drawn on the work of Hawley and the work of the CASE team at Kings College London in developing an approach that teaches primary school children how to identify rocks. CASE, or Cognitive Acceleration through Science Education, was first developed in secondary schools in the 1980s, but later the CASE team turned its attention on the impact of cognitively stimulating activities on primary school children and published two intervention programmes for Year 1 and Year 3 children (Adey et al. 2001, Adey et al. 2003). Each activity is based around the 'five pillars of cognitive acceleration':

1. Concrete preparation: setting the scene for the problem.
2. Cognitive conflict: the learner is presented with an activity which challenges their current understanding.
3. Social construction: children are actively encouraged to work together to solve the problem.
4. Metacognition: learners are asked to reflect on the thinking they employed to overcome a problem.
5. Bridging: identifying where else similar thinking could be used and applied.

Moreover, the CASE approach involves general ways of thinking that can be applied in many different contexts. These schemata are referred to in Table 3.1.3. So, the thought process that goes into putting a series of pictures in chronological order can also be applied to ranking a series of rocks in order of hardness. Drawing together the work of Hawley, ESEU and the CASE team, along with that of the authors of this book, an approach to teaching about rocks in the primary classroom that enables children to develop a sound conceptual framework about rocks has been developed and is summarised in Table 3.1.4. Note that a number of schemata are developed through this approach including, most obviously, skills in classifying objects, and concrete modelling of different rock types. The pillars of 'metacognition' and 'bridging' relate most closely to 'review' and 'application' stages although the table as a whole is included in this section for the sake of completeness.

Table 3.1.3 General ways of thinking suitable for primary school children

Schema	Characteristic features
Classification	Putting into groups that have some common characteristics.
Causality	Understanding the relationship between variables so that what is the cause is distinguished from what is the effect.
Combinatorial thinking	Thinking of as many different combinations from a limited number of variables, and doing so in a systematic way.
Seriation	Developing the general ability to put things in order.
Concrete modelling	Building simple models to explain observations.
Relationship between variables	Deciding if there is a relationship between one variable and another.
Conservation	Developing the understanding that the amount of many materials stays the same even though their shape or location may change.

After Adey et al. 2003.

After children have gained a basic understanding of some of the differences between rocks formed by sedimentary, metamorphic and igneous processes, it is illuminating for them to look at these rocks in thin, translucent sections. An alternative to buying expensive microscopes and thin sections is to visit one of the many websites that display stunning images of sandstones, granites and the like. Can children speculate from the images the processes that led to the rock's formation? Sandstone images may show very clearly in cross-section grains that have been rounded by erosion as they were moved about by wind or water. By contrast the grains making up granite are tightly interlocking and are a result of minerals crystallising from molten rock.

Summary

In this chapter we have presented some key concepts about materials, reviewed curriculum progression, and examined ways in which teachers can help children become more informed about the materials – natural and manufactured – that make up their world. We have considered engaging, meaningful contexts in which to introduce this topic and how we might contribute towards building children's science capital. The ideas and alternative frameworks that children might bring to the study of materials have been explored. We have emphasised developing substantive knowledge and the role of working scientifically, with a particular focus on observation, sorting and classifying, and comparative/fair testing. The relationship of conceptual understanding and skills has been explored, for example, by considering how simple tests can be planned and carried out by pupils to determine a range of properties of materials. Approaches to assessing children's knowledge have been suggested, with a focus on ensuring that children receive ongoing feedback throughout sequences of lessons, and that they play an active role in their learning. This has been exemplified in the CASE approach, where children are encouraged to engage in metacognitive thinking throughout the process and to apply this learning in a range of contexts. With growing understanding of the variety of materials, the uses to which they are put and, particularly, the finite nature of the Earth's resources, one of our aims must be that children retain some of the curiosity and 'awe and wonder' they exhibit when young. Contexts in which children might be encouraged to retrieve and apply their learning in meaningful contexts have been explored. If this results in adults prepared to take action to ensure a sustainable future for our world, we will have achieved a great deal.

Everyday materials and their properties

Table 3.1.4 An approach to teaching rocks in the primary classroom

Stage description and aim	Concrete preparation	Social construction and cognitive conflict	Metacognition	Bridging	Teaching points
1 What is a rock? Clarify ideas of what constitutes a rock and focus on the idea of grains.	Activity focuses on finding a way to sort a collection of rocks.	Find a working system to sort rocks, considering those rocks that don't easily fit into it.	How well do the rocks fit the system?	Is it okay for our class to have several different rock identification systems?	7-11-year-olds most frequently sort using colour, shininess, speckliness and roughness.
As a follow up to 1 above.	An observer needs to be nominated.	To move thinking on, one member of the group listens and the remaining members discuss their approach. What is it that makes a rock shiny/colourful/etc.? What can you see? Observer identifies commonly used words.	Which words were most commonly used? Is it apparent now what element of a rock is most important when classifying rocks?	Geologist uses the bits of a rock, their relationships and arrangement, to classify them. We can take this further with other activities.	Often word 'bits' is used although the correct scientific term is grains.
2 Are there differences between grains? Focus attention on just two very different rocks, such as sandstone and granite.	This activity studies in more detail the differences between the grains in each rock. Model the use of magnifying aids (hand lenses).	Begin by encouraging close observation of the grains of the two rocks. Invent a name for each to forestall the need to name each. Observe and describe the grains of each sample. What differences do you note?	What helped you to observe the rocks more closely? How has your thinking developed? What were the challenges?	Why do you think there are differences between the rocks?	Children most commonly describe the samples as having sharp edges and rounded grains. Responses may include ones about the differences being due to the way the rocks were formed.

Stage description and aim	Concrete preparation	Social construction and cognitive conflict	Metacognition	Bridging	Teaching points
3 Predictions and explanations Give children a concrete experience to reason about differences in textures.	Model how to use scales. Predict what will happen to the mass of each sample when it is immersed in water. This prediction should be based on experience gained in the workshop so far.	Carrying on with only the sandstone and granite, measure the mass of each before and after immersing in water. Note masses on the board. How closely did the changes noted match the predictions? How did the water penetrate the sandstone?	What process did you go through when predicting what you thought would happen?	Which other rocks in the collection do you think water would be able to penetrate?	
4 Modelling Help understand about grain relationships.	This activity uses a model to demonstrate the grains in rocks. Show the paper shapes and demonstrate the tessellation activity.	Complete a tessellation activity to answer questions: 1. How do grains fit together with no space between them? 2. How do they fit together with spaces? Children are provided with two sets of paper shapes (circles/ovoids, and angular shapes) and are challenged to stick each set together to minimise space between the pieces. Next children model the structure in 3D using either marbles or LEGO. Why don't the grains fall out of rocks like sandstone?	How has this activity refined your earlier understanding of grains in rocks?	Can knowledge of interlocking and glued together grains be applied to other rocks? Look at a conglomerate. Is it most like an interlocking or non-interlocking rock?	Grains are stuck together by 'rock glue' in rocks such as sandstones and conglomerates. This precipitates naturally between the grains during rock-forming processes. Although grains don't readily fragment, the conglomerate is most similar to the non-interlocking group of rocks.

Everyday materials and their properties

5. Classifying rocks Consolidate new understanding; introduce concept of grain arrangement.	Provide a selection of rocks. Show how to use a frame to focus observation on a small area.	Grain relationships (how grains fit together) are reviewed. Does grain shape help us decide if a rock is interlocking or non-interlocking? Can a selection of rocks be sorted into crystalline and fragmental? Grain arrangement – introduce two forms of arrangement: 1) random, and 2) aligned, using samples of schist and granite, drawing a sketch of each through a frame. Can children now classify a selection of rocks?	What approach did you adopt when confronted with a new rock?	Can the new approach be applied to any rock sample?	Some rocks such as gritstone have angular grains but with pore spaces filled or partially filled with rock glue. Frequently the fine-grained rocks cause confusion. Slate and mudstone are often put to one side and returned to later. Children could be asked to scrape these and use knowledge about crumbliness to draw conclusions. Most students sort the rocks into three categories based on textural relationships. The names igneous, metamorphic and sedimentary can be introduced at this stage.
6. Names	Now it is time to name the rocks by pairing each with a prepared description.	Which rocks continue to present difficulties and why?	Did using only the way grains are joined together provide enough information? What other criteria did you use?	Use your new understanding to set up a building stone trail.	

Based on the work of ESEU and Hawley 2002

Discussion questions

1. Explain the relationship between working scientifically and conceptual development in the topic of materials and their properties.
2. How might teachers encourage children to discuss their ideas about materials through opportunities for dialogue?
3. What importance should teachers attach to making the topic of materials relevant to children's experiences and why?
4. How can cross-curricular projects in the topic of materials encourage children to take action for sustainable development?
5. To which other topics in science could the CASE approach to teaching thinking skills be meaningfully applied?

Further reading

Explorify website provides ideas for investigations linked to materials, as well as activities such as 'Odd one out' for comparisons, 'Zoom in, zoom out' for observation skills and 'What if…?' to consider materials and their properties from a different perspective: e.g. What if… Every material was stretchy?

Primary Science Teaching Trust's (PSTT) website has a range of fantastic free resources for schools, including a free booklet of activity ideas to support children to explore the properties, uses and benefits of glass through meaningful investigations.

University of York's Centre for Industry Education Collaboration (CIEC) web page has links to free resources for schools, including ideas for materials investigations linked to different enquiry types.

WWF 'Schools Sustainability Guide' and resources, provide tips on how to take action for climate, nature and sustainability.

References

Adey P., Nagy F., Robertson A., Serret N. & Wadsworth P. (2003) *Let's Think through Science: Developing Thinking with Seven- and Eight-Year-Olds*. London: Nfer Nelson.

Adey P., Robertson A. & Venville G. (2001) *Let's Think: A Programme for Developing Thinking with Five and Six Year Olds*, London: Nfer Nelson

Archer, L., Dawson E., DeWitt, J., Seakins, A. & Wong, B. (2015). 'Science capital': a conceptual, methodological, and empirical argument for extending Bourdieusian notions of capital beyond the arts, *Journal of Research in Science Teaching*, 52(7), 922–948.

Association for Science Education (ASE) (2011) *Be Safe!: Health and Safety in School Science and Technology for Techers of 3- to 12-year-olds* (4th ed.), Hatfield: ASE.

Bianchi, L. (2016) *Smart Pickings*, Millgate House Publishers.

Bryon, N. & Adeola, D. (2020) *Clean up!*, UK: Puffin.

Cole, B. (1986) *Princess Smartypants*, London: Hamish Hamilton.

Department for Education (2013) *Science – Programmes of study for Key Stages 1–2*, London: DfE.

Department for Education (2020). *Development Matters: Non-statutory Curriculum Guidance for the Early Years Foundation Stage*. https://assets.publishing.service.gov.uk/government/uploads/system/uploads/attachment_data/file/1007446/6.7534_DfE_Development_Matters_Report_and_illustrations_web__2_.pdf

Department for Education (2021) *Statutory Framework for Early Years Foundation Stage*, London: Crown. https://assets.publishing.service.gov.uk/media/659d3e68aaae22001356dc46/Early_years_foundation_stage_statutory_framework_for_group_and_school-based_providers.pdf

Earle S. (2022) Early science research summary: Use of play and role of the adult, *Journal of Emergent Science* 22, 5–12.

Goldsworthy, A., Watson, R. & Wood-Robinson, V. (2000) *Investigations: Developing Understanding*, Hatfield: ASE.

Guillain, C. & Zommer, Y. (2017) *The Street Beneath My Feet*, London: Words & Pictures.

Hawley, D. (2002) Building conceptual understanding in young scientists, *Journal of Geoscience Education*, 50(4), 363–371.

Howard-Jones, P. (2018). *Evolution of the Learning Brain: Or How You Got to Be So Smart…*, London: Routledge.

Howe A. J. (2004), *Play Using Natural Materials*, London: Collins Educational.

Layton, N. (2019) *A Planet Full of Plastic*, London: Wren and Rook.

McCullagh, J., Walsh, G. & Greenwood, J. (2010) Books and stories in children's science, *Primary Science*, 111(1), 21–24.

Paul, M. (2015) *One Plastic Bag: Isatou Ceesay and the Recycling Women of the Gambia*, Minneapolis: Millbrook Press.

Roberts, S. & Peck, H. (2019) *Somebody Swallowed Stanley*, London: Scholastic Children's Books.

Russell. T., Bell D., Longden K. & McGuigan L. (1993) *Primary SPACE Project Research Report: Rocks, Soil and Weather*, Liverpool: Liverpool University Press

Russell, T., Longden, K. & McGuigan, L. (1991) *Primary Science Processes and Concept Exploration (SPACE) Project Research Report: Materials*, Liverpool: Liverpool University Press.

UN General Assembly (2015) *Transforming Our World: The 2030 Agenda for Sustainable Development*, A/RES/70/1. https://www.refworld.org/docid/57b6e3e44.html

CHAPTER

3.2

Changing materials

Purpose of this chapter

After reading this chapter you should have:

- an understanding of how the study of changing materials will progress from early childhood until the beginning of secondary education;
- knowledge of key concepts and strategies for developing children's understanding of these concepts;
- an understanding of how to design engaging, meaningful learning experiences to develop children's science capital;
- an appreciation of an approach to science education that begins with exploring children's existing ideas to develop or challenge their understanding;
- an understanding of how to involve children in the development of meaningful enquiry through encouraging questioning and dialogic talk;
- an awareness of the key role science plays in the teaching of issues of global significance.

Introduction

In this chapter we explore how to teach about the changes that happen to materials in a way that is matched to children's experiences, by returning to the essential ideas and concepts that underpin our understanding of the particulate nature of materials. Before reaching a point where changes can be explained in terms of particles, teachers can engage younger pupils through a range of exciting and developmentally appropriate investigations that are matched to pupil needs. These include observing over time, conducting comparative/fair tests and engaging in research using secondary sources. We emphasise the importance of relevant, meaningful enquiry linked to children's questions and ideas. Then we take the idea that all materials are made of particles because, as well as helping us understand how properties of materials are determined, this idea also helps us to visualise what happens when materials change state, which in turn helps us to explain *reversible* processes such as freezing, melting and condensing. Relevant contexts for learning and progression in key concepts through primary school are at the heart of this chapter. One particular theme that is discussed in detail is the contribution of science education to debates about environmental issues. We take issues such as waste management and climate change and consider how these could be taught in a meaningful and engaging way at primary level, with purposeful connections to the sustainable development goals (UN General Assembly 2015). There can be few concerns greater than

Changing materials

the impact we are having on our planet, so an education that explains the science behind climate change and considers how we can make a positive difference is hard to overstate.

Planning for progression

In the EYFS, through a wide and varied range of experiences with changing materials, children develop an awareness of change using all their senses and ask questions about why change has occurred. A balloon or rubber glove, as large as possible, filled with water and frozen to make an ice-balloon or ice-hand will immediately focus attention and give rise to questions such as: What will happen if we leave it in the classroom? How long will it take to melt? How can we make it melt more slowly? Work with food can provide further opportunities for finding out how materials change; baking biscuits, making jelly, porridge, ice-lollies or chocolate cakes are guaranteed to motivate. Provided health and safety is kept in mind with the risk of allergic reactions assessed and controlled, such activities never fail to interest children and allow for endless questions to be asked, answered and explored. Understanding some important processes and changes, including changing states of matter, is part of the early learning goal for 'The Natural World' (DfE 2021). Later at KS1 in Year 2 (Uses of everyday materials) pupils should be taught to find out how the shapes of solid objects made from some materials may be changed by processes such as squashing and bending. A topic related to changing materials is covered in the Year 2 (Seasonal changes) Programme of Study (PoS), which requires pupils to observe and describe weather associated with the seasons.

At lower KS2 in Year 4 (States of matter) pupils are taught to compare and group materials according to whether they are solids, liquids or gases; and to note changes of state when materials are heated or cooled. They identify the role played by evaporation and condensation in the water cycle, including associating the rate of evaporation with temperature. This develops pupils' observations of changes in the weather that was part of their KS1 education by requiring them to understand the scientific processes that lead to these changes.

In upper KS2 Year 5 (Properties and changes of materials), pupils are taught to use their knowledge of solids, liquids and gases to decide how mixtures might be separated for example through filtering, sieving and evaporating. They will know that some materials dissolve in a liquid to form a solution and that the original material can be recovered from that solution by evaporation. They should demonstrate that dissolving, mixing and changes of state are reversible changes. They should also be taught that some changes (such as those associated with burning) result in the formation of new materials, and these changes are not usually reversible. Furthermore, related to this area of the science curriculum is the Year 4 PoS for science (Living things in their habitats) in which pupils are asked to explore examples of human impact (both positive and negative) on environments.

In KS3 pupils are introduced to the way in which the particle theory of matter can be used to explain changes of state, gas pressure and diffusion, although teachers do find it useful to introduce this to pupils in a simplified form in upper KS2. They study physical, geological and chemical reactions in some detail and learn about the production of carbon dioxide by human activity and the impact of this on climate. However, pupils will be receiving messages about environmental issues before reaching KS3 so it is important that teachers are able to provide a scientific explanation for climate change at an earlier age (Table 3.2.1).

Table 3.2.1 Changing materials: progression in key concepts

Key concepts	Teachers' background knowledge
All materials are made up of particles	According to kinetic theory, all material is made up of particles too tiny to see. We use the particle model, where particles are represented by small, solid, inelastic spheres, to help describe and explain the properties of solids, liquids and gases. This is a helpful but simplified model, which assumes that all particles are the same. In reality, 'particles' are different (e.g. atoms, molecules) and different forces exist between them.

(Continued)

Table 3.2.1 (Continued)	
Key concepts	**Teachers' background knowledge**
In theory all materials can exist as solids, liquids or gases (kinetic theory)	For most materials it is not easy to demonstrate their different states, but water provides an example that can be used relatively easily. An ice cube, as it is warmed up, changes from a solid to a liquid (water). If it is heated further, the liquid will turn into a gas (water vapour). The temperature at which a solid melts to form a liquid is called its melting point. For pure water this is 0° Celsius. This is the same as the freezing point; the temperature at which pure water turns to ice when it is cooled.
	Boiling point is the temperature at which a liquid turns to a gas. For pure water this is 100° Celsius. If steam is cooled below 100° Celsius it condenses back to a liquid again.
	Change of state can be explained by the particles from which they are made and the arrangement of these particles.
	In a solid the particles are:
	■ closely packed; ■ arranged in a regular pattern; ■ able to vibrate about a fixed point but not move from place to place; ■ strongly bonded by forces of attraction to neighbouring particles.
	The properties of a solid (ice for example) are:
	■ not easily compressed so have a fixed volume; ■ fixed shape.
	In a liquid the particles are:
	■ fairly closely spaced; ■ in a random arrangement; ■ bonded to neighbouring particles by weaker forces, so able to move from place to place.
	The properties of a liquid (water for example) are:
	■ not easily compressed so have a fixed volume; ■ no fixed shape.
	In a gas the particles are:
	■ widely spread out; ■ in a random arrangement; ■ moving about at high speeds; ■ not bonded to neighbouring particles by forces of attraction.
	The properties of a gas (water vapour for example) are:
	■ able to be compressed so have a variable volume; ■ no fixed shape.
	This simplified mental model of the structure of solids, liquids and gases helps to explain some of their properties. In the examples, the particles in the ice, water and vapour are the same particles (water molecules). The arrangement of these particles is what determines the different properties of the ice, water and vapour.

(*Continued*)

Changing materials

Table 3.2.1 (Continued)	
Key concepts	**Teachers' background knowledge**
Materials can be changed by being pulled or pushed	In the case of solid materials, strong bonds exist between neighbouring particles holding them together. However, it is possible to change the arrangement of particles of materials by force. Although squashing, bending, twisting and stretching changes the form of the material, no new material is created. A lump of dough is still a lump of dough after it's been pushed and pulled even if its shape has changed. In some materials the bonds between particles are so strong they don't yield to the manual handling described but instead retain their shape.
Freezing, melting and boiling, condensation and evaporation, are reversible changes	When a solid is heated, the heat energy transferred causes the particles in the solid to vibrate more rapidly. In doing so they move apart, causing the solid to expand. If enough heat energy is transferred, the particles vibrate rapidly enough to break free from their fixed positions and they are able to move around each other. At this point the solid melts and becomes a liquid.
	If heat energy is transferred to a liquid, the particles move increasingly rapidly until they are able to separate and move in all directions as a gas. The escape of gas particles from the surface of a liquid is known as evaporation. The temperature at which gas forms inside the body of a liquid (and escapes as bubbles) is known as the boiling point. To bring about the reverse changes of condensation and freezing, the movement of particles must be reduced, and this is done by cooling – removing energy from the particles.
	Evaporation, condensation, melting and solidification are examples of reversible change. Physical changes can be fairly easily reversed. This is because the particles that make up the materials are simply rearranged without fundamentally changing them. During physical change, the mass of the material remains the same before and after the change. Simple processes such as warming, cooling or mixing can reverse the change. Melted chocolate can be cooled until it sets as a solid once more. Water evaporated can be condensed to a liquid again, as when water vapour condenses on cold glass. Clay that has been shaped into a pot and left to harden can be reconstituted by adding the water that has evaporated.
	Evaporation and condensation are important processes in the water cycle. A simplified model that ignores evaporation from the solid land surface and from plants has energy from the Sun driving water evaporation from the surface of an open body of water such as an ocean. Here water changes form from a liquid to a gas (water vapour). The water vapour is held within the atmosphere as a gas until it is cooled, when it will condense forming tiny droplets of water now suspended in the atmosphere as a cloud. In certain circumstances the tiny droplets coalesce forming larger droplets. When the droplets become sufficiently large they will fall to the ground as rain (or hail, sleet or snow depending on temperature). Sooner or later precipitation falling on the surface of the Earth will return to the ocean via streams and rivers and the cycle is complete.
Dissolving is a reversible change	If a material can be completely absorbed within a liquid so it becomes invisible, we call this dissolving. One liquid can dissolve in another liquid or a solid (or gas, such as oxygen) can dissolve in a liquid. A solution (a completely uniform mixture) is formed. The **solvent** is the liquid that does the dissolving. The **solute** is the material dissolved. The **solution** is the mixture of the two. Something that dissolves in a solvent is described as soluble. Those that do not dissolve are called insoluble. Salt and sugar are soluble in water. There is a limit to the amount of solute that can be dissolved in a given volume of solvent. The solution eventually reaches a point where no more solid can dissolve. This is called a saturated solution. The saturation limit depends on the solvent and solute concerned and also on the temperature. Usually, as the temperature is increased, the mass of solute that can dissolve increases.

(*Continued*)

Key concepts	Teachers' background knowledge
	Dissolving and melting are frequently confused. Dissolving: ■ can happen without heat, whereas heat is needed for melting to take place; ■ requires two or more substances, whereas melting involves only one; ■ involves substances mixing; in melting the substance remains pure; ■ cannot be reversed by cooling whereas melting can; ■ involves two different kinds of particles mixing whereas melting involves the rearrangement of one kind of particle.
Chemical changes are non-reversible	Chemical changes are usually permanent. A new substance is produced which is not easily returned to its original form. Chemical change can be accelerated or caused by heat. For example, an egg once boiled cannot be made soft again by cooling, nor dough baked into bread returned to the original flour and water. Once it has been fired in a kiln, clay cannot be returned to its original state. During chemical changes, a chemical reaction takes place in which the particles involved undergo significant changes. In the example of a candle burning, new chemical bonds are formed between carbon atoms and oxygen atoms to make carbon dioxide molecules. The carbon atoms are firmly bound to the oxygen atoms inside the carbon dioxide molecules and cannot easily be separated. A new compound has been created. During a chemical change no new matter is created or destroyed. The same number of atoms exists, but they have been redistributed between the new materials formed. Therefore the mass or amount of 'stuff' after the chemical change is the same as the mass before the change. The mass remains constant. Decay is another form of permanent change often brought about by the actions of micro-organisms. If a material decays in this way it is biodegradable.
Burning is a non-reversible change, resulting in the formation of new materials	Burning (combustion) is a familiar chemical reaction, in which particles from a material combine with oxygen from the air. When a candle burns, some of the wax (fuel), made from atoms of hydrogen combined with atoms of carbon, becomes a liquid and melts. Some is drawn up the wick, evaporates and becomes a gas. This gas combines (burns) with oxygen from the air to form carbon dioxide and water droplets, together with soot (carbon). Heat and light is generated and a flame can be seen. Burning of fossil fuels from the time of the Industrial Revolution onwards is seen by many to be responsible for the rise in carbon dioxide in the Earth's atmosphere, from around 280 parts per million (ppm) in the eighteenth century to around 400 ppm today. Along with other greenhouse gases such as methane, carbon dioxide traps the Sun's energy on the surface of the Earth and its lower atmosphere leading to warming of around 1° Celsius to date and associated climate change.
Mixtures and solutions can be separated	When two or more substances are combined together without a chemical reaction taking place, a mixture is formed. If the mixture is a solid in a liquid, it will either form a suspension or a solution. Suspensions appear cloudy and eventually the solid material will settle out. On the other hand, solutions are clear and never settle out. Examples of solutions are given in the above (see 'dissolving is a reversible change'). Examples of suspensions include muddy water and flour mixed with water. Mixtures do not form new substances: they can have a variable composition and have similar properties to those of the original constituents. It is possible to separate a mixture using physical techniques. Sieving can separate a mixture of solids such as sand and rice. Insoluble solids can be separated from a liquid by filtration (e.g. some components of soil from muddy water). Soluble solids can be recovered by evaporation. In the case of instant coffee, you could in theory boil away the water and get the coffee grains back. When a solvent is evaporated the solute (solid) remains behind. The solvent can be collected by allowing it to condense on a cold surface such as glass, a process known as distillation. Some mixtures of solutes can be separated into their components by paper chromatography. For example, to separate ink into its constituent colours, the solvent soaks through filter or blotting paper and the coloured components with differently sized particles separate out as they travel different distances through the microscopic holes in the paper.

Table 3.2.1 (Continued)

Teachers' self-assessment questions

1 Grains of sand seem to flow to fill the bottom of the container they occupy. Is sand therefore a liquid?
2 Can you describe what happens to the particles of sugar when it is added to hot tea in the cup?
3 What is happening when a candle is alight? What new materials are formed and from what are these new materials formed?

Engage

Situating the topic

The study of changes in materials provides an ideal opportunity for children to prepare and cook food. Take for example the possible learning opportunities presented by something as simple as making bread. Initially, flour and dried yeast – both solids which seem to behave like liquids as they 'flow' into the bowl – are mixed with liquid water to form dough, a material that behaves like a liquid in that given time it will flow into the spaces of a bread tin. Too much water and the dough is too sticky to knead; too little and it resists our attempts to squash it. After kneading, the yeast will respire using the sugars in the flour and oxygen from the air to produce carbon dioxide, a gas, which leads to the dough rising. During baking, chemical changes will occur in the risen dough that result in bread being made, a change that cannot be reversed. Bake the bread for too long and it will be dry and burnt. If an oven is not available, making cheese with warm milk and white vinegar in the classroom allows children to observe the changes as the hydrogen ions in vinegar react with the casein protein in milk to form lumps or 'curds'. This mixture can be sieved to separate the curds from the whey. In cheese making, rennet is used in the curdling process rather than vinegar. Discussions and observation can support children to make connections to similar cheeses, such as cottage cheese, and they can find out more about these processes by researching using secondary sources.

For examples from the kitchen of changes that can be reversed, making ice cream or melting chocolate to form a sauce will prove to be popular choices with children. For very energetic children, vigorously shaking double cream will form a lump of butter and buttermilk. This activity, as well as many others, can be found on the Science Sparks website.

Many different subject areas and learning environments can provide engaging contexts for exploring changes of state. For example, the energy required for the process of evaporation can be demonstrated during PE, when sweat evaporates from the body, cooling us down. A similar effect can be felt by licking the back of your hand and blowing on it. In the winter, salting the playground or roads around the school can lead to discussions around the melting point of ice, how sea salt is collected from the oceans and investigations into separating materials. Observing water vapour condensing on cold classroom windows or children seeing their breath outside on a cold day, all provide relevant contexts for discussing changes of state. Stories such as the Gingerbread Man, Goldilocks and The Snowman (Briggs 2010) provide familiar contexts for exploring chemical changes in cooking and heating/cooling.

Breaking down barriers

Education for sustainable development

The study of changing materials provides many opportunities to focus on citizenship and issues such as sustainability. Burning a candle could lead to a discussion about the impact that burning fossil fuels is having on the Earth's atmosphere. Investigating a collection of packaging or 'clean' waste products might encompass the life cycle of manufactured objects from 'raw materials' and leads naturally to the environmental impact caused by 'waste' materials. There are a number of videos on YouTube showing how materials are produced, which are fascinating to watch and can spark discussion about the energy used to create the materials, as well as their impact on the planet. The history of different materials can be investigated, including reference to scientists, such as the chemist Ruth Benerito, who is best known for inventing wrinkle-free cotton.

The concept of biodegradability can be introduced through an investigation of food waste (which does degrade) and plastic, which does not. Continuing the theme of waste materials, a discussion can be structured around the concept of recycling – which materials can be recycled and which can't? Why is it only possible to recycle some of our waste? Collecting the class or school waste for one week could lead to a discussion on landfill sites. Some sites welcome visitors, such as the Wood Lane Nature Reserve in North Shropshire or the Carymoor Environmental Trust in Somerset.

At Carymoor, during a visit to a working landfill site pupils can discover much about waste disposal and recycling including:

- finding out where their rubbish goes and what happens to it after it is dumped;
- discovering the financial costs of landfilling and who pays for it;
- considering how waste can be recycled into compost;
- discovering how gases from the landfill site can be used to generate electricity;
- which liquid pollutants come out of our rubbish, how they are cleaned and why this is important;
- the uses to which old landfill sites can be put.

Activating children's ideas

The SPACE project (Russell and Watt 1990) probed children's understanding of evaporation and condensation by getting them to monitor the change of water level in a large container over a five-week period. For many KS1 children, the reason that the water level declined over that period was described through the use of non-technical terms such as 'dried up'. At KS2 'evaporated' was used by children much more frequently as a way to explain their observations. When questioned further on the reason for the change, the great majority of children in both KS1 and KS2 did not discuss water as a substance having different states. Only a minority of children understood that water could undergo a transformation from liquid to gas.

Research into children's ideas about global warming (Palmer and Suggate 2005) shows that at KS1 most children understand what effect warming would have on snow and ice. However, for some children, it was not a clearly held view that this warming could transform ice to water. Short-term effects on animals were described ('The penguin would have to go in the water'), and some children revealed a general understanding of the dependence of living things on their particular habitat. However, when questioned about the impact of deforestation, children believed that animals would simply move on somewhere else if their forest was destroyed. As for the reasons why the Earth is getting warmer, about one-third of children knew something about greenhouse gases or pollution by the end of KS2, but there was confusion between the greenhouse effect and the hole in the ozone layer (which is actually shrinking owing to the restrictions on use of chlorofluorocarbons (CFCS) since the 1990s). Other explanations for global warming given included the Sun getting nearer to the Earth and that it was simply as a consequence of seasonal change. Eliciting children's prior knowledge so that misconceptions can be identified and addressed has been identified as a key theme in effective climate change education (Monroe et al. 2019). (See 'Further reading' at the end of the chapter for guidance on subject knowledge for teachers on this topic.)

A formative assessment of children's current understanding of changes in materials can be made by noting what children say and the questions they ask. A particular material or object might be presented to the children, and their ideas elicited about how it might change. Such items could be an ice cube or ice balloon, a puddle of water, a burning candle, chocolate, perfume, clay, an egg, a rubber band, sugar, a rock or a coin. Key questions could include:

> *How could you change this material?*
> *Could you get the material to change back?*
> *Would any new materials be made?*
> *If we warmed the material, what would happen to it?*

To elicit children's ideas about environmental issues, stories and images can provide useful starting points for dialogue. For example, the picture book *Hunter's Icy Adventure: A True Story About the Global Problem of Climate Change* (Jackson & Callwood 2020) provides an introduction to the melting of the polar ice caps and the impact of climate change. Photographs within a theme such as 'climate change' might include influential people, such as Greta Thunberg, extreme weather events and changing landscapes. Using local images might help to make the learning more relevant and meaningful, although these must be carefully chosen according to the teacher's knowledge of the class to avoid causing undue anxiety. Asking children to make connections to their prior knowledge and experiences of these issues will enable the teacher to assess their starting points.

Build

Constructing new knowledge

Material transformations

Careful observation over time and conducting comparative/fair tests can support children to build new knowledge about changing materials. Key questions to pose during these investigations include:

> *How do materials change?*
> *Which materials change?*
> *What makes materials change?*
> *Could they be changed back to their original state? If so, how?*

Activities that involve physical changes that address the key ideas above include:

> *Melting*: close observation of ice cubes, chocolate or cheese in plastic bags immersed in hot water encourages the development of vocabulary to describe what is happening. Teacher questions can help to focus on change of shape or colour and on what happens when the substance cools again. Keeping the sample in a bag throughout can show that no material is added or taken away. Another 'un-bagged' sample can be melted to allow children to feel and smell as well as see the changes.
>
> *Dissolving*: investigating what happens when sugar, jelly, paint or baking powder are dissolved in small amounts of water encourages prediction and hypothesis about what will happen; where the substance has gone; whether we could show it is still in the water (for example a taste test); how we could make it dissolve more quickly; and whether it can be retrieved. Other insoluble powders or grains such as flour, sand or talc can also be tested to encourage further questioning and thinking.

Investigations that involve chemical changes of materials as well include:

Cooking: making toast provides a simple example, with the advantage that the product can be eaten! There are lots of independent variables to explore: try making toast on different time settings, with different breads or with bread that is fresh or stale. Encourage children to observe the changes closely with a hand lens or microscope. Create a 'colour chart' that relates time to colour change. Investigate how long before the butter will not melt on the toast. Do different spreads have different melting points?

Burning: ask the children to draw a lit candle placed in a dish of sand. Encourage close observation of the flame, wick and wax – ask them to identify what is seen, what changes and what 'disappears'. Encourage them to generate questions: *Do different-coloured waxes burn in different colours? Do thick candles have thick flames? What happens when a saucer is held over the flame? What happens when a flame is 'blown out'?* A video could be taken and reviewed frame by frame. Children can be asked if they think we could get the wax back again, which other materials they think will burn easily and which will not.

Decaying: provide opportunities to observe over time the decay of substances such as milk, bread, cheese, yoghurt or apple, carefully sealed in dishes or bags. Looking at leaves in autumn or objects buried outside can be used to introduce the concept of biodegradability. Record the changes through drawing or photography, keeping careful note of time elapsed. What changes can be seen? Do different materials decay differently? Do all materials decay? Do things go rotten faster if they are wet, hot or buried? How can we keep things fresh longer? What is causing the decay?

Rusting/corrosion: a walk around the school and playground or observation of a bicycle could be the starting point for identifying materials that rust or corrode. A collection of materials, some coated with paint or galvanised and clean and some rusty, can be used to find out what happens when metals are left in air or water or oil. The coins chosen by one trainee teacher for children to investigate rusting proved a poor choice since these are made from or coated with metals which do not rust! Investigations might determine which metals will rust, which conditions are necessary, how long it takes for iron or steel to rust and how we can stop things rusting.

Children's health and safety are of particular concern when teaching about the way in which materials change since heat is often involved. A risk assessment will identify the need to ensure careful adult supervision of any activity involving the use of hot water or a naked flame. Teacher demonstration of the use of hot water for melting materials is probably safest. If children are to use water for melting it should be warm, not hot and take place under strict supervision with a ratio of no more than six children to one adult. Lighted candles should always be placed in a container of sand and again require careful supervision. Children should know what to do if the candle is knocked over – do not try to stand it up but place a wet towel over it and allow it to cool (the sand should extinguish it in any case). Children should also know how to deal with a burn or scald – run the affected part under cold water for 5 minutes. Burning other materials, such as fabric and paper, should be done by the teacher as a demonstration, and care should be taken to ensure that substances that produce unpleasant or dangerous fumes are not used. Decaying matter should be carefully sealed in small dishes or plastic bags. Refer to the ASE's *Be Safe!* booklet (ASE 2011) for definitive guidance.

Addressing global issues

As a starting point to gaining an understanding of global issues, younger children can study the weather. However, to do this meaningfully teachers do need to be flexible in their planning so that spontaneous opportunities for learning are not lost. Equally and for the same reason it helps if resources are prepared in advance and are ready to use. Over the years, the authors have developed a range of activities for different weather conditions, organising them into separate weather boxes, one for each weather type, with each box helpfully containing all the resources needed to carry out the activities and intervention cards.

The ranges of activities for each weather type include:

> **Rain**. **Box contents:** chalk, wipeable pens, rain catchers, powder paint, fabric squares, paper boats, paper towel strips. Activities: make different shaped rain catchers from plastic bottles, and use them to collect rain; form a shelter from the rain using a plastic sheet; create pictures using powder paint and investigate what happens to them in the rain; investigate what happens to a range of both waterproof and non-waterproof fabrics in the rain; make a range of boats to play with in the puddles; draw patterns on paper towels using felt-tip pens and investigate what happens to them in the puddles.
>
> **Wind**. **Box contents:** pegs and washing line, streamers, plastic bag wind socks, windmills, paper kites, balloons and pump, bubble making, parachute. Activities: wash, wring out and peg out bits of cloth; play with the kites, windsocks and balloons, investigating what makes them fly, turn and move; stand in a group around the edge of the parachute feeling the force of the wind; play with bubble-making equipment, watching the bubbles move in the air.
>
> **Snow**. **Box contents:** black card t-shapes, paper cups, gloves, magnifiers, scissors, white paper, track makers. Activities: fill up cups with snow and place around the school in the Sun and shade; catch snowflakes on the black card and observe them using a magnifier; make different tracks in the snow; make or follow a trail around the school; investigate which glove is the best; investigate which movements keep you warm outdoors.
>
> **Sun**. **Box contents:** chalk, collection of shapes, brushes and buckets, sand and trays, sunglasses, hat instructions, paper, UV beads, sun cream. Activities: trace chalk shadows of people and objects; observe the shadow created by a shape stuck to a sunny window over the course of the day; draw and write with water and brushes on walls and the playground, observing what happens to them after they are finished; feel the change in temperature of a sand tray placed in the Sun; evaluate the effectiveness of a range of sunglasses (but do not look directly at the Sun); make a range of paper hats and establish which is the best; observe the UV beads in different places around the school and test the effectiveness of a variety of sun creams in blocking UV light.

A physical model can be used with older children to develop their awareness of the greenhouse effect. This activity has clear links to the D&T curriculum as well. Children are set the challenge on a sunny day to raise the temperature of a beaker of water by as much as they can, using only the heat from the Sun and a solar collector. What they use to create their solar collector is up to them, but typically children will be provided with a large clear plastic container such as an aquarium, tin foil and possibly cling film and mirrors. Turning over the aquarium alone creates an effective solar collector which models the greenhouse effect by allowing solar energy to pass through it but only letting a limited amount of the energy escape. On a sunny day in the summer, expect temperatures in excess of 40° Celsius to be reached.

Dataloggers/apps can be used to support a variety of investigations that promote awareness of global issues. Detailed measurements of temperature inside and outside the solar collector along with light measurements can be gathered using a datalogger, and these readings can be displayed on a graphing package. The traces tell a story. For example, if the temperature rose steadily but suddenly dropped at the same time as the light intensity fell, this could be interpreted as the Sun was initially out warming up the 'greenhouse' but then went behind a cloud. Giving children an opportunity to tell these stories provides them with an opportunity to develop data interpretation and reasoning skills, so called 'data literacy'. Dataloggers can also be used to monitor energy usage, for example, by tracking classroom temperature over the course of a day. This in turn may lead on to a discussion about times during the day when the classroom thermostat could be turned down and energy saved.

For all ages, children need an opportunity to discuss the messages about global climate change that they will inevitably hear through the media and friends, because, as was mentioned earlier, possibly two-thirds of 10-year-olds may still not fully understand the link between climate change and burning fossil fuels (Palmer and Suggate 2005). Children may hear arguments that question this link, which provides an opportunity to discuss how science works, and that science is about gathering evidence and establishing links between cause and effect. Research suggests that environmental education, with a particular focus on climate change, is most effective when information is personally relevant and meaningful to learners (Monroe et al. 2019). Messages about thinking globally while acting locally can be supported in the classroom by children monitoring their use of energy, and interesting debates can be had around children changing their lifestyles. For example, would they be prepared to play on their games console for less time each day if it saved energy? The BBC Bitesize website contains useful information and videos explaining climate change, its effects on the planet and what we can do to help. Useful primary science session materials, as well as videos for teacher professional development can be found on the Primary Science Teaching Trust's 'Climate Science Education' page. Try to avoid 'doomsday' scenarios, which may cause undue 'climate anxiety'. Instead focus on positive action children can take to reduce their carbon footprint; walking to school, learning to cycle safely, switching off unneeded electric lights and so on.

Solids, liquids and gases

During KS2 children are expected to begin to differentiate between solids, liquids and gases, particularly in terms of flow and maintenance of shape and volume. Exploring and sorting a collection of solids and liquids will stimulate thinking and raise a number of questions. Collections could include objects made from metal, plastic, wax, chalk, paper and wood, for example. More problematic solids that may raise questions include powders such as flour and dry sand, fabrics, wool and cotton wool, steel wool, playdough or Blu-Tack. Liquids could include water, washing-up liquid, honey, milk and cooking oil. Discussion about the viscosity, or ease of flow, of a liquid can be encouraged and apparent anomalies explored. Dry sand might be seen to 'flow' like a liquid, and children need help to recognise that the individual grains have the properties of a solid. Substances which may cause difficulties include foams, where gas is trapped in a liquid or solid. These include closed-cell substances, such as shaving foam, and open-cell substances, such as a bath sponge, where the air pockets connect to one another. In colloids, such as gels and toothpaste, one substance is suspended within another (in toothpaste, a solid in a liquid). They will therefore display properties of both states of matter. An emulsion is a mixture of two immiscible liquids which will separate out, such as vinegar and oil. The scientist Alice Ball, who developed a new way to blend oil and water to make injections to treat leprosy, can be discussed in this context.

In KS2 pupils are required to learn about gases and that liquids evaporate to form gases. Providing examples of gases in the primary classroom is difficult but not impossible. Blowing up balloons, cans of fizzy drink and air fresheners can be used to introduce the concept of gas and associated vocabulary: air, carbon dioxide, oxygen. Although they are usually invisible, gases sometimes have a smell, which is a helpful way to introduce this concept. For example, by spraying some perfume at the front of the room and having children raise their hand when they smell it. Children may think that there is 'nothing' around us, so it is useful to point out their breath on a cold day (the water vapour), to consider how sailing boats move and to carry out exploration of the air around us by making paper aeroplanes, flying kites, using wind socks and dropping sycamore seeds. Laying an 'empty' bottle on its side and placing a small ball of paper in the neck, then blowing into the bottle will cause the ball to fly towards the child, which is a surprising demonstration of the air in the bottle. This surprise at experiencing a counter-intuitive concept can be a memorable and engaging experience. Creating lava lamps with water, oil and Alka-Seltzer (see Science Sparks website) or creating a fizz by mixing vinegar and bicarbonate of soda, can all provide demonstrations of the production of a gas. If you can get your hands on a film cannister, adding water and half an Alka-Seltzer tablet before replacing the lid can achieve a more dramatic demonstration. Stand well back, ensure children are out of range and wait for the lid to be 'blown off' as a result of the large volume of carbon dioxide gas produced by the chemical reaction. The explosion occurs because the gas is compressed until the pressure is too much and the lid pops off. Sticking the tablet to the lid and turning the canister upside-down produces a more spectacular 'rocket'.

Another demonstration of gas production can be set up by putting a mixture of warm water, sugar and a teaspoon of yeast in a bottle with a balloon fixed tightly over the neck. Left in a warm place the balloon should begin to inflate as a result of the carbon dioxide produced by the yeast. Placing raisins in a bottle of soda water will 'pick up' the raisins as they are lifted by the bubbles of carbon dioxide, giving the impression that they are dancing. The aim of these activities is to help children to identify criteria that can be used to distinguish between solids, liquids and gases. For example, solids have a fixed shape and volume, liquids have no fixed shape but a fixed volume, and gases have no fixed shape and variable volume. It is important to support children to make these connections and to reflect on their learning, so that these engaging experiences are not only memorable, but meaningful, and help to develop their schema.

Changing state

From an early age, children meet examples of materials changing from solid to liquid, liquid to gas and vice versa. Helping to bake biscuits and cakes, making jelly, melting chocolate and ice cream, burning candles, watching ice form or puddles evaporate, observing steam come from a kettle and condensation form on car windows all provide everyday experience of materials changing state. As children become older, this is developed through observation, questioning, demonstration and investigation in order that children begin to understand the role of heating and cooling in bringing about these changes. An investigation into ways in which ice could be made to melt more slowly could involve a discussion of how to make the test fair, using ice cubes of the same size, drawing a table to record results and deciding what the results show.

With older children the activities in Table 3.2.2 could be used to develop the understanding that the same material can exist as both solid and liquid and the role of heat energy in this. Dataloggers with temperature sensors or spirit thermometers can be used to demonstrate the rise

Table 3.2.2 Activities for exploring particles

Activity	Questions
Observation of an air freshener	What do you notice when the lid of the air freshener is opened?
Observation of ice cubes on a dish	What will happen if these ice cubes are left on a work surface for several days?
Put ice cubes into a screw-top jar. Dry the outside of the jar with a cloth and leave for 15 minutes. Observe the water vapour (condensation) that forms on the outside of the jar.	Why do you think this has happened?
Observe chocolate squares inside a sealed plastic bag placed in a dish of hot water	What is happening to the chocolate? What will happen if it is left to cool?
Seal three plastic syringes, one containing air, the second water and the third sand.	What happens when you press down the plunger of each syringe? What are your explanations for what happens?
Based on Johnston and Scott 1990.	

in temperature of water at intervals until it boils, or to plot the warming of ice and water over a period of several hours. Secondary sources such as video and images of molten metals and lava can be used to extend children's understanding that different solids melt at different temperatures. This could be accompanied by a visit to observe glass blowing at places like Bath Aqua Glass or Bristol Blue Glass, or to see a farrier shaping horseshoes, demonstrating the high temperatures which need to be reached to melt different solids. Time-lapse images can capture changes in superb detail. See YouTube for many examples including what happens when a match is struck or for a speeded-up film of ice melting. Alternatively children could make their own videos by using the time-lapse option available with tablets, digital cameras and microscopes.

An understanding of evaporation and condensation supports children's comprehension of the water cycle. One way they can investigate the water cycle is by setting up a physical model in the classroom. A shallow layer of water is added to the bottom of an aquarium, with a playdough 'model mountain' in the middle. The top of the aquarium is sealed by a layer of cling film on which is placed some ice. A strong lamp provides the source of heat. The lamp is shone on the water and after a while the processes of evaporation, condensation and precipitation are set in motion. First the water evaporates. Then the moist air that is created condenses as it comes into contact with the cold cling film. Water droplets tend to collect in the centre of the cling film where there is a slight dip owing to the weight of the ice. 'Rain' then falls from the underside of the cling film onto the summit of the 'mountain', before running down its flanks back to the water layer below and the cycle is complete. Water cycle models can be constructed by the pupils themselves or purchased ready-made from suppliers of primary school curriculum resources.

Particles

There is controversy among science educators about the teaching of the kinetic theory of matter at KS2 since in the NCE this is placed in KS3. However, many primary teachers believe that the concepts of solid, liquid and gas, change of state and reversible and irreversible changes cannot be easily explained without reference to a particle model, albeit a much simplified one.

We suggest that efforts should be made to help children appreciate the microscopic size of the particles which make up all matter, perhaps by imagining or trying to find out what would happen if we cut something in half, in half again, and again . . . What would we end up with? To appreciate the structure of solids, liquids and gases and the energy transfer needed to change from one state to another, drama might be used, with the children in the playground 'being' particles tightly packed but 'vibrating' in a group with elbows linked, to represent a solid. When the teacher applies (imaginary) heat energy the 'particles' become a little excited and move slightly apart – their bonds constantly break and reform so the particles of a once-ordered solid mix and flow into the spaces of a container (for example, a shape drawn on the ground) rather like a liquid. As more heat is applied, some particles have sufficient energy to break loose and run off (evaporate) as 'gas particles' to distant parts of the playground. Other ideas include making a 'mobile' for the classroom using polystyrene balls, glued together for the solid, connected with short lengths of dowel for the liquid and hung freely to represent the gas.

Understanding of this model of the nature and behaviour of matter might be developed by asking children to apply it in a series or circus of activities developed by the Children's Learning in Science Project (Johnston and Scott 1990). Children work in pairs or small groups and are asked to produce a poster or drama, with or without words, explaining their ideas about one of the activities. They then present their explanations to the whole class. Possible activities are outlined in Table 3.2.2.

Working scientifically

We saw in the previous chapter that studying the properties of materials can develop the important scientific skill of raising questions for further investigation. This applies equally well to investigations into the changes that materials undergo. Presented with an ice balloon, quizzical children can be encouraged to think:

What happens if powder paint is sprinkled on its surface?
How can the ice be made to melt faster?

Children will observe – intuitively even if they do not have a full conceptual grasp – that cornflour mixed with water acts like a liquid until it is hit, at which point it behaves like a solid: *What happens if it is poured, or scooped, or mixed in different proportions?*

Questions may also be raised in response to concept cartoons on phenomena such as evaporation and dissolving. In response to a cartoon on where to hang the washing, investigations could examine the factors involved in drying laundry (air temperature, wind/air flow, type of material, etc.). A cartoon on getting sugar to dissolve in tea may lead to questions about the size of sugar granule, the temperature of tea, and the amount of tea/sugar. Encouraging children to ask questions is part of the Working Scientifically strand of the NCE at KS1 and lower and upper KS2 (DfE 2013).

These questions can lead children to carry out comparative/fair tests with a genuine purpose, to set up investigations which require careful observation over time, to carry out research using secondary sources or a combination of these. Children may need to be supported to refine their questions and to consider how best to seek answers. Investigations such as observing the effect of a variety of liquids (water, juice, fizzy drinks) on eggshells to mimic the effects of teeth will provide children with understanding about dental hygiene and allow them to make connections to other areas of science learning and their own lives. This not only makes science learning more meaningful and relevant, increasing engagement and motivation, but having clear aims for practical work helps to mitigate against the concern that it does not always support learning to the extent that we would hope (Bianchi et al. 2021, Ofsted 2021).

The value of providing pupils with freedom to choose their own ways of working scientifically was illustrated in a Year 6 class in a Somerset primary school. Presented with the provocation of separating a mixture of solids (sand, salt, objects of different sizes, magnetic and non-magnetic objects, etc.), the class were given leeway to choose their own equipment. As a consequence, each group of pupils employed a range of different approaches and techniques to meet the challenge – sieving, filtering, passing a bar magnet over the materials, even using tweezers to pick out larger objects. The simple act of the teacher providing the pupils with freedom to choose meant a range of innovative approaches to solve the problem ensued. It allowed children greater ownership of their learning and opportunities for reflecting on their approaches through metacognitive thinking. If the teacher had directed the pupils to use particular approaches and apparatus, a valuable opportunity for children to learn creatively and reflectively as they worked scientifically would have been lost.

Monitoring and feedback

Concept cartoons, developed by Naylor and Keogh (2014) provide a great starting point for eliciting children's ideas in science, promoting dialogic talk (Alexander 2020) and challenging misconceptions. They are a useful way to formatively monitor and assess ongoing learning. The cartoons present various plausible opinions about scientific phenomena, drawing on common misconceptions and alternative frameworks, and invite children to agree with one of the characters or to propose their own views. The depersonalising of ideas encourages children to take risks when sharing their ideas, which reduces anxiety amongst children and gives the teacher a better picture of the thoughts of individuals who might not typically be willing to share.

Naylor (2015) emphasises that the dialogue generated through concept cartoons encourages children to support their responses with reasoning and evidence, to consider alternative viewpoints and to think critically about scientific ideas. These align with the spoken language requirements of the PoS for English, including articulating and justifying answers, arguments and opinions (DfE 2013). As the different perspectives often contain some truth, discussion highlights the uncertainty often associated with science, and encourages metacognitive thinking as children reflect on the merits of their own ideas and those of others. This dialogue naturally promotes self- and peer-assessment, providing children with immediate feedback and generating cognitive conflict. To ensure that this is constructive, it is important that a classroom climate is developed where children are provided with time, space and ground rules for talk (Naylor 2015). Disagreement amongst the class can lead to meaningful follow-up enquiries, taking children's ideas into account in a way that is manageable for the teacher. For example, a concept cartoon about a snowman melting can draw out ideas about clothing keeping us warm, and cause children to question the reasons for this. It may lead to an investigation into the insulating properties of different materials, where children design their own enquiries to test their ideas. Starting from children's ideas and experiences in this way provides opportunities for meaningful ongoing feedback, giving pupils ownership of their learning.

To assess specific disciplinary skills alongside relevant substantive content, the *Assessment in Primary Science* (TAPS) materials (see the PSTT's web page) provide free one-page focused assessment plans, which support teachers to identify suitable activities, questions, adaptations and assessment criteria to assess children in a way that is valid, reliable and manageable. Plans are provided for all topic areas and age groups, as well as exemplification materials. Those relating to changes of state include assessing children on their ability to set up a fair test to explore the best place to dry materials by evaporation (Year 4), and evaluating the reliability of methods in the context of cleaning coins using a variety of different substances and approaches (Year 6-7).

Consolidate

Retrieve

To support children to rehearse their learning in a variety of contexts, they can take part in investigations linked to environmental sustainability. This will help to ensure that children are equipped with the knowledge and skills to promote a more sustainable world, as outlined in Sustainable Development Goal 4, quality education (UN General Assembly 2015). An example of one such project from the Centre for Industry Education Collaboration (University of York) is an enquiry into different packaging materials for a soap or shampoo bar. After receiving a letter from a company specifying certain desirable properties for the packaging, such as flexible, light and able to dissolve in water, children investigate and test different types of paper to make comparisons. This encourages them to draw on both their existing substantive knowledge about the properties of different materials, as well as their disciplinary knowledge about how to carry out successful science enquiries to answer questions. Children decide how to present their findings and write back to the company to make their recommendations. Through investigation, they consider questions such as 'Why should we attempt to reuse and reduce, rather than recycle?' and 'How can we help to tackle environmental problems?'. Links to other subjects include investigating packaging materials for different personal care products in D&T, exploring sources of ingredients in geography and advertising products in English. This activity, and many more linked to sustainability, can be found in the freely downloadable activity pack *Sustainable Stories and Solutions for Our Planet: A science investigation pack for teachers of 9-11-year-olds* (Centre for Industry Education Collaboration).

Apply

Through applying their knowledge to current issues with relevance to their own lives, children can find out about Green Chemistry, a branch of science which develops sustainable solutions to environmental challenges. The *Potatoes to Plastics (*Centre for Industry Education Collaboration 2021) resource makes this accessible to children and aims to build their science capital through introducing a range of scientists and scientific innovations. Children take part in an activity to produce and test bio-plastic from waste potato peelings. This is an excellent opportunity to invite a scientist into the classroom for children to talk to about their work (see the STEM learning website for the contact details of your local STEM Ambassador hub).

A number of challenges which encourage children to apply their learning in new contexts can be found on the Practical Action website, the STEM learning website and through resources provided by the British Science Association and the National Association for Environmental Education. One such activity, from the Practical Action charity, challenges children to extend their knowledge and understanding of plastic waste around the globe. In addition to sorting, identifying and making plastics, application activities include designing, making and evaluating products from waste plastics for a predetermined audience.

Review

Talk has a prominent role to play when working scientifically. As well as helping with the planning and carrying out of investigations, it also helps children draw conclusions from their science enquiries and for them to review their work by suggesting improvements (NCE Working Scientifically KS2). Children's thinking can be improved by encouraging them to reflect actively on their progress in solving a problem, on 'wrong turns' taken and on how they got back 'on track' (Adey et al. 2003). It is important that we allow children to make mistakes; if we always step in, children will not be able to meaningfully reflect on their process or understand why investigations may need to be repeated. Articulating their own thinking can support children as they evaluate their investigations into changing materials. For example, pouring water from one beaker to another and back again to confirm that the volume remains the same despite 'changing shape', can be supported by children reflecting on the results of the investigation and explaining them. Going further they might be able to also explain what the decisive factor or factors were that helped them construct new meaning. Was it, for example, through discussion of their ideas with other people, or did someone say something that helped move their thinking forward? Explicitly knowing how a problem was solved supports metacognitive processes and provides a child with a 'learning tool' that can be employed on any similar problem she or he encounters in the future.

Summary

In this chapter we have seen how an understanding of what happens to materials when they are changed can lead to an appreciation of issues of global significance. We have considered curriculum progression and key concepts, including particle theory, with an emphasis on children's ideas and starting points. Throughout, we have emphasised the importance of ensuring that science is seen as having relevance to everyday life, so that teaching about global issues begins with studying the weather and reversible and irreversible changes are taught through everyday experiences, including cookery. We have considered how children can build new learning through investigations including observation, comparative/fair tests, research, outdoor activities and drama. The emphasis when working scientifically has been on encouraging children to generate meaningful questions and providing opportunities for purposeful discussion and choice. This is supported through the use of formative assessment tools, such as concept cartoons, which encourage dialogic talk and metacognitive thinking. We discussed ways in which pupils might apply their learning to investigations linked to environmental sustainability. It is our hope that children will make choices about their lifestyle now and in the future for the good of the planet. Our teaching should contribute to them making these choices in a more informed way.

Discussion questions

1. What arguments are there for and against teaching children about the particulate nature of matter at KS2?
2. How can teachers build children's science capital through the study of materials?
3. How can we provide children with choice when planning materials enquiries?
4. How will teaching about materials contribute to education for sustainable development?
5. How can we encourage dialogic talk and metacognition through the study of changing materials?

Further reading

NASA Global Climate Change: Vital Signs of the Planet web pages provide useful information for teacher subject knowledge on the evidence for climate change, its causes, effects and solutions.

Science Sparks website contains many ideas for engaging practical science activities for both inside and outside of the classroom. These are accompanied by simple scientific explanations to ensure that children and teachers understand the science behind these memorable activities.

Strachan, A. & Davey, J. (2022) *Saving the Planet One Science Lesson at a Time*, Hatfield: Millgate House. Based on the Sustainable Development Goals, this book provides a framework for embedding global issues into primary science teaching through meaningful enquiry.

References

Adey P., Nagy F., Robertson A., Serret N. & Wadsworth P. (2003) *Let's Think through Science: Developing Thinking with Seven- and Eight-Year-Olds*, London: Nfer Nelson.

Alexander, R. J. (2020) *A Dialogic Teaching Companion*, London: Routledge.

Association for Science Education (ASE) (2011) *Be Safe!: Health and Safety in School Science and Technology for Techers of 3-to 12-year-olds* (4th ed.), Hatfield: ASE.

Bianchi, L., Whittaker, C. & Poole, A. (2021) *The 10 Key Issues with Children's Learning in Primary Science in England*, The University of Manchester and the Ogden Trust. 3634_Childrens_Learning_in_Primary_Science_Report_2020_v8.pdf (scienceacrossthecity.co.uk)

Briggs, R. (2010). *The Snowman*, UK: Penguin.

Centre for Industry Education Collaboration (2021) *Potatoes to Plastics: A Science Investigation Pack for Teachers of 9-11 Year Olds*. https://www.york.ac.uk/media/ciec/potatoestoplastics/fullpdf/Potatoes%20to%20Plastics%20Full.pdf

Department for Education (2013) *Science – Programmes of study for Key Stages 1–2*, London: DfE.

Department for Education (2021) *Statutory Framework for Early Years Foundation Stage*. London: Crown. https://assets.publishing.service.gov.uk/media/659d3e68aaae22001356dc46/Early_years_foundation_stage_statutory_framework_for_group_and_school-based_providers.pdf

Jackson, E. & Callwood, L. (2020) *Hunter's Icy Adventure: A True Story About the Global Problem of Climate Change*, UK: Ellie Jackson.

Johnston, K. & Scott, P. (1990) *Children's Learning in Science Projects: Interactive Teaching in Science – Workshops for Training Courses*, Hatfield: ASE.

Monroe, M., Plate, R., Oxarart, A., Bowers, A. & Chaves, W. (2019) Identifying effective climate change education strategies: a systematic review of the research, *Environmental Education Research* 25(6), 791–812.

Naylor, S. (2015) Talking and thinking using concept cartoons: what have we learnt?, *School Science Review*, *97*(359), 61–67.

Naylor, S. & Keogh, B. (2014) *Science Concept Cartoons: Set 1 - Revised Edition*, Sandbach: Millgate House.

Ofsted (2021) Research Review Series: Science. https://www.gov.uk/government/publications/research-review-series-science/research-review-series-science

Palmer J. & Suggate J. (2005) Children's reasoning about global environmental issues: deforestation and global warming, *Primary Science Review*, 87, 12–16.

Russell, T. & Watt, D. (1990) *Primary Science Processes and Concept Exploration (SPACE) Project Research Report: Growth*, Liverpool: Liverpool University Press.

UN General Assembly (2015) *Transforming Our World: The 2030 Agenda for Sustainable Development*, A/RES/70/1. https://www.refworld.org/docid/57b6e3e44.html

SECTION 4

Teaching physics topics

Introduction – the big ideas

Ever since the emergence of primary science from 'nature study' in the late 1980s, the inclusion of 'physics' topics such as forces and electricity – introduced in the National Curriculum for England and Wales in 1990 – has caused anxiety among many teachers. This may be because they have negative memories from their own secondary physics education or fear that children will have difficulty grasping such abstract and counterintuitive concepts. However, when they have been reintroduced to such topics through simple, hands-on approaches – whether during initial teacher education or professional development courses – many primary teachers have discovered the 'Wow! Factor' of understanding concepts they had not previously grasped and the joy of seeing children engage enthusiastically. The seemingly magical behaviour of magnets and light, spectacular flight of 'stomp rockets' and harmonious movement of the celestial spheres can all be harnessed to promote more exciting and engaging lessons. Concerns over primary teacher subject knowledge have remained, which may have contributed from the removal of nearly all 'physics' topics from Key Stage 1 of the 2013 National Curriculum for England (NCE). This is a great shame because, as we shall see, there are plenty of wonderful science activities young children will enjoy which are entirely conceptually appropriate for their age range.

Physics claims to be the most fundamental of the sciences, because it deals with the basic building blocks of the universe – energy, matter and forces. The 'big idea' here – which does not appear in the NCE until Key Stage 3 – is that of energy transfer. The abstract concept of energy can be explained simply as 'what makes things happen'; without energy the universe would be completely dead as literally nothing would happen. Energy can exist in many forms, from chemical energy in our muscles enabling us to move; light and sound energy enabling us to see and hear; electrical energy flowing through our many appliances and gadgets, to the kinetic energy possessed by the Earth, Moon and planets as they rotate and orbit the Sun. Forces are often confused with energy – it's perhaps easiest to differentiate between the two by thinking of forces as a means of transferring energy from one place to another. So, for example, if I use the energy in my muscles to push a trolley, I'm transferring that chemical energy to kinetic (movement) energy of the trolley by means of the force (push) I'm exerting. Other kinds of energy transfer are also possible; you may have heard it said that 'energy is never created or destroyed, simply changed from one form to another'. All the topics in this section can be seen as different kinds of energy transfer. In the Earth and space, gravitational potential energy of the Sun, Earth and Moon is transferred to the kinetic energy of orbits; while light and heat energy from the Sun gives us daylight and seasons. Sound and light are both forms of energy transfer from sources to receptors (our eyes and ears), while chemical energy stored in batteries is transferred through electrical energy in circuits to light and heat (lamps), sound (buzzers) or movement (motors). While we don't need to mention energy with primary-aged children, it's a big idea we can build towards when examining the particular phenomena of seasonal change, light, sound, electricity and forces; ultimately it's a unifying concept which brings them all together.

Although energy takes many forms, not all of them are useful to us as sources that humans can use to power our modern lives. So, energy is also a precious resource to be managed, it is sometimes fought over, and, as we think about how to live more sustainably, an understanding of energy and its manifestations is important for us all.

CHAPTER

Earth and space

Purpose of this chapter

After reading this chapter you will have:

■ gained an overview of progression in the main concepts in relation to the relative movement of the Earth, Sun and Moon

■ developed your understanding of commonly held alternative frameworks in explaining night and day, movement of shadows, seasons and phases of the Moon

■ considered ways of working scientifically to support children to engage with their learning, and to build and consolidate their knowledge and understanding of the Earth and space

Introduction

Unless you have the financial means to secure a place on one of the commercial flights to space that are available to the lucky few, it can be challenging for us to directly observe close hand the ways in which the Earth, Sun and Moon move in relation to each other to give us day and night, seasons and lunar phases, which are the 'big ideas' in this topic. This is hardly surprising since most people believed that the Earth was flat (although ancient Greeks had discovered its spherical shape) and at the centre of the universe until the end of the sixteenth century, when global circumnavigation and Copernicus' observations of planetary motion challenged science and church teaching. A few decades later, Galileo famously got into trouble with the Pope for suggesting that his telescope observations supported Copernicus' ideas. It is very difficult to move away conceptually from our position on the surface of the Earth and to see it as part of a bigger system. We need as many models and hands-on experiences as possible to help us envisage the three-dimensional movement of the solar system. However, do not let this put you off teaching about the Earth and space: it is an extremely motivating topic which appeals to children of all ages, and a great deal can be done through working scientifically, including using secondary sources and modelling.

In the UK, our fascination with the night sky and what lies beyond our own atmosphere has been reignited in recent years through the missions to the International Space Station that Tim Peake participated in. He communicated with school children from space and held an online meeting with the late Professor Stephen Hawking. Since his return to Earth, he has continued to champion the need for trips to space to further our understanding of science in space and here on Earth. Another great ambassador for all things related to space is Dr Maggie Aderin-Pocock, MBE. Her enthusiasm is contagious, and she is an excellent example of the diversity of scientists who currently work in this field. She has been highly successful in making space accessible to adults and children alike by bringing this field of science to mainstream audiences through her work on *The Sky at Night* and her engaging children's book, *Am I Made of Stardust?*. There is even a Barbie doll based on her.

There are plans for humans to return to the Moon, with a race between NASA, India and China to be the first to return. Robots have landed on Mars and are exploring it to investigate the possibility of humans setting foot on our closest planetary neighbour. The future is exciting and one that the children we currently teach will watch unfold over the coming decades. Who knows, you could be teaching a future astronaut, astronomer or Martian explorer.

Planning for progression

If you searched the Early Years foundation stage (EYFS) curriculum guidance and primary science National Curriculum for England (NCE), you might think that children only need to know about the Earth and space once they reach Key Stage 2. However, think about your own childhood or young children you know. A fascination with the stars and the Moon is present from a very young age. Nursery children listen to stories which feature the Sun, Moon and stars. They also associate bedtime stories with night-time. Producers of children's streaming content and television programmes use images of dark skies and stylised representations of the Moon and stars to indicate to children that the story they are about to watch is part of the bedtime ritual when the Sun has 'gone to sleep' and the 'Moon and stars have come out'. Of course, this means that children often develop misconceptions and alternative frameworks about the relationship between the Earth, Sun and Moon, so planning carefully sequenced learning opportunities to address these alternative schemas is essential and certainly begins before KS2.

In the EYFS, stories are a great provocation for children's play and learning. *The Darkest Dark* by Chris Hadfield, a Canadian astronaut, explores how a small boy is inspired by the lunar landing of 1969 to become an astronaut. Chris makes cardboard box space rockets, explores space as a child and, as an adult, orbits the Earth as an astronaut. There is also a useful section at the end of the book for practitioners to give context to the race to the Moon of the 1960s and Chris's biography.

Moving into KS1, children develop their understanding of the passage of time through the concept of day and night, as children may count time to an event in 'sleeps'. Our whole notion of passing time is so closely related to the periods of rotation and orbit of the Earth around the Sun that no study of 'Ourselves' or 'Autumn' is complete without some link to these concepts, however implicit. This is reflected in the seasonal changes element of the Year 1 programme of study requiring children to be taught to:

- observe changes across the four seasons;
- observe and describe weather associated with the seasons and how day length varies (DfE 2015.)

Although an explanation for seasonal changes in terms of the tilt of the Earth's axis relative to the plane of its orbit is clearly inappropriate for this age group, teaching about 'day length' without reference to the Sun as a source of light (the foundation concept in this topic) is impossible. While we would argue that an understanding of how the Earth's spin gives us day, and that night comes next, this does not appear in the NCE until Year 5, where children are to:

- use the idea of the Earth's rotation to explain day and night and the apparent movement of the Sun across the sky (DfE 2015).

This statement embeds two concepts – the idea that the Earth spins so that half is always in darkness and the related idea that the apparent movement of the Sun is actually us moving on a rotating surface. Children may not have noticed that the Sun 'moves', so first need to link this to the change in direction of shadows over time on a sunny day. The Year 5 programme of study for Earth and space – the only time this topic features in the primary NCE – also requires children to:

- describe the Sun, Earth and Moon as approximately spherical bodies;
- describe the movement of the Earth and other planets relative to the Sun in the solar system;
- describe the movement of the Moon relative to the Earth (DfE 2015).

Progression beyond the primary phase includes the concept of gravitational attraction between the Earth, Sun and Moon; the strength of gravity on other planets relative to their masses; and the Sun as a star, part of a galaxy of other stars with huge distances between them measured in 'light years'. Even though these more cosmological concepts appear in the post-primary curriculum, they will be of great fascination to some children in upper KS2.

The key concepts to be taught at KS1 and KS2 are identified in Table 4.1.1, along with some notes to inform the teacher's understanding.

Table 4.1.1 Key concepts for teachers: Earth and space

Key concept	Teachers' subject knowledge
The Sun is a source of light	The Sun is a medium-sized star that produces light and heat energy from a process of nuclear fusion. It is ultimately the source of nearly all the light around us. Most combustible materials (e.g. wood) burn because of the energy stored in them from the Sun via photosynthesis. 'Artificial' light sources transform electrical energy, much of which was generated from either fossil fuels or 'renewable' resources, again powered by the Sun. Only the other stars, volcanic eruptions and nuclear, have non-solar origins.
Day and night happen because the Earth spins on its axis	The Earth's period of rotation is exactly 24 hours (give or take some slight 'wobbles'). This is a terrestrial 'day', made up of variable periods of light and dark, because only those parts facing the Sun are illuminated.
Shadows of still objects move during a sunny day because the Sun appears to 'travel' in an arc across the sky	The Sun only appears to move; in reality it is us who move because of the rotation of the Earth. Because we move in an arc, the Sun appears to us to move in an arc, starting low in the East, rising to its zenith at midday GMT and 'setting' low in the West. The position of this arc in the sky changes constantly through the year (see seasonal changes below): it reaches its highest point at the summer solstice (usually 21st June) and is at its lowest at the winter solstice (usually 21st December). We can use this predictable movement to tell the time using a sundial – this will differ depending on our longitude because different points on the Earth's surface are directly opposite the Sun at different moments, giving us time zones.
The Earth, Sun and Moon are approximately spherical	Nearly all heavenly bodies (planets, stars, etc.) are approximately spherical, which is because they are pulled together by gravitational attraction; a sphere contains a given mass or volume within the smallest possible surface area. A bubble is a useful analogy; although it is potentially misleading.
We have years because the Earth moves around the Sun	The Earth orbits the Sun once every 365 and a quarter terrestrial days. Because this period is rather inconvenient, we 'save up' the four extra quarter days and add an extra day (29th February) once every four years (the leap year).

(Continued)

Table 4.1.1 (Continued)	
Key concept	**Teachers' subject knowledge**
We have seasons because of the tilt of the Earth's orbit	The Earth's axis of rotation makes a constant angle of approximately 66.5° with its plane of orbit (i.e. 23.5° from vertical). This means that as it moves in its orbit, the sunlight strikes any particular point on the Earth's surface at constantly varying angles. The higher the sun's position at midday, the more intense its energy at this point, so summer tends to be warmer than winter.
The Moon has phases because we see differing amounts of the side lit by the Sun	Half the Moon is always illuminated by the Sun (it is not a source of light but reflects sunlight). Because the Moon orbits the Earth (approximately once every 29.5 days – a lunar month), we see differing proportions of this lit half. For example, when the Moon is on the same side of us as the Sun, we see none of the lit half – a 'new' Moon.

Teacher self-assessment questions

1. Why does the Sun appear to move from east to west across the sky?
2. How do you account for the different time zones around the world?
3. Why are our shadows shortest in the middle of the day and longer in the evening?
4. 'In summer it's hotter because the Earth is nearer to the Sun' – what's wrong with this statement?
5. 'The Moon has different phases because the Earth blocks some of the light from the Sun' – true or false?
6. When and why do we have 'equinoxes'?
7. What's the difference between a lunar eclipse and a solar eclipse?

Engage

Situating the topic

When planning for learning, we need to consider how we will engage the children in their learning and situate the topic for them within their knowledge and understanding of their world. Young children's familiarity with day and night, sleeping and waking, the Moon and the stars can be used to initiate a discussion about why it gets dark at night. Stories such as Maudie Puwell Tuck's *The Moonlight Zoo* (2014), Nicola O'Byrne's *The Rabbit, the Dark and the Biscuit Tin* (2019) or Martin Waddell's *Can't You Sleep Little Bear?* (2001) can be used to discuss children's fears and link the topic to that of light. Plenty of children's stories, comics and films feature space travel. Older children might want to assemble a collection of ideas about space from computer games, films, cartoons and theme park rides and use them to discuss the differences between 'science fiction' and established scientific ideas in this area. They could compare the portrayals of space and identify how these may lead to alternative frameworks or misconceptions. A good example of this would be any portrayal of an explosion in space which is accompanied by an explosion sound effect; the *Star Wars* franchise of films, animated series and live action series often draw upon this dramatic convention and compound the misconception that we would hear the explosion. There are lots of models of the solar system available online, but do not underestimate the power of a globe which can start children thinking about their position on Earth and the movements it might make through space. For older children, making a table of the relative sizes and distances of planets from the Sun, then modelling them with different-sized fruit, beads, marbles and balls can offer a mathematical challenge and provide a graphic illustration of the sheer scale of the solar system.

The topic of Earth and space has clear links with Religious Education (RE). Children's sense of awe and wonder at the night sky – perhaps as part of a 'night walk' on a residential school trip in a rural area with low light pollution – can readily lead to a discussion of 'the big questions' about life, the universe and everything. Creation stories from different cultures can be compared with the current scientific story of the big bang, and children can also explore the origins of the signs of the Zodiac in the patterns humans have seen in the arrangement of stars. If your school is in an urban area with little opportunity to see the stars, a visit by an inflatable planetarium dome can be an excellent substitute for the night walk. In history, children can look at the different ways humans have interpreted the motions of the spheres over the centuries including the appearance of astronomical signs at significant events such as Halley's comet at the Battle of Hastings.

Although climate change is not introduced in geography until KS3, we believe that this is an essential aspect of children's education to safeguard the future of our planet. An image of the Earth from space is an essential resource if you want to use this topic as a way of addressing issues of sustainability and distribution of resources. It is the fragile beauty of such images of a blue-green 'pearl' in space, suggesting a small planet with strictly limited resources, that arguably first kick-started the environmental movement in the late 1960s. By comparing photographs of the Earth with other planets and moons, children can come to appreciate the uniqueness of this environment in our solar system, as the only place that, as far as we know, can support life through its liquid water and oxygen-rich atmosphere. The dangers of turning our own atmosphere into something like that of our neighbour Venus, full of carbon dioxide and sulphuric acid, producing an inhospitable environment of intense global warming and acid rain, can be used as the starting point for an exploration of the possible effects of human influences on our environment. It is important here not to use shock tactics to frighten or indoctrinate children, but to enable them to collect data from various sources and to evaluate them. There are numerous websites and projects which explore sustainability which teachers can use with all ages of children. Rarely a week goes by without some astronomical or environmental programme or article appearing, so there should be plenty of material to choose from.

Breaking down barriers

Until very recently, space-themed books, toys, soft furnishings (such as duvet covers) and room decor were marketed for boys. When we consider the characters from mainstream science fiction, they have been dominated by white heterosexual males. Out of the fifteen canon portrayals of the long-established fictional Time Lord and space traveller, The Doctor, from *Doctor Who*, it has only been in the past decade that a female actor was cast to play the thirteenth Doctor, with the fifteenth Doctor as the first portrayed by a Black actor. When exploring Earth and space with children, it is therefore important to introduce them to a range of diverse influential scientists. Children should be introduced to scientists of ancient times, such as Ptolemy, Alhazen and more recently, Copernicus, who helped develop our ideas of a heliocentric model of the Sun, Earth, Moon and our neighbours in the solar system to broaden their experiences of scientists as more than white men in lab coats.

When we consider twentieth century space exploration, almost all teachers will be aware of Neil Armstrong and company, but how many will be aware of Katherine Johnson, a gifted African-American mathematician who worked for the National Aeronautics and Space Administration (NASA) of the US federal government? During her time at NASA, she worked on projects including the Apollo program which saw the first humans land on the Moon in 1969. We believe it is essential to broaden children's knowledge of influential scientists and include a diverse range of individuals. We want children to learn about scientists who look like them. Dr Maggie Aderin-Pocock and Professor Stephen Hawking have already been mentioned in this chapter and are good examples of the diversity of influential scientists in this field. Another example could be Jocelyn Bell

Burnell, who is an astrophysicist from Northern Ireland. She was part of the team who discovered the first radio pulsars but was not one of the scientists who received the 1974 Nobel Prize in Physics for this discovery. The reasons given for her exclusion have been debated over the decades, and the fact that she was an undergraduate researcher and woman are often cited as contributory factors. Her career went from strength to strength, and she used prize money from a prestigious physics award, the Special Breakthrough Prize in Fundamental Physics, to set up a fund administered by the Institute of Physics to support females, refugees and minorities to become physics researchers.

Activating children's learning

To fully engage children in their learning, it is essential to elicit their prior knowledge. What do they already know and understand about the Earth and space? What misconceptions or alternative frameworks do they have? It is important to consider children's science capital and what experiences of space exploration they have encountered beyond the classroom. Do any of the children have family members or carers who work in the field of space science who could come into school and discuss what they do? Do the children, or someone they know, have a telescope and regularly stargaze? Who has been on a trip to a science museum and engaged with the exhibitions and artefacts? Has anyone travelled across different time zones or knows someone who lives in a different time zone? Time zones can be a challenge for children to understand, so linking with a school in a different country and having an online meeting could be a good way to elicit children's understanding, for example, of why it may be the end of the school day in our classroom but the start of the school day in our friends' classroom in the US. Much of the formative assessment within the topic of Earth and space can be done by asking children questions, or by listening to the interesting snippets of information they bring in from home, media and other sources. For example, if you are beginning to explore children's concepts about the relationship between our notions of time and the movement of the Sun, Moon and Earth, the following starter questions could be helpful:

- How long is a day? (Explore the difference between daylight hours and period of rotation.)
- How long is a month? (Explore the difference between calendar and lunar months.)
- How long is a year? (Do children relate this to Earth's orbit?)
- How can we work out what time it is? (This could lead to discussion of sundials.)

Children's ideas about seasonal changes (Osborne et al. 1993) parallel many adults' alternative frameworks concerning this difficult concept, raising some doubts about the effectiveness of science education in this area:

> 'It's hotter in the summer because the Sun is closer to the Earth.' (The Earth's orbit is slightly elliptical, but it is closer to the Sun during northern hemisphere winter.)
> 'It's hotter in summer because the Earth is facing the Sun.' (This notion is worth exploring further, since it could imply an appreciation of the 'height' of the Sun in summer but may equally suggest that the child is confused about the Earth's rotation.)
> 'The Sun doesn't shine in the winter.' (Not a bad generalisation in England but will not stand up to sustained observation.)

Children do not tend to mention changing daylight hours or 'height' of the Sun between seasons – perhaps these changes are too gradual or subtle to be easily observable?

We need to consider the cognitive challenges that some children may face when thinking about the Earth in space and how we can reduce cognitive overload by scaffolding their learning with meaningful models and representations. Before these models are used, asking the children to make a model of the Earth, Sun and Moon with modelling clay is an effective strategy for eliciting children's ideas about the shapes of these bodies. The Earth may well be represented as a sphere, whereas some children may model the Sun as a flat disc (as it appears in the sky) or the Moon as a crescent. The phases of the Moon do tend to be noticed and commented on by children, who may offer the following observations (Osborne et al. 1993):

> 'The Moon really changes shape.' (Influenced perhaps by storybook representations of the Moon. It is actually possible to see the whole disc faintly on a clear night even when it is not full.)
> 'The Moon looks like it changes shape because of clouds getting in the way.' (Perhaps a confusion of time frames here, easily challenged by observing the Moon on a partially cloudy night.)
> 'The Moon looks like it changes shape because the Earth casts a shadow.' (This is another idea held by many adults; it confuses the Moon's phases with much rarer lunar eclipses, when the Moon does indeed pass through the Earth's shadow.)

From these examples you can see why it is important to elicit what children already know about the Earth and space, so that you can address any misconceptions and build on children's prior learning.

Build

Constructing new knowledge

So that children can effectively make connections with their prior learning and construct new knowledge, it is important to consider how you will scaffold children's learning. Some of the ideas you will explore with the children are challenging and cannot be experienced practically at first hand. For example, through your elicitation, you may have assessed that children are not secure with the concept of the Earth as a sphere. As mentioned earlier, it is important to consider children's cognitive load. When learning about objects that are so enormous, we need to remember that to a child when they view the Earth, it could appear to be hilly or flat, depending on where they are positioned. From the child's viewpoint, one thing it does not appear to be is a sphere. Video clips of the Earth from space or clips from science fiction films showing spacecraft approaching a planet from space and then landing on the surface, can help to reinforce the idea of the Earth as a sphere. Giving the children the opportunity to handle globes and locate where we, friends and family live is a good way to scaffold this concept. Making links with geography topics to help children to transfer their knowledge to a new context is important as children find it challenging to transfer learning from one context to another.

Using a dialogic approach is important to support children to develop their knowledge and understanding of the Earth and space. Allowing children time to talk about their ideas and pose questions they want to find out is essential. As the teacher, you will model how to use the correct science vocabulary and will need to give the children opportunities to try using the vocabulary for themselves. There should be an ebb and flow to the dialogue where sometimes the teacher models, explains or questions and at other times the learners take the lead. For example, when discussing the apparent movement of the Sun across the sky, the teacher could pose the question, 'In your group, can you use the globe and the lamp to demonstrate how the turning of the Earth creates day and night? I used turning, is there a more accurate word we could use? What other science terms should we listen for?' A child, or group of children, will then model to each other using the resources. Hopefully the science vocabulary 'rotate' and 'axis' will be used correctly; if not the teacher can introduce them by monitoring the conversations, interjecting with questions, prompts or answers to the children's questions, to support connections to prior learning and constructing new knowledge.

Teaching physics topics

Working scientifically

The focus of working scientifically within this topic of science is very much centred around observation over time, using secondary sources and modelling. The purposeful practical work examples below illustrate how working scientifically can be incorporated into this topic without having to charter one of the private companies travelling into orbit or hitching a ride with NASA.

Day and night

To relate day and night to the rotation of the Earth, children can work in groups with one seated on a chair while another child first walks clockwise around the chair shining a torch at its occupant (Figure 4.1.1). This simulates what appears to be happening from our Earth-centred view – that the Sun moves around us, and when it is behind us (on the other side of the Earth) we experience night. The seated child needs to keep their head still and describe what they observe (the light from the torch moving across their field of view, then disappearing) and the others keep a record on an individual whiteboard of when it is day and when it is night for the 'Earth'. Next, the child in the chair rotates anticlockwise while the torch-bearer stays still – this should produce a similar observation from the chair occupant and the others in the group can confirm this by referring to their individual whiteboards.

Children could also use the internet or the World Clock app on tablets or laptops to find out the time in different places in the world. Do they have friends or family who live in another country? What time is it there when it is playtime, lunchtime, learning time in the UK? Is it day at the same time all over the world? Can the children use a torch and globe to model what they find out?

Seasonal changes

The NCE requires that Year 1 children should be taught to:

- observe changes across the four seasons
- observe and describe weather associated with the seasons and how day length varies (DfE 2015).

1. First move the torch in a clockwise circle around the chair to show the apparent movement of the sun.

2. Next rotate the chair anti-clockwise whilst keeping the torch still, to show that it is the Earth that is moving.

Figure 4.1.1 Modelling day and night.

This seems relatively simple and will encourage lots of talk and exploration; a good basis to build on as the children grow older and start to learn about the Earth and space in Year 5. There are numerous models and cartoons illustrating this on the internet. However, you need to be cautious that they do not lead to, or compound, alternative frameworks and misconceptions. An example of this could be the relative sizes of the Earth and Sun and the distances between them, as the animations will often show them relatively similar in size and close together (to fit on the screen). Set out below is one way to involve the children more directly in modelling this phenomenon is by using a strong torch and a globe, which consolidates the idea of the Heliocentric model suggested by Ptolemy, Alhazen and Copernicus.

However, there are a few things to consider before embarking on this activity. Importantly, to avoid cognitive overload, we recommend that seasonal change and day and night are tackled separately. It is also important to remind the children that when we use strong torches to model the Sun, a limitation is that torchlight is unidirectional by design, whereas light travels from the Sun in all directions. Another limitation is similar to that of the animations described above, i.e. the relative size of the Earth and Sun and the distance between them. Also, it can be tricky for some children to hold the globe in the correct orientation and describe how the sunlight appears on the globe and what this illustrates in relation to the seasons. Again, considering cognitive overload, a simple adaptation is to have the children seated on the floor and the globe standing on the floor in front of them. To avoid confusion, it is also important to check that the children have a firm understanding of surface area before embarking on this modelling activity.

Modelling the seasons

1. The children form a circle to model the orbit of the Earth around the Sun. The Sun is represented by a child in the centre of the circle holding the strong torch.

2. The children will be asked to pass the globe around the circle anti-clockwise, if viewed from above, to model the orbit of the Earth around the Sun. By placing the globe on its stand on the floor, the correct 23.5° tilt of the Earth on its own axis will be maintained.

3. Start with the globe positioned in the circle so that the tilt is towards the Sun. The frame of the globe can be used to help position it. All of the children should note the position of the frame in relation to a fixed point in the classroom, e.g. the frame of the globe will always point towards the display directly behind the child who is the Sun. By using this starting point, the season being modelled is the summer for the UK (and the northern hemisphere). The chosen country (we recommend the country which the school is in) should always be facing the Sun, to illustrate midday for each day in the orbit around the Sun.

4. The globe is passed around the circle, anticlockwise, modelling its orbit of a year around the Sun. The children observe and describe how the Sun shines on the globe. As the Earth orbits the Sun, the children should observe that different amounts of the Earth's surface are illuminated. During the summer, the Sun shines more directly on the UK and a smaller surface area is illuminated, focussing the Sun's light and heating that part of the Earth more intensely, leading to warmer days. However during the winter, more surface area is illuminated; the Sun's light is spread out, less focussed on the UK and the heat from the Sun's light will be less intense, resulting in cooler days.

5. Once the Earth has orbited the Sun once, you've addressed any misconceptions and any questions from the children have been answered, send it on another orbit. Stop at key positions to illustrate the solstices and equinoxes. You can use the globe to illustrate the change in the length of days – summer solstice (usually 21st June) the UK is in daylight for the longest time and winter solstice (usually 21st December) the UK is in daylight for the shortest time. Ask the children why this happens and if they can predict what will happen to the length of the day during the spring and autumn equinoxes (usually 20th March and 20th September,

respectively) – the day lengths should be equal, shorter than the summer solstice but longer than the winter solstice. Ask them to check what they have observed about the lengths of the days using the internet.

Apparent movement of the Sun

Perhaps the most common pattern seeking element of working scientifically undertaken during this topic is an activity in which children place a stick in the playground on a sunny day, marking the position and length of the shadow every hour using either chalk directly onto the asphalt or marker pen on a large sheet of paper. They should notice a change in shadow angle, and this can be related to the study of sundials to tell the time, noting that a sundial gnomon is actually angled rather than vertical (to give accurate time at a particular location, the gnomon's angle should equal the latitude, for example, 51.5° for London).

Once children have noticed a pattern in their observations and offered hypotheses to explain it, this activity can be followed up by simulating the Sun's 'movement' using a torch in the classroom (Figure 4.1.2). They should notice that they need to move the torch in an arc to produce the same changes of shadow length observed in the playground, but of course this could reinforce the notion that it is the Sun that moves. So the third part of this teaching sequence should be to make a mini shadow-stick for a classroom globe, using half a matchstick. If the globe is then rotated in a strong unidirectional light source, the same pattern of changing shadow length can be observed (see Figure 4.1.3). Although not proving that the children's observations of shadows in the playground are related to the Earth's rotation, this demonstration does at least provide some evidence in that direction.

Another way to illustrate this apparent movement of the Sun is to record on a south facing window the position of the Sun at the start of the day, at lunchtime and at the end of the day. Circles of paper, with the time clearly written on them, can be stuck on the window to show the approximate position of the Sun. It is important to remind children that they should not look at the Sun directly, even if they wear dark glasses; an adult can record for the class where the Sun is in relation to the window (see Figure 4.1.4).

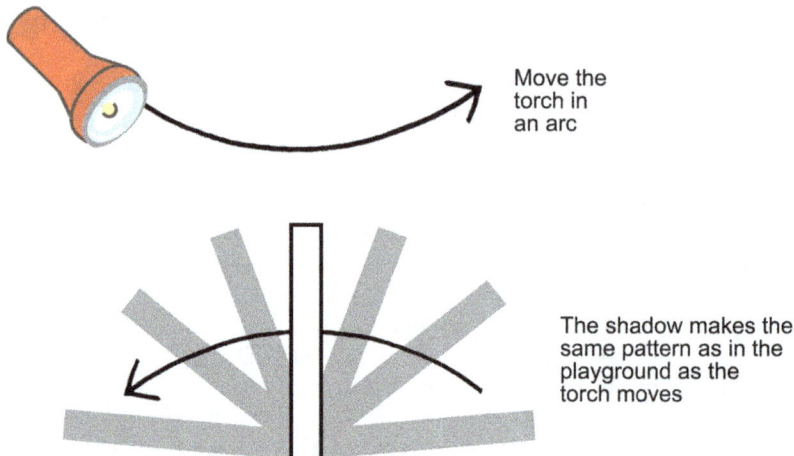

Figure 4.1.2 Modelling the apparent movement of the Sun.

Earth and space

The shadow makes the same pattern as in the playground as the globe rotates

Figure 4.1.3 Modelling the relationship between shadow movement and the rotation of the Earth.

Figure 4.1.4 Modelling the phases of the Moon.

Phases of the Moon

Children can observe a whole cycle of lunar phases over a month. Make sure you consider the time of year so they do not need to stay up too late to see it. Asking children to draw the apparent shape of the Moon in a lunar diary is an excellent way to start the discussion of what might be causing this phenomenon. The National Geographic for Kids website could be a good secondary source of information for the children to research about the phases of the Moon. However, to demonstrate the mechanism clearly, we can engage children in a simulation using a strong light source, a white ball on a stick (a table tennis ball is ideal) and a swivel chair. A child sits in the chair, representing the Earth, and observes the ball held at arm's length and slightly above head height in the beam of light (a relatively dark room is required). By rotating slowly, a complete cycle of lunar phases can be observed, starting from the position where the ball is on the same side as the light source (though not blocking its beam – this would be a solar eclipse). The rest of the class can see that half the ball is illuminated, but the child on the chair sees none of this 'lit half' – for them this is a 'new moon'. Rotating a quarter-turn anticlockwise brings us to the 'first quarter' in which half of the lit face is visible to the chair's occupant. This is about seven days into the cycle. Turning further we pass through 'waxing gibbous' to 'full moon' when the ball is on the opposite side of the chair from the projector and the child can see the whole of the lit face (provided the beam is not blocked by their head – a lunar eclipse). Completing the cycle, the white ball passes through 'waning gibbous' and 'third quarter' back to the new moon position. Again, it may be necessary to repeat this several times to accommodate the child's mental model to this new representation, and you will certainly need to allow every member of the class to try it for themselves. A further refinement is to draw a 'crater' on the ball and demonstrate that we always see this same face throughout the cycle. The far side of the Moon was only first seen by astronauts from Apollo 8 in 1968. This peculiar phenomenon occurs because the Moon's period of rotation is exactly the same as its period of orbit.

Our solar system

The highly detailed simulations of lunar changes described above can be generalised by letting children 'become' the inner solar system in the school hall. You can support this with simple models, posters or elaborate costumes. A child or group representing the Sun stands in the centre, perhaps shining torches in various directions. At its simplest, another two children represent the Earth and Moon – the Moon orbiting the Earth approximately 12 times as it orbits the Sun once. You can also introduce Mercury and Venus both orbiting the Sun within the Earth's orbit, and Mars outside it. If you want to introduce more mathematics, you could position the orbits at roughly the correct relative distances from each other. If Sun to Mercury is one unit, Sun to Venus is roughly two, Sun to Earth three, Sun to Mars five – the Fibonacci series, although this breaks down at Jupiter. For the periods of orbit, Mercury goes round the Sun four times for every Earth year, Venus nearly twice, Mars about half. You could add the outer planets but if you want to keep the orbit distances accurate you will need a very large playground. An alternative which requires less space, is the Ogden Trust's 'Solar system in my pocket' (a video demonstration is available on their website) which uses coloured stickers and a strip of till receipt paper. This is a very low tech way to demonstrate a complicated natural phenomenon. Caution is needed, however, as possible misconceptions could be taught, for example, that the planets are 2D or, their relative sizes are not represented accurately, depending on the size of the stickers used.

Feedback

As mentioned previously in this chapter, much of the formative assessment opportunities within this topic are gained from asking children questions and listening to what they say. Feedback to the children about their learning should be linked to the assessment pedagogy adopted, so the most effective ways to give feedback to children for this area of science could be in-the-moment oral feedback. As with any topic, when giving feedback to children, it is important to focus the feedback on the learning rather than the learner and to be most effective, by using feedback which gives information rather than that which is judgemental (Harlen with Qualter 2018).

We will use an example from the Bright Ideas Time, available via the Primary Science Teaching Trust (PSTT) website, to illustrate this idea. In the first activity, children are presented with three images and are asked to discuss the odd one out. The images are of the Sun, Moon and Earth and children discuss which is the odd one out. The children will come up with numerous answers and the role of the teacher is to give feedback on how closely their ideas mirror the current accepted scientific thinking, e.g. the Sun is the only star, the Moon is the only one which orbits the Earth, the Earth is the only one to support life (as far as we know). Focussing in on what the children say and the questions they ask each other should be used to give feedback. If a child suggests that the Earth is the odd one out because it does not shine, the teacher could ask if both the Sun and Moon shine because they are sources of light or do they shine for different reasons? If the child suggests that both are light sources, the teacher could point out the Sun is a source of light but that the Moon reflects the sunlight and only appears to shine. This could be illustrated using a torch and circle of paper in a darkened room, shining the light to the side of the circle and then directly onto the circle, demonstrating that we see the circle when the light is shone directly onto it. Another example could be that a child suggests that there isn't an odd one out as they are all (approximately) spherical and are in space. This could be followed up with confirmation that they are all roughly spherical and are in space and then scaffolding the child's thinking by asking a two-step targeted question which is less open, e.g. Which one is the only planet? (Earth), What are the other two? (the Sun is a star and the Moon is a moon/a natural satellite).

Consolidate

Retrieving and applying

It is important that children are given opportunities to retrieve and apply their learning about the Earth and space so that learning can become embedded. Opportunities for children to retrieve what they have learnt about the Earth, Sun and Moon and applying this to new contexts can be challenging and will require engaging activities and thoughtful scaffolding. The use of low stakes or no stakes quizzes has become common practice and by sitting these quizzes learners consolidate their learning (Weinstein et al. 2019), but these are not the only forms of retrieval which can support learning about the Earth and space.

As discussed earlier, presenting children with images and asking them which is the odd one out requires them to retrieve their prior learning about the images and apply it to the context of the discussion. Another good example from the Bright Ideas Time section of PSTT website is the Big Question. These questions work as great discussion topics. If you know the children have previously learnt the knowledge needed to answer the questions, these questions can act as a good retrieval and application activity. An example from the Big Ideas Time is 'Why do the Sun and Moon appear the same size in the sky?'. For the children to answer the question, they will need to be able to retrieve some key facts: the Sun's diameter is 400 times greater than the Moon's, and the distance from the Earth to the Sun is 400 times greater than the distance from the Earth to the Moon.

There is an opportunity with this topic for children to apply their understanding of sustainability and environmental issues beyond our planet. Children can consider the amount of space debris that has accumulated due to the numerous missions beyond our atmosphere. The European Space Agency (ESP) have produced a short cartoon animation 'Paxi and cleaning up space' (ESP 2022) in which an alien explores the problems caused by satellites in low Earth orbit which have completed their missions. This could be a good starting point for children to design more sustainable ways to launch satellites into orbit or ways to help to dispose, repair, recycle or reuse decommissioned satellites. However, you need to be aware that there is a possibility of children developing misconceptions due to the personification of the satellites and an alien helping to clear space debris. To avoid this, specific adult input will be needed.

The Education Endowment Foundation (EEF) funded an efficacy trial of the Stop and Think: Learning Counterintuitive Concepts project led by the Centre for Educational Neuroscience team from Birkbeck University London and UCL Institute of Education (EEF 2019). The intervention used whole-class computer-based learning at the start of mathematics and science lessons with KS2 children, for no more than 15 minutes, two to three times per week (EEF 2019). The premise was that children are often limited in their learning by drawing on their intuition when thinking about some tricky science (or mathematics) concepts. An example relevant to the Earth and space is that the horizon of the Earth looks flat, yet we teach the children that the Earth is round. This is a counter-intuitive concept. The trial found that children who participate in the project made 'two additional months' progress in science, on average, compared to the children in the control group' (EEF 2019). It would suggest that allocated time spent on teaching specific counter-intuitive concepts, in the way proposed by the Stop and Think project, helps children to retrieve knowledge and apply it to different contexts.

Reviewing

It is important to review with the children the learning they have retained and think about any gaps in their knowledge. Using assessment in a summative way to track attainment and progress in understanding and applying learning about Earth and space can be test-based. Of course, tests or quizzes are one way to collect summative data but the Focussed Assessment Tasks from the TAPS project can offer a manageable, reliable and valid alternative. We will use a *TAPS Plan for Focussed Assessment of Science: Space travel questions* (PSTT 2023) as an example. The resource outlines the disciplinary (working scientifically) and substantive (concept context) knowledge that is the intended learning focus. In this case, using research to plan different types of scientific enquiries to answer the children's questions can help assess whether they know that the Earth, Sun and Moon are approximately spherical and the movement of the Moon relative to the Earth. A specific assessment focus is given so that the children and adults are clear what is to be assessed – designing questions about the Moon or space travel and focussing their research to answering their questions. The plan gives a suggested activity, including adaptations for different learners and, importantly, questions to support discussion. There are clear assessment indicators which can be used by the children and adults to establish whether the assessment focus has been met, not yet met or the learning has gone further than the specific focus. By collecting summative assessment data in this way, teachers and children can review what the children have retained and identify any gaps, alternative frameworks or misconceptions that need to be addressed by the current or future teacher.

Teachers might also ask the children to review how they feel about this topic now: are they more interested in it than before, is it something they would like to learn more about, do they have questions that haven't been answered yet. Invite children to give examples of jobs or hobbies for which knowledge of the Earth and space might be helpful and to consider whether these are things they can see themselves doing in the future.

Classroom management

Because so much of Earth and space is taught through observation – demonstrations, models and simulations – it is essential to have a really good collection of resources so that several groups can be working simultaneously on the same or related activities. Of course, some of the class can be finding out information from secondary sources (books, websites, charts) and it is important to discuss the main ideas, but everyone needs to get hands on with equipment as often as possible to aid spatial concept development. This could be supported through activities in which children explain concepts to each other using the models and simulations they have experienced. Below is a sample list of resources you may wish to accumulate:

- chart of solar system;
- globes (including inflatable), LEGO figures;
- modelling clay for imitating the shapes of the Sun, Moon and Earth; powerful torches, bike lights or lamps;
- polystyrene balls; clocks and watches; sundial, shadow-stick; squared paper;
- books on space; compass;
- video clips of Earth, Moon, planets;
- data-logging equipment, including temperature and light sensors

A room you are able to darken is desirable, though not essential provided that you have sufficiently bright light sources. There are few health and safety issues associated with this topic, although you will definitely want to remind children about not looking directly at the Sun.

Many websites contain such animations to help children understand the movement of the Earth and Moon in relation to each other and the Sun. However, make sure that you are aware of misconceptions so that you can address these if you choose to use an animation. Children can be asked to spot the misconception and be asked to work together to formulate an explanation which is in line with current scientific thinking. The NASA Solar System Exploration website has 'real time simulations' of spacecraft orbiting the Moon, a complete lunar phase cycle (to reinforce the scientific explanation as the pattern appears so beautifully regular and the 'dark' portions of the Moon are clearly visible throughout) and other high-quality simulations and images.

To help children understand how the angle of the Sun in the sky affects the temperature on the Earth's surface – the explanation for seasonal changes (see above) – they can use a temperature or light sensor connected to a datalogger, demonstrating that the highest temperature and light levels occur when the source of light (e.g. a torch) is directly overhead.

Summary

In this chapter we hope we have communicated some of the excitement of teaching and learning about the Earth and space, a topic which remains at the cutting edge of science. It requires imagination and the ability to visualise in three dimensions, resulting in numerous alternative frameworks held by children and adults. We have discussed how to use assessment pedagogies formatively to elicit these misconceptions, and suggested a series of observations, demonstrations, models and simulations to help children to engage with, build and consolidate their learning about this exciting area of science education. The importance of working scientifically – in its broadest sense – in this area has been emphasised, offering the concrete and engaging experiences children need to make sense of the counter-intuitive explanations for seasonal and lunar changes. We have suggested some useful links with other areas of the wider school curriculum, including the use of technology to enhance children's learning.

Discussion questions

1. What are the strengths and limitations of using models and simulations to help engage children in their learning about the Earth and space?
2. How can formative assessment pedagogies be used to effectively support children to consolidate their understanding of this relatively abstract area of science education?

Further reading

Allen, M. (2019) *Misconceptions in Primary Science*. (3rd ed.), London: Open University Press. (This is a very useful book that provides a summary of common alternative ideas held by children, and also many teachers!)

Chambers, P. & Souter, N. (2020) Space, in Chamber, P. & Souter N. *Explaining Primary Science* (2nd ed.), London: SAGE, pp. 305–323 (Use this to develop your subject knowledge on space further.)

References

DfE (2015) National Curriculum in England: Science Programmes of Study. https://www.gov.uk/government/publications/national-curriculum-in-england-science-programmes-of-study/national-curriculum-in-england-science-programmes-of-study#year-1-programme-of-study

Education Endowment Foundation (2019) Stop and Think: Learning Counterintuitive Concepts. https://educationendowmentfoundation.org.uk/projects-and-evaluation/projects/learning-counterintuitive-concepts

European Space Agency (2022) Paxi and Cleaning Up Space. https://www.youtube.com/watch?v=dhZ2T2sxeoE

Harlen. W. with Qualter, A. (2018) *The Teaching of Science in Primary Schools*. (7th ed.), Abingdon: Routledge.

Osborne, J. F., Wadsworth, P., Black, P. J. & Meadows, J. (1993) *SPACE Research Report: The Earth in Space*, Liverpool: Liverpool University Press.

The Primary Science Teaching Trust (2023a) Teacher Assessment in Primary Science (TAPS). https://pstt.org.uk/unique-resources/taps/?_sft_taps_topics=space-and-seasons

The Primary Science Teaching Trust (2023b) Bright Ideas Time. https://pstt.org.uk/resources/bright-ideas/?_sft_science_topics=space&_sft_activity_types=assessment

Weinstein, Y. & Sumeracki, M. with Caviglioli, O. (2019) *Understanding How We Learn: A Visual Guide*, Abingdon: Routledge.

CHAPTER

4.2

Light and sound

Purpose of this chapter

After reading this chapter you will have:

- gained an understanding of progression in the main concept areas of light and sound
- become aware of a variety of ways of working scientifically to develop children's understanding of the concept areas of light and sound
- appreciated ways of making cross-curricular links more explicit

Introduction

Light and sound are sources of energy that surround us all and which we interact with from the moment we awake until the time we fall asleep. They are used and manipulated for the purposes of communication, entertainment and to support us to live our lives. For those who have a visual or auditory impairment, developments in understanding how we interact with these forms of energy has meant that adaptations and modifications can be made to include far more individuals in everyday interactions with light and sound than ever before. Light and sound are often engaged with simultaneously: to warn us of danger (a flashing light and siren); entertain us (streaming content on a personal device or trips to the cinema); to communicate in short video clips on social media rather than only relying on text messages or phone conversations. Of course, we engage with light and sound separately: reading texts on e-readers; streaming music; turning the lights on to see in a dark space or listening for the teacher's footsteps as they come along the corridor.

It seems undeniable that light and sound are highly important, but what are they? As mentioned above, light and sound are forms of energy. The current scientific explanation for how each travel points to their similar nature in the sense that they are believed to travel as waves from a source. Sound is caused by the vibration of an object: the source. As the object vibrates, the molecules in the particles of the medium the sound is travelling through also vibrate, affecting the neighbouring particles. In this way the sound is dispersed throughout the medium. We usually hear sounds that travel through air and into our ears. The further we are from the source, the quieter the sound is due to the reduction in intensity of the vibration as it travels from the source. Light is thought to be made up of photons (light particles) which travel from a source in waves; it is said to exhibit wave-particle duality. We see the things around us because light travels from a source directly to our eyes – for example, our mobile phone displays – or it is reflected from an object and then enters our eyes; for example, when we see another person, the light is reflected off them and into our eyes.

One of the tricky concepts for children to understand is that light and sound do not travel at the same velocity. Light travels at approximately 300,000,000 m/s and sound much slower, travelling at approximately 340 m/s. You can model this for children by using two wooden blocks and a large open space, for example, a school field or playground. Line the children up along the edge of the field/playground, facing towards the open ground. An adult stands about 100 metres away holding the two wooden blocks. The children are asked to raise one hand when they see the blocks being struck together and then raise the other hand when they hear the blocks striking each other. There should be enough of a delay between seeing the impact and hearing it for the hand which indicates seeing to be raised before the hand which indicates hearing.

An interesting idea from neuroscience linked to how we process what we see and hear, and how we learn, is the idea of dual coding. Part of the wider cognitive theory of multimedia learning (CTML) (Mayer 2005), dual coding is concerned with how children's working memory has two distinct processing channels – auditory and visual/spatial. 'It is thought that given the specialised nature of the two subsystems of working memory, a larger amount of content can be understood with more richness when conveyed through multiple formats without overloading working memory' (EEF 2021). We will look at this idea in more detail when we discuss planning for progression.

Planning for progression

The EYFS builds on children's natural curiosity to explore the world around them through play and by offering them more structured experiences. Practitioners can help young children to develop observational skills and awareness of their senses. They need to be given opportunities for play that develop their experience of light through exploration of collections of shiny, transparent and translucent objects, mirrors, kaleidoscopes and torches, making shadows on a sunny day, making dark dens and looking at the world through different colour filters. They will begin to learn the vocabulary to enable them to describe their observations: light, dark, shiny, dull, smooth, rough, mirror, shadow, reflection. The exploration of sound in the EYFS can be achieved through 'listening walks', identifying sounds with eyes closed, circle games such as 'keeper of the keys', and through using musical instruments such as drums, shakers and scrapers. The excitement of experiencing a fireworks display (at a safe distance) immerses children in both light and sound and can be the stimulation for creativity in their play as they create the sounds, movements and shapes of fireworks. Children can also create artwork and models inspired by the light from the fireworks as they explode. It is during EYFS that children start to learn songs about stars and rainbows.

There are no specific topics related to light or sound in the Key Stage 1 programmes of study of the primary science national curriculum (DfE 2015). However, with a more holistic view when learning about the properties of materials and how we link these properties to their use, children cannot learn about glass without learning the substantive knowledge that glass is a good material to use for windows because it is transparent and lets light pass through it. When singing and playing instruments, children in Key Stage 1 will experiment with, describe and mimic sounds with different volumes and pitch. So, although light does not appear in the primary science national curriculum until Year 3 and sound until Year 4, children will learn about these phenomena from a very young age. It is our role as educators to make links with this prior knowledge and use it to support children to learn about light and sound as they progress through school.

The key concepts to be taught at KS1 and KS2 are identified in Table 4.2.1, along with some notes to inform the teacher's understanding. We have organised them into light and then sound, and ordered them to illustrate a progression in conceptual understanding. Although the concept of colour does not feature in the primary science national curriculum, it is an interesting topic and one that lends itself to some intriguing science activities through concepts such as 'white light is a combination of different light colours'. For this reason, we have included it.

Table 4.2.1 Key concepts for teachers: light and sound

Key concept	Teachers' subject knowledge
Light	
There are many different light sources, including the Sun	Light is a form of energy; it is the energy source that keeps our planet alive. Only objects that emit light are sources, and these include the diode in an LED, a mobile phone or tablet screen, a fire and the Sun.
Darkness is the absence of light	Light illuminates objects; in the absence of light nothing is visible to our eyes.
Light travels from a source in straight lines	Light travels in straight lines from its source. Light travels at 300,000,000 metres per second. Light is the visible part of the electromagnetic spectrum. This spectrum also contains radio waves, microwaves, infrared light, ultraviolet light, X rays and gamma rays. Scientists describe light as having wave particle duality – it can behave as both a particle and a wave.
Light cannot pass through some materials which leads to the formation of shadows	Light can travel through transparent materials. Some light passes through translucent materials, which may cast grey or coloured shadows. Light cannot travel through opaque materials, and black shadows are formed because they block the path of light.
Light is reflected from surfaces	When light hits an object, it can be absorbed, reflected or scattered. If the surface (in a microscopic sense) is uneven, the light will be scattered (reflected in all directions). If the surface is smooth, the light will be reflected evenly in the same direction giving the image we refer to as 'a reflection'. When light meets many materials, it is partly scattered and partly absorbed.
We see things when the light reflected from them enters our eyes	Light passes through our cornea and then our pupil. Our lens focuses it onto our light sensitive retina at the back of our eye. The retina sends electrical messages to our brain via the optic nerve.
Visible light consists of different wavelengths which we see as different colours	White light can be split into a spectrum or 'rainbow' by using a prism that refracts (redirects) different wavelengths by different amounts. The colours that are visible are (according to Newton) red, orange, yellow, green, blue, indigo and violet. The process can be reversed by adding coloured lights together to create white light. Mixing paint is a different (subtractive) process: each time a paint colour is added to a mix, fewer wavelengths of light are reflected by the pigment.
We see objects as coloured because they reflect different wavelengths of light	When we see an object as red it is because only red wavelengths from the object have been reflected and reached our eyes. White objects reflect all visible wavelengths. Objects that appear matt black absorb most of the light that hits them.
Sound	
There are many kinds of sound and sources of sound	Sound is produced when an object vibrates; the molecules in the particles of the medium the sound is travelling through (e.g. air) also vibrate, which we call sound waves.
Sounds travel away from sources getting fainter the further they travel	Sounds travel as waves in all directions outwards from the source, similar to ripples when you drop a pebble in a pond but 3D. Sound waves can travel through the air at approximately 340 metres per second. Hard surfaces such as walls reflect sound waves. When you hear an echo, you are hearing a reflected sound a short time after the original sound.
Sounds are made when objects vibrate but vibrations are not always directly visible	Vibrations are (often minuscule) backwards and forwards movements of materials. Some hard materials are 'resonant' – vibrations are amplified, making them easier to hear (e.g. placing a tuning fork on a wooden table).
Vibrations from a sound source require a medium through which to travel to the ear	Sound waves require materials to travel through: they can travel through gases, liquids and solids but not through a vacuum.

(*Continued*)

Table 4.2.1 (Continued)

Key concept	Teachers' subject knowledge
Sounds are heard when they enter the ear	Sounds are heard when vibrations from an object travel through a medium, usually air, and enter the ears, causing the eardrums to vibrate. There are three bones in the middle ear: the hammer, the anvil and the stirrup. The vibrations from the eardrum cause these bones to move, and the sound then travels round the cochlea where thousands of hairs containing nerve endings carry impulses to the brain.
The pitch and loudness of some vibrating objects can be changed	The number of waves per second is called the frequency (pitch) and is measured in hertz (Hz). Sound waves can differ in amplitude (size) and frequency and this leads to differences in loudness and pitch, respectively.

Teacher self-assessment questions

1. How are light and sound similar, and in what ways are they different?
2. What is the difference between a reflection and a shadow?
3. Why do reflections from some surfaces form an image, whereas others don't?
4. Why can't we see things in the dark?
5. How are the pitch and loudness of sounds related to the wavelength and amplitude of their waves?
6. Sound can only travel through air. True or false?
7. How do ear defenders reduce what we hear?

Engage

Situating the topic

Children engage with light and sound every day; it is how we interpret the world around us and communicate with each other. For some children this can be more challenging due to a visual or hearing impairment, which we will discuss more in the next section (breaking down barriers). From an early age, children will associate light and sound with celebration. In the UK we sing happy birthday and put candles on a birthday cake. There are numerous religious festivals which celebrate light – in Hinduism, Jainism and Sikhism, Diwali is the 'Festival of Lights'. During Eid-al-Fitr, lights and decorations are used to celebrate the end of the Islamic month of Ramadan; and in Christianity Jesus is celebrated as the light of the world. Candle lighting ceremonies mark the major Jewish holidays, for example Hanukkah, and Holi, the Hindu festival of colours, celebrates the coming of spring. These celebrations and religious festivals are good ways to promote discussion around light and sound, and can be referred to when teaching children more explicitly about the science of light and sound.

Creating a dark area such as a cave can give children first-hand experience of darkness and of how the introduction of light enables them to see objects. Stories such as the classic *Can't You Sleep Little Bear?* by Martin Waddell (2001), *The Dark* by Lemony Snicket (2014) or *I'm Not (Very) Afraid of the Dark* by Anna Milbourne (2019) can be used to set the context for young children. The cave could have curtains to open and let in the light from the classroom, or children could use torches to help them find objects in the cave. Topics on 'The Victorians' or trips to mines and caves also give opportunities to explore various sources of light and to demonstrate how we need to shine light onto objects to be able to see them.

NASA's *Black Marble project* (NASA 2016) shows images of the Earth from space at night and allows the viewer to identify the areas of high light density. Images such as these can be used as provocation for discussion about light pollution and how it can affect our sleep patterns, and the impact on ecosystems and wildlife. However, if you use a map of the Earth showing everywhere at night, you will need to ensure you are clear the image has been fabricated from several photographs, to avoid misconceptions about day and night (see the previous chapter, Earth and space). These satellite images of the world at night are a good starting point for raising questions about the impact and effects of how light is used by different people.

- Where is the most light? Can you explain why?
- Is it good to make so much light?
- How is most of the light made?
- Are there more eco-friendly ways to make light?
- Why are some local authorities in the UK turning street lamps off when it is very late at night/very early in the morning?

Breaking down barriers

Most of us will be aware of Isacc Newton and Albert Einstein, who were among the scientists who are credited with theories associated with light. You may even be aware of ancient mathematicians and philosophers, such as Ptolemy, Euclid and Pythagoras, who understood that light travels in straight lines. However, are you aware of Ibn al-Haytham (known in the West as Alhazen), a tenth century scientist from what is now known as Iraq? It is important that we introduce children to diverse scientists and Ibn al-Haytham is a great example of how tenth century Middle Eastern theories about light were ahead of Western ideas. Until approximately the twelfth century, in Western society, the accepted scientific understanding of light was that seeing was an active mechanism; your eyes emitted rays, a bit like Superman and Supergirl from DC Comics. However, these rays were not focussed light energy from the Sun (as is the case with the superheroes) but were invisible active search beams seeking out things that we see. Our use of language adds to the misconception of seeing as an action we perform, for example, we 'look' at a picture. This idea was centuries old and came from the ancient Greeks – Ptolemy, Pythagoras and Euclid. Translations of Ibn al-Haytham's tenth century work has shown that he theorised that we see things because light from a source was reflected off objects and entered our eyes – which aligns with the current scientific explanation.

It is also important to introduce the children to contemporary role models linked with light or sound. A great example is Evelyn Glennie the hearing impaired Scottish percussionist. Although she is a musician rather than a scientist, her understanding of sound and how to manipulate it is outstanding. Glennie often plays barefoot to feel the vibrations, the sound, and in her 2003 TED Talk explains how she uses different parts of her body to listen. It would be interesting to talk to the children about how they can feel sound. A quick example is by asking them to close their mouths very lightly, so their teeth just touch, and then ask them to hum. They should be able to feel the vibrations created by their humming. We will look at other examples of seeing sound in the purposeful practical work section of this chapter.

Activating children's learning

When eliciting children's understanding about light or sound, the use of annotated drawings can be particularly useful for helping them to communicate what they know and can become a focus for the discussion of ideas with the practitioner or with peers. The children can label their drawings and write explanations of what is happening or discuss their drawing with the practitioner who can scribe their explanation. As always, teacher questioning is important, to establish what the children have experienced in relation to understanding the substantive knowledge of light and sound that children need to know. Are there any children who have family members who are engineers, musicians, artists or architects? How does an understanding of light and sound help an architect design a building that will allow its occupants to have well-lit rooms that are insulated from the sounds of the street outside? How does a musician's understanding of how sound travels, help them to perform in different environments for different audiences? What scientific knowledge do we think a music technician needs for their job?

Questioning children while they are engaged in an exploratory activity will extend their ideas, reveal their level of understanding and give opportunities for assessment. For example, when looking for light sources in the classroom or in the school, teachers could ask:

- Can you find any areas that are very light? Where is the light coming from?
- What about the dark places, why are they dark?
- What happens to bright-coloured things when we put them in a dark place? What is getting in the way of the light?

Sorting and classifying objects or pictures can be another starting point for discussion or for questioning about existing ideas. After looking at a range of objects or pictures, including some light sources, some very good reflectors and some light-coloured objects, ask the children if they can sort them, e.g. source of light vs not a source of light or sorted by their reflectiveness. Use a variety of materials and objects that reflect light in different ways, e.g. spoons (concave and convex surfaces), shiny objects and dull objects. Asking children questions such as, 'What happens when you shine the torch on the shiny objects?' may provoke a response such as, 'the shiny things light up.' This could lead to a rich discussion about the light source, reflections and how light travels. Another question you may wish to ask the children is, 'Why can you see your reflection in some things and not in others?' This could provoke a series of responses, which could include:

- because they are shiny
- because they are different shapes and sizes
- because you can see through some things
- because some are the right colour for reflection

Again, there is a good opportunity for a dialogic pedagogical approach by asking probing questions to elicit further the children's understanding.

Making sounds with a drum, 'elastic-band guitar' or by 'twanging' a ruler on the edge of a table can offer opportunities for probing children's understanding about sources of sound. Some children may observe the vibration of the drum skin or elastic band, but not make a connection between this and the sound they hear. Others may suggest that the sound 'causes' the vibration or vice versa, implying that sound and vibration are separate phenomena (Allen 2019). To help to assess what children know about how sound travels, children can explore how far the sound of a clock, a telephone or an alarm will travel. Where is the best place to put a smoke alarm or an intercom for a baby to make sure they can be heard? Which materials can be used to make a room soundproof? By investigating solutions to these questions, you can elicit what the children know about how sound travels and uncover possible misconceptions, such as that sound can only travel through air or that the volume of a sound is not affected by the distance the sound travels from the source to our ears.

Hinge questions are a good way to ascertain if children are ready to move onto the next step in their learning. In our experience, a well-constructed, specific question posed during the lesson, ideally after an initial modelling and explanation, rather than at the start or end of a lesson, can uncover if children are ready to move on. The DfE's frameworks for initial teacher training and induction of beginning teachers, the Core Content Framework (DfE 2019b) and Early Career Framework (DfE 2019a), state that children may develop misconceptions if their subject knowledge is weak and new ideas are taught too soon. So, not only planning what to ask in a hinge question but when to ask it in the sequence of learning is important. Goalby (2020) suggests that, 'the best hinge point questions are multiple choice questions where the wrong answers are common misconceptions', helping to identify any misconceptions currently held by the children and giving the opportunity to address these and hopefully prevent any of the common misconceptions developing. An example related to this topic is set out below.

A common misconception is that sound cannot pass through obstructions (Allen 2019). After the initial input and modelling that sound travels in waves, the children are asked to think about this question and the three possible answers:

Can sound waves outside of our classroom be stopped by the closed doors, closed windows and walls?

a) Yes. Sound waves cannot pass through closed windows, closed doors and walls. (Linked to the misconception that sound can only travel through air.)

b) No. They are not stopped but we cannot hear the sound because they are reflected away when they hit closed doors, closed windows and walls. (Linked to a misconception about echoes and reflecting sounds – this is a partial understanding and needs to be addressed.)

c) No. The sound waves hit the windows, doors and walls, and some sound energy is reflected away, some is absorbed by the material, and some travels through the material and can be heard by the people in the room. (Aligned with current scientific thinking.)

A good way to address this question is to use one minute from playtime, close the windows and doors and listen to the other children outside. Make sure you 'pay back' the missed playtime; science should never be seen as an alternative to playtime.

Build

Constructing new knowledge

As light and sound are integral to a child's life from the moment they are born – and in the case of sound, even before they are born – children will come to their learning about light and sound with some established schemata that many not be aligned with current scientific thinking. It is important that children's understanding of light and sound are elicited so that teachers can address alternative ideas and misconceptions and build on the children's prior learning. Thorough planning carefully sequenced learning experiences, children can work scientifically to build a secure understanding of light and sound.

Working scientifically

Working scientifically within light and sound requires children to plan and carry out comparative and fair tests, and to pose questions they can find the answers to using secondary sources as well as their own investigations. There are also opportunities for pattern seeking, making systematic and close observations, recording and presenting data in a variety of ways. Children can also explore how they group and classify materials dependent on how the materials respond to light and sound. We've included some ideas for working scientifically when learning about light and sound, in the purposeful practical work section.

Light

Comparing sunglasses for teddy

You can pose the problem that teddy wants to go out for a walk but that they find the Sun too bright. Which material could we use to make the lenses for a pair of sunglasses for teddy? Children can be given a range of materials to compare. It is important to ask the children why it is important that the sunglass lenses let some light through but not all? You can ask the children how we can find out which material would make good sunglass lenses. This is a good opportunity to ensure children understand and use the vocabulary *opaque, translucent* and *transparent*. To extend this enquiry, children can use a datalogger to measure the light that travels through each material. It would be interesting to measure the amount of light that travels through a pair of real sunglasses first as a goal to aim for. You should also discuss the other properties of the materials used to make sunglasses and the lenses to help children make informed decisions when finding out which material is better.

Observing colour

Spectra or rainbows can be created in the classroom using a strong light source and a prism – a glass bowl of water can work, as can water mist and some plastics. Light can be 'mixed' by making colour wheels divided into the six primary and secondary colours and spinning them quickly, by mounting them on a motor, for example. If you have access to coloured lights such as stage lights, discoveries to be made include the fact that shadows will be the complementary colour to the light source (for example, red light creates a green shadow) and some objects lit with coloured light will appear to change colour.

How much light is needed before we can see an object?

For this investigation you will need:

- a large cardboard box
- a blanket to cover the box and observer
- a collection of reflective and non-reflective objects of different colours (they need to be able to be placed in the box and be seen when the box is open)
- a dimmable light source (that does not create much heat) such as a torch on a smart phone or tablet

The box is placed on a table or the floor and the objects are placed inside. Do not let the observer know which objects have been chosen. One side of the box is open so the observer can see into the box. The dimmable light source will be used to increase the amount of light in the box. The blanket is draped over the box and observer to make the interior of the box dark. The observer is asked to name the objects and their colour as the amount of light is slowly increased. This effect can also be achieved by raising the blanket to allow an increased amount of light into the box, if a dimmable light source is not available or it would create heat that could cause injury or damage. Children can record when they see each object and what happens to the colour of the objects as the light increases. You could vary this enquiry by changing the colour of the light source. How does this change the appearance of the objects or how soon they can be seen?

Sound

Sound travelling through a solid/liquid

Children often think that sounds will not travel through solids or liquids. Our hearing system is designed to efficiently hear sounds which travel through air but that does not mean that sound does not travel through other media (materials). If that was the case, aquatic animals would not be able to hear sounds, and we know that whale song can travel many miles under water and be heard by other whales. A simple way to address the question, 'Can sound travel through solid materials?', is to ask children to do the following. Before you start this activity, it is important to remind children that they should only place their ear on a clean, clear surface. Ask the children to gently tap the tabletop with their fingernail and listen. They should hear the tapping but it should be quiet. They place their ear directly on the tabletop and tap again, trying to tap in the same way as before. The sound should be louder. Ask the children to continue tapping, trying to maintain a steady tap. They should lift and replace their ear to the tabletop, comparing the difference in loudness of the tapping sound. This can then be extended to the school hall (this works best on a wooden floor). Children are at one end of the hall and the teacher the other. The teacher gently taps the floor using a key or other hard object. The children place their ears on the floor and compare the sound. It should be louder when their ear is directly on the floor. This is particularly effective if the teacher can tap the floor so that it can only be heard if the children's ears are placed directly on the floor. You may want to relate this to the saying, 'keep your ear to the ground' to ascertain what might be ahead. It is thought that people would put their ear to the ground to listen for stampeding herds or put their ear to the early train tracks to listen for an approaching train. The sound travelling through the solid will be heard more easily than relying only on hearing it through the air. Of course, children should not be encouraged to try this for themselves, however, it is possible to hear the sound in the rails as a train approaches a station platform.

It is important to carry out an appropriate risk assessment for the next activity and ensure that all health and safety requirements are fully met. If children are competent in the water and feel safe putting their head underwater, during a swimming lesson you could ask them to duck underwater as you tap a metal object, such as a relay baton, against the side of the pool. Children should be able to hear the sound that travels through the water.

Nosiest classroom

Ask children to predict which classroom is the nosiest in the school. This can be recorded individually, in groups or as a whole class straw poll and recorded on a science working wall. Children can then work in groups to measure the volume of sound in each classroom using a data logger. The results from the groups can then be collated and recorded on a class graph. This is a good opportunity to reinforce the difference between discrete and continuous data. Some children will think that a line graph is the correct way to record their data because of the numerical readings on the datalogger. However, as each classroom is a discrete entity, the data should be recorded as a bar chart. For older children, you could ask them when a line graph would be the best way to present sound data. Hopefully, some will know that observing the change in volume over a given period of time in a classroom would produce continuous data for a line graph. Data logger software will record and present this data so you could use it to monitor the noise level in your own classroom and share it with the children live and/or the next day.

Big Ben

We like to call this enquiry Big Ben as a nod to the bell in the Elizabeth Tower of the Houses of Parliament in London. You will need a metal object and some string. We have found that a metal coat hanger with two pieces of string tied to it works well.

1) The child stands by a table, holding the ends of the string at chest height and gently knocks the hanger against the edge of the table. They describe the quality of the sound (e.g. quiet knocking sound).

2) The child then holds the ends the strings to their ears, pushing their fingers against their ears. Remind the children not to stick anything into their ears. This will need to be modelled for them and reference to how a stethoscope is worn by medical professionals may be helpful.

3) They now gently knock the hanger against the edge of the table and describe the quality of the sound. It should be louder and reverberate like a large bell – Big Ben.

Once the children have mastered this, they may wish to carry out a comparative test with different types of string, different lengths of string or different numbers of strings at each end of the coat hanger.

Changing the pitch of sounds – noticing patterns

Pitch, or the frequency of sounds, measured in hertz (Hz) or vibrations per second, can be explored in many different ways. Generally, the smaller or shorter the object or material vibrating, the higher will be its pitch. For example, if children 'twang' a ruler on the edge of a table but move it towards the centre of the table during the vibration, they can hear and see how the vibrations become more frequent as the length free to vibrate shortens. A lovely and simple way of showing this is to make a paper straw 'oboe' by cutting one end into a 'v', flattening it and blowing through. It takes a bit of practice to get the lip position and force of breath right, but children should soon be able to produce a 'toot', a little like the sound some people can make by blowing over a blade of grass held between thumbs. Making 'oboes' of various lengths or cutting pieces off the other end of the straw as they blow, very clearly demonstrates pitch rising as the length shortens.

Another simple demonstration is to stretch an elastic band while a child plucks it near their ear. However, this can be confusing, as the pitch rises as the elastic band is stretched (i.e. gets longer!), so might be better as an activity to challenge those ready to move on. Similarly, the familiar row of glass bottles with differing amounts of water can be a tricky example. Blow across the top of each one and the pitch gets higher as the amount of water increases. However, hit each gently (bearing in mind health and safety precautions) and the pitch decreases. The explanation, that some children may come up with, is that when you are blowing, the column of air in each bottle vibrates, whereas when you strike the bottles, it is the column of water that vibrates – as one increases the other decreases.

Seeing sound

These activities give opportunity for close observation, making predictions and asking questions. There are several clips available on the internet which demonstrate movement of materials caused by sound. We think the video 'CYMATICS: Science vs. Music' by Nigel Stanford is a fun way to demonstrate to children that sound is an energy form and can affect how materials behave. You can use sections of the clip with the children to prompt discussion about how the materials react to the different volume and pitch of the sounds created. This can then be recreated in class by covering a speaker or tablet with tissue paper (to protect the speaker) and placing dry sand on it. What happens when the speaker is switched on? What is causing the sand to move? Can the children describe how the sand moves? Does it always move in the same way? How can we change the way the sand moves?

Noticing patterns with reflections and echoes

The use of torches with mirrors can demonstrate how light can 'bounce off' a mirror; children enjoy using mirrors to send light round a corner or under a table. Ask children to talk about what is happening from the point of view of the beam of light – can they tell the story of its journey? This can be extended by making kaleidoscopes and periscopes. There are obvious links with mathematical work on symmetry; the awe and wonder of counting the images when children look at an object between two hinged mirrors can be extended by relating the number of images observed to the angle between the mirrors, and perhaps establishing a general rule, e.g. the number of images = 360 degrees divided by the angle between the mirrors, minus one. Sound too reflects; children will probably have noticed echoes in the school hall or when walking through a pedestrian underpass,

Light and sound

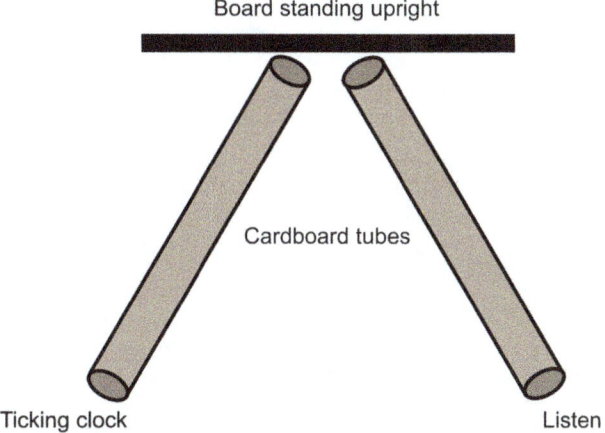

Figure 4.2.1 Bird's-eye view of enquiry to investigate angles of reflection of sound (echoes).

so the idea of sound travelling until it is absorbed or 'bounces off' (reflects from) hard surfaces may be worth exploring here. A pattern-noticing activity to investigate angles of reflection using two cardboard tubes and a hard surface can be used to explore the way in which sounds reflect from a surface, by putting a ticking clock at the far end of one tube while the other is moved until the optimum angle for hearing the clock is achieved (see Figure 4.2.1).

Feedback

As with the previous topic, Earth and space, much of the formative assessment opportunities within this topic are gained from asking children questions and listening to what they say. However, there is also the opportunity to give children feedback on their written work. We will start by looking at the formative assessment opportunities that can be afforded when using images to promote children's scientific discussion. In a similar way to the previous chapter, we will use an example from the Bright Ideas Time, available via the Primary Science Teaching Trust (PSTT) website. Children are presented with three musical instruments, images or preferably the real thing: a piano, a drum and a guitar. In the previous chapter we suggested that in this type of activity, the children are asked to suggest the odd one out. They would use their science knowledge about how each instrument creates sound to give reasons why it is, or is not, the odd one out.

Another way to use these artefacts/images is for the teacher to suggest that one instrument is the odd one out and to ask the children to offer reasons why. An example could be that the teacher says, 'I think the piano is the odd one out,' and the children suggest their reasoning. The piano is considered both a percussion instrument (like the drum) and a stringed instrument (like the guitar). The children may come up with a range of reasons, and your role as the teacher is to use a dialogic pedagogical approach. Ask questions and offer alternatives for the children to consider, without completely closing the children's discussion, unless a misconception is offered. At this point, clear feedback, including the current scientific thinking should be given.

Giving feedback on children's written work, including diagrams, tables and graphs, should focus on the science learning not the presentation. After some practical experience and exploratory activities, such as going for a 'shadow hunt' around the school grounds, ask children to make annotated drawings to explain what a shadow is and how they are made. Figure 4.2.2 is from a child 'Adam' explaining what a shadow is.

Feedback to Adam, preferably at the point of learning, could be either oral or written. It should focus on his correct explanation about his body blocking the sunlight to cause a shadow and that

Teaching physics topics

Figure 4.2.2: Adam's annotated drawing to explain a shadow.

the shadow is in the shape of him. To develop his thinking further, he could be asked to give a name to materials that block light and model for him that shadows are caused due to an absence of light. 'Well done, Adam, you have explained that your body blocks the light, so the shadow is dark. You got the shape right too. Scientists say that the shadow is where there is no light and that is why it is dark. Do you know what the science vocabulary is for a material, like your body, which blocks the light?'

Consolidate

Retrieving and applying

A good way for children to retrieve and apply their learning about light and sound is through cross curricular activities. When designing and constructing during design & technology lessons and art and design lessons, children can apply what they have learnt in science to the task in hand. This is a powerful low stakes form of retrieval which the children will be highly invested in as they want to complete their project. Below are some examples we think are worth considering.

Shadow puppets

Through devising and performing shows using shadow puppets, children can explore transparent, translucent and opaque materials and can learn that light travels through some materials but not others. Stretching white fabric over a rectangular frame can make a simple screen. Children can learn how light is blocked by some objects, how shadows are formed and how to make coloured shadows. There are good opportunities here for cross-curricular work, for example with storytelling in Literacy: children can either dramatise their own stories or retell stories from around the world. There are also possible links with D&T: making their own shadow puppets and putting on a show for others, making posters, selling tickets, selling popcorn at the show and evaluating the event.

Children could make sound effects for their shadow puppet play, exploring the qualities of sound to create a certain atmosphere or to describe the movement of an animal or character. A good starting point for this might be to listen to a recording of Prokofiev's *Peter and the Wolf*, in which every character has a different theme tune, or to watch an episode of *Phineas and Ferb* in which sound effects are used to create the sounds of their inventions. Children could discuss the choice of sounds for each effect – Why do we associate certain sounds with a particular action, for example a 'boing' for a spring?

Musical instruments

There is so much potential in this cross-curricular context because it is possible to engage children of all ages and levels of attainment, returning to this theme often by focusing on a different aspect of sound or music each time. There is a wide variety of instruments from all over the world that make sounds in different ways – usually through either beating (includes plucking and strumming), blowing (e.g. recorder), shaking (e.g. maracas) or scraping (e.g. violin). Children can explore ways to make sounds with instruments, feel the vibrations when sounds are being made and explore pitch and loudness. They can examine how an instrument is made, noting which materials have been used, identifying the parts that vibrate and the parts that amplify the vibration. Later they could try to identify a range of instruments while blindfolded. Children usually enjoy making and decorating their own instruments such as shakers, drums and 'box guitars' – this provides a natural link with D&T.

Houses and homes

This theme provides a relevant context for developing awareness of sources of sound, the variety of sounds in our environment and sound travelling through different materials. Children enjoy identifying a range of 'mystery' household sounds from a tape, for example, filling a kettle, shutting a door and cleaning teeth. The story *Peace at Last* by Jill Murphy (1995a) or the poem 'The Sound Collector' by Roger McGough (2003) are good starting points when working with young children. You could discuss with the children when a sound becomes a 'noise' – is this just to do with whether we like the sound or not, or is it about loudness?

Art and colour

Activities such as colour mixing, mixing dark and light colours, and using paint colour charts to stimulate colour hunts outside are examples of cross-curricular activities. Teachers need to be aware that mixing paint colour is a different phenomenon to mixing light (see Table 4.2.1). Light can also be mixed 'in the eye' – artists such as Seurat made use of this phenomenon by painting coloured dots (pointillism) that merge together when viewed from a distance, so an orange hat is in fact created by a juxtaposition of red and yellow dots.

Reviewing

It is important to give children the opportunity to review their learning about light and sound and for you and them to see what has been retained and what has been forgotten. As the children engage in these activities, you will be able to identify any misconceptions that still need to be addressed. As in previous chapters, we will use a TAPS Plan for Focussed Assessment of Science. The theme this time will be: Investigating Shadows (PSTT 2023). The lesson plan outlines the disciplinary (working scientifically) and substantive (concept context) knowledge that is the intended learning focus. In this case, the focus is on taking accurate measurements and recording data on a graph, and – using the idea that light appears to travel in straight lines – to explain why shadows have the same shape as their objects. Children are asked to select a question from a set they generate as a class focussing on how they could change the shadow of an object, which has a torch shone on it. The children are guided to choose a question that will give them continuous numerical data that can be plotted and presented as a line graph. The clear assessment indicators, which are linked to the assessment focus, 'Can children make accurate measurements?' and 'Can children plot their results accurately on a line graph?' can be used by the children and adults to establish whether the assessment focus has been met, not yet met or the learning has gone further than the specific focus.

Another example is the String telephones lesson plan (PSTT 2023). After an initial exploration of how string telephones work, children are asked to make the 'best' string telephone. Children are asked to demonstrate their telephones to the class, explaining improvements they have made and reasons for making those improvements. This links with the specific assessment focus, 'Can the children explain how to make the best possible string telephone?' and 'Can the children suggest reasons for the improvements?'.

You could review the topic as a class, thinking together about the parts that were the most enjoyable, the most surprising, or puzzling. Support children in making the shift from seeing this as school topic to thinking about how it might be relevant to them in their future lives. Maybe they might become an audiologist and test people's hearing. Perhaps they can imagine themselves designing the lighting for a music festival!

Classroom management

Health and safety issues should be brought to children's attention at an early stage in any work on light or sound. It is essential for them to know that they should never look directly at the Sun, even through coloured filters. When using magnifying glasses outside, children should be reminded not to look up at the sky. Teachers need to be alert to the possibility that magnifying glasses could become 'burning glasses' if they focus the Sun's rays. If observing each other's eyes, children should not point or have a pencil in their hand during the activity. If children are holding listening devices up to their ear such as 'ear trumpets' or 'string telephones', others must be warned not to shout into the device no matter how tempting it seems as this could damage the eardrum. Children should be informed about the dangers of putting things in their ears and of damaging them by listening to loud music using headphones both over the ear or in the ear. They should also exercise care when striking a bottle 'xylophone'.

It can sometimes be a problem creating sufficient darkness in the classroom for working with light. If there are no blackout curtains or blinds, then spaces such as stock cupboards could be used, under careful supervision and following safeguarding procedures, or mini darkrooms can be created by using cardboard boxes with holes cut in them and curtains or 'flaps' to look through or shine torches through. To collect resources cheaply, encourage parents to donate old decorations from festivals and celebrations. Mirrors can be made from bathroom mirror tiles but need to be backed by sticking them onto cardboard, so that if they break the glass stays in place.

Given the potential for noise in much of the practical work in the topic of sound, it may be best to focus the noise within a few sessions, perhaps by organising a carousel of activities, around which groups of children move during one lesson. Below is a useful set of equipment for the activities suggested in this chapter:

- Sources of sound: different types of musical instruments, demonstrating four different ways of making sounds: bang, scrape, shake, blow.
- Sound travels: Slinky spring, string telephones, water-filled balloon, metal metre rule, metal coat hanger.
- Hearing: sheets of card to make ear trumpets, blindfold, cotton wool, sound sources, cardboard tube with piece of burst balloon stretched over one end (model ear drum).
- Vibrations: drum, rice, balloon, paper and comb, tuning fork, bowl of water, ping-pong ball on thread.
- Volume (amplitude, loudness): guitar, Slinky, sound-insulating materials to make ear muffs, data-logging equipment set up to measure sound level, buzzer and circuit.
- Pitch (frequency): ruler, metal tube in water-filled beaker, elastic band, milk bottle xylophone, art straws, scissors.

There are many opportunities for exciting uses of technology to learn more about light and sound. Comparing the reflective or sound-insulating properties of materials is greatly enhanced for older children if they use a datalogger to measure the amount of light that is being reflected or sound transmitted. In answering the question 'which material would be the best sound insulator for a pair of ear defenders?' children can think of a good way to make a 'standard' sound (perhaps a simple circuit including a buzzer) and can set up the sensor and material being tested in the same place each time to make a comparative test. Unfortunately, because sound sensors tend to be rather sensitive to extraneous noises, it is rather difficult to obtain reliable results, although this can be a useful point for discussion. Children can apply their ideas about light in topics on ecosystems, using light meters to measure the amounts of light in different habitats and linking this to the plants that live there. They could also monitor noise levels around their school, producing an environmental map as part of a study into noise pollution.

Summary

In this chapter we have explored the subject knowledge needed to teach this topic either through discrete science learning or in more cross-curricular contexts. A range of possibilities for observation, pattern-noticing and fair tests to develop children's understanding of light and sound has been suggested. We have looked at various ways of making sounds, finding out children's ideas about how these sounds travel through air and enter our ears. The potential for working scientifically in a range of ways and through using data logging equipment has been explored.

Discussion questions

1. In what ways are sound and light similar, and in what ways are they different?
2. In what ways does our language to describe volume and pitch of sounds risk confusing children? What words would help them distinguish between these concepts?
3. What are the pros and cons of teaching the science topics of light and sound together at primary level?
4. How can we include children who have visual and/or hearing impairment in the study of light and sound?

Further reading

Allen, M. (2019) *Misconceptions in Primary Science*. (3rd ed.), London: Open University Press.

Chambers, P. & Souter, N. (2020) 'Light', in Chamber, P. & Souter N. *Explaining Primary Science* (2nd ed.), London: SAGE, pp. 355–371; 373–388.

All of these books will support you in identifying where you need to strengthen your own subject knowledge and provide helpful explanations.

References

DfE (2015) National Curriculum in England: Science Programmes of Study. https://www.gov.uk/government/publications/national-curriculum-in-england-science-programmes-of-study/national-curriculum-in-england-science-programmes-of-study#year-1-programme-of-study

DfE (2019a) *Early Career Framework*, London: Crown.

DfE (2019b) *ITT Core Content Framework*, London: Crown.

Education Endowment Foundation (2021) *Cognitive Science Approaches in the Classroom: A Review of the Evidence*. https://educationendowmentfoundation.org.uk/education-evidence/evidence-reviews/cognitive-science-approaches-in-the-classroom

Goalby, N. (2020) *How to Use Hinge Point Questions Effectively*. https://edu.rsc.org/ideas/how-to-use-hinge-point-questions-effectively/4011966.article

Mayer, R. E. (2005) Cognitive Theory of Multimedia Learning, in Mayer, R. (ed.) *The Cambridge Handbook of Multimedia Learning*, Cambridge: Cambridge University Press, pp. 31–48.

NASA (2016) *NASA's Black Marble*, https://blackmarble.gsfc.nasa.gov/

The Primary Science Teaching Trust (2023a) *Teacher Assessment in Primary Science (TAPS)*. https://pstt.org.uk/unique-resources/taps/?_sft_taps_topics=space-and-seasons

The Primary Science Teaching Trust (2023b) *Bright Ideas Time*. https://pstt.org.uk/resources/bright-ideas/?_sft_science_topics=space&_sft_activity_types=assessment

CHAPTER 4.3

Electricity

Purpose of this chapter

After reading this chapter you will have:

- an understanding of children's development in electrical concepts from early childhood until the beginning of secondary education
- an awareness of a range of strategies for eliciting children's understanding of electricity, and for building on their ideas using illustrative activities, models and analogies
- an appreciation of a problem-based approach to working scientifically with electricity, involving a series of progressive challenges to engage children's enquiry skills

Introduction

When exploring electricity with children, teachers often think it's one of the easier topics to cover until a child asks a simple question such as, 'How does the electricity get from the battery to my toy?' The phenomenon of electricity is abstract and requires models and analogies to help children understand it. However, we need to be careful that the model or analogy we use does not inadvertently confirm alternative frameworks or misconceptions held, or arguably even worse, lead to new misconceptions being formed. We will explore this in more detail later in this chapter. If we can come to appreciate how children make sense of what is going on inside a circuit, while at the same time coming face to face with our own 'alternative frameworks', we can plan activities that challenge those understandings: do they really accord with evidence? It helps, of course, to have some ways of making the abstract concrete, the invisible 'visible'.

Chambers and Souter (2020) suggest that a sound understanding of particle theory can help children to make sense of electricity. A good grounding to build on, is helping children to understand and accept that the current scientific model is that all matter is made up of tiny particles that we cannot see and that some of these particles hold a negative charge and are called electrons. The chemistry chapters in this book share ideas about teaching particle theory to primary aged children which will be useful to read before embarking on an exploration of electricity. Once we are sure that children have grasped this idea, we can help them to understand that the flow of the negatively charged particles, the electrons, is electricity. We can then explore electricity in different contexts and use purposeful practical work to support the children's learning.

It is essential to consider the health and safety aspect of teaching electricity practically. Electricity is one of the most overtly 'dangerous' science topics; children need to become aware of the hazards and know how to avoid them as part of their science and PSHE education. We need to teach children about the dangers of electricity while reassuring them that resources we provide for their classroom-based activities are safe. We will discuss this in the classroom management section later in this chapter.

When we consider planning for progression, we will discuss how to ensure progression in learning and avoid the trap of mastering how to make a simple circuit but never going further either cognitively or scientifically.

Planning for progression

Some of the things for children to 'do' with electricity, for example, make a bulb light up using a simple circuit, could be achieved during the Early Years, while the understanding to underpin it may develop much later. As with other physics topics, there is no coverage of electricity at KS1 in the national curriculum for England, so the conceptual sequence below has been linked to the two electricity units within the Years 4 and 6 programmes of study.

The application of these electrical principles is mentioned in the programmes of study for design and technology at KS2. Children are required to 'understand and use electrical systems in their products' (DfE 2013, p. 3). At KS3 children will be introduced to the electric current as flow of charge measured in amperes; series and parallel circuits; potential difference measured in volts; battery and bulb ratings; resistance measured in ohms and differences in resistance between conducting and insulating components. In relation to static electricity, they will cover the separation of positive or negative charges when objects are rubbed together, forces between charged objects and the idea of an electric field. We have included commentary relating to static electricity in this chapter as many children will have experienced static electricity, for example, as a shock between them and another person, or when they have rubbed a balloon on a jumper and 'stuck' it to a wall or used it to make their hair 'stand up straight'.

The key concepts to be taught at KS1 and KS2 are identified in Table 4.3.1, along with some notes to inform the teacher's understanding.

Teacher self-assessment questions

1. What are the differences between electricity conductors and insulators?
2. How does the idea of microscopic particles called electrons help us understand the flow of electricity?
3. What is the difference between current and voltage?
4. If you were to measure the flow of electricity at different points in a simple circuit, would you expect it to be the same or different? Why?
5. Why do electric bulbs become hot in use?
6. Why is it helpful to understand the difference between charged and uncharged materials when exploring 'static' electricity?

Engage

Situating the topic

Electricity is a source of energy that dominates our lives. Electrical impulses speed through our nervous system, controlling our bodies and helping us to make sense of the world we live in. It is hard to find a community of people who do not depend on electricity for at least some part of their

Table 4.3.1 Key concepts for teachers: electricity

Key concept	Teachers' subject knowledge
Electricity is a form of energy that has a wide variety of everyday uses	Electricity (current) involves the flow of billions of tiny particles (electrons) through conducting materials (e.g. metals). This movement can be generated by converting another form of energy (e.g. chemical energy in batteries, heat energy in power stations, wind energy in wind turbines).
Materials can become charged and attract or repel other materials	The negative and positive charge of particles in objects usually cancel each other out – objects have a neutral charge overall. Rubbing a balloon or other plastic object can cause the material to become charged. The charge is localised and does not spread throughout the object. The charged area can attract uncharged objects, such as small pieces of tissue. Two similarly charged objects will repel each other.
We need a complete circuit to make a bulb (lamp) light up	There needs to be a complete circuit for the electricity (electrons) that are already in the battery, wires and bulb to flow. The bulb has two connections (base and side) so electrons can flow through the filament, heating it until it glows.
Switches can control the flow of electricity in a circuit	A switch acts like a gate, stopping the flow of electrons by introducing a gap in the circuit of conducting material. At low voltage, electrons do not usually flow through air, though they can 'jump' a very small gap, making a spark.
Changes to the resistance of a circuit (e.g. by altering the number or type of components or the circuit layout) will alter the flow of current	Adding more bulbs to a series circuit increases the resistance ('difficulty of electron flow' measured in ohms) and hence reduces the current. Adding cells (batteries are a series of 1.5V cells) increases the voltage ('push') and thus increases the current. Making a parallel circuit in which each bulb has its own supply from the battery increases the overall current, since there are more pathways through which electrons can flow.
Circuits can be represented using circuit diagrams, which can be used as a plan to construct new circuits	Circuit diagrams are a standard way of representing circuits, using a standard set of symbols and conventions to indicate connections. They have evolved to enable people all over the world to communicate electrical information precisely.

lives. There are, however, some communities who choose not to use high voltage mains electricity to remain a step removed from the wider world. An example is the Amish community who believe that only the use of electrical equipment that adds value to their community is to be embraced, so an electric iron would be acceptable. Some Jewish communities do not use electrical devices on Shabbat, but it is not always clear to the outsider if it is the electricity causing the automation or the task being undertaken which is not allowed. An example is the use of an electric lawnmower. It is not the fact that the mower is powered by electricity which inhibits its use but the mowing of the lawn itself which is forbidden. A manual lawnmower, therefore, would also be against the rules.

Oscar and the Bird: A Book about Electricity by Geoff Wring is an accessible way to introduce young children to electricity, including how to stay safe and different ways electricity is generated and stored. Oscar and the bird explore the machinery and environment they live in, identifying sources and the uses of electricity.

Readily available online and reasonably priced, 'energy sticks' can be used to engage children in thinking about electricity and circuits. Children stand in a circle holding hands to make a circuit. Two children hold the energy stick between them. If there is a complete circuit, the energy stick will be activated; they usually light up and buzz. When the circuit is broken, by two children letting go of each other's hands, the energy stick switches off. Different children can break and make the circuit at different points of the circle. Our bodies are good conductors of electricity due to the high levels of electrolytes they contain. The energy stick has a very low power cell so is safe for children to make a human circuit. This is also a good way to start the conversation about the flow of electricity being instantaneous and happening in all parts of the circuit at the same time. Links should also be made to the nature of our bodies as conductors of electricity and the health and safety rules around using electricity domestically and in school. We discuss this further in the classroom management section of this chapter.

It is becoming commonplace to see electric vehicles (EVs) on our roads as they become more widely available to consumers. Most, if not all, major car manufacturers across the world have at least one fully electric car in their range. Several automotive manufacturers have stopped the manufacturing of long running and popular models, explaining that they have decided to focus on new and innovative fully electric cars. It is usually the smaller models which have been stopped as they simply do not have the space for the driver, passengers and the batteries on the chassis and within the body work of the traditional smaller car design.

There are exciting developments too in the aviation industry with aeroplane manufacturers looking to develop fully electric passenger aeroplanes. In September 2022, an eight-passenger electric aeroplane, developed by an Israeli company, had its inaugural flight in the United States. Children can explore how this technology is developing using secondary sources. Questions that could prompt discussion, research and engage the children could be:

- Why can't electric aeroplanes fly as far as fossil fuel powered ones?
- Electric cars are cheaper to run than fossil fuelled ones. Would it be the same for electric aeroplanes?
- Which is heavier: an aeroplane with full tanks of aviation fuel or an aeroplane with batteries? Does this make any difference to the design and performance of an aeroplane?
- What are the current barriers to fully electric commercial passenger flights?

Another opportunity to make links with the children's lives beyond their classroom is through an exploration into alternative ways to generate the electricity much of the world relies on to function within modern society and simply live our lives. Are there wind turbines in the local area? Is the school on the coast and near an offshore wind farm? Do any of the class have solar panels on their roofs at home? There are strong links between geography and science when exploring the pros and cons of renewable energy. The use of books to engage children in their learning can often be a less threatening way to engage in complex real-world issues. The picture book *The Boy Who Harnessed the Wind* by Brian Mealer and Elizabeth Zunon (2012) is the true life story of a twelve-year-old boy who saved his village in Malawi by researching and building a wind turbine to generate electricity. It is also available as a novel by William Kamkwamba (the boy from the story) and Brian Mealer (2009) and a 'young reader' by William Kamkwamba and Brian Mealer (2019). The film adaptation directed by Chiwetel Ejiofor was released in 2019 by Netflix, and short clips could be used to inspire engineers in your class to invent and construct their own renewable energy generators.

Breaking down barriers

When learning about the scientists who were influential in our understanding of electricity, we should introduce the children to a diverse range of physicists, engineers and other scientists. Table 4.3.2 is not an exhaustive list but is intended as a place to start.

Activating children's learning

For young children, talking to them and observing what they do with components while they play with a torch or with wires, battery and bulb, is probably the most direct form of assessment used formatively. Questions that could be asked in this context include:

Table 4.3.2 Influential scientists in the field of electricity

Scientist	How they influenced our understanding of electricity
Alessandro Volta (1745–1827)	An Italian chemist and physicist who is credited as one of the first to invent the electric battery – the Voltaic Pile. He alternated discs of copper and zinc, with cardboard between, and soaked it all in brine (salt water) to create an electric current.
Thomas Edison (1847–1931)	An American inventor of many things that have greatly influenced the world: the first commercially practical lightbulb and the power station are most relevant to the topic of electricity. Some historians have suggested that Edison was home schooled by his mother as he found school challenging, due to ADHD and dyslexia.
Lewis Latimer (1848–1928)	Latimer was an American inventor whose parents escaped slavery. He was credited with several inventions. His work that has had the most impact on our lives is the improvements he made to lightbulb filaments.
Nikola Tesla (1856–1943)	A Croatian inventor, diagnosed with dyslexia, Tesla invented a coil which produced high voltage low amperage electricity. He contributed to the alternating current (AC) system that we use in our homes, schools and workplaces today. Elon Musk named his electric cars after Tesla.
Hedy Lamarr (1941–2000)	Lamarr was an Austrian-born film star and engineer. She held a patent on technology that is the foundation for advanced wireless networks and communications that we use today (e.g. Bluetooth and Wi-Fi).
Mária Telkes (1900–1995)	Known as the 'Sun Queen', Telkes was an Hungarian-American biophysicist and inventor who worked on solar energy. She collaborated with others to design the first house that generated both heat and electricity from the Sun and so was a pioneer of sustainable electricity.

- What things do we have in our classroom or at home which use a battery?
- What are the smallest/biggest electrical things you can think of?
- What is electricity like?
- Where does it come from?
- Can you name and describe some of the things in front of you?
- What materials are used to make the wire?
- Why are there metal pieces on the bulb-holder, battery and wire?
- What would happen if you took out the battery/loosened the wire?

A collection of torches, while offering rich evaluation potential for design and technology, can also be used to focus children's attention on the electrical concepts they embody:

- How do you make the torch switch on?
- What do you think it's got inside to make the light come out?
- Can you open the torch and tell me (or draw) what it's like inside?
- What are the batteries (cells) for? Why do you think some torches have more than one?
- Can you make the bulb (lamp) light outside the case?
- Can you use wires to make the bulb (lamp) light?
- What do you think the torch has inside instead of wires to complete the circuit? How do you think the switch works?
- What does the switch do to the circuit when you press it?

Teaching physics topics

Allen (2019) considers the common misconceptions children have about electricity and builds on the work of Osborne et al. (1991) to help teachers plan for engaging learning opportunities to identify whether children hold these alternative frameworks and to support their learning to address any identified misconceptions. Below are some of the common ideas about the nature of electricity Osborne et al. (1991) identified:

- Children linked their ideas about electricity to the (domestic) purposes it serves ('electricity comes out of the plug').
- It is strongly associated in children's minds with gas, heat or burning.
- Electricity is thought of as moving very fast.
- Children are generally aware of the uses and dangers of mains electricity but do not always associate it with batteries, which are seen as 'safe, because all the electricity is inside them'.

The source–sink model

In this common idea, the battery is seen as the 'source' of the electricity for the circuit, literally a store of electricity that is released down a wire and used up in the bulb (the 'sink' – think of electricity flowing down a plughole) (see Figure 4.3.1). It is easy to see where this misconception comes from: we commonly plug one flex into the wall (though it is actually composed of two or three strands of wire) and think of the electricity coming out of the socket and down into our appliance. We have electricity bills that invite us to pay for the electricity we have 'used' – surely the electricity in the battery must get used up in the same way, so they go 'flat'? The usual indicator for this concept is a drawing showing one wire connecting the battery to the bulb (a 'circuit' which clearly does not work if you try it, even though the child may have had to use two wires to make their bulb light up). Because in the source–sink model there is no need for a second wire to carry electricity back to the battery, children do not include it, introducing an inconsistency between their actions and the way they record them.

Figure 4.3.1 The 'source-sink' model.

Electricity

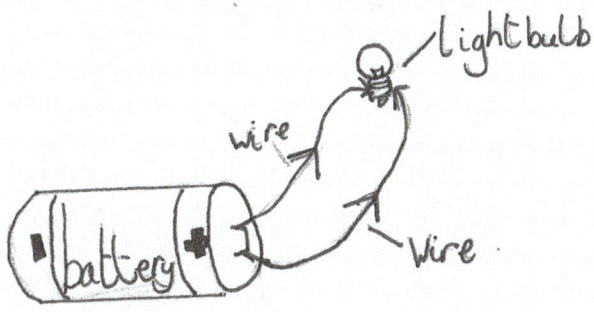

Figure 4.3.2 The 'clashing currents' model.

The clashing-currents model

Children holding this idea generally draw two wires connecting the battery and bulb, though the positioning of these on the correct terminals may be rather vague. If, however, we ask them to draw arrows to show the direction of flow of electricity in the wires, they tend to draw it flowing away from the battery towards the bulb in both cases (see Figure 4.3.2). If asked about what makes the bulb light, children with this model commonly refer to the two flows 'crashing together', likening it to the crashing together of clouds to make lightning and thunder. The clashing-currents model is really another version of the source–sink idea; children have often only added another wire because they've observed that the circuit would not work without one.

The consumption model

The consumption model contains a key feature common to scientific explanations of simple circuits – that the electricity flows in the same direction all the way round the circuit (see Figure 4.3.3). However, when asked to indicate using the size of arrows how much electricity is flowing

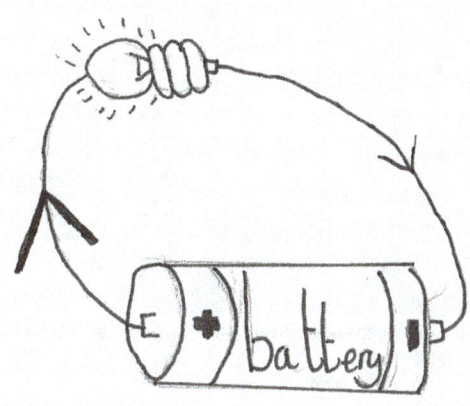

Figure 4.3.3 The 'consumption' model.

197

in different parts of the circuit, children holding this model tend to draw a bigger arrow 'upstream' of the bulb – the idea underlying this is that some of the electricity is 'consumed' by the bulb'.

Build

Constructing new knowledge

To support children to build new knowledge about electricity, teachers should be clear about the misconceptions and alternative frameworks the children have. Using children's annotated diagrams, observation of children exploring circuits and asking children carefully planned questions, teachers can elicit what knowledge the children have and plan how to either address misconceptions or build on sound understanding. Working scientifically is a good way to scaffold children's learning, help them to make connections to accurate scientific ideas and build new knowledge in line with current scientific thinking.

Working scientifically

When learning about electricity, children can group and classify materials into conductors and insulators. There are also opportunities for comparative and fair tests. Research using secondary sources can support children to learn about the mains electricity and the environmental impact of fossil fuel power stations. Children can also research about energy poverty and the impact it has on people's lives in the UK and around the world.

Grouping and classifying electrical appliances

A display of battery toys and other small mains appliances (not to be plugged in!) can be used for sorting activities; perhaps leading towards a Venn diagram using overlapping hoops for mains, battery and 'both' (for example a radio that can be plugged into the wall or used unplugged). When using Venn diagrams, it's always good to include objects that are cannot be categorised using the hoops, so include a 'wind-up' radio or toy. Children could also sort and classify torches, for example, in order of brightness (an opportunity for data-logging).

Exploring circuits

Supply children with sets of components to make circuits and then pose them with a range of challenges. They can complete them as a carousel, or you could direct groups to each task.

Using analogies to model current flow in a simple circuit

An analogy is a way of linking an idea or example from a different field, one that may be more familiar to the children, such as the flow of water through pipes. Powerful learning tools as they

Table 4.3.3 Electricity challenges

Challenge	Teaching and learning points to consider
Can you make the bulb light or buzzer sound?	Children could draw a working circuit and annotate it, explaining the purpose of different parts. Introduce vocabulary: ■ cell (a single 1.5 volt battery) ■ lamp (the bulb is actually the glass part – the whole component is called a lamp) ■ wire ■ connection Find as many ways as possible to break the circuit in preparation for Challenge 2.

(Continued)

Table 4.3.3 (Continued)	
Challenge	**Teaching and learning points to consider**
Can you find the fault in the circuit? Can you make a fault?	Suggestions for a 'fault' the teacher (or another child) could introduce to the circuit include: ■ ends of wire not bared ■ bulb/lamp not screwed in properly ■ blown bulb ■ flat battery/cell ■ two cells opposing each other ■ buzzer wrong way around
Can you make something with your circuit?	This is a good example of a design and technology activity used to apply children's understanding of circuits towards the end of a unit. Examples are a house with light, warning device, quiz board, novelty greetings card, steady-hand game.
Can you predict which of these circuits will work?	Provide the children with drawings of circuits, some with only one wire, some with both wires at the same end of cell, or same contact on bulb, some with open switches.
Can you make a circuit to test whether materials conduct electricity?	This is a comparative test. We could use this challenge to introduce some specialist vocabulary (e.g. open, closed, terminal, electrical insulator, electrical conductor). This could be followed by a session identifying conductors and insulators in electrical fittings (e.g. plugs, cable). Before they use their circuits to test conductivity, encourage children to make predictions such as an ordering of the materials from the 'best' to the 'worst' conductor. Encourage them to describe the evidence they will look for to support or challenge their predictions. Look for children's questions which are framed with both an independent and a dependent variable. Some questions may be framed with only a dependent variable (DV) (for example 'does the bulb light?') while some questions may not be expressed in a testable form. Identify which children are aware of the independent variable (IV) (kind of material) in this investigation.
Can you make a working switch?	A range of commercial and 'home-made' switches can be provided to stimulate children's ideas, together with materials such as aluminium foil, paper clips, lolly sticks and paper fasteners. Children could incorporate their switch into working models.
How many ways can you find to change the brightness of a lamp or the speed of a motor?	Some children will know that increasing the number of bulbs in a circuit has the effect of making each bulb individually less bright. Some may assume a difference in the brightness of two bulbs in the same circuit (indications of a consumption model, see above). Children may be aware of the effect of increasing the number of batteries but may be unsure about polarity (the way round you put the cells in series).
Can you find two different ways of lighting two lamps in one circuit?	This is an introduction to parallel and series circuits (covered in the national curriculum for England at KS3). Children can be shown how to record their circuits as diagrams with conventional symbols. They could relate this to discussing commercial circuit diagrams using examples from the home.
Can you control two lamps each with its own switch? What about one lamp using either of two switches? Any other combinations?	This is a classic problem-solving activity, and children can have great fun considering the circuit needed for, say, a stair light that needs to be switched from either end. Increasing the complexity of the scenario will provide extension and challenge in this area and will develop creative-thinking skills.

Teaching physics topics

are, all analogies carry a health warning. de Boo and Asoko (2001) remind us that children may not be familiar with the 'domain' from which the analogy is drawn. It is not much use likening an electric circuit to a central heating system unless you have a class full of plumbers' children. They may remember the event but not what it represents. Before selecting an analogy for use in your own teaching, ask yourself the following questions:

- Is it within children's experience?
- What do the components represent?
- What is not represented?
- What misconceptions does it challenge?
- What misconceptions might it reinforce?
- What are the other possible dangers of this analogy?

The rope or hoop analogy

Join two ends of a piece of rope to make a loop large enough for your class (or a group) to hold while standing in a circle (see Figure 4.3.4). This represents the 'electricity' (actually the electric charge carried by electrons) that is already present within the wire, and that starts to flow once the circuit is connected up to a source of energy. Most children hold the rope loosely, palm up, allowing it to slip through their fingers (warn them not to hold it too tightly to avoid rope burns). One child, representing the 'cell' passes the rope through their hands so that it moves around the circuit. Alternatively, a small group of say four children could hold a PE hoop, which has the advantage that it is easier to hold loosely and therefore less tempting for everyone to become the battery, which could then be confusing. This makes the point that the cell/battery gives the 'electricity that's already there' a 'push/pull' to get it moving around the circuit (strictly speaking it gives energy to the electric charge to produce a current or flow). One or more children can now grip the rope lightly (again, avoid rope burns) to represent components that place a 'load' on the circuit (e.g. lamps, buzzers, motors). They do not 'use up' the electric current – there's still just as much rope after it has passed through their fingers as before – but they do take energy from it (represented by the warming of their hands) because they 'resist' the flow. So we have within this analogy both a challenge to the source–sink, clashing-currents and consumption models, together with an introduction to the key electrical concepts of charge, voltage (the 'strength' of

Figure 4.3.4 The rope analogy.

the cell/battery in 'pushing/pulling' the charge around the circuit), current (the flow of charge) and resistance. Use your judgement and the age of children to decide how many (if any) of these terms to introduce.

The bicycle-chain analogy

This is very similar to the rope analogy. It introduces the notion of particles within the circuit so is probably more appropriate for older children. Turn a bicycle upside down (on a table if necessary for children to see) and rotate the pedals: these represent the cell/battery, giving energy to the charge (chain) in the circuit to flow (see Figure 4.3.5). You can liken the individual links of the chain to free electrons moving from atom to atom, though this may be pushing the analogy a bit far (the electrons are not actually joined together). The rear axle and wheel represent the load (lamp, buzzer or motor) and you can increase the resistance by applying the rear brake gently. This can be used to introduce the relationship between voltage, current and resistance: the more resistance, the less current (slower movement of chain) given that the voltage (push on the pedals) remains the same. You can also talk about how the electric current (movement of charged electrons) transfers or 'carries' energy from the cell/battery (pedals) to the lamp/buzzer/motor (rear wheel), though this may be beyond the conceptual development of some Year 6 pupils.

Feedback

Observing children and asking them questions provides clear opportunities for formative assessment opportunities. Asking children what they notice and why they constructed their circuit in a particular way can support teachers to elicit children's understanding.

Another assessment pedagogy that can be used is annotated drawings. Children can be asked to create drawings, either directly illustrating the components of the circuit or by using standard symbols in a circuit diagram. They then annotate their work to explain what is happening in their circuit at different points, for example, when the switch is open or closed, if they add a new component, why their circuit is not working. Feedback from the teacher or a peer can focus on the

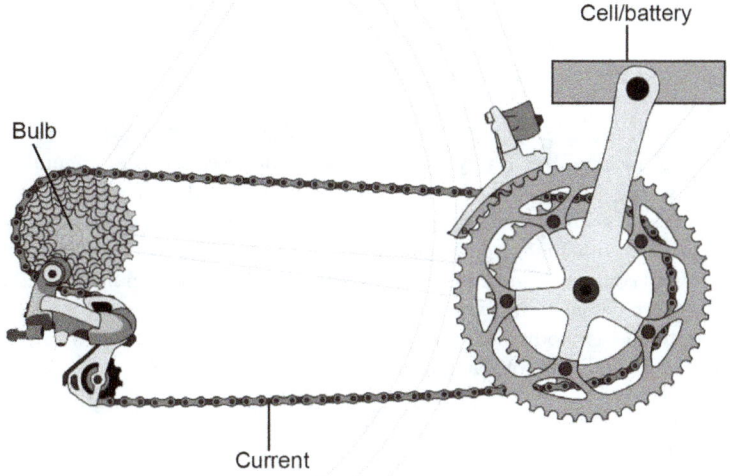

Figure 4.3.5 The bicycle-chain analogy.

Teaching physics topics

application of correct scientific understanding, the use of appropriate vocabulary and pose next step questions to support the thinking and progress of the children.

On the PSTT website there is a free resource 'The Big Questions' (PSTT 2019) which contains a set of images and questions together with ideas and possible misconceptions. The one relevant to electricity, 'Why are insulators as important as conductors?' challenges children to consider what would happen if we did not use insulators in our electric appliance and devices.

Consolidate

Retrieving and applying

As with other science topics, a good way for children to retrieve and apply their learning is through cross curricular learning experiences. Design and technology is a good subject to plan purposeful opportunities for children to retrieve and apply what they have learnt in science. Below are some examples we think are worth considering.

The Lighthouse Keeper's Lunch by Rhonda and David Armitage (2022)

This well-loved picture book has had a makeover to celebrate 45 years of the series of humorous stories about a lighthouse and its keeper. As a simple application of their knowledge about electricity, children can be tasked with creating the lighthouse and the light within. To add challenge, the children can be posed with the task of creating a motorised pulley system to deliver the lunch basket to the lighthouse keeper. How will they start and stop the pulley system? Can they control the speed so it can speed up to escape the hungry gulls?

Electric buggies

Once the children have mastered how to build a simple axle and chassis construction to create a buggy, can they add an electric motor to power their buggy? This can lead to races and adaptations to their buggies to improve aerodynamics and give them the advantage in a race. Can they create a track with hills and different surfaces for their buggies to traverse? Dataloggers and speed gates can be used to capture accurate timings of the races to create a league table.

Torch disassembly

Using concrete examples of everyday appliances (e.g. a torch), either through disassembly or designing and making, the 'reality' of design and technology can assist scientific concept formation. Most young children will have seen, and may have played with, a torch – the ability to shine a light where you want it is fascinating and seems like magic. Manufacturers have cashed in on this sense of wonder with a range of different styles, some based on cartoon characters and featuring various battery configurations and switch mechanisms. Once children have found out how a torch works, they can design their own, or think about another person's need for a controllable light. Of course, torches and other lights are not the only electrical appliances with which children are familiar, though they are probably the simplest.

Sustainable energy

Many of the gadgets children use during their leisure time (games consoles, computers, electronic toys, mobile phones, etc.) rely on electrical energy, so any of these could be used as a motivating starting point, but why not embed the study of electricity within a topic on sustainability? Thinking about how electricity is generated, distributed and transformed into storable sources of energy (e.g. chemical energy within batteries) could lead to a link with global warming – the burning of fossil fuels to generate electricity contributing to carbon dioxide emissions and hence the 'greenhouse effect'. Older children could explore alternative methods of generation (wind turbines, wave and tidal harnessing, solar panels, hydroelectric and geothermal sources), evaluating the environmental impact of each. The STEM Learning website has some great resources and ideas to support. The disposal of batteries is also an environmental issue. Household batteries contain a variety of chemicals including heavy metals (nickel, cadmium, mercury), which can pose serious environmental health hazards. By 2020, the UK was recycling 27 per cent of its batteries; approximately 40,000 tonnes of batteries were sold in 2020 but only approximately 18,000 tonnes were recycled (recyclingbins.co.uk 2023).

Children could investigate how much electricity is used by computers and tablets and consider ways to reduce the school's electricity bill. Energy use is one of the key environmental topics that schools are asked to investigate to achieve 'Eco-School' status. Eco-Schools report that some schools will spend four times more per pupil on energy than similar schools in the same region. The difference is often to do with how effectively schools manage their energy use.

Reviewing

As with all learning, it is important to give children the opportunity to review their learning about electricity. As the children engage in the activities we have described in this chapter and the others, you will be able to identify any misconceptions that still need to be addressed. As in previous chapters, we will use the TAPS Plan for Focussed Assessment of Science. The two examples below give good opportunities for children to apply their learning and for you and them to assess what they know and can do.

Does it conduct electricity? (Primary Science Teaching Trust 2023)

The context for this learning could be that soldiers, athletes and other sporting professionals wear 'smart' clothes which conduct electricity. For the military this is used to get power to mics, GPS and other electrical equipment needed. For sports professionals it is used to give feedback to their coaches to help improve performance. The TAPS lesson plan outlines the disciplinary (working scientifically) and substantive (concept context) knowledge that are the intended learning foci:

- Can children explain results and their conclusions?
- Can children recognise common conductors and insulators?

The context for the learning is that a soldier is stranded in the dessert with a ripped uniform, breaking the circuit to the GPS. The soldier has a pack containing a variety of objects which could be used to complete a circuit to activate the GPS. Children work in groups using the contents of the 'soldiers rucksack' to investigate if materials are conductors or insulators. Groups test by putting materials into a gap in a circuit with a bulb or buzzer, recording their results and explaining what they show.

Conductive dough (Primary Science Teaching Trust 2023)

The disciplinary and substantive knowledge that is the intended learning foci of this activity are:

- Can children use the conductive dough to make a circuit?
- Can the children systematically troubleshoot if something is not working?

Children make salt dough and then test to see if their dough is conductive by using a battery, wires, an LED and balls of dough to make a circuit. They could try different recipes and amounts of salt in their salt dough. In the plan the advice is to remind children that the electric current will take the path of least resistance, so they should check for shortcuts such as no gaps between the dough balls. Children could take photos or draw diagrams of different designs.

Reviewing is also about looking back on learning and supporting metacognition. In this topic, children may have had to be patient, to manage frustration when electric components didn't work, or persist with finding a break in an electric circuit. They may have been creative in applying their knowledge in designs. You might ask the children how those attributes might be useful to them in the future. Help children to see the potential for using their knowledge about electricity in their later lives. Ask whether they can see themselves as electricians, as kitchen designers or helping to fit solar panels.

Classroom management

One of the greatest barriers to effective teaching of electricity is resourcing: 'flat' batteries, 'blown' bulbs and loose connections can bedevil the most carefully planned lessons. Our recommendation is to buy the 4.5 V batteries (they are genuinely batteries consisting of three cells joined together), which have two copper strips (terminals) projecting from the top to facilitate easy connections. These have the advantage of being relatively long-lasting, and of 'driving' 3.5 V bulbs quite 'hard' so they are very bright. When you start making circuits with children, it is probably best to avoid crocodile clip leads and bulb-holders, lest the children come to believe that there is something magic in these components that makes the circuit work. They need to find the two terminal connections to a lamp themselves, before you introduce bulb-holders to facilitate easy connections, particularly if using crocodile clips. Older children will be able to make more permanent connections by using wire strippers to bare the ends of wire that can then be screwed into the bulb-holder terminals (so pliers/wire strippers and mini screwdrivers become very useful). Organise all your components into easy-access open trays, so children can collect and return the pieces they need and encourage them to dispose of non-working bits rather than putting them back for someone else to struggle with. You may need to check the numbers of components such as motors, counting them in at the end of each lesson.

Effective teaching of electricity – as of many other areas of science – depends upon the following factors (Summers et al. 1997):

- controlling the scope of the session by restricting teaching to those aspects of subject knowledge with which you feel comfortable (for example, not pushing analogies too far)
- controlling the content (try not to cover too much)
- getting the right mix between demonstration, explanation, exploration and investigation
- conceptual focus (trying to deal with only one concept per lesson)
- progressive development of ideas
- use of visual aids
- using a variety of approaches and contexts
- linking experiences and discussion closely
- making new ideas relevant
- timing (making time to discuss findings and new learning)

We also need to consider issues such as grouping, resourcing and health and safety. Electricity is one of the most overtly 'dangerous' of science topics, and it is worth starting each unit of work with a reminder of some basic rules for keeping safe. Children tend to know that electricity is dangerous; in discussion they might suggest that it can give a shock or kill. While they may know not to touch electrical appliances with wet hands, the dangers of long cables or pylons (e.g. when kite-flying) may be less familiar. Below are some safety tips for teachers to consider in planning a unit of work.

- Never use mains electricity (the types of power supply used in secondary science laboratories are not appropriate for primary).
- Never use rechargeable batteries (if 'short-circuited' – connected in a circuit without any other components – they may become so hot they burst into flames).
- Check bulb voltage ratings (if you connect a 1.5 V lamp to a 4.5 V battery it will become very hot and not last long).
- Do not use a mains plug as part of a display (it may be too tempting for children to plug into a socket).
- Any mains electrical appliance brought in (e.g. a hair dryer) needs to be checked for electrical safety by a qualified person – usually the school premises officer.
- Never cut open batteries (they contain chemicals which may irritate skin or eyes).
- 'Button' batteries could be demonstrated but are not suitable for use by small children (swallowing hazard).
- Dispose of batteries carefully and recycle them if possible.

Further safety information can be found in Be Safe! (ASE 2011). There is a danger of making children so nervous about electricity that they refuse to engage in practical activities, so you may need to reassure them at the beginning that the equipment is safe to use.

Summary

In this chapter we have considered some of the main conceptual and practical barriers to teaching about electricity effectively. We have examined some common alternative frameworks held by children and how to use assessment for formative purposes. We have suggested some cross-curricular contexts through which children can be introduced to this topic, promoting the potential for links with geography, literacy and design and technology by using everyday technology. We have considered progression in electrical skills and understanding, proposing a progressive sequence. We have explored the potential for making some of the abstract and difficult electrical concepts more concrete for children using analogies, while being aware of some of the potential pitfalls in this pedagogy. Finally, we have given some thought to appropriate uses of digital technologies and the safe organisation of classroom resources, to make our teaching of this topic as enjoyable, engaging and trouble-free as possible.

Discussion questions

1. What issues arise when constructing a progressive sequence of electrical concepts for children to be introduced to?
2. How well do the analogies described above correspond to a scientific model of electric circuits? What might be some of the dangers of this approach?

Further reading

Allen, M. (2019) *Misconceptions in Primary Science*. (3rd ed.), London: Open University Press.

Chambers, P. & Souter, N. (2020) Electricity, in Chamber, P. and Souter N. *Explaining Primary Science* (2nd ed.), London: SAGE, pp. 339–354.

These books are very helpful for developing your own understanding of electricity.

References

Association for Science Education (ASE) (2011) *Be Safe!: Health and Safety in School Science and Technology for Teachers of 3- to 12-year olds* (4th ed.), Hatfield: ASE.

de Boo, M. & Asoko, H. (2001) *Analogies and Illustrations: Representing Ideas in Primary Science*, Hatfield: ASE Publications.

DfE (2013) National Curriculum in England: Design and Technology Programmes of Study: Key Stages 1 and 2. https://assets.publishing.service.gov.uk/media/5a7ca43640f0b6629523adc1/PRIMARY_national_curriculum_-_Design_and_technology.pdf

Osborne, J. F., Black, P. J., Smith, M. & Meadows, J. (1991) *SPACE Research Report: Electricity*, Liverpool: Liverpool University Press.

Summers, M., Kruger, J. & Mant, J. (1997) *Teaching Electricity Effectively: A Research-Based Guide for Primary Science*, Hatfield: ASE.

The Primary Science Teaching Trust (2019) The Big Question, https://pstt.org.uk/resources/bright-ideas/?_sft_science_topics=space&_sft_activity_types=assessment

The Primary Science Teaching Trust (2023) Teacher Assessment in Primary Science (TAPS), https://pstt.org.uk/unique-resources/taps/?_sft_taps_topics=space-and-seasons

CHAPTER

4.4
Forces and magnets

Purpose of this chapter

After reading this chapter you will have:

- An understanding of how children's knowledge and understanding of forces (including magnetic forces) will develop from early childhood until the beginning of secondary education
- knowledge of research into children's ideas about forces and strategies for eliciting children's understanding
- knowledge of a range of appropriate activities to teach about forces through working scientifically and whole-class interactive teaching

Introduction

Through play, children become experts in understanding the basic principles of forces at a very young age. Many of us have seen children who have learnt that if they hold their food or eating utensil out to the side of their highchair and let go, it will fall and make an interesting noise and pattern on the floor. They have learnt that an object will continue to fall until it reaches another object to stop its acceleration – usually the floor. This is their introduction to the effects of gravity. As they learn to move around, they become experts in working with the pull of gravity on their bodies and how to control their movements in particular ways, so they do not fall over but move from A to B. As they grow, they use their knowledge of forces to help them play and improve at sports – making quick fire decisions about how hard to kick the football so it is passed to their teammate, how to strike the tennis ball with the racket softly enough for it to just go over the net – making it tricky for their opponent to return it. They learn that pushing their hands into dough can change its shape and that pulling it can stretch it more thinly. Children learn how to use forces to their advantage and accept that their actions can cause an effect.

As teachers, we need to understand how and when to teach children the science behind their play and how to use this foundational understanding to build on creating new understanding at a deeper level. We must address misconceptions that we uncover through our use of elicitation and other assessment pedagogies and use this information in a formative way so that children's understanding of forces can progress towards current scientific thinking. The skilled teacher will be able to do this by tapping into the excitement and sense of wonder the children had when the 'best thing in the world' was to be sat in your highchair and drop your spoon on the floor.

Forces can be a difficult area of science to teach for two reasons. The first is that forces seem a bit abstract – we cannot see, hear, smell or touch them. The second is that some ideas associated

Teaching physics topics

with forces can be tricky because they seem not to fit with 'common sense'; teachers may be concerned about their own knowledge and understanding. This chapter alerts you to some of these counter-intuitive bits of science and discusses the importance of contexts in making forces interesting and understandable. These contexts include water-play, toys and PE. It goes on to show how children can develop an understanding of forces appropriate to various phases of primary schooling through explorations and investigations. Part of the fascination of forces is that they are able to act over a distance without direct contact between objects – an example of this is magnetism, which tends to be grouped with forces in primary science, though its close relationship with electricity is emphasised from KS3 onwards. The chapter includes discussion of how whole-class interactive and dialogic teaching can support children's learning in this area.

Planning for progression

The key concepts to be taught at KS1 and KS2 are identified in Table 4.4.1, along with some notes to inform the teacher's understanding.

Teacher self-assessment questions

1. What is the difference between mass and weight?
2. What effects can forces have?
3. Does force always cause movement?
4. Give examples of forces that act through contact and those which act remotely.
5. What are the main similarities and differences between the forces of gravity and magnetism?

Table 4.4.1 Key concepts for teachers: forces

Key concept	Teachers' subject knowledge
All movement begins and ends with a force	Whenever something starts moving, speeds up, slows down, stops or changes direction, a force is involved. Forces can also change the shape of an object – this can be seen when a pull stretches an elastic band or a push squashes some clay.
Forces are pushes and pulls	A push, a shove, a twist, a jerk, a nudge – all these are words to describe a force – a push or a pull. As we twist something in both of our hands, we push with one hand and pull with the other.
When things speed up, slow down or change direction, there is a cause	Forces are invisible, although the causes and effects of forces can be seen. When an object is speeding up, a force is acting on it in the direction of motion; when it is slowing down a force is opposing motion. Changes in direction are caused by lateral (sideways) forces.
Gravity is a force	We experience gravity as a pull towards Earth. Gravity is a force of attraction (a pull) between all objects. Its strength depends on the masses of the objects and their distance apart. Since the Earth is a very massive object very close to us, in practice this is the only gravitational pull we experience. The size of the force of gravity on an object depends on its mass (the amount of matter in the object, measured in grams). A more massive object is pulled towards the Earth with a greater force. We call the size of this pull towards the Earth the object's weight (measured in Newtons) – so a more massive object weighs more in Earth's gravity. If gravity changes, weight changes. Imagine you could turn a knob and turn up gravity. If you did this, you would get heavier. If you could turn down gravity you would get lighter. If you stood on the Moon, which has only one-sixth of the Earth's mass and therefore one-sixth of its gravitational pull, you would only weigh one-sixth of your weight on Earth. Your mass would not have changed.

(Continued)

Table 4.4.1 (Continued)

Key concept	Teachers' subject knowledge
Friction is a force	Friction in solids is caused by an interaction between two surfaces. It is a force that slows objects and can also prevent them from moving. Friction increases with the speed of movement between the objects, e.g. the faster a car engine runs, the greater the friction between the moving parts.
Air resistance is a special name for friction between an object and air	Air resistance is caused by air 'rubbing' on an object moving through it. There is no air resistance on still objects in still air. Faster moving objects will experience greater air resistance (observe a dog with floppy ears with its head out of a car window – the faster the car goes, the more its ears will be pushed back). Children will begin to learn about the effects of air resistance and identify it in different contexts such as when running or cycling, and when dropping light objects such as spinners, parachutes and dandelion and sycamore seeds. Air resistance should be distinguished from wind – we can still experience air resistance cycling on a perfectly still day, although a headwind will tend to increase its effect. As objects fall they gather speed (accelerate) and the air resistance on them increases. In some situations, the air resistance (push) will come to balance their weight (pull) and the object will not fall any faster. This happens with parachutists. It does not mean parachutists float – it means that they will not accelerate past the point of balanced forces. This point is called terminal velocity.
When objects are pushed or pulled, an opposing force can be felt	When you sit in a chair, your body exerts a downward force on the chair and the chair exerts an upward force on your body to support you (otherwise you would fall through). These two forces are called action and reaction forces.
When objects float, forces are balanced	Water is displaced when an object is placed in it. The water then 'pushes up' objects in it (upthrust). If the weight of the water displaced is equal to the weight of the object, it will float. In other words, the upthrust is equal to the weight of the object. Some light objects that are denser than water (e.g. a needle) can be made to float because they rest on the 'skin' of the water (surface tension). The phenomenon of 'floating magnets' is caused by the repulsion force between the magnets balancing the weight of the upper magnet.
Force is measured in Newtons	Weight is expressed in Newtons (N). The weight of an object is calculated by the formula $W = m \times g$ (weight equals mass multiplied by gravitational field strength). This tells us that an object will not have any weight if it is not experiencing a pull of gravity. For most people, mass and weight will mean the same thing, as we are not likely to be in situations where a distinction is necessary. It is therefore unlikely a primary-aged child will grasp the distinction between mass and weight, but a teacher should be aware that mass is a measure of the amount of matter in an object. We express this in grams and kilograms.
Forces are represented by straight arrows	An arrow can be used to describe the size and direction of a force. The longer the arrow, the greater the magnitude of the force.
Magnetism is a force	You may find magnetism teamed with electricity in many textbooks as they are linked by the concept of 'electromagnetic' fields. In the science national curriculum for England, magnets (permanent magnets, to be precise) can be found in 'Forces' at KS2 because the most visible property of such a magnet is that it can exert a push or a pull on another magnet, or a pull on anything containing iron, nickel, cobalt, (steel due to its iron content) and some other rare metals. When a magnet pulls on such an object, it is said to be a force of 'attraction'. Magnets have two poles: north and south (strictly speaking, north-seeking and south-seeking). These are so named because the Earth is a huge magnet (it contains a spinning iron core) and all permanent magnets tend to align with its magnetic poles. The only true test of a magnet is that it will push away or repel another magnet if the two like poles are aligned: like poles repel and opposites attract.

Engage

Situating the topic

Children will have lots of experiences of forces during their early years through playing in the bath or the park; in fact, in any situation where they are making themselves or objects move, float or fall. They may have developed some language to describe forces – push, pull, twist, turn – and the effects of forces: go, stop, start, faster, slower. EYFS activities such as construction, play with vehicles, water-play and play with mouldable materials will have given them appropriate first-hand knowledge of forces and their effects. Although, unfortunately, the science topic of forces is not explicitly included in KS1 programme of study in the national curriculum for England (though the effects of forces on materials are mentioned), we believe that there is a need during this key stage to formalise some of the intuitive understanding gained during the EYFS and for children to begin to develop the big idea of 'forces' that brings all the earlier experiences together. It is not the time, however, to set aside those contexts in which children have learned about forces. It is much better to use experiences which children have found 'naturally' relevant and motivating. This bridging between play-based learning in the EYFS and the more formal learning of primary school needs to be done skilfully so children continue to see relevance and enjoyment in what they are asked to learn. We need to ensure that our teaching allows children to incorporate new ideas into their existing conceptual understanding, such as the realisation that when things speed up, slow down or change direction there is always a cause. Children should begin to distinguish between a push and a pull and recognise that forces can change the shape of some materials such as modelling clay. Always this conceptual understanding must be developed through working scientifically in appropriate contexts: investigations into their own bodies and movements, vehicles moving and rolling, objects floating and sinking, toys flying and falling.

At KS2 the national curriculum for England combines forces with the study of magnets (an example of forces acting over a distance with no direct contact). At Year 3 this includes being able to:

- compare how things move on different surfaces;
- notice that some forces need contact between two objects, but magnetic forces can act at a distance;
- observe how magnets attract or repel each other and attract some materials and not others;
- compare and group together a variety of everyday materials on the basis of whether they are attracted to a magnet, and identify some magnetic materials;
- describe magnets as having two poles;
- predict whether two magnets will attract or repel each other, depending on which poles are facing.

The focus shifts again in Year 5 away from magnets towards other types of force, such as gravity, and the effects of air resistance, water resistance and friction, that act between moving surfaces. There is an explicit link with design and technology in considering the role of forces in simple mechanisms, including levers, pulleys and gears, which allow a smaller force to have a greater effect. During this key stage, children may be able to understand science in new ways; they move from being rooted in the world of objects to the world of pictures and diagrams that can 'stand for' a real event. Some children will be able to think about forces as represented by numbers and measured in standard units (Newtons).

At KS3, children will move on to learn more about the relationships between speed, distance and time for moving objects, together with the idea of pressure as a force over a given surface area.

They will begin to use force arrows in diagrams, considering balanced and unbalanced forces; moment as the turning effect of a force; and the effects of forces in changing the shape of materials including the force-extension linear relation. Concepts relating to magnets gradually move away from forces and towards the link with electricity at KS3, including plotting magnetic fields with a compass; relating this to Earth's magnetism and navigation; and relating the magnetic effect of a current to electromagnets and motors.

Rhett Allain's *National Geographic Angry Birds Furious Forces!: The Physics at Play in the World's Most Popular Game* (2013) can be used as a hook to engage children in this science topic. There are also numerous non-fiction books for KS1 and KS2 children which are accessible; *Motion* by Darlene Stille (2004) is just one example. The picture book *The Boy Who Harnessed the Wind* by Brian Mealer and Elizabeth Zunon (2012), referred to in the previous chapter on electricity, is a good way to make links between forces and electricity.

Breaking down barriers

It is important to introduce children to a diverse range of scientists so that they can recognise and identify people like them who are working in this field. Two contemporary scientists who use their knowledge and understanding of forces in their daily lives are:

- Aprille Ericsson, PhD, Aerospace Engineer and Instrument Manager at NASA. She has made significant contributions towards NASA's projects gathering data about the Moon and the ice sheets on Greenland and Antarctica.
- Emma England, MEng, Handling Qualities Design Engineer for Airbus. She has worked on projects which include flight test aerodynamic modelling and was awarded the Best of British Engineering at the Semta Skills Awards in 2016.

When learning about forces, Galileo Galilei and Isaac Newton are often the 'go to' scientists whose ideas children can discuss. The image of Galileo dropping two equal sized balls of different mass from the tower of Pisa to prove that they accelerate at the same speed is intriguing and seems to go against what children perceive to be true. Surely, Aristotle's theory of gravity which states that objects fall at a speed proportional to their mass, is correct? The heavier the object the quicker it will fall? There is a useful YouTube clip from the BBC2 series *Human Universe* (2014) in which Professor Brian Cox demonstrates this phenomenon and the impact air resistance has on falling objects with a large surface area and low mass. Inside a vacuum chamber (initially with none of the air removed), an ostrich feather and bowling ball are dropped simultaneously from the same height. As expected, the bowling ball hits the floor first. The test is repeated once almost all the air is pumped out and a near vacuum is created. The bowling ball and feather accelerate and land together. The removal of (almost) all the air has eliminated the air resistance, so the only force acting on the falling objects is gravity. It really is a fascinating watch, even when you understand the science at play!

Activating children's learning

As force is such an abstract theme, it is not surprising that children and adults have misconceptions embedded within their schema about this area of physics. Allen (2019) dedicates two chapters to these misconceptions. Elicitation can be achieved by using a range of pedagogical approaches, including discussions of the children's play and planned learning experiences, drawing and writing (plus the use of arrows to represent forces, even though this is not required until KS3) and the discussion of concept cartoons (Naylor and Keogh 2000). For example, at the playground we could ask children questions such as:

- Can we see anyone pushing?
- Why did the seesaw go up and down?
- What did it feel like on the swing?

Children's ideas about forces are a very well researched area of science education. Key research reports have been published by Driver et al. (1985), Kruger et al. (1991), Russell et al. (1998) – the Science Processes and Concept Exploration (SPACE) project report – and built upon by Allen (2019). This body of research throws fascinating light on teachers' and children's misconceptions and alternative frameworks and some of these are outlined below. The first alternative idea to be aware of is that 'force' can have other meanings, and it is more likely that children know these meanings than the scientific one: for example 'he forced me to do it', 'I want to join the Air Force', 'may the Force be with you'. Driver et al. (1985) identified the main types of alternative ideas a teacher is likely to encounter:

- Forces are to do with living things, for example, the object is 'fighting against' gravity.
- Constant motion requires constant force, rather than recognising that an object will continue moving unless other forces (e.g. friction) slow or stop it.
- If an object is not moving, there are no forces acting on it, rather than seeing balanced forces keeping something static.

Kruger et al. (1991) added other groups of ideas, including:

- A force is contained within a moving object, for example, 'the force is in the ball' (a confusion between force and kinetic energy).

The research of Russell et al. (1998) and later work by Allen (2019) added further insights into children's thinking. They found, for example, that children believed that when an object is falling there is no visible cause so children will apply their prior knowledge to develop an alternative explanation: 'the air pushed it down' or 'the wind made it fall'. Children may not recognise cause and effect – saying for example 'it stopped because it slowed down' – or they may confuse effect with cause – 'the car made a push', 'the pedals made the bike move'. There seems to be a particular problem in recognising that a force is the cause of an object's slowing down; the push to start movement may be far more obvious than the forces causing the object to stop.

Build

Constructing new knowledge

The use of arrows to represent forces is a scientific convention which is now located in KS3 of the NC in England but may still be useful for children to learn in upper KS2. More generally, the representation of ideas plays an important part in developing scientific understanding. It was Bruner (1966) who first described the three modes of representation with which learners need to engage before full understanding is reached. The first mode is 'enactive' where representation, and thus learning, occurs through interactions with physical objects, the second is 'iconic' (for example, the use of pictures and diagrams) and the third is 'symbolic' where representation occurs in the abstract, justifying the need for pupils to describe/annotate the meaning behind the force arrows they draw. During KS2, when many children will be learning to represent the world in iconic and then symbolic ways, we can support them in doing this by focusing their attention on the 'iconic' conventions in science. Furthermore, we have already discussed how the teacher can use children's

Forces and magnets

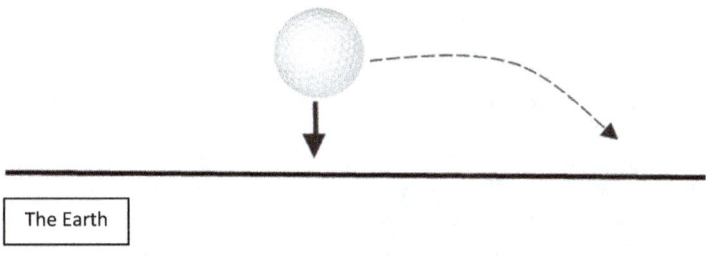

Figure 4.4.1 Which arrow is correctly showing the direction of the force of gravity, and which indicates the movement of this golf ball? (Note: Air resistance is not shown.)

drawings to gain insights into pupils' thinking and understanding. Consequently, teachers should help pupils to make their drawings and diagrams more scientifically accurate and complete by adding arrows and other annotations. It is important to note that arrows can actually mean many things in science, for example:

- direction of movement
- size or magnitude
- energy transfer in a food chain
- position or location of a feature

When forces are being described, however, an arrow represents the size and direction of a push or pull (Figure 4.4.1). It is very important to note at this stage that the arrow is describing the direction of the force, not necessarily the direction of movement of the object. In Figure 4.4.1 the dashed arrow has been used to describe the trajectory of the golf shot that has just been played. It is the solid arrow that correctly describes the force of gravity acting upon the ball. (Note that the force of air resistance opposing the motion of the ball has been omitted in this example.)

Working scientifically

When learning about forces, children can notice patterns, and group and classify objects relating to the way they fall, move or change shape when a force acts on them. There are opportunities for comparative and fair tests.

Swings and roundabouts – observation, sorting and classifying

Within the context of the playground, children should use their observation skills to identify apparatus that can be pushed or pulled, and that moves in different ways (e.g. goes up and down, round and round, back and forth). Children could be encouraged to make models of such apparatus with construction kits that reflect these types of movement. Photographs taken during the visit to the park could be sorted by the children using similar criteria and labelled accordingly. Children might make a comparison between, say, a swing and a slide, and identify how each is used differently and what happens: 'I climbed up the slide and went down fast but on the swing, I needed a push.' This kind of statement would show an understanding that a force (push) is needed to make something move, although the child does not recognise that gravity (pull) is acting on them in the case of the slide. If the children are asked to make some record of their findings, such as an annotated drawing of how they made the apparatus move, and to report on their findings to others, this will help to cement their learning.

Toys – fair test

It requires a good deal of planning – ideally by the children, supported by the teacher – to carry out a fair test of toys rolling down a slope. The suggestion about using collections of toys discussed earlier will have given the children the opportunity to explore a collection of toys. The next stage is to raise a question to investigate. Children might initially ask 'Which toy is the best?' which could be developed into 'Which toy goes the furthest?' With further guidance an investigable question such as 'Does the size of wheels (or weight of vehicle, or shape of vehicle) affect the distance that a toy rolls?' can be developed. Rolling two or three different toy cars down a slope seems a straight-forward way to answer the question, but is fraught with problems as the cars may differ in all sorts of ways – weight, diameter of wheel, width of wheel, length, shape, etc. To help children control variables a construction kit can be used, such as Lego, where test vehicles can be constructed that are nearly identical, apart from the factor under investigation. Keeping the slope fairly short will ensure more manageable measurements either in centimetres or non-standard units, although very short or shallow ramps will not give enough variation in the data to compare and contrast. This is another area where the teacher will need to help children in their investigation design. The investigation could be developed through different groups investigating different factors and reporting back to each other during a plenary session.

Floating and sinking – comparison

To understand the reason why objects float or sink, a number of subsidiary concepts need to be in place:

- some light objects sink and some heavy objects float
- water 'pushes up' objects in it (upthrust)
- objects 'light for their size' (with a density less than water) float and objects heavy for their size (with a density greater than water) will sink in water
- water is displaced when an object is placed in it
- if the weight of the water displaced is equal to the weight of the object, it will float

This suggests a sequence of comparison activities to help children develop their thinking rather than a fair test. The teacher will need to decide on activities which best address children's level of understanding. Such activities include:

- hanging objects from elastic bands or force meters, then lowering the object in water to demonstrate that objects weigh less in water
- measuring displacement by observing levels rise on a graduated tank or measuring jug
- using 'push-meters' to investigate how much force is needed to make floating things sink

Whose trainers have the most grip? – fair test

Young children can begin to understand the concept of friction, though they do not need to name it. Children will also come to realise that there can be a 'grip' between two surfaces, such as shoes and a floor. They will notice that different surfaces might be 'grippy' or slippery. Bumpy soles may be grippy, but water will make a floor slippery. Friction between solids is caused by an interaction of two surfaces. Imagine pushing a heavy box across the floor. A force will oppose this movement: this is friction. In some cases, friction will prevent movement from starting. A child may get stuck on a slide because the interaction between their coat and the dirty slide produces a frictional force equal to their weight due to gravity, so the child stays still. A clear demonstration of friction as a force between surfaces can be given by pulling the bristles of two hairbrushes against each other.

The interlocking bristles model the microscopic unevenness of any two surfaces acting against each other.

You might let children put sand, water, talc, hand cream or cooking oil on their hands to experience the reduction of friction by lubricants. Lubricants act by filling in those uneven surfaces so small particles that do not soak in or evaporate as the surfaces get hotter tend to work better, though even large objects such as marbles, rollers and wheels can be effective since they reduce the area of contact between the surfaces. A common idea held by children is that friction does not act on still objects. One experience that will help to challenge this is to set up a slope that can be slowly raised at one end. An object such as a coin is placed on the slope. As the slope is raised the coin will eventually slide down. Changing the material on the slope will help to show that friction can be changed to prevent or allow movement: higher angles can be reached with 'rougher' or 'stickier' surfaces. The key question is 'What stops the coin from moving?' This experience can be used to make effective links with the properties of materials.

How do we go about answering the question 'Which trainer provides most grip on the school hall floor?' The challenge arising with this investigation is that each shoe tested will vary in a number of ways. This will give children the opportunity to think creatively about how to control factors such as the size of the shoe, its mass and how a push or pull is applied and measured. Newton meters (which come in both pull and push varieties) will be required if children are to make measurements using standard units. If children have little experience of using newton meters, time will need to be spent on teaching them how to take accurate measurements. Once the children have had practice using the meters, then they will be more likely to make accurate measurements and understand what the numbers mean. Teaching points would include ensuring the scale and divisions are understood, and recognising inaccuracies can be minimised by taking a number of readings and being consistent about the point at which readings are made (for example, as the shoe begins to move). The data gained could be represented in graphical form. Children should be encouraged to use these graphs to point out patterns in the data, for example, 'The bumpier the sole of the trainer, the harder it was to pull.' They should also be able to relate this to scientific knowledge and understanding by statements such as, 'There was more friction between the bumpier sole and the ground, which stopped the shoe from moving', and to suggest improvements in their investigation.

Rolling bottles – comparative test

Children can observe and compare how 500ml plastic water bottles move down a ramp, when they contain different materials. We recommend that one set of bottles are filled with different volumes of water ranging from 0ml to 500ml. Another set of bottles (partially filled) contain equal volumes of water, sand, golden syrup and vegetable oil. Initially, the children roll each bottle of water in turn down a fixed ramp and compare how the bottles move and the distance they roll using standard or non-standard units. Questions about why some bottles roll further than others can be posed and discussed. Children should be encouraged to consider the forces acting on the rolling bottles. Questions such as 'How does the volume of water change the way the bottle rolls?' or 'Do the heavier bottles roll further? Why?' The second set of bottles can then be compared and the effects of friction, as well as gravity can be explored. It would be interesting ask the children to predict what might happen before the second set of bottles are tested.

Feedback

Observing children and asking them questions provides clear opportunities for formative assessment opportunities. As discussed in previous chapters, feedback in the moment is powerful in supporting children to make connections to their prior learning, current thinking and the accepted scientific explanation. The 'Odd one out' from the PSTT (2023) are a range of three images (or better still the actual objects) that can support teachers to identify misconceptions and the next steps in learning. Although these examples focus on the properties of materials, they can also be used to support the understanding of forces. The first can be with younger children. Three images of objects – sand, sawdust and paperclips – are presented to the children. The children are asked to identify the odd one out, stating their reason. To ensure the children are thinking about the properties of the materials in relation to forces, teachers should make this clear before showing the images. If children do not suggest the paperclips are attracted to a magnet so are the odd one out, teachers should ask the children to consider the properties of the materials. For older children the images (or objects) are aluminium (baking foil), copper (1 cent Euro coin or penny), gold (a ring) and iron (nails or tacks) could be used. Through careful listening and questioning the teacher can spot misconceptions and scaffold the children's learning to understand the correct scientific concept.

Consolidate

Retrieving and applying

As with other science topics, a good way for children to retrieve and apply their learning is through cross curricular learning experiences. Below are some ideas with clear links with other curriculum areas which can be used to support children to consolidate their learning within the theme of forces.

Visiting the playground

Many schools have on-site play equipment or are likely to be located near a play park with access to a slide, swings, a roundabout, seesaw and climbing frame (see the classroom management section for guidance on risk assessment). A pre-visit discussion will help children to think in terms of pushes, pulls, starting, stopping, speeding up, slowing down and changing direction when they are on the equipment. Perhaps organise one group to play while another group watches and get the children to describe what is happening: 'Karla is pushing the roundabout', 'Abdul is sliding down', 'Safia will fall down when they let go'. Take some photographs or videos of the children and discuss these afterwards. The topic provides opportunities for work in design and technology – the designing and making of play equipment as models or with large-scale construction kits.

Dance and gymnastics

Following a similar pattern to the last example – a short preliminary talk and a follow up – children can again be involved in learning about pushes and pulls on their own bodies. Working in pairs, children can co-operate to balance pushes or pulls – by leaning into each other or pulling away from each other to create body shapes and dance movements. When jumping and landing, the children can experience large and small pushes and their effects. There is even potential for talking about gripping (more friction) and slipping (less friction) in relation to appropriate shoes for gym, or when trying to hold on to a smooth bar. There is clearly potential to link with PE objectives. Children could also compose and perform music to accompany dance or gym routines.

Toys

Gather a collection of toys that can be pushed or pulled in some way. The best way to make such a collection is to ask children to bring in toys from home – simple toys such as those for toddlers, or wind-up toys are ideal. Avoid complex or battery-operated toys as these may confuse. The toys can be displayed and played with in the class and added to over a few days. Questions such as: How do we make the toy move? How do we make the toy stop? can begin to elicit children's understanding. The collection can be sorted into toys that are pushed, pulled or both. Other categories might be toys that can move fast, toys that can only go slowly, toys that float, toys that fly. Designing and making toys provides a motivating context for learning across the curriculum. The project could begin with some research (e.g. KS2 children observing and interviewing KS1 children). It could then proceed with some idea generation and trialling and conclude with manufacture of toys, marketing and evaluation.

Floating and sinking

As with the previous context, make a collection of objects on a theme – this time it could be toys that float, or things that float and sink. You could ask children to bring in groups of three items – one that will float, one that will sink and one that can float or sink. Initially, allow children to play and explore: can they make 'floaters' sink or vice versa? Introduce some challenging items such as very light objects that sink (for example, paper clips); objects that are heavy but float (for example, a large off-cut or log of wood); objects that are obviously very light for their size (for example, a balloon); and objects that can be made to float or sink (for example, a foil tray or a lump of modelling clay that can be made into a boat). There are opportunities here to link with mathematical understanding – measurements of capacity.

Stopping and starting

Bicycles are ideal props to stimulate thinking about forces. With due care and appropriate permission from parents and the head of school, ask some of the class to bring in bicycles to elicit a discussion about how a rider starts, stops and stays at a steady speed. You might extend this to other wheeled vehicles, perhaps by observing the reception class at play or a teacher's car as it starts and stops. This topic may be developed alongside a road-safety theme, asking Why do we wear seatbelts? Why do we wear cycle helmets? Why does a car skid in the rain? Another angle could be to look at air resistance on moving objects (aerodynamics). Running along with an open umbrella is a good way to demonstrate the forces involved, but may be hazardous – perhaps it is better to run with a large sheet of corrugated card or plastic. Cycling is seen as a 'green' way to get around. This assertion could form the basis of an investigation into the environmental effects of travel – carbon 'footprints', CO_2 emissions and atmospheric pollution. Children might be motivated to develop a campaign to encourage more pupils (and teachers) to cycle to school. They could also investigate the reasons why many people prefer to get in their cars.

Whose trainers have the most grip?

The work could begin with a look at a collection of shoes from a number of perspectives – their uses, materials, ways of fastening, construction. The focus could then move to asking questions about the collection, for example What sports could they be used for? What differences are there between the design of the sole? After the class has generated a list of questions, those that could be answered scientifically could be identified. Finally, those questions that would involve investigating friction are identified and refined – perhaps rephrasing them as Which trainers grip best on the school hall floor? or Will a shoe grip more if the sole is dry or wet? Such questions could lead to the planning and carrying out of a fair test.

Reviewing

As stated before, we believe it is essential to give children the opportunity to review their learning. As the children engage in the activities we have already described in this chapter and the ones

Teaching physics topics

below, you will be able to identify any misconceptions that need to be addressed. As in previous chapters, we will use the TAPS Plans for Focussed Assessment of Science. The examples below give good opportunities for children to apply their learning and for you and them to assess what they know and can do. There are many examples on the PSTT website for the topic of forces. We have chosen three, one from each age phase of primary but as with all of the TAPS Plan for Focussed Assessment of Science, each can be adapted to give further support or extension, meaning they can be adapted for other age ranges.

Testing the strength of magnets for 7–9-year-olds (PSTT 2023)

The disciplinary and substantive knowledge that is the intended learning foci of this activity are:

- Can children decide on an approach to compare magnet strength?
- Can children recognise and control variables where necessary?
- Some forces need contact between two objects but magnetic objects can act at a distance.

Children are given a range of magnets and other materials (both magnetic and non-magnetic) and asked to find ways to test whether all of the magnets have the same strength. As with all TAPS plans, questions to support discussion are included as are examples to support their investigations – testing then magnets through paper/card or layers of each, how close the magnet needs to be before it attracts a paper clip. As this assessment focuses on planning, the children can report their findings orally and the teacher can collect responses for the class, for example on a science working wall.

Spinners for 9–12-year-olds (PSTT 2023)

Making links to Emma England (see the breaking down barriers section above), the children will be aeronautical engineers. The assessment foci for this TAPS Focussed Assessment of science are:

- Can children systematically collect results?
- Can children improve accuracy by repeating measurements?

Children make and drop their spinners to gauge how they move through the air, consider what the variables could be and to formulate a question to be investigated. The examples given are 'How does the length of wing/number of paper clips/size of paper affect the time it takes to fall?' In groups, the children decide what apparatus they need to use, how they are going to record and collect their data and then discuss patterns and accuracy in results. The substantive knowledge that will be applied by the children is the effect of air resistance acting between moving surfaces – the air and the spinner.

Reviewing is also a time to help build children's 'science capital' (see section 1); we want children to see science as 'for me'. As a class you could review the topic and consider the skills and attributes that were developed. Ask question such as: when did you need to make careful measurements? can you think of any times you had come up with a good idea to solve a problem? There is a need for engineers of many different kinds and to become resilient to climate change. We will need many creative people who understand physics. Teachers can help children to see themselves using science in the future.

Classroom management

There will be occasions during the teaching of a sequence of learning about forces when the teacher wishes to teach the whole class through questioning, discussion or demonstration.

Whole-class dialogic teaching (Harlen with Qualter 2018), when the teacher is seeking to value as wide a range of children's ideas as possible can be used to good effect when exploring children's ideas about forces. The teacher helps the children to reason and test their ideas, rather than favouring the teacher's 'authoritative' version at the outset (which would close the discussion). Interactive whole-class teaching is not a return to a purely didactive pedagogical approach where the teacher transmits information to the learner from the front of the class, nor is it a 'question and answer' session where the teacher quizzes the children on their understanding nor even a demonstration session where the children are passive onlookers. We should see whole-class dialogic teaching as interactive and an opportunity to use a pedagogy which involves every child in the social learning of the whole group. It may take place during any part of the lesson, but any decision on how much to use this pedagogy is likely to be based partly on the age of the children – it should not be seen as a substitute for the hands-on experiential learning so vital to younger children. Perhaps the most important reason to use some of the pedagogies outlined below is that they will help to establish a culture of dialogue about scientific thinking in the classroom.

1. Provide children with a scenario to consider or a concept cartoon (Naylor and Keogh 2000) and three alternative points of view. For example, three children are watching a friend come down a playground slide. Child A says 'I think our friend will stop at the bottom because the slide levels out.' Child B says 'I think she will stop because of the rubbing between her coat and the slide', while Child C comments 'I think she will stop because the air stops her.' Ask the children to discuss with a partner the merits of each comment and what they think the explanation might be, then to share their choices and reasons with the whole group, perhaps by means of mini-whiteboards.

2. As part of a demonstration, ask children to make a prediction, for example 'Will this object float or sink?' Ask them to discuss with a partner, then make a prediction by holding up their mini-whiteboard with 'float' or 'sink' written on it. Older children could make a prediction in graph form to a question such as 'If we plotted the surface area of parachute against time taken to fall, what would the graph look like?' The teacher could then plan part of an investigation with the class using a 'Post-it planner' or a similar planning format in which children have to decide on:

   - a question that can be investigated (e.g. Whose trainers are best?)
   - variables to change (the independent variable) and keep the same (control)
   - a prediction
   - an explanation (hypothesis)

At each stage, ask the children to discuss their ideas with a partner and to record them as notes on a small white board or as notes pm a shared sheet of sugar paper. Then ask all groups to share their ideas by holding them up. The ideas are quickly collated and recorded by the teacher on a science working wall, for example.

Health and safety

There are few dangers associated with forces in the primary classroom. Several of the activities suggested in this chapter involve dropping things with the obvious risk to toes. Ensure children keep away from the drop zone, perhaps by cordoning off the area with a table, or by arranging a drop into a large cardboard box, which might also protect the floor. Floating and sinking activities will inevitably lead to a wet floor; the children need to know where to find the mop and how to clear up spillages. Further safety information can be found in Be Safe! (ASE 2011).

Summary

In this chapter we have argued that the conceptual difficulties in the topic of forces can more easily be overcome if the topic is taught through contexts that are familiar and motivating for children. A range of contextualised activities has been suggested. There is a wealth of research into children's ideas about forces, from which we have identified some clear teaching sequences. Concepts that prove more difficult to grasp and the alternative ideas held by learners are well known. Some of the 'trickier' forces concepts can safely be left for specialist teachers at KS3, although primary teachers will need to have a secure understanding of these ideas to avoid reinforcing children's misconceptions. Perhaps one of the best ways to ensure learning is through genuine opportunities for children to discuss their ideas while working scientifically with peers and teachers.

Discussion questions

1. The topic of forces has been removed from KS1 in the NC for England, and the representation of forces using arrows has been moved from KS2 into secondary education. What are the arguments for and against these changes?
2. What is an appropriate balance between 'working scientifically' and 'whole-class dialogic interactive teaching' in helping children to understand the concept of a force?

Further reading

Allen, M. (2019) *Misconceptions in Primary Science* (3rd ed.), London: Open University Press.

Chambers, P. & Souter, N. (2020) Forces, in Chamber, P. & Souter N., *Explaining Primary Science* (2nd ed.), London: SAGE, pp. 389–406.

Chambers, P. & Souter, N. (2020) Gravity and weight, in Chamber, P. & Souter N., *Explaining Primary Science* (2nd ed.), London: SAGE, pp. 407–424.

References

Allen, M. (2019) *Misconceptions in Primary Science*. (3rd ed.). London: Open University Press.

Association for Science Education (ASE) (2011) *Be Safe!: Health and Safety in School Science and Technology for Teachers of 3- to 12-year olds* (4th ed.), Hatfield: ASE.

BBC (2014) Human Universe, https://youtu.be/E43-CfukEgs?feature=shared

DfE (2013) National Curriculum in England: Design and Technology Programmes of Study: Key Stages 1 and 2. https://assets.publishing.service.gov.uk/media/5a7ca43640f0b6629523adc1/PRIMARY_national_curriculum_-_Design_and_technology.pdf

Driver, R., Guesne, E. & Tiberghien, A. (eds.) (1985) *Children's Ideas in Science*, Milton Keynes: Open University Press.

Harlen. W. with Qualter, A. (2018) *The Teaching of Science in Primary Schools*. (7th ed.), Abingdon: Routledge.

Kruger, C., Palacio, D. & Summers, M. (1991) *Understanding Forces: Understanding Science Concepts: Teacher Education Material for Primary School Science*, Oxford: Oxford University and Westminster College.

Osborne, J. F., Black, P.J., Smith, M. & Meadows, J. (1991) *SPACE Research Report: Electricity*, Liverpool: Liverpool University Press.

Russell, T., McGuigan, L. & Hughes, A. (1998) *Science Processes and Concept Exploration (SPACE) Project Research Report: Forces*, Liverpool: Liverpool University Press.

The Primary Science Teaching Trust (2019) Odd One Out, https://pstt.org.uk/resources/bright-ideas/?_sft_science_topics=forces&_sft_activity_types=assessment

The Primary Science Teaching Trust (2023) Teacher Assessment in Primary Science (TAPS), https://pstt.org.uk/unique-resources/taps/?_sft_taps_topics=space-and-seasons

SECTION 5
Supporting science across the school

Introduction

If children are to have the best science education during their primary years, then their school will need to have a co-ordinated approach to planning, pedagogy and assessment. The role of the subject leader is key in inspiring and supporting colleagues, together with identifying areas for development. Both senior leaders and classroom practitioners also play an important part in ensuring any initiative is implemented across a school. In this section we consider ways that the development of primary science can be promoted across and between schools.

We know that effective assessment can drive teaching and learning, so in Chapter 5.1 we will consider a whole school approach to assessment put forward by the Teacher Assessment in Primary Science (TAPS) project.

In Chapter 5.2, we will explore the important role of science subject leader in raising and maintaining the profile of science and how external agencies like the Primary Science Quality Mark can support this.

In Chapter 5.3, we will explore how science can be used to support transition into primary school and beyond into secondary education.

CHAPTER

5.1

A whole-school approach to assessment

Purpose of this chapter

After reading this you will have:

- Explored key concepts in assessment
- Become familiar with the Teacher Assessment in Primary Science (TAPS) approach
- Gained an understanding of how to actively involve pupils in assessment
- Reflected on the use of assessment for responsive teaching
- Considered the role of moderation

Why is teacher assessment important?

Assessment is the way we adapt our teaching to meet the needs of the children in our care. Assessment is a 'fundamental competency' that needs to be actively practised (DeLuca and Johnson 2017). Every interaction we have with children can potentially provide useful information that can help us to decide what to do next. Listening to children's talk, looking at their drawing, writing, making and the expressions on their faces can all help to make judgements about their level of understanding. Skilled practitioners may do this so quickly that it is often difficult to separate the processes; assessment can be an embedded part of teaching and learning within the classroom. Assessment information can also help us to plan ahead and to reflect on our teaching and the success of the learning experiences we are facilitating. Much of what is being described here could be termed formative assessment, so let us pause to consider different uses of assessment information.

A common way to think about assessment is whether the aim is formative or summative. The purpose of formative assessment is to find out about current understanding so that next steps can be formulated. Whilst summative assessment is aiming to summarise learning at the end of a topic or year, which might be used for reporting to parents, senior leaders or the next class teacher.

Many authors use the term 'Assessment for Learning' (AfL), when describing formative assessment since it emphasises that the endeavour is to support learning and is an integral part of classroom practice. The Assessment Reform Group defined AfL as: *'the process of seeking and interpreting evidence for use by learners and their teachers to decide where the learners are in their learning, where they need to go and how best to get there'* (ARG 2002, p. 2). A key point here is that it is a process, the assessment task is not the end of the story. In fact, more recent definitions strengthen the need to act upon the information, claiming that assessment can only be formative if the information gathered through assessment is used to advance further learning. For example:

> Assessment for learning (AfL) is a group of classroom practices that are utilised to help students in their learning and so bring about improvement in their achievement.
>
> (Harrison 2012, p. 142)

> An assessment functions formatively to the extent that evidence about student achievement is elicited, interpreted, and used by teachers, learners and their peers to make decisions about the next steps in instruction that are likely to be better, or better founded, than the decisions they would have made in the absence of that evidence.
>
> (Wiliam 2017, p. 43)

Also important is the active role of the learner. Self-assessment, identified by Black and Wiliam (1998) as an important facet of formative assessment, and has become increasingly centre stage as pupils are 'activated as owners of their own learning' (Wiliam 2017). This active role is in line with insights from cognitive science, which as discussed in the rest of the book, propose that the learner needs to actively engage with the information to be able to build connected schema.

The relationship between formative and summative assessment is not simply that one takes place during the school term and the other is at the end of term, or even, that one is good and the other is bad (since a focus on high stakes testing skews the curriculum). The line between the two is blurred when summative assessments are then used to inform later teaching, or when formative assessment outcomes are gathered to provide an ongoing record of progress. A particular activity or strategy is not formative or summative in itself, most can be used for either purpose and it is their use that decides their label. For example, a child's drawing of how shadows are made can be used formatively to decide on whether to explore shadow shape or size next, but it can also be used summatively to judge that the child has demonstrated understanding that a shadow is formed when light is blocked.

Teacher assessment is seen as a more valid way of assessing a practical subject like primary science because it can draw upon a wider range of pupil performance across a broader range of contexts than is possible if judgement relies solely on performance in one-off tasks (Gardner et al. 2010). This is an essential part of validity: to assess children's performance in science, not in something else, such as the ability to read the question or perform well in exam conditions. Teacher assessment can draw evidence from classroom practice to consider how knowledge, understanding and skills have been demonstrated in a range of situations and topics. This does, however, present a challenge to teachers in relation to manageability and to support this practical guidance is explored below.

The reliability of teacher assessment may be questioned because it is open to teacher bias and inconsistency (Black et al. 2011). For a summative judgement to be reliable there needs to be a shared understanding and agreement between teachers on what meeting any objective would 'look like' in terms of children's performance, either orally, in writing or by some other way of representing understanding and attainment. This agreement needs to happen within and between schools. Harlen (2007) argues that with moderation, teacher assessment can be reliable enough for the purposes of primary science.

An expert group convened by the Nuffield Foundation (2012) suggested that the same assessment evidence could be used for both formative and summative assessment purposes. They proposed a pyramid-shaped model of whole-school assessment whereby there is a foundation built of a range of rich formative information from everyday classroom activities which was progressively summarised for reporting purposes within and beyond the school. The Teacher Assessment in Primary Science (TAPS) project has operationalised this model into a school self-evaluation tool with examples of classroom practice at each layer (TAPS 2020). Figure 5.1.1 summarises the model. The arrow moving up through the model represents the flow of information gained from teacher assessment activity. At the base of the TAPS pyramid, the active pupils and responsive teaching layers are where evidence is generated through 'everyday' classroom activities such as those presented in sections 2, 3 and 4 of this book. The middle layer requires moderation and

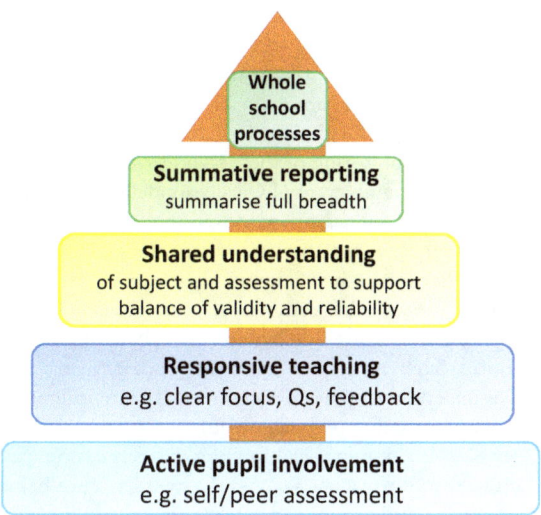

Figure 5.1.1 The Teacher Assessment in Primary Science (TAPS) 'formative to summative' pyramid.

shared understanding across the school; and the upper layers represent a distillation of a range of information for summative assessment. Examples of practice linked to each of the layers can be found on the TAPS pyramid website (https://taps.pstt.org.uk). We will use its structure here to explore practical ways to support a whole-school approach to assessment.

Assessment in practice

Active pupils

For pupils to be actively involved in assessing their own learning, they need to know the focus for the lesson and what it looks like to get better. Involving pupils in discussion of learning objectives and success criteria can support active pupil involvement and ownership of their learning. However, this does not mean that every piece of information needs to be shared at the beginning of the lesson, for example, to tell the children that they will be learning that *light travels in straight lines* might 'give the game away' if the intention is to initially explore children's ideas about how light travels. In this case, a more open objective like *to explore how light travels* might be appropriate at the start of the lesson, or a skills-focused learning objective could be *to draw conclusions from observations*. It is also possible that the learning within a lesson takes an unplanned trajectory and the teacher may decide that a different learning objective is more suitable. For example, a lesson about interpreting graphs may need to change if it becomes apparent through formative assessment that the pupils are unclear about using a thermometer to gather the data in the first place. For teachers to be flexible or responsive in this way, it is useful to have a sense of the sequence of learning objectives within the topic (for example, see Table 4.2.1). Whilst the children focus on the objective for the lesson, the teacher needs an overview of where the topic is leading and the progression of science skills. Each of our previous sections has outlined this progression for you.

To help children to consider how successful they have been in the lesson, it can be useful to develop success criteria. Such a list can be developed with the pupils by looking at a previous 'good' piece of work such as conclusion to an investigation or a labelled observational drawing, and identifying the features which make it successful. Such discussions about what it 'looks like' to succeed not only support a clear focus in the lesson, it also means that pupils are better equipped

> **BOX 5.1.1 SHAW PEER ASSESSMENT CASE STUDY**
>
> At Shaw Primary school there is a strong emphasis on speaking, listening and group work. The emphasis on talk, combined with a focus on self and peer assessment, points to the way pupils are involved in the monitoring of their own learning. For example, in a Year 5 (age 9–10) lesson on Space, the pupils were physically modelling the orbit of the Earth around the Sun using different sized balls. As they moved the 'Earth' they gave a commentary on what was happening, which was then peer-assessed for clarity and accuracy. The groups gave advice to each other for how to improve their explanation. The teacher emphasised that they should aim to use scientific vocabulary accurately, so the pupils listened out for the word 'orbit' in the explanations and watched to check that the Earth ball was moving whilst the Sun remained still. Such use of peer assessment appears manageable because it all takes place within the lesson, and the focus on accurate use of scientific vocabulary provides clear criteria for reliable teacher and pupil judgements.
>
> In a Year 4 (age 8–9) lesson pupils had found it difficult to construct branching identification keys for animals, so the teacher adapted the next lesson to begin with pupils making keys with sticky notes in small groups. After talk partners had formulated yes/no questions to divide the animals, pupils identified for themselves whether they felt confident in this activity or not, which the teacher then used to group them. Pupils were given time to look at others' work, being asked to pick out elements of a successful key before returning to improve their own key. This was a manageable way for the pupils to give and act on feedback, with the teacher noting on her plan pupils who 'stood out' – those who struggled and those who exceeded expectations. The class had constructed the success criteria for what constituted an effective branching key within the lesson, which supported reliability of pupil and teacher judgements as everyone now had a shared understanding.

to make *self or peer assessments*. This could take the form of highlighting where they have met the success criteria, identifying 'two stars and a wish', adding new learning to a 'thought-shower' display, or completing an exit card *'I used to think this and now I think this… because…'*. If the children are clear about how to make progress, then they can assess their own and others' learning. Further examples of peer assessment can be found in the Shaw case study (see Box 5.1.1).

Responsive teachers

Responsive or adaptive teaching requires action on assessment information. For teacher assessment to be formative, the information collected needs to be put to use: the teacher responds. Responsive teaching could involve adapting the pace, challenge or content of the lesson. For example, when the majority of a Year 6 class could make and adapt a circuit at the beginning of the term, then future lessons could challenge the children to apply their knowledge by making an electrical model (see chapter 4.3).

To be responsive in teaching, an important part of the lesson or sequence is the elicitation of current understanding, as discussed in section 1. Elicitation has the dual purpose of providing the teacher with information about the child's thinking, and supporting the child to consider what they already know (Ollerenshaw and Ritchie 1997), so it is also integral to self-assessment. There is a wide range of elicitation strategies, from observing children making circuits or sorting a collection, to recording ideas in a floor book or annotating a drawing (see Table 5.1.1).

We have explored the importance of talk and dialogue in section 1. A number of the elicitation strategies can be based around talk rather on the production of a written piece of work. As well as being arguably more immediate, accessible and reciprocal, talk also provides opportunities for

Table 5.1.1 Elicitation strategies

Elicitation strategy	Explanation
Observing a child	Observation is a powerful way of getting an insight into the ideas of young children: the way they handle objects, whether or not they show interest, what they can do alone or with help, what they do and for how long. Observing also includes listening carefully to what children are saying when they talk, in play or in groups.
Talk: questioning and discussion	Talking with children is perhaps one of the most obvious ways of finding out their ideas. This can be questioning individuals or groups, or holding a whole-class discussion. However, closed questions will reveal little more than whether or not children know certain facts. It is more productive to ask open person-centred questions: *What can you tell me about… ? Why do you think it does that… ? Can you give me another example of* that? Active listening by the teacher is vital so that the focus is on finding out what the child thinks, rather than asking leading questions to 'guess what is in the teacher's head'. Talk is discussed further below.
Sorting a collection	The ways in which children sort a collection of objects or pictures helps us to understand how their ideas are organised, and the kinds of mental categories that they have developed. This can be extended by asking children to sort in a different way, or add further objects to their groups.
Annotated drawing	Often a visual representation communicates an idea well. Annotating a drawing with labels or a few sentences to explain what it shows makes it even more helpful. This is not a formal 'diagram', but is a different way of representing the mental picture that a child holds. If a child's writing skills are limited, someone else can scribe their ideas on the drawing for them.
Floor books	Floor books got their name because they are books made out of large sheets of paper that an adult or children write on while sitting on the floor in a group. There are many possible variations on this format, but the important idea is that an adult (or child) records exactly what various children say, probably noting their name or initials. (This strategy is explored further below.)
Concept mapping	Concept mapping is a way of representing connections and relationships between different ideas. Key words are either given or generated by the children and are joined with lines. Phrases are written along the line to explain how the key words are linked.
Concept cartoons and other prompts for thinking	You can buy publications (Naylor and Keogh 2000, Naylor et al. 2004) containing cartoons in which a central problem is posed in the form of a cartoon, and the responses of different children are shown in speech bubbles around it. For example, one shows a drawing of a tub of ice cream that has just been taken out of the freezer and has droplets of moisture on the outside of the tub. The speech bubbles contain the children's suggestions about where the droplets have come from. They are very useful starting points for discussions, particularly with groups of children who are reluctant to express their own ideas or find it difficult to articulate them, as they can choose the idea that best matches their own. The BEST resources is also a growing bank of freely downloadable prompts to support exploration of children's ideas: https://www.stem.org.uk/primary/resources/collections/science/best-evidence-science-teaching

immediate feedback. Listening to an individual, group or a class, can be a productive way of eliciting ideas. By initiating open-ended questions where children need to draw on both their scientific knowledge and creative thinking skills, understanding can be revealed and shared. For example, discussing the implications of a life without friction reveals a lot about what the children understand. Concept cartoons (Naylor and Keogh 2000) also place discussion at the heart of the learning.

Such discussions can be recorded in a floor book or on a flipchart (electronic or paper), which can be used to record progress if contributions are named. Floor books (or other ways of publicly recording children's ideas) is a way of valuing children's ideas and can encourage children to 'open up' about their ideas. Such interactions can be time consuming, so it may be that a different group becomes the focus for each occasion. If the adult working with the group has been provided with key questions to stimulate the discussion, this can enhance consistency (therefore reliability) of data collection. The floor book will also contain an accurate record of the pupil utterances for review and evidence of learning.

Person-centred questioning (Harlen 2006) and dialogic talk have been recurring themes throughout this book as teachers strive to move away from the Interaction-Response-Evaluate triads discussed in section 1. Dialogic teaching in science often involves making shifts from talk as part of elicitation, where the aim is uncovering the child's thinking, to more scaffolded dialogue moving the learning forward by relating the child's ideas to a more scientific perspective. Alexander (2008) characterises dialogic talk as cumulative, with purposeful and deepening lines of enquiry as both the teacher and pupils build the learning together. In such interactions the teacher leads the discussion by responding to the pupils ideas or acts as 'chairperson' as children challenge each other. Sustained shared thinking (Siraj-Blatchford et al. 2002) similarly looks at building ideas together, but with perhaps a more even footing for children and adults. In all of these classifications of talk, every interaction can provide more information about the child's thinking which the teacher can respond to formatively either 'on the hoof' or in another lesson.

There is a danger at this point of feeling overwhelmed: how can a teacher respond to every interaction with every child, let alone the children who they have not been able to speak to in that lesson? This is where we return to a discussion of manageability: it is not possible for every interaction with every child to be dialogic or lead to sustained shared thinking. However, across the topic there will be different opportunities for discussion with different children and sometimes such discussions will happen between children or with other adults. Where such discussions lead to significant information about a child's learning, this can be noted on planning, in floor books or in children's workbooks. To decide whether the event is significant, the teacher will use their knowledge of the child and of curriculum progression, for it is not necessary or possible to record every interaction.

In summary, responsive teaching might involve responding to children's ideas through talk, planning or adjusting a specific learning activity or even deciding not to do something that was planned if the children are already secure with that concept. To be responsive, we must value and act upon children's ideas, but this may be at the level of the whole class, as we seek a general impression of how the lesson needs to be tweaked.

Focused assessment

Focus is a key word for assessment; this section began by noting its importance for learning objectives and success criteria. Lesson aims can also be maintained through focused recording and feedback. This is particularly the case for skill development, for example, if the aim is to develop conclusions that emerge from a discussion of data, then assessment should focus on the drawing of conclusions. This is a core principle of the TAPS Focused Assessment approach, to be clear about the focus for teacher attention and any pupil recording (McMahon 2018). It can be easy for a lesson to become diverted when problems arise around investigation planning or data gathering. Maintaining a focus, within the context of a whole enquiry, helps to manage the cognitive load of both the teacher and the pupils (Earle and McMahon 2022).

The TAPS focused assessment online database on the Primary Science Teaching Trust website contains plans for assessing an element of working scientifically within a conceptual context. The approach embeds assessment within classroom activities with the plans describing the activity, key questions and assessment indicators. Specific areas for children's development can be identified and subsequent teaching can take this into account, using the information for formative decision-making (Earle 2021). The focused assessments can also contribute to an ongoing summative record of children's attainment in scientific enquiry since any recording of children's learning is around the focused element. Ideally, the focused assessments should occur about two-thirds of the way through a topic – far enough that the children have had the opportunity to develop their understanding and skills, but allowing sufficient time to act on the assessment information. The discipline-specific examples are helpful because: *'many teachers find it difficult to translate generic principles into their own practice'* (Quinlan and Pitt 2021). The Focus4TAPS professional learning programme supports teachers to implement the TAPS principles and has been found to have a positive impact on pupil attainment (Mujtaba et al. 2022).

Moderation

So far the discussion has been very much based in the classroom, but it is only through the support of the subject leader that these approaches occur consistently across the school. We will return to the role of the subject leader in the next section, but first end this section with a brief discussion of moderation, which is one way to support a shared understanding of progression.

Moderation discussions, across Year groups, schools and clusters, support consistency of expectations and judgements, and can take many forms. Informal moderation could simply be a comparison of work with a colleague after a lesson to consider whether the children have 'got it'. More formal moderation could take place in a staff or network meeting, where work from different Year groups or schools is brought together to consider attainment and progression. Often work is compared to a set of criteria, like a National Curriculum; or work can be compared to publicly available exemplification material (for example the PLAN materials at www.planassessment.com). A non-threatening approach to moderation, which contained a clear focus on progression, was developed by a classroom teacher and is explained in our Moderation Graffiti Wall case study (see Box 5.1.2). Such moderation is less about checking that the assessment is 'right' and more about developing a whole-school understanding of progression in scientific enquiry.

BOX 5.1.2   WORLEBURY CASE STUDY: MODERATION GRAFFITI WALL

Worlebury St Paul's Primary used the TAPS school self-evaluation pyramid to explore their assessment processes. They were confident with the way they used formative assessment, for example, using a range of different ways to elicit children's understanding like concept cartoons or KWL grids (Know, Want to know, Learnt) and then using these to plan the topic. However, staff wanted to be sure that there was consistency in teacher assessment, and in particular in the reliability of their judgements for Working Scientifically.

In response, the subject leader, Kate Porter, ran a staff meeting to address the concerns about explicit teaching and assessment of Working Scientifically. The staff were asked to bring examples of enquiry work from each Year group and lay these along a roll of paper from Year 1 to Year 6. This enabled teachers to discuss skills progression and development of independence in investigations. Judgements regarding attainment were discussed in relation to statements in the National Curriculum. The teachers considered what it was about the work which signified whether the child was developing, secure or exceeding the objective. This helped to make explicit what progress looked like within the Year group, and the staff developed a more shared understanding of how Working Scientifically developed through the school. Staff commented on how supportive they had felt the process had been and how it was useful look at investigations from different classes which were recorded in different ways. It was agreed that there would be a whole school termly skills focus and that they would repeat the moderation activity later in the year to look at progression. The termly skill would define the focus for the teaching and recording, rather than recording the whole investigation each time, which meant more time for hands on science.

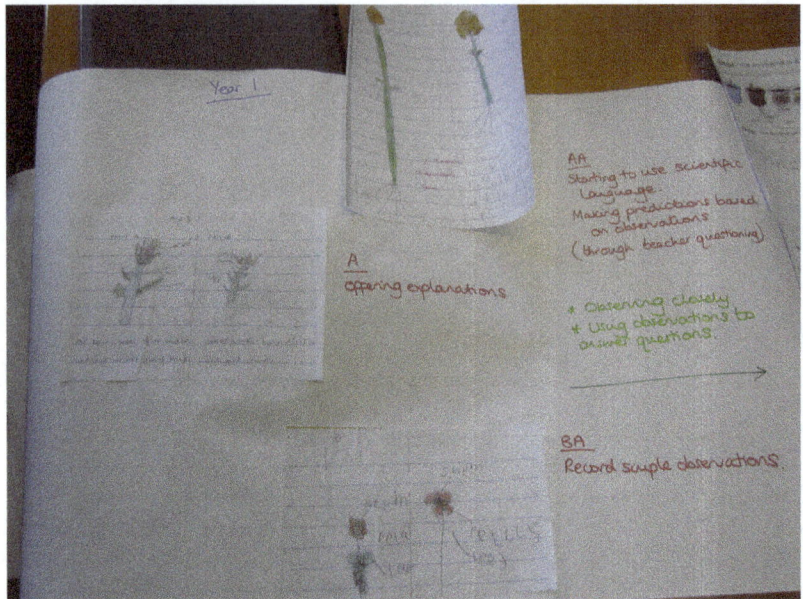

Figure 5.1.2 Staff created a moderation graffiti wall to consider progression from Y1 to Y6.

Summary

Teacher assessment which utilises a range of sources of information on children's learning has been put forward as a valid means of assessing primary science, although moderation discussions are needed for it to be reliable enough for the purposes of summative reporting. The Teacher Assessment in Primary Science (TAPS) project has developed a pyramid-shaped structure to inform school assessment processes and an online database of focused assessment plans and examples. Such examples include a wide range of strategies for elicitation, self and peer assessment. The importance of talk, active pupils and responsive teaching has been explored to enable assessment information to be used formatively to drive teaching and learning forward.

Discussion questions

1. Do you agree with Harlen (2007) that teacher assessment can be 'reliable enough'?
2. What is the purpose of self and peer assessment?
3. Which of the TAPS resources and assessment examples could you add to?

Further reading

The black box series of booklets give very user-friendly introductions to assessment:

Black, P. & Wiliam, D. (1998) *Inside the black box*. London: GL Assessment.

Black, P. & Harrison, C (2004) *Science inside the Black Box*. London: GL Assessment.

Harrison, C. & Howard, S. (2009) *Inside the Primary Black Box*. London: GL Assessment.

The Teacher Assessment in Primary Science (TAPS) project guidance documents, lesson plans and pupil work examples can all be found on the TAPS page of the PSTT website:

TAPS website https://pstt.org.uk/unique-resources/taps/

References

Alexander, R. (2008) *Towards Dialogic Teaching – Rethinking Classroom Talk*, Cambridge: Dialogos.

Assessment Reform Group (ARG) (2002). *Assessment for Learning: 10 Principles: Research-based Principles to Guide Classroom Practice*, Cambridge: University of Cambridge School of Education.

Black, P., C. Harrison, J. Hodgen, B. Marshall & N. Serret (2011) Can teachers' summative assessments produce dependable results and also enhance classroom learning? *Assessment in Education: Principles, Policy and Practice*, 18(4), 451–469.

Black, P. & Wiliam, D. (1998) *Inside the Black Box*, London: GL Assessment.

DeLuca, C. & Johnson, S. (2017) Developing assessment capable teachers in this age of accountability, *Assessment in Education: Principles, Policy & Practice*, 24(2), 121–126.

Earle, S. (2021) Formative decision-making in response to primary science classroom assessment: What to do next?, *Frontiers in Education*, (5) 584200.

Earle, S. & McMahon, K. (2022) *Cognitive Science and TAPS: Guidance from the Teacher Assessment in Primary Science (TAPS) Project*, Bristol: Primary Science Teaching Trust.

Gardner, J., Harlen, W., Hayward, L., Stobart, G. with Montgomery, M. (2010) *Developing Teacher Assessment*, Maidenhead: OUP.

Harlen, W. (2006) *Teaching, Learning and Assessing Science 5–12 (4th ed.)*, London: Sage.

Harlen, W. (2007*) Assessment of Learning*, London: Sage.

Harrison, C. (2012) Assessment for Learning: Classroom Practices That Engage a Formative Approach, in J. Oversby, (Ed), *ASE Guide to Research in Science Education*, Hatfield: ASE.

Mujtaba, T., Sheldrake, R., Hodgen, J. & Reiss, M. (2022) *Focus for Teacher Assessment of Primary Science (Focus4TAPS): Evaluation Report*, London: Education Endowment Foundation. https://educationendowmentfoundation.org.uk/projects-and-evaluation/projects/focus4taps

Naylor, S. & Keogh, B. (2000) *Concept Cartoons in Science Education*, Sandbach: Millgate House.

Naylor, S., Keogh, B. & Goldsworthy, A. (2004) *Active Assessment: Thinking, Learning and Assessment in Science*, London: David Fulton.

Nuffield Foundation (2012) *Developing Policy, Principles and Practice in Primary School Science Assessment*, London: Nuffield.

Ollerenshaw, C. & Ritchie, R. (1997) (2nd ed.) *Primary Science: Making It Work*, London: David Fulton.

Quinlan, K., & Pitt, E. (2021). Towards signature assessment and feedback practices: a taxonomy of discipline-specific elements of assessment for learning, *Assessment in Education: Principles, Policy & Practice* 28 (2): 191–207.

Siraj-Blatchford, I., Sylva, K., Muttock, S., Gilden, R. & Bell, D. (2002) *Researching Effective Pedagogy in the Early Years*, DfES Research Report 365. London: HMSO.

TAPS (2020) *TAPS Focused Assessment: Teacher Assessment in Primary Science (TAPS) support for Working Scientifically*, Bristol: Primary Science Teaching Trust.

Wiliam, D. (2017) *Embedded Formative Assessment* (2nd ed.), Bloomington: Solution Tree Press.

CHAPTER

5.2
Subject leadership

Purpose of the section

After reading this you will have:

- an understanding of how class teachers can be supported by science subject leaders
- considered the wider role of the subject leader
- become aware of further sources of support for science subject leaders

Introduction

The science subject leadership role within a primary school is an important one because it is their job to argue for science: to maintain its status as a core subject in the face of pressures for time and resources. The Wellcome Trust's state of the nation report noted that the 'passion' of the science lead was seen to be 'pivotal in raising and sustaining science's profile across the school' (CFE Research 2019, p. 2). This chapter aims to provide an overview of subject leader responsibilities and consider ways they could support class teachers. We will consider how teachers can work together with science subject leaders within their own schools to develop teaching and learning in science through dialogue and collaboration.

Sometimes the science subject leader in a school will have particular expertise in science and/or science teaching, perhaps through their own education or previous work, but more often the role is taken on by a generalist primary teacher who then develops their expertise in the area of science teaching. This is one reason why it would not be appropriate to see science subject leaders as a source of authoritative answers, but it is not the main reason. Just as children need to be actively involved to engage and build their learning, we see teachers as active learners, and argue that professional development is most likely to be successful when it is meaningful to the individual teachers concerned and when they are able to initiate changes themselves. Increasingly, professional development is recognised as part of a whole, as a community of practice or professional learning community (Admiraal et al. 2021). This complexity means that science leadership and professional development need to recognise the context within which they take place, to both select and effect change.

In section 1 we introduced the term 'dialogic teaching' to explore how teachers can work with children's ideas and encourage children to use talk productively with each other. The central idea here is that people will have different ideas and we need to find out what they are and use them to develop a better shared understanding. Dialogic discussions are: collective, reciprocal, supportive, cumulative and purposeful (Alexander 2008). This concept can be usefully applied to discussions between colleagues as they work together with the common purpose of improving the learning of children in their school.

From subject management to subject leadership

The first task of this section is to explain why we have chosen to use the term 'subject leader' rather than 'co-ordinator' which is the term used in many schools. The term 'co-ordinator' is often preferred because it implies a role in which one teacher supports colleagues in their work, without taking a position of power. The term 'leader' implies a sense of direction and purposefulness that the term 'co-ordinator' lacks; a co-ordinator keeps things ticking over smoothly, whereas a leader thinks strategically to take things forwards. The term 'leadership' can seem threatening if it is associated with hierarchy and telling others what to do. Alternatively, leadership can be viewed as distributed through a school, with colleagues taking on responsibility for leading different aspects of the school curriculum within an ethos of collaboration and culture of shared ownership.

Key areas of responsibility for a science subject leader are monitoring, management and the strategic direction of the subject (Bell and Ritchie 1999). These areas are exemplified in Table 5.2.1 and further explored below.

Management

The management role of the science subject leader is likely to be the first one that a class teacher encounters directly. The subject leader can provide help with locating existing planning documentation and resources. It might be helpful to discuss flexibility in planning, for example, to what extent are class teachers expected to follow existing medium-term planning and how can they introduce new ideas of their own and be responsive to the classes they are teaching. Science resources may be stored in classrooms or centrally and the science subject leader can explain procedures for borrowing and returning books and resources. They will be able to provide information on health and safety policies, although they may well need to direct teachers to further sources of information (see Be Safe, ASE 2011) to answer specific questions: the class teacher needs to take responsibility for making judgements about managing risks within the context of their own classroom.

Table 5.2.1 Key responsibilities of the science subject leader

Strategic direction	leading the development of a vision for science in the school
	promoting values, high expectations, inclusion
	action planning and writing policies
	organising staff development
	communication beyond immediate colleagues, e.g. governors, Ofsted, ASE
Monitoring	checking curriculum coverage
	collating and analysing data, e.g. pupil voice, learning walks, staff audit
	evaluating progress, e.g. implementation of new learning from training
Management	day-to-day support of colleagues
	ordering and storage of resources
	maintaining an overview of health and safety in science
	providing guidance for planning and record keeping for science, e.g. format and amount

Beyond being a source of information about school processes, it may be helpful to seek out the science subject leader to discuss planning ideas, perhaps for teaching a Year group that is unfamiliar, or to consider the pros and cons of different ways of introducing a new topic. As all teachers are very busy, asking others for their valuable time can sometimes seem like an unreasonable demand. However, colleagues coming forward with ideas and talking openly about the practice of teaching science actually helps the subject leader to monitor what is happening in classrooms and to maintain the profile of science. It contributes to a positive culture within a school in which teachers discuss how they are teaching to support children's learning. Of course, there are limits to available time, and subject leaders are not expected to do their colleagues' planning for them, but most will be only too pleased to discuss ideas with an interested colleague.

Beyond the immediate advice and support in getting started with teaching science in a school, the subject leader will be looking at the longer-term picture for science and it is part of their role to support colleagues in the development of their practice. Different ways in which this might happen are considered below.

Monitoring and mentoring

A key role for subject leaders is to monitor what is happening across the school. This could begin with mapping the science content being taught across the school to ensure coverage and progression. This is particularly important in schools where there is cross-curricular topic-based teaching since it may not be clear where science is taking place (Harlen 2006). Coverage or sequence maps are useful to share with all staff so that they know what has come before, or what will come after, which helps avoid repetition. When building a curriculum map for topics and Year groups, or for a rolling program where there are mixed age classes, it is also important to consider the development of Working scientifically knowledge and skills. Some schools choose to have a termly Working Scientifically focus to ensure that by the end of the year all skills have been covered. This does not mean that they only do part-investigations, it means that when carrying out a full investigation only part of it will be the focus for teaching and recording – read more about the focused assessment approach in chapter 5.1.

Once the subject leader has an idea of what is to be taught at different times across the school, there are a number of ways of checking how this is happening. For example: the subject leader could look at a sample of books (a work scrutiny) or planning; discuss these or other issues with pupils (pupil voice) or staff; or carry out a learning walk to look at displays or drop into science lessons. This information gathering will help the subject leader to determine how to develop their subject and whether it is a case of organising a science event to raise its profile, or planning some professional development of particular concepts or skills.

Subject leaders may have the opportunity to observe teachers in the classroom as part of 'monitoring'. Although this can be very valuable for all parties if it is well focused and everyone knows what the purpose of the observation is, and trusts that the information gained will be used constructively, it can still be an unsettling experience. Class teachers can regain some control of an unfocused 'monitoring' visit by asking in advance for the observation to concentrate on some specific aspects of what is going on in the classroom, providing them with some ownership of the experience (Porritt 2014). Arranging an exchange observation visit to the subject leader's class can help develop an approach in which two colleagues are discussing a matter of professional practice rather than one making an authoritative judgement on another. Likewise, team teaching provides opportunities for developing teaching together.

Approaches to working directly with an individual to support their development include coaching or mentoring. Coaching is focused on a specific aspect of a job, often involving ongoing feedback on the way an individual is carrying out a task and can be a collegial process between peers. In mentoring, one person is offering their expertise and experience to another, usually less experienced, colleague. In the context of a class teacher working with a science subject leader, either mentoring or coaching may be more appropriate, depending on the need that has been identified, and the relationship between the individuals.

The first step in making any change is identifying needs. This may sound straightforward and reflective practitioners will generally have a good sense of where their practice can be developed, but it may be that someone else might be able to contribute a further insight into what is happening and come up with different ways of addressing the situation. For example, a teacher might identify support for high attaining children as an area for development, but through discussion with a colleague about the issue may conclude that presenting starting points for scientific enquiries in a more open– ended way would benefit not only the high attainers, but the whole class. Or, a teacher may want to improve the children's use of scientific vocabulary, and the science subject leader may initially be at a loss for ideas, but after talking to another colleague who is responsible for English in the school, all three teachers work together on strategies to improve oral work in science and alternative forms of recording outcomes. Or, a teacher might decide they want to improve their questioning skills when they work with a group of children and ask the science subject leader to listen in so that they can reflect on it together later. In all of these cases the subject leader is likely to learn as much as the class teacher concerned. It is this sense of 'learning together' that is central to success.

Having analysed the situation, and planned some ways forward it is a good idea to consider how to identify whether changes in classroom practice have been made. Again, subject leaders might be very helpful in gathering evidence to review changes and give some feedback. Successes are best shared! Where things have not worked as hoped, discussion with colleagues can explore reasons and provide motivation to try something different. Fullan (2016) points out that having a clear sense of the particular change that should happen at the outset can actually present a barrier to productive development if it means that people are too rigid to listen and look at the evidence of what is really happening to everyone during a process of change.

Professional development within a staff team

Schools have to balance the development needs of individual teachers with maintaining a whole school approach to professional learning. This means that the priorities of one teacher are sometimes in line with the plans for whole school development but sometimes they are not, and so teachers need to take responsibility for identifying their own needs. The science subject leader will also want to take responsibility for their subject, working with staff to map out a vision and strategic direction for science in the school.

Personal change and development can come within a whole school focus for development, such as improving assessment, developing cross-curricular approaches or broadening children's reading. In these examples it is possible to see how there might be room to adjust the focus according to the interest of different teachers: e.g. assessment for learning in science, exploring links between science and art or investigating the use of poetry texts within science teaching. Professional development can also be very much tailored to an individual and their needs. This might involve going on external courses, but making use of the expertise and experience of colleagues within school is also a good option as they are able to give support over a longer period of time and have a good understanding of the context in which they are working.

Different ways in which science subject leaders can support colleagues include:

- Introducing ideas or inviting discussion at staff meetings
- Leading or arranging INSET (In Service Training) days
- Observing others teach and feeding back
- Having other teachers observe their teaching
- Team-teaching/teaching alongside colleagues

- Setting up working groups to focus on an issue
- Induction of new staff/trainees
- Informal discussions

The success of these strategies for change depends on the attitudes of and relationships between the people concerned. Staff meetings can be a time for issuing instructions or a forum for open discussions. There may be occasions when subject leaders are simply giving information or asking other teachers to carry out a task, perhaps completing a quick audit of resources in their room, or providing assessment information, but generally they are more productive if there is a dialogue between staff about an issue. By definition, the subject leader can't achieve a dialogue on their own and the thoughtful contributions of colleagues are vital. Differences between ideas can be constructive and creative. When taking part in discussions, as well as expressing your own ideas, there is a genuine opportunity to understand better those of others. It helps to develop a collaborative culture if all members of staff are aware of the wider roles and relationships of colleagues and support dialogues that are open and honest, but also caring and professional (Bell and Ritchie 1999).

Whole school INSET days will only provide lasting impact on teachers' practice if they find them relevant and are committed to implementing the changes.

> Educational change is a process of coming to grips with the multiple realities of people who are the main participants in implementing change.
>
> (Fullan 2016, p. 83)

Fullan's (2016) view of educational change means that it is not something that leaders in schools can plan for without being open to the ideas and experiences of all the people involved. Although leaders with a clear vision and sense of purpose can be powerful in leading change, they cannot do it alone. Fullan also stresses the importance of understanding cultural contexts of schools and how the people within them will respond to any innovations. This gives a valid reason for individuals to voice their ideas and take an active role in discussions about changes.

Subject leaders will need to consider how to 'bring staff on board' with new initiatives, for example, by basing the training around areas which have collectively been identified in previous discussions with colleagues or an audit of staff needs. Porritt (2014) describes the importance of collaboration, engagement, ownership and reflection for professional learning opportunities. One implication of this is the need to provide time for staff to reflect on what they will take from the training and where they will make changes in their classrooms.

Where the training focus is more of a 'top-down' initiative, then staff engagement is even more important. This could be achieved by making the initiative immediately relevant, for example, introduce a new strategy which they will try out in a Science Day later in the term. 'Putting knowledge to work' is an effective way of thinking about the impact of professional learning and development (Porritt 2014). The Education Endowment Foundation propose that implementation of professional learning should be viewed as a process, something that will take time for planning, executing and sustaining (EEF 2019).

The overriding focus for school development should be on supporting children's learning and the test for any investment in professional development is whether the outcomes will ultimately benefit the children. Guskey (2002) proposed five increasingly complex levels of professional development evaluation from participants' reactions and learning, to use of knowledge and student outcomes. For the planning of professional learning he suggests reversing the order:

> because the primary goal is to improve student learning outcomes, so planning must begin with clarifying those outcomes. This means we must plan backward, beginning where we want to end and then working our way back to the processes that will get us there.
>
> (Guskey 2014, p. 13)

Porritt (2014) also suggests that to demonstrate change and development in response to professional development activities, subject leaders should be clear about what they are trying to improve and collect baseline information to enable evaluation of impact. For example, when working towards the Primary Science Quality Mark (PSQM), subject leaders begin with a self-assessment against the PSQM criteria to consider current practice in the school, before creating and implementing an action plan, then finishing the year with reflections on the impact which changes have had for science in the school.

> **CASE STUDY: MONITORING AND PARENT INVOLVEMENT AT HOLT**
>
> Pauline Rodger, experienced science subject leader and PSTT Fellow from Holt Primary School, uses a range of monitoring techniques to find out about science across the school. For example, a scrutiny of pupil work accompanied by the relevant teacher planning can be used to identify areas for development, or evaluate the embeddedness of new initiatives like a push to record science differently, using more creative approaches. Other monitoring includes: curriculum walks to look at current topics accompanied by the link governor for science; informal 'drop-ins' to talk to staff or pupils; staff requests for clarification or support; and the occasional science-focused lesson observation.
>
> Whilst working towards the Primary Science Quality Mark, Pauline added a parent survey to her monitoring repertoire. She found that parents would like to find out more about science in the school and planned for a number of actions to address this. Science was included in parent events, for example, to the annual Christmas Fair was added a science stall for which the children made gifts along a changing materials theme: salt dough decorations, mixed wax candles, dyed baubles and pots of slime. Home learning was adapted to include details of the science covered in class and opportunities for practical science at home. Parents have been invited into school to support their children make rockets during science week and family teams were set catapult challenges on a Family Fun Evening. To evaluate whether these actions had had the desired effect, science books were sent home containing a feedback form for parents, whose responses indicated that they felt much more involved in their children's science learning.

Becoming a science subject leader

It is not obvious how to go about becoming a science subject leader. Sometimes job advertisements do include something about science subject leadership, but this is not common. The role is usually an internal appointment within a school, and a responsibility allocated by the head teacher. This means that the first step to becoming a subject leader for science is making your interest known in the school. This can be done in a professional way that does not threaten the position of the existing science subject leader, but is supportive, by offering to help out and perhaps 'shadowing' them to learn more about what the responsibility entails. It is worth taking up available opportunities to lead other subjects as there is much generic learning to be done about the leadership role and how to work with colleagues.

The desire to become a science subject leader, may be rooted in a passion for the subject, or perhaps having seen how positively children can respond to imaginative science lessons a teacher may want to share this with others. It can also be seen within a wider view of career development as a teaching professional in which supporting colleagues and leadership become increasingly important.

Support for subject leadership

Although most of this chapter has emphasised the opportunities for development that exist within school, there is a wide range of organisations that provide support for primary science. The following organisations may provide a starting point for exploring the available resources.

The Association for Science Education www.ase.org.uk

The Association for Science Education (ASE) is the national professional association for primary and secondary teachers of science in the UK. It offers conferences regionally and nationally and publishes a range of journals, teaching resources and books. Members can get involved in local and regional networks of other science educators, and this is a really good way of getting to know some key national people at a personal level. Nationally it also frequently advises the government on matters concerned with science education. The ASE is the awarding body for CSciTeach, or Chartered Science Teacher, which is a chartered designation in line with other awards, such as Chartered Accountant or Chartered Surveyor, that recognises the professional standing of an individual working in that field.

Primary Science Teaching Trust www.pstt.org.uk

The Primary Science Teaching Trust (PSTT) supports teachers and schools across the UK. It sponsors of the Primary Science Teacher Awards who then continue to be supported through the Primary Science Teacher College to develop science in their region. PSTT also supports groups of schools working together through the Cluster Programme and the research of Academic Collaborators. The website contains a range of resources from previous and ongoing projects, including the Teacher Assessment in Primary Science (TAPS) project.

Primary Science Quality Mark www.psqm.org.uk

The Primary Science Quality Mark (PSQM) is an award scheme to enable primary schools across the UK to evaluate, strengthen and celebrate their science provision. Across the course of a year schools can work towards PSQM, PSQM Gilt (for embedded leadership) or PSQM Outreach (for impact beyond the school). The PSQM programme is recommended by subject leaders, head teachers, Ofsted, the Royal Society and other members of the primary science community because of the way it raises the profile of science and supports systematic whole school development. The process consists of: auditing existing provision in science; creating and implementing an action plan to develop science teaching and learning; completing a reflective submission with key pieces of evidence to demonstrate the impact of their leadership.

STEM Learning www.stem.org.uk

STEM learning is a large organisation which provides both online and face-to-face professional development opportunities, including a database of resources for STEM subjects (science, technology, engineering and maths). Support is provided through the National STEM Learning Centre at York, a network of 28 Science Learning Partnerships across England and partners in Scotland (SSERC), Wales (Techniquest) and Northern Ireland. Many of the courses are eligible for additional funding so that your school may not need to pay the full price for training.

Hands-on science and technology centres

Around the country there are a large number of centres dedicated to developing the public understanding of science and technology. Some examples of science and discovery centres are: the Eden Project in Cornwall, the National Space Centre in Leicester, Stratosphere in Aberdeen, Centre for Alternative Technology in mid-Wales and Investigate in the London Natural History Museum. As well as being educational to visit, these centres often run sessions for teachers and have useful websites reporting on their latest projects.

Higher education

Many universities have outreach departments who lead knowledge exchange partnerships and engagement activities for children. For example, Bristol ChemLabs deliver science workshops to support widening participation in science. Some education faculties also run courses for primary teachers to support primary science or subject leadership. They may also be leading research projects locally and may be interested in hearing from local teachers who are keen to be involved with new initiatives.

The above is not an exhaustive list. For example, other notable groups include: the Great Science Share for Schools which is a national campaign to support children sharing science each year (greatscienceshare.org), the Ogden Trust help to set up partnerships for groups of schools (ogdentrust.com) and Explorify which provides a range of online activities to prompt science discussions (explorify.uk). The wide range of campaigns, organisations and resource banks demonstrates the interest and importance of primary science.

Summary

In this chapter we have considered ways in which class teachers might be supported in their work from science subject leaders in school. We have emphasised how a two-way, or dialogic relationship with the subject leader is more productive than seeing them as an authoritative source of information. This supports our view of the importance of developing a collaborative culture in schools in which colleagues learn together. Through discussion of this we have introduced a view of the roles of the subject leader and finally provided information about how this could be developed further.

Discussion questions

1. What opportunities can you identify (or create) for working with colleagues to develop science teaching in your school?
2. Which elements of your role are more subject management, and which are more subject leadership?
3. Which subject organisation is active in your area?

Further reading

Association for Science Education (2011) *Be Safe* (4th ed.), Hatfield: ASE.

This will support you to answer any health and safety queries.

Education Endowment Foundation (2019) *Putting Evidence to Work: A School's Guide to Implementation: Guidance Report*. London: EEF.

This report provides guidance and prompts to support thinking around the implementation of new initiatives in school.Education Endowment Foundation (2023) *Improving Primary Science Guidance Report*, London: EEF.

References

Admiraal, W., Schenkeb, W., De Jonga, L., Emmelotb, Y. & Sligteb, H. (2021) Schools as professional learning communities: what can schools do to support professional development of their teachers? *Professional Development in Education*, 47(4), 684–698.

Alexander, R. (2008) *Towards Dialogic Teaching – Rethinking Classroom Talk*, Cambridge: Dialogos.

ASE (2011) *Be Safe* (4th ed.), Hatfield: Association for Science Education.

Bell, D. & Ritchie, R. (1999) *Towards Effective Subject Leadership in the Primary School*, Buckingham: Open University Press.

CFE Research (2019) *Understanding the 'State of the Nation' Report of UK Primary Science Education: A Baseline Report for the Wellcome Trust*, London: Wellcome Trust.

Education Endowment Foundation (2019) *Putting Evidence to Work: A School's Guide to Implementation: Guidance Report*, London: EEF.

Fullan, M. (2016) *The New Meaning of Educational Change* (5th ed.), London: Routledge.

Guskey, T. (2002) Does it make a difference? Evaluating professional development, *Educational Leadership*, 59(6), 45–51.

Guskey, T (2014) Planning Professional Learning, *Educational Leadership*, 71(8), 10–16.

Harlen, W. (2006) *Teaching, Learning and Assessing Science 5–12 (4th ed.)*, London: Sage.

Porritt, V. (2014) Evaluating the impact of professional learning, in Crowley, S. (Ed) *Challenging Professional Learning*, Abingdon: Routledge.

CHAPTER 5.3

Transitions

Purpose of the chapter

After reading this you will have:

- Developed an understanding of potential barriers to successful transition
- Explored ways to support transition
- Considered the use of transition or bridging units

Introduction

Starting a new school can be a nerve-wracking experience for pupils and their parents (and for teachers too!). It feels a little like leaping into the unknown because we assume everything will be different, and this lack of continuity between phases is a main cause of anxiety. With different curricular, organisation, teaching approaches and environment, a pupil can very quickly feel lost in an unfamiliar world. Galton and McLellan (2018) studied transition across five decades and concluded that practice in England had regressed, due to an emphasis on performativity, more distributed intakes and increasingly decentralised academisation, leading to loss of local links.

Research consistently shows a dip in attainment and enthusiasm for science at the beginning of secondary school (Galton 2002; Royal Society 2010). A poorly managed transition can also affect wellbeing and mental health (van Rens et al. 2018). Braund (2016) cites repetition of work, a change in teaching and lack of use of information about prior experiences and attainment as causes for post-transfer regression. Increasingly, it is argued that children decide whether science is 'for them' at an early age (ASPIRES 2013; Nag Chowdhuri et al. 2022). So for science, such negative attitudes may lead to the low uptake of science in later years, which has been attributed to an 'engagement problem' (EEF 2018).

In this chapter there is not the space to fully cover all issues of transition, instead we will focus on those which specifically relate to science. Some authors separate discussions of transfer (between schools) and transition (between Key Stages and Year groups), but since the changes at the beginning and end of primary school usually include both, these terms will be used interchangeably within this chapter. Both transfer into and out of primary school will be discussed, with greater depth on the latter since Early Years transitions are covered more fully in our companion text (Davies et al. 2019). We will consider ways to potentially alleviate some of the transition anxiety, noting that such strategies can also stimulate effective professional learning for teachers who gain knowledge of other phases when working together on a smoother transfer.

Transition barriers

The reasons why children could find transition to a new phase or school difficult can be grouped into the following areas, which will be explored briefly below:

- Environment
- Relationships
- Pedagogy
- Curriculum
- Assessment

The school **environment** varies widely between different settings, but this can be more pronounced when considering different phases. Free-flow Early Years settings are vastly different from most Year 1 classrooms when more desks and chairs take over. Equally the all-purpose space of the primary classroom is in stark contrast to the secondary school science lab. These differences signify more than a change in furniture, they also signal a change in **pedagogy**. Whilst Early Years practitioners are likely to employ more play-based and child-initiated teaching approaches, primary school teachers make more use of whole class teaching and focused group activities. The exploration of Early Years, leads to the enquiries of primary, to the more content-driven experiments in secondary (Hoath and Shields 2015). The **curriculum** and **assessment** for each phase is quite different, with Early Years considering development towards Early Learning Goals using a range of ways to document learning; whilst the National Curriculum for England lists more content and end of Key Stage objectives. In earlier years science could be seen as Piagetian child-led practical exploration, by secondary school the body of scientific knowledge is more at the forefront with a focus on conceptual development and argumentation (Davies and McMahon 2011). Statutory revisions of curriculum and assessment arrangements for each phase happen at different times, which does not help with continuity, and practitioners may not be aware of new expectations for the phase which precedes or follows theirs.

Relationships with adults also change dramatically across this time: from the keyworker responsible for the whole child in the Early Years, to the primary teacher responsible for the academic achievement of the whole class, to the specialist secondary teacher who may only spend a couple of hours with the class each week. Relationships also become more distant for parents as daily contact is gradually replaced by written or electronic feedback. Smith (2011) argues that the Early Years practice of keyworkers could be utilised in supporting secondary transfer, with a key person tasked with building relationships with children and their parents.

Some would argue that many of these 'barriers' are necessary for pupils; discontinuity provides children with a reason to develop useful life skills to cope with change, together with the opportunity for a fresh start, so perhaps some 'planned discontinuity' is not all bad (Braund 2007, p. 921). Changing schools could be a time for growth; transition can be seen as an opportunity for development (Gale & Parker 2014). However, Howe (2019) questions whether 5- and 6-year-olds are really so different that they need different types of schooling, and perhaps the same could be argued for 11- and 12-year-olds. In addition, those born at the end of the school year cut off point (Summer-born in the UK, November/December elsewhere), are more likely to struggle with transitions and: *'the effects of transition could be cumulative – the legacy of a badly managed move early on could damage children's abilities to make successful transition throughout their school career'* (Alexander 2010, p. 370). As in most educational debates, solutions rely on a balance between enough change to enable the child to move forward, and not so much change that they feel lost. Next we will turn to strategies for smoothing transition.

Supporting transition

Improvements to transition are often framed in terms of the building of bridges (e.g. Howe and Richards 2011; Galton and McLellan 2018). These authors propose the development of five bridges:

- The **administrative bridge** is about developing a process for the transfer of information between schools, e.g. deciding what data will be transferred and when, providing information to parents.
- The **pastoral bridge** concerns the social and emotional needs of the child, e.g. stakeholder meetings, induction visits.
- The **curriculum bridge** is about balancing continuity and progression, e.g. curriculum mapping, subject visits.
- The **pedagogical bridge** concerns teaching strategies, e.g. meetings to discuss common strategies and language.
- The **student bridge** considers the point of view of the child, e.g. induction programmes, pupil voice at each stage.

The curriculum and pedagogy bridges are particularly relevant to science transition. For both of these, communication between settings is integral, for example, there could be: joint meetings to consider content and progression in the curriculum; moderation meetings to discuss expectations for pupil work; reciprocal school visits to see primary and secondary science in action; invitations to a science day or STEM event. Secondary science teachers may actively link with their primary feeders through initiatives such as Ogden Trust Partnerships (ogdentrust.com) or the Great Science Share for Schools (greatscienceshare.org). This list has so far only concerned the meeting or movement of teachers, but it is perhaps here that efforts may have more lasting impact, with long-term relationships being developed. If practitioners are able to meet and learn from each other about the pedagogy, curriculum and assessment in the other phase, then they are better equipped to support progression and smooth transition.

Transition activities for pupils need not be restricted to the entry and exit years. For example, many secondary schools invite Year 5 pupils (age 9–10) to a taster day. Although in some cases this may be an effort towards recruitment in advance of school applications, it can also give pupils a valuable experience of the look and feel of a secondary school. Often such days include subject tasters and the exciting experience of sitting in a lab and wearing a lab coat. Whilst it is important to make the experience a fun and interesting one, care also needs to be taken to avoid setting up false expectations that secondary science will always contain burning and explosions. Braund and Driver (2005) found that one of the reasons Year 6 pupils looked forward to secondary science was because they were expecting to use more equipment for more dangerous experiments, but it is an unreasonably high expectation for this to be the case in every lesson.

If previous experiences and attainment are to be understood and utilised by the receiving setting, there need to be discussions about content and progression. There needs to be a shared understanding of attainment for data passed to be meaningful (Davies and McMahon 2011). This goes beyond the passing of individual data regarding whether the pupil is meeting or not yet meeting the end of Key Stage statutory expectations. There needs to be an understanding of what the data means, particularly in a time of changing assessment practices. Perhaps a discussion of coverage is the simplest place to start, mapping out the topics covered in each year could avoid the annual growing of cress for example. Discussions about progression and development of skills can then follow, which could lead to involve moderation discussions, schools visits and lesson observations further down the line. Readers are directed to chapter 5.1 for a discussion of whole school approaches to assessment and to the Meadowbrook case study below to see how development of focused assessments can support a growing shared understanding between phases.

Transition projects

A transition or 'bridging unit' is one way to smooth transfer between settings. A topic or set of lessons begins in one setting and is continued in the next. For example, a nursery could begin a topic on dinosaurs with children collecting and exploring figures in different media, then the feeder Year 1 class can continue the theme by exploring where the dinosaurs lived or what they ate. In later primary the STAY project (Science Transition AstraZeneca York) produced a bridging unit on why Fizzy Drinks taste better cold, with the Year 6s exploring the drinks at different temperatures, whilst Year 7s investigated the heating rates of different coloured cans (Braund 2007).

This kind of collaboration is made much more difficult in areas where many settings feed into one, or where children from the Year 6 class scatter into a wide range of secondary schools. Watkins (2010) also raises the issue of those schools with mixed-age classes who may struggle to complete bridging units. Nevertheless, teachers are encouraged to make contact: the suggestion here is that any collaboration between settings can provide the opportunity for professional learning which feeds into a better understanding and ability to ameliorate transition issues. The increasing number of all-through schools could mean that transition between Key Stages becomes less of an issue, but that will only be the case if the dialogue between colleagues of different phases is maintained.

Galton (2002) found that transition units are not always as effective as hoped both because of timing and repetition. Teachers and pupils in Year 6 were less keen to complete projects after the intensive preparation for end of Key Stage assessments, especially if they were already doing transition units for English and Maths. There was also a question over repetition, by revisiting a topic which had previously introduced in primary school, pupils felt that they were repeating work. It appears that a revisiting of topics could support continuity, but if activities are too closely matched then the repetition is bad for motivation.

Whilst the STAY project provided bridging units to the schools, Davies and McMahon (2004) took a different approach by developing units with the teachers. They aimed to: *'construct a continuous curriculum experience in science across transfer, and engage primary and secondary teachers in dialogue concerning teaching styles and expectations of learners'* (p. 1010). The collaborative planning exercise included reciprocal teacher visits to science lessons to promote greater mutual understanding. Whilst productive for the teachers, there were some pupils who saw the unit as repetition of primary school learning and were keen to move on, they expected a degree of discontinuity as they passed from childhood into adolescence (Galton 2002, p. 262). Nevertheless the process of teachers collaboratively working together to develop the unit was found to develop teacher understanding of the other phase and paved the way for developing greater continuity in pedagogy.

The Primary Science Quality Mark recommends that links are made with secondary schools. Such mutually beneficial links can be made even when there is no organised transition project, for example, inviting secondary colleagues to a science day or asking to borrow their hall for a science event. Bianchi and Turford (2022) found that a key factor in supporting primary-secondary progression was to develop a common understanding of different types of vocabulary in science and strategies for teaching vocabulary. Such pedagogical approaches could be the kind of practical sharing of ideas which teachers gain by meeting and talking with colleagues.

> **CASE STUDY: TRANSITION AT MEADOWBROOK**
>
> Asima Qureshi, science subject leader at Meadowbrook primary school and the Olympus Academy Trust, developed a transition project to improve progression and continuity from Year 6 to Year 7. After using TAPS (Teacher Assessment in Primary Science) focused assessment activities for Working Scientifically with her Year 3 class, she set about using the structure to develop a set of activities which would promote collaboration between primary and secondary teachers in the Trust. The cross-curricular activities were based around 'Itch' by Simon Mayo, which tells of the explosive adventures of Itchingham Lofte, whose love of the periodic table has led him to become an 'element hunter'. This provided an opportunity to link the Chemistry of Year 7 to some new teaching in Year 6. Primary and secondary teachers met to plan the activities, taking a different Working Scientifically focus for each. The project provided a stimulus for professional dialogue and collaboration for the teachers involved.

Summary

School transfer or transition to a new phase of education can lead to a dip in enthusiasm and attainment in science as pupils struggle to understand a different environment and pedagogy. Where schools have not worked in partnership, there can also be the risk of curricular repetition as the feeder school starts from scratch, assuming nothing has come before. Such barriers can be broken down when settings work together to consider how the curriculum can provide progression for the pupil. Transition projects can help to smooth the transfer, but it is perhaps the developing professional partnerships which will bring the long-term rewards, rather than the specific activities themselves. Practitioners on both sides of the divide can learn a lot from discussions, meetings and visits, gaining both an understanding of their pupils' path, but also alternative ways of teaching. Communication and collaboration leads to continuity where what came before is not repeated, but built on.

Discussion questions

1. What links can you find between the primary and secondary science curriculum?
2. How could you develop communication between teachers on either side of a transfer divide?
3. What would help your pupils to develop a realistic expectation about secondary science?

Further reading

Galton, M. & McLellan, R. (2018). A transition Odyssey: pupils' experiences of transfer to secondary school across five decades, *Research Papers in Education*, 33(2), 255–277.

This article provides a review of the last five decades of research.

Howe, A. (2019) Moving on – transitions in Early Years science and technology, in Davies, D., Howe, A., Collier, C., Digby, R., Earle, S. & McMahon, K. (2019) *Teaching Science and Technology in the Early Years (3-7) (3rd ed)*, London: Routledge.

This chapter explores issues particular to transition from Early Years.

References

Alexander, R. (Ed) (2010) *Children, Their World, Their Education. Final Report and Recommendations of the Cambridge Primary Review*, Abingdon: Routledge.

ASPIRES (2013) *Aspires: Young People's Science and Career Aspirations, Age 10 –14*, Kings College.

Bianchi, L. & Turford, B. (2022) *Shining a Light on Inclusive Science Teaching and Learning (7-14 years)*, The University of Manchester.

Braund, M. (2007) 'Bridging work' and its role in improving progression and continuity: an example from science education, *British Educational Research Journal*, 33(6), 905–926.

Braund, M. (2016) Improving continuity and progression from primary to secondary science, *School Science Review*, 362, 19–26.

Braund, M. & Driver, M. (2005) Pupils' perceptions of practical science in primary and secondary school: implications for improving progression and continuity of learning, *Educational Research*, 47(1), 77–91.

Davies, D., Howe, A., Collier, C., Digby, R., Earle S. & McMahon, K. (2019) *Teaching Science and Design and Technology in the Early Years (3–7)* (3rd ed.), London: David Fulton.

Davies, D. & McMahon, K. (2004) A smooth trajectory: developing continuity and progression between primary and secondary science education through a jointly planned projectiles project, *International Journal of Science Education*, 26(8), 1009–1021.

Davies, D. & McMahon, K. (2011) Smoothing the trajectory: primary-secondary transfer issues in science education, in Howe, A. & Richards, V. (2011) *Bridging the Transition from Primary to Secondary School*, Abingdon: Routledge.

Education Endowment Foundation (EEF) (2018). *Improving Secondary Science: Guidance Report*, Education Endowment Foundation.

Gale, T. & Parker, S. (2014) Navigating change: a typology of student transition in higher education, *Studies in Higher Education*, 39(5), 734–753.

Galton, M. (2002) Continuity and progression in science teaching at key stages 2 and 3, *Cambridge Journal of Education*, 32(2) 249–265.

Galton, M. & McLellan, R. (2018). A transition Odyssey: pupils' experiences of transfer to secondary school across five decades, *Research Papers in Education*, 33(2), 255–277.

Hoath, L. & Shields, T (2015) Transitions in science education, in Dunne, M. & Peacock, A. (Ed), *Primary Science: A Guide to Teaching Practice* (2nd ed.), London: Sage.

Howe, A. (2019) Moving on – transitions in Early Years science and technology, in Davies, D., Howe, A., Collier, C., Digby, R., Earle, S. & McMahon, K. (2014) *Teaching Science and Technology in the Early Years (3-7)* (3rd ed.), London: Routledge.

Howe, A. & Richards, V. (2011) *Bridging the Transition from Primary to Secondary School*, Abingdon: Routledge.

Nag Chowdhuri, M., King, H. & Archer, L. (2022) The primary science capital teaching approach: building science engagement for social justice, *Journal of Emergent Science*, 23, 34–38.

Royal Society (2010) *Science and Mathematics Education, 5–14: A 'State of the Nation' Report*, London: The Royal Society.

Smith, H. (2011) The emotional impact of transfer: what can be learned from early years practice, in Howe, A. & Richards, V. (2011) *Bridging the Transition from Primary to Secondary School*, Abingdon: Routledge.

van Rens, M., Haelermans, C., Groot, W. & Maassen van den Brink, H. (2018). Facilitating a successful transition to secondary school: (how) does it work? a systematic literature review, *Adolescent Research Review* 3, 43–56.

Watkins, R. (2010) Primary-secondary transfer, *Primary Science*, 111, 33–34.

Index

Page numbers in italic indicate a figure and page numbers in bold indicate a table on the corresponding page

accuracy 35, 106, 218, 228
active environmental scientists 52
active pupils 227–228
adaptations 48, 51, 55, 61–62, 77, 152, 172, 175, 202
adaptive teaching 34
Aderin-Pocock, Maggie 159–160, 163
administrative bridge 245
adolescence 96, 105, 246
AfL *see* Assessment for Learning
Agyakwa, Pearl 122
air: effect on plant growth 81; fresheners 148–149; resistance 209–211, 213, 217–218
alcohol 94–96, 101, 111
al-Haytham, Ibn 179
alternative frameworks 8–9, 55, 102, 129, 132, 151, 159–160, 162, 164, 167, 191, 196, 198, 212
alternative ideas 23
animal life, diversity of 90
animal(s) 8, 12, 15, 24, 37, 43–44, 47–52, 54–56, 59–66, 70, 72, 80, 84, 120, 129–130, 144, 187, 228; approach to understand 90; bones 106; classification of 91–92, 99, 103; ethical and values-based questions to study 89–90; growth and reproduction 90; materials 120; parts of 89, 92; and plants 48, 51, 59, 61–63, 91; protected by law 66; relevance of 89
animals including humans, learning about 90; body functions 99–100, 103–104; body parts 99–100, 103–104; breaking down barriers to 98–99; classification of animals 99, 103; classroom management 111–113; foods 100, 104; growth and reproduction 102, 105; health and safety issues 112–113; key concepts for teachers **92–96**; KWL grids for 104; monitoring and feedback 110; orientation to topics 97–98; progression planning 91, 96; retrieval strategies 111; reviewing 111; scientific enquiry 105–110; secondary sources of information 102, 104; sensitive issues 111–112; staying alive and healthy 100–101, 104–105; using secondary sources and models 102

annotated drawings 101, 186, 201–202
'appropriation,' stages of 27
ARG Assessment Reform Group 225
Aristotle's theory of gravity 211
Armitage, David 202
Armitage, Rhonda 202
Armstrong, Neil 163
art and colour 187
art curriculum 75
ASE *see* Association for Science Education
assessment 4, 22, 25, 30–33, 63–64, 84, 110, 129, 172, 180, 194, 218, 230, 236, 244–246; electricity, learning about 201–202; and feedback 30–33; focus 172, 188, 218; focused 32–33; formative 32; forms of 30; importance of 30; indicators 33, 130, 172, 188, 230; information 33, 110, 225, 228, 238; as learning 30; pedagogies 170, 201, 207; planning sequences of lesson 31–33; processes 20, 30, 231; self/peer 31, 227; summative 225–227; teachers and pupils role in 31; whole-school 226
Assessment for Learning 30, 63, 225–226, 237
Assessment Reform Group 225
Association for Science Education 56, 64, 128, 146, 235, 246; cross curricular set of upper KS2 resources 99; guide to health and safety 64–65, 128
Attenborough, David 52, 77
attention 7, 11–12, 17, 19, 21, 23, 25, 33, 35, 52, 55, 86, 103, 111–112, 131, 212
attitudes and enthusiasms 5
attraction 140, 208–209
authoritative talk 13
automaticity 26

bacterial microbes 55
bag gardens 75
balanced diet 100–101
bar chart *108*
bath-time collection 121
batteries 157, 191–200, 203–204

249

Index

battitudes **62**
BBC Bitesize website 148
Bell, Jocelyn 163–164
Benerito, Ruth 144
bicycles 146, 217
Big Ben 183–184
'Big Questions, The' 202
biodegradability 144
biodegradable materials 61
biodegradation and microorganisms 55
biology/living things topics, learning about 43; adaptation 55, 61–62; application of 63–64; biodegradation 55; breaking down barriers of 52–53; classroom management 64–66; ecosystem surveys 58–60; environment and law 65–66; evolution 61–62; food chains 54–55, 60–61; food webs 60–61; inspirational scientists 52–53; key concepts for teachers **49–51**; living and non-living collection 53–54; microorganisms 55, 61; monitoring and feedback 63; needs of life 56–58; orientation to topics 51–52; outdoor education 51–52; progression planning 48–51; retrieval of 63–64; reviewing of 64; seasonal change 54
bio-plastic from waste potato peelings 153
birds' needs, understanding of 56
birdwatching 56
Black Botanists Week (event) 76
Black Gardener see Clarke, Danny
Black Marble project 179
body parts and functions: digestion 103–104; elicitation strategy 99–100, 103; 'multimodal' approach to explain 103; teeth 103–104
bones 94, 98, 100–101, 106, 112, 178
Boy Who Harnessed the Wind, The (Mealer & Zunon) 194
brain 4, 11–13, 19, 23, 25, 30, 92, 95, 100, 177–178; cells 11–12, 94; changes during interaction 13; interconnected networks in 11–12; pathways of connections across 12, *12*; processes for reasoning and memory 19; and spinal cord 92
brainwaves 13
bread, learning opportunities in making 143
breathing 15, 77, 93, 98, 100, 105
British Hen Welfare Trust 105
build element of EBC model: for animals including humans 102–110; for changing materials 146–152; for earth and space 165–171; for electricity 198–202; for forces 212–216; for light and sound 181–186; for materials 123–129; for plant biology 77–84; for primary science 22–25; *see also* EBC (Engage, Build, Consolidate) model
burning 146

carbon dioxide 15, 72, 77, 82, 91, 93, 95, 139, 142–143, 148–149, 163
Carroll diagrams 127
cartoons 151, 162, 167, 229
CASE *see* Cognitive Acceleration through Science Education
categoric variables 107–108
cave 178
Centre for Industry Education Collaboration 152
changes of state, contexts for exploring 143
changing materials, teaching about 139; addressing global issues 146–148; applying to current issues 152–153; change of water level 144; changing state 149–150; deforestation 144; formative assessment 145; global warming 144; key concepts **139–142**; material transformation 145–146; misconceptions, identifying 144; monitoring and feedback 151–152; orientation to topics 143; particles 150; progression planning 139–140; retrieval of 152; reviewing 153; scientific enquiry 150–151; seasonal change 144; solids, liquids and gases 148–149; for sustainable development 143–144
changing state 149–150
charts 10, 79, 101, 108, 122, 129, 172
chemical changes: contexts for exploring 143; of materials 146
chemical energy 157
chemistry 115
'child-centred' education 21
children's ideas 9–10, 13–14, 22–23, 69, 76–77, 89, 100–102, 123, 144–145, 151–153, 164–165, 199, 207, 212, 227, 229–230, 234; activation of 22; adaptation 55; body parts 99–100; building and rebuilding 23; challenges to 25; changing materials 144–145; classification of animals 99; condensation 144; constructing 22–23; dialogic talk to explore 13–17; eliciting 22; evaporation 144; food chains 54–55; global warming 144; growth and reproduction 102; health 100–101; living and non-living 53–54; materials 122–123; microorganisms and biodegradation 55; plants 76–77; reviewing 28; seasonal change 54; sorting of foods 100
chlorofluorocarbons (CFCS) 144
CIEC *see* Centre for Industry Education Collaboration
circuit diagrams 193, 201
citizenship 47, 53, 64, 89, 97, 143
Clarke, Danny 76
clashing-currents model 196–197
class discussion, science-based questions for 74
classroom 3–4, 10–11, 13–14, 18, 22, 33, 55–56, 60–61, 70, 75, 104–105, 112, 127, 130, 139, 143, 148, 150, 164, 167–168, 178, 180–183, 188, 194–195, 219, 225, 231, 235–236, 238, 244
classroom management 4, 64, 86, 111–113, 127, 172, 188, 204, 218; animals including humans 111–113; biology/living things topics 64–66; Earth and space 172–173; electricity 204–205; forces 218–219; health and safety issues 112–113; light and sound 188–189; plant topics 86; risk assessment 64–65; sensitive issues 111–112
classroom temperature 148

Index

clay modelling 164, 172, 210, 217
CLEAPSS *see* Consortium of Local Education Authorities for the Provision of Science Services
climate change 43, 47, 53, 63, 69, 84–85, 115, 138–139, 144, 145, 148, 163, 218
Cognitive Acceleration through Science Education 131–132
cognitive conflict 131, 133–135
cognitive overload 11, 29, 129, 164, 167
cognitive psychology 1, 8, 10–11, 25, 29
cognitive psychology and neuroscience 10–13
cognitive science 2, 10, 13, 226
cognitive science views of learning 10–13; connections between neurons 11–12; emotion 13; knowledge as interconnected networks 11–12; memory model 10–11; *see also* EBC (Engage, Build, Consolidate) model
Cole, Babette 105
collaboration 234–235, 238
collection of objects 121, 124, 127, 217, 229
colour: art and 187; observation 182
communication 13, 19, 52, 62, 175, 195, 245
communities 8, 18, 21, 23, 47, 50, 52, 56, 63, 69, 75, 83, 85, 90, 98, 122, 130, 192–193, 234; local 20–21, 85, 98, 122; professional learning 234
comparative tests 37, 118, 121, 123, 129, 138, 145, 151, 153, 184, 199, 215
compare and contrast 26, 27
concept cartoons 63, 77, 151–152, 151–153, 211, 219, 229, 231
concept map 101
concept mapping 229
concepts 7–9, 11, 17–19, 22, 26, 32, 34, 36–37, 48, 55, 60–62, 64, 70, 77, 82, 84, 117, 119, 124, 130, 135, 138, 144, 146, 148, 150, 159–161, 165, 171–172, 176, 196, 204, 209, 211, 214, 230, 235; abstract 90, 102–103, 157; biological 43–44; counter-intuitive 148, 171; substantive 32
conceptual development 35, 43, 201, 244
conceptual knowledge 102
conceptual learning 12
conceptual understanding 7, 17, 36, 43, 63, 91, 132, 176, 210
concrete preparation 131, 133–135
condensation 139, 141, 144, 149–150
conductive dough 203–204
conductivity 119–120, 123
consolidate element of EBC model: for animals including humans 111–113; for changing materials 152–153; for earth and space 171–172; for electricity 202–205; for forces 216–218; for light and sound 186–189; for materials 129–132; for plant biology 85–87; for primary science 25–28; *see also* EBC (Engage, Build, Consolidate) model
Consortium of Local Education Authorities for the Provision of Science Services 56
constructivism 8, 28–29, 28–30

constructivist learning 22
constructivist theories of learning 8–10
consumption model 197
content knowledge 8
continuous variables 108–110
corrosion 146
COVID-19 pandemic 90, 97
Cox, Brian 211
cross-curricular activities 186–187
cross-curricular contexts 20, 74, 118, 187
cross-curricular links 81, 97, 105, 130, 175
cross-curricular projects 74–75
cross-curricular work 27
cultural context for learning 9–10
culture 7, 14, 29, 70, 163, 219, 235
curriculum 6, 8, 10, 21, 31–32, 34, 36, 48, 74, 91, 96, 111, 121, 129, 199, 217, 226, 239, 244–245; and assessment 244–245; bridge 245; map 236; planning 37; post-primary 161; primary 35; progression 153, 230

dance and gymnastics 216
dark area, creating 178
darkrooms 188
data-handling skills 107
dataloggers/apps 60, 147–148, 149, 182–183, 202
Davies, Nicola 98
day and night and rotation of Earth 166
decaying 146
deforestation 144
Dehaene, Stanislas 30
Department for Education 7, 10, 34–35, 48, 91, 102, 105, 111–112, 118, 126–127, 139, 151, 160–161, 166, 176, 181, 192
dependent variable 146, 199, 219
Design and Technology 24, 75, 192, 195, 202, 210, 216
Designated Safeguarding Lead 112
DfE *see* Department for Education
dialogic approach 13–14, 16–17, 54, 129, 138, 151, 165, 180, 185, 230, 234
dialogic talk and learning in science 13–17, 230; case studies 14–17; 'IRE triads' 14
dialogic teaching 208
digestion 91, 95, 100, 103–104
digestive system 49, 92–93, 95, 110–111
digital images of plants 79–80
digital technologies 77
disciplinary knowledge 7–8, 36, 84, 110, 118, 126, 129, 152
discrete variables 108
domino game 125
dough 118, 141–143, 204, 207
drama 75, 83, 85, 129, 150, 153
DSL *see* Designated Safeguarding Lead
D&T *see* Design and Technology
DV *see* dependent variable

Index

Early Years Foundation Stage (EYFS) children 48, 91, 118, 122, 124, 126, 139, 160, 176, 210; learning about animals 91; learning about changing materials 139; learning about earth and space 160; learning about electricity 192; learning about forces 210; learning about light and sound 176; learning about materials 118; statutory framework for 91

ears 103, 105, 111, 157, 175, 177–178, 180, 183–184, 209

Earth 7, 24, 70, 98, 119, 141–142, 144, 157, 159–167, 169–174, 179, 208–209, 213, 228; orbit 162, 164, 170; rotation 160, 164, 168; surface 115, 119, 161–162, 167

Earth and space, learning about 157, 179, 185; apparent movement of Sun 168–169; breaking down barriers to 163–164; classroom management 172–173; day and night 166; dialogic approach 165; elicitation strategy 164–165; feedback 170–171; key concepts 157, 159, **161–162**; links with Religious Education 163; orientation to topics 162–163; phases of Moon 169–170; progression planning 160–161; questions to activate 164–165; retrieving and applying 171; reviewing 172; scientific enquiry 166–170; seasonal change 166–167; seasons, modelling 167–168; solar system 170

Earth Science Education Unit 131, 135

Earthwalks activities 48, 52, 56–58, 63; leaf matching 58; matching colours 57; nature mini-safari 58; nature palette 57; outdoor artwork 57; perfume potion 58; photo-quiz 58; pick and mix activity 57; skywalkers 57; sound symphony 58; Squirrels hide their nuts 56

Eatwell Guide 104

EBC (Engage, Build, Consolidate) model 18, 20; activating children's ideas 22; applying learning 27–28; breaking down barriers 21–22; build element of 19–23; consolidate element of 19, 25–28; constructing new knowledge 22–23; engage element of 19–22; monitoring and feedback 25; retrieval of learning 25–27; reviewing 28; situating the topic 21; Vygotskian constructivist approach 20; working scientifically 23–25; *see also* build element of EBC model; consolidate element of EBC model; engage element of EBC model

echoes, patterns with 184–185

ecosystems 44, 47–48, 50–52, 54–55, 58–63, 70, 90, 179

ecosystem surveys 58–60; ideas for 59, **59**; plant and animal identification 60; questions 58–59

Eden Project 70

education 8, 30, 47, 58, 75, 91, 117, 139, 163, 171; climate change 144; environmental 148, 153; primary 7, 18, 52, 91, 102, 126; secondary 47–48, 52, 91, 117, 138, 157, 191, 207, 223; for sustainable development 58, 143

educational neuroscience 1

Education Endowment Foundation 171, 176, 238

EEF *see* Education Endowment Foundation

Einstein, Albert 179

Ejiofor, Chiwetel 194

elaboration 14, 26

elasticity 120, 123

electrical concepts 191, 195, 200

electrical energy 157

electric buggies 202

electric circuit 13, 32, 200, 204; making 204, 228; parallel 192–193; series 193, 199; simple 37, 123, 192, 197–198

electricity 2, 37, 127, 130, 144, 157–158, 208–209, 211; alternative ways to generate 194; challenges **198–199**; common ideas about nature of 196; communities not using 193; definition of 192; effective teaching of 204; importance of 192–193; influential scientists in field of **195**

electricity, learning about 191; analogies to model current flow 198, 200; bicycle-chain analogy 201; breaking down barriers to 194; circuits, exploring 198; clashing-currents model 196–197; classroom management 204–205; consumption model 197; electrical appliance, grouping and classifying 198; feedback 201–202; key concepts for teachers **193**; misconceptions 196; orientation to topics 192–194; progression planning for 192; questioning 194–195; retrieving and applying 202–203; reviewing 203–204; rope or hoop analogy 200–201; scientific enquiry 198–201; source–sink model 196

electric passenger aeroplanes 194

electric vehicles (EVs) 194

elicitation 22, 32, 77, 99–100, 102, 165, 207, 211, 228, 230

elicitation strategies 22, 77–78, 99, 110, 128, 228–229, **229**; body parts 99–100; Earth and space 164–165; forces, learning about 211–212; growth and reproduction 102; light and sound 179–181; for plants 76–77; questioning 101; sorting of foods 100; staying alive and healthy 100–101

emotion 13

encounters with real animals 56

energy 7, 43, 49, 61, 71–73, 81, 92–94, 101, 104, 141, 143–144, 148, 150, 157–158, 161–162, 175, 177, 193, 200–201, 203; abstract concept of 157; chemical 43, 50, 157, 193, 203; electrical 157, 161, 202; forms of 157–158; kinetic 157, 212; solar 147, 195; source of 94, 175, 177, 192, 200; sticks 193; transfer 50, 55, 150, 157, 213; understanding of 43

engage element of EBC model: for animals including humans 97–102; for changing materials 143–145; for earth and space 162–165; for electricity 192–197; for forces 210–212; for light and sound 178–181; for materials 121–123; for plant biology 74–77; for primary science 21–22; *see also* EBC (Engage, Build, Consolidate) model

England, Emma 211

enquiries 23–25, 33, 35–38, 52, 74, 78, 83–84, 89–90, 102, 104, 110, 121–122, 126, 152, 182, 185, 230, 244
enquiry skills 32, 126, 191
environment 6, 8, 11–12, 14, 21, 25, 44, 47–48, 50–53, 55–59, 62–66, 70, 75, 85, 90, 92, 98, 103, 120, 122, 139, 163, 180, 187, 193, 243–244; natural 35, 43, 48, 51–52, 56, 105; physical 59–60
environmental impact 43, 47, 69, 121, 130, 138–139, 144, 145, 171, 198, 203
environmental measurements 60
environmental protection 63–64
environment and law 65–66
epistemic knowledge 8
Ericsson, Aprille 211
error feedback 25
ESEU *see* Earth Science Education Unit
evaporation 115, 139, 141–144, 150–152
evaporation and condensation 139, 141, 144, 150
'everyday knowledge' 13
everyday materials 118
evidence 1, 6–11, 15, 17, 23, 26, 28, 30, 35, 37, 58, 60, 63–64, 79, 92, 97, 102, 106, 110, 119, 148, 151, 168, 199, 226, 230, 237, 240
evidence-based practice 2
evolution 7, 25, 44, 47–48, 51, 61–63, 90, 92
exercise 44, 65, 89–91, 94, 97–98, 101, 108–109
experiential learning 75
explicit memories 11
exploration 24–25, 35, 47, 56, 69, 77, 106, 118, 121–122, 126–127, 148, 163, 167, 176, 191, 194, 204, 208, 244; and investigation 69, 204; open-ended 10, 100; simple 77; to systematic investigations 47
exploratory or epistemic play 8
Explorify website 63, 85, 123
eye colour 107–108
eyes 57, 60–62, 91, 103, 105, 111, 157, 175–177, 179, 188
EYFS children *see* Early Years Foundation Stage (EYFS) children

fair tests 16, 36–37, 60, 89, 106, 118, 119, 121, 122–123, 126, 128–129, 138, 145, 151, 152, 153, 181, 184, 198, 199, 213–214, 215, 217
feedback 3, 20, 25, 28, 30–31, 33, 63, 82, 84, 85, 86, 97, 110, 128–129, 131–132, 151–152, 170, 185–186, 201, 203, 215, 227–230, 236–237; biology/living things topics 63; changing materials 151–152; Earth and space 170–171; electricity 201–202; electricity, learning about 201–202; forces 215–216; light and sound 185–186; materials 128–129
first-hand exploration 77
first-hand observation 105–106
floating and sinking 217
floor books 76, 228–230
flowering plants 70–71, 73–74, 82–85
focused assessment 32–33

food 6, 13, 15–17, 23–25, 43–44, 49–50, 53, 55–56, 60–61, 69–75, 77–78, 81–83, 90–97, 100–101, 103–104, 115, 118, 122, 139, 207; chains 43–44, 48, 50–51, 54–55, 59–61, 60–61, 213; plants 83; social meanings attached to 101; sources 48–49; webs 44, 48, 50, 60
forces: of attraction 140, 208; balanced 209, 212; and electricity 157, 211; *vs.* energy 157; of gravity 208, 213; magnetic 207, 210; use of arrows to represent 212–213
forces, learning about 207; breaking down barriers to 211; classroom management 218–219; elicitation strategy 211–212; feedback 215–216; floating and sinking 214; friction 214–215; key concepts for teachers **208–209**; orientation to topics 210–211; progression planning for 208; retrieving and applying 216–217; reviewing 217–218; rolling bottles 215; scientific enquiry 213–215; swings and roundabouts 213; toys–fair test 214
formative assessment 3, 20, 22, 25, 30, 63, 82, 84, 99, 110, 128, 145, 164, 185, 225–227, 231; changes in materials 145; electricity, learning about 201–202; evidence for 226; forces 215–216; multimodal approaches 63, 84; and summative, relationship between 226
'formative to summative' model 31
fossil fuels 44, 50, 115, 119–121, 142, 161, 194, 203
friction 23, 209–210, 212, 214–217, 229
fruit 10, 26, 65, 70–72, 74–76, 83, 86, 94, 101; salad, making 75; and vegetables 75–76, 94, 101
funding 5

Galilei, Galileo 211
games, sorting and classifying 124–126
gases, learning about 148
germination 72, 81–82, 86
Glennie, Evelyn 179
global issues 47, 75, 146–147
global warming 144
Goldsworthy, Andy 57
Goodall, Jane 53
government regulation 5
graphs 59, 81, 107, 130, 185, 188, 215, 219
gravity 49, 73, 161, 207–211, 213–215
Green Chemistry 152
green-house effect: and hole in ozone layer 144; physical model to understand 147
Grenfell Garden of Peace 76
grids and carroll diagram 126
group discussions 33, 63, 101, 126
Grow2Know 76
'growth mindset' 19
gymnastics and dance 216

habitats 6, 8, 17, 24, 32, 44, 47–67, 55, 58–60, 70, 84–85, 103, 115, 139, 144
hands-on science and technology centres 241

Hawking, Stephen 159, 163
health 1, 4, 6, 34, 43–44, 52, 56, 64, 74, 94–95, 97, 100, 111–113, 139, 172, 183, 188, 191, 194, 235; aspects of 100; biological dimension 90; challenges to 90; importance of 90; needs, understanding 97
health and safety issues 111–112; animal materials 112–113; animals including humans 112–113; electricity 205; forces 219; internet usage 112; light and sound 188–189; materials change 146; teaching about plants 87
healthy diet 101, 104
heat 37, 43, 77, 119, 142, 146–147, 150, 157, 167, 182, 195–196
heat energy 117, 141, 149–150, 157, 161, 193
higher education 241
histogram 108–109, *109*
historical-based thinking 7
hot water for melting materials 146
houses and homes 187
human 12, 43, 51, 61, 72, 89–113, 130, 158, 160, 163; growth 102, 105; life cycle 105; relevance of 89; reproduction: children's ideas about 102; scientific study of 89; *see also* biology/living things topics, learning about
Human Connectome project 12
humans, learning about *see* animals including humans, learning about

illegal drugs, teaching about 111–112
implicit memories 11
inquiry-based instruction 29
inspirational scientists: for learning about animals 98–99; for learning about Earth and space 163–164; for learning about forces 211; for learning about light and sound 179; for learning about living things 52–53; for learning about materials 122; for learning about plants 75–76
interactive teaching 207
interactive whiteboard 101, 123
interdependence 8, 44, 47–48, 50
internet 29, 90, 112, 166–168, 184
Investigating Shadows 188

Jenner, Edward 98–99
Johnson, Katherine 163
judgements 7, 24, 30–31, 64, 95, 97, 201, 225–226, 231

Kamkwamba, William 194
keyhole gardens 75
Key Stage 1 (Early Years of primary school) children 48–49, 77, 81–82, 91, 118–119, 122–124, 126, 139, 144, 151, 160, 161, 176, 192, 208, 211, 217; learning about animals 91; learning about electricity 192; learning about forces 210; learning about light and sound 176–178; learning about materials 118
Key Stage 2 (Early Years of primary school) children 48–49, 70, 72, 77, 82, 91, 96, 119, 122–124, 131, 144, 148, 150, 160–161, 171, 176, 192, 208–212, 217; kinetic theory of matter 150; learning about changing materials 139, 144, 148; learning about earth and space 160; learning about electricity 192; learning about forces 139, 144, 210–211; learning about light and sound 176–178; learning about materials 118–119; teaching about plants 70, 77
Key Stage 3 (Early Years of primary school) children 48, 70, 119, 139, 150, 163, 192, 199, 208, 210–212
knowledge 1–3, 6–8, 10–12, 18–19, 25–27, 29–30, 32, 43, 48, 50, 63–64, 73–75, 78, 99, 101, 104, 111–112, 117–118, 129–130, 134–135, 139, 152, 165, 171–172, 188, 198, 202–204, 207, 211, 226, 228, 230, 236, 238, 243; as interconnected networks 11–12; process of building 19; and understanding 97, 100, 153, 159, 162, 165, 207, 208, 211
KWL grids 104

landfill site 144
leadership 235, 239–240
leaf: matching 58; photographs showing diversity of 79, *79*; veining and patterns 79, *79*
learning: models 10–11; objectives 33; pillars of 25; visual representations of 11
learning in science, constructivist theories of 8–10; 'alternative frameworks' 8–9; cultural position 9–10; hands-on experiences 8; interaction with physical world 8; play 8; practical investigations 9; socio-cultural views 9; talking 9
lenses 182
lesson planning 33–34; medium term 31–33; middle section of lesson 33; objectives 33; risk assessment 34
life cycle of flowering plants 82
light 157; colours 81, 176, 187; effect on plant growth 81; 'mixing' 182; scientific understanding of 179; to see object 182; sources 160–161, 169–170, 178, 180, 182
light and sound, learning about 175–176; Big Ben 183–184; breaking down barriers to 179; classroom management 188–189; colour observation 182; dialogic pedagogical approach 180; elicitation strategy 179–181; equipment for activities 189; feedback 185–186; key concepts for teachers 176, **177–178**; lenses 182; light to see object 182; misconceptions 180–181; nosiest classroom 183; orientation to topics **178**, 179; patterns with reflections and echoes 184–185; pitch of sounds 184; progression planning 176–178; questioning 180; retrieving and applying 186–187; reviewing 188; scientific enquiry 181–185; seeing sounds 184; sorting and classifying objects 180; sound travel through mediums 182–183; sunglasses 182
Lighthouse Keeper's Lunch, The (Armitage) 202
line graph *109*
liquids 7, 49, 104, 118–119, 121, 123, 139–144, 148–151, 177, 182; learning about 148; sound travelling through 182–183

listening devices 188
living and non-living collection 53–54
living things 2, 77; characteristics of 15, 43, 51; diversity of 43–44; interdependence of 44; sorting activity 80–81; and their habitats 48, **49–51**
living things, learning about *see* biology/living things topics, learning about
long-term memories 11; attention and effort in creating 12–13; retrieval practice and 25–26
lunchtime food 101

Maathai, Wangari 53
magnetism 208–209
magnets 1, 24–25, 37, 119, 123, 157, 207–221, 210, 218; *see also* forces
magnifying glasses 188
Makuyana, Ntombizodwa 98
MARGE (Motivate, Attend, Relate, Generate, Evaluate) 19
matching colours 57
materials, teaching about 117; applications 123; breaking down barriers to 122; choice of objects 121; comparisons 122; key concepts 119, **119–120**; local community 122; monitoring and feedback 128–129; orientation to topics 121–122; picture books 122; progression planning 118–119; properties 123; questioning 118; retrieval practice 129–130; rocks **133–135**; scientific enquiry 126–128; sorting activities 126–127; sorting and classifying games 124–126
material transformation 145–146
mathematics 48, 105, 107, 130, 170–171
matter: changing states of 118, 139; particle theory of 119, 139; particulate nature of 115
medicines 69, 74, 76, 89, 91, 94, 98, 101
medium term planning 31–33
melting 145
memory 1, 10–13, 19, 26, 85; based views of learning 29; basis of 12; model 11; as 'residue of thought' 12; retrieval 26; selective and organised 12; working 10–12, 23, 29, 176
mental health 89
mental structures 9
metacognition 4, 19, 22, 28, 64, 131, 133–135, 204
metals 37, 117, 120, 122, 128, 130, 146, 148, 193
microorganisms 48, 51, 55, 61, 90, 95–96, 98, 142; and biodegradation 55; learning outcome in relation to 61
mind 8–9, 11, 18–19, 23, 30, 74, 139
'mirror neuron systems' 19
misconceptions 9, 77, 85, 102, 110, 129, 144, 151, 160, 162, 164–165, 167, 170, 179–181, 185, 188, 191, 196, 198, 200, 202–203, 207, 211, 215, 218; and alternative frameworks 160, 198; common 151, 181
modelling 19, 118, 134, 159, 163, 166–169, 181, 228
models 10–11, 18, 23, 25, 28, 37, 44, 75, 90, 102–105, 110–111, 121, 129, 133–134, 147, 150, 159, 162, 164–167, 176, 186, 191, 194, 197–198, 213, 216, 226; and analogies 25, 102, 111, 191; consumption 197, 199–200; electrical 228; heliocentric 163, 167; particle 119, 150
moderation 225–226, 231–232, 245
monitoring and feedback 3, 20, 25, 63, 82, 84, 110, 128, 151; animals including humans 110; changing materials, teaching about 151–152
monitoring and parent involvement 239
Moon 157, 159–165, 169–173, 208, 211
motion 150, 163, 208, 211, 213
motors 157, 182, 199–201, 204, 211
mouth 60, 92–93, 100, 103, 179
movement 43–44, 49, 73, 92, 94–95, 100, 141, 147, 157, 160–162, 164–165, 168, 176, 184, 187, 193, 201, 207–210, 213–215, 245
multimedia learning 176
multimodal approaches 63, 84, 103, 110
muscles 13, 49, 92, 94, 100, 157
musical instruments 187
mystery object 124

nail-biting and blood pressure 106–107
NASA *see* National Aeronautics and Space Administration
National Aeronautics and Space Administration 160, 163, 166, 179, 211
National Curriculum in England 7, 32, 34–36, 43–44, 48, 70, 105, 117–118, 157, 160, 161, 176, 192, 209–210, 212, 231, 244
natural materials 56–57, 118–119, 131
natural objects 122
natural systems 106–107
natural world 29, 44, 47, 91, 139
nature: mini-safari 58; palette 57
nature of science (NoS) 7, 8
NCE *see* National Curriculum in England
neurodiversity 21
neurons, connections between 11, 12
neuroplasticity 12
neuroscience 8, 10–13, 12, 19, 176
Newton, Isaac 179, 211
night walk 163
noise 189
nosiest classroom 183

objects 15, 24, 57, 60–61, 78, 118, 120–127, 129–130, 145–148, 151, 165, 175, 177–180, 182, 184, 187–188, 192–193, 198, 203, 207–218, 229; choice of 121; moving 209–210, 212, 217
observational drawings 78–79, 85–86, 106
O'Keefe, Georgia 106
online resources 32
orbits 24, 157, 160, 162, 166–167, 170–171, 228
organisms 24, 43–44, 49–51, 60–61, 63, 73, 80, 84, 90
organs 90–92, 94, 100, 103

Index

orientation to topics: animals including humans 97–98; biology/living things topics 51–52; changing materials 143; Earth and space 162–163; electricity 192–194; forces 210–211; light and sound 178–179; materials 121–122; plant biology 74–75
Oscar and the Bird: A Book about Electricity (Wring) 193
outdoor artwork 57
outdoor education 20, 48, 51–52, 121

packaging materials, enquiry into 152
palm oil sector, impact of 64
particles 115, 138–143, 149–150, 175, 177, 191, 193, 201; activities for exploring **149**; model of 150
particulate nature of matter 115
pastoral bridge 245
pattern-seeking enquiries 60, 78, 105–107, 109
Peake, Tim 159
pedagogical approaches 180, 185, 211, 219, 246
pedagogical bridge 245
pedagogical constructivism 28–29
pedagogy 5, 18, 29, 219, 223, 244–247
peer assessment 110, 228
personal, social, health and economic education (PSHE) 44, 89, 97, 102, 192
person-centred questioning 230
photo-quiz 58
photosynthesis 15–16, 49, 55, 70, 72–73, 77, 161
physical changes of materials 145
physical experiences 9
physics 2, 18, 34, 43, 164, 211, 218; joy of understanding 157; negative memories 157
pick and mix activity 57
pictogram *107*
picture books 105, 121–122, 145, 194, 211
pie chart *108*
pitch 37, 58, 176, 178, 184, 187
PLAN 63, 64, 84, 110, 119
planet 18, 43–44, 50, 52, 62, 64, 74, 85, 115, 122, 130, 139, 144, 148, 152–154, 157, 161–163, 165, 170–172, 177
plant growth 17, 70, 74, 77, 82, 84, 119; leaves, flowers, stems and roots role in 82; light, air, water and temperature effect on 81; material for 82
plants 43; adaptations 77; and animals 43–44, 48–52, 54–55, 59–61, 65, 80, 105, 120, 129; diversity of 69; functions of 82; green 50, 73, 83; growing 70–71, 83, 86; importance of 69–70; key concepts for teachers 70, **71–73**; life 69–70, 85; orientating children to 74–75; poisonous 87
Plants in Motion website 87
plants, teaching about: activating children's idea for 76–77; breaking down barriers to 75–76; classroom management 86–87; climate change impact 85; digital images 79–80; elicitation activity for 77–78; elicitation collection for 76–77; external parts 82; goals of 69–70; growing plants for 74–75; health and safety considerations for 87; lesson resources 75;

observational drawing for 78–79; progression planning 70; seeds 82; sorting activity 80–81; *see also* plant growth
plant time lapse clips 87
plastic bags 55, 65, 122, 145–146
play and learning 8
pollination 82
Potatoes to Plastics 152–153
Potter, Beatrix 79
Practical Action schools 75
practical work 3–4, 20, 23, 33, 36–39, 86, 151, 179, 181, 191; planning for 36–38; plant topics 86–87; purposes of 37, **37**
primary classroom 26, 34, 43, 75, 90, 105–106, 131, 133, 148, 219, 244
primary school science 34, 47
primary science 1–2, 5–6, 20, 25, 28, 31, 44, 64, 84, 90, 99, 110–111, 130, 152, 157, 176, 208, 223, 225–227; aims of 5–6; development of 223; education 1
Primary Science Quality Mark 223, 239–240, 246
Primary Science Teaching Trust 21, 31, 33, 52, 75, 84, 98, 111, 118, 122, 130, 148, 152, 170–172, 185, 188, 202–203, 215, 218, 221, 230, 240, 246; 'A Scientist Just Like Me' website 21, 52, 75; 'Big Questions, The' website 202; Just Like Me website 98; resources for developing science 118
primary teachers 1–2, 4, 32, 91, 119, 150, 157, 234, 244
procedural knowledge 8
process skills 35
professional development 148, 234, 236–238, 237–239
professional judgement 30
professional knowledge 1
professional learning 237–238, 246
provocation for learning 21
PSQM *see* Primary Science Quality Mark
PSTT *see* Primary Science Teaching Trust
psychology 1, 8, 10–11, 25, 28–29
public health measures, COVID-19 pandemic 97

QCA *see* Qualifications and Curriculum Authority
Qualifications and Curriculum Authority 54–55
questioning 101

rainbows 182
rain box contents 147
real foods 100
reasoning 6–7, 9, 19, 151, 185
recall of facts *vs.* understanding 26
recycling, concept of 144
reflections, patterns with 184–185
relationships 14, 23–24, 59, 97, 105, 107, 111, 132–133, 160, 164, 169, 201, 210, 226, 229, 237–238, 244
relationships and sex education (RSE) 105
reliability 24, 31, 90, 104, 152, 226–227, 230–231
Religious Education (RE) 163
religious festivals and light 178

renewable energy 194
reproduction 44, 49, 51, 70, 72–73, 85, 90–91, 94–96, 99, 102, 105
reproductive technologies 90
responsive teachers 228–230
responsive teaching 31, 63, 225–228, 230
retrieval practice 3, 11, 20, 25–26, 30, 47, 63, 69, 85, 111, 117, 129–130, 132, 152, 171, 186, 202, 216; biology topics 63–64; changing material 152; forms of 111; plant topics 85
retrieving and applying: electricity, learning about 202–203; forces, learning about 216–217; living things topics 63–64
reviewing 4, 20, 22, 28, 64, 85, 111, 172, 188, 203–204, 217–218; animals including humans 111; biology topics 64; changing materials 153; earth and space 172; electricity, learning about 203–204; forces, learning about 217–218; light and sound, learning about 188; living things topics 64; plant topics 85–86
revision strategies 26
'reward' brain networks 13
Rice crop 81
'Rich Retrieval' project 26
Ripple Effect 75
risk 7, 34, 57, 63–65, 95, 139, 151, 219
risk assessment 34, 65, 146, 216
rocks 37, 48, 115, 118–121, 123, 128, 131–135, 145; classifying 133, 135; metamorphic 119
role models 52
rotting or decay, conception of 55
'rubbish,' collection of 121
rusting 146

safety 34, 57, 64, 111, 128, 139, 146, 219, 235; information 219; issues 4, 34, 112, 172, 188; precautions 56, 184
SAPS *see* Science and Plants for Schools
schema 9, 11
school environment 244
'school knowledge' 10
school visits and communications 52
science 6; big ideas in 7–8; capital 1, 18, 20–21, 47, 52, 69, 75, 117–118, 121–122, 132, 138, 152, 164, 218; connections 75; contribution to decision making 97; critical understanding of 7; curricula 2, 8, 32, 52, 105, 129–130, 139; education 1, 3, 5–6, 8, 18, 22, 27–28, 34, 36, 64, 89, 91, 115, 117, 131, 138, 164, 212, 223, 240; education research, Ofsted's review of 7; enquiries 34–35; knowledge 7, 27, 86, 103, 129, 185; leadership 234; learning 18, 25, 29–30, 110, 151, 185, 239; lesson 13, 17, 33, 64, 75, 85, 102, 110, 171, 236, 239, 246; status in primary schools 6; teaching 1, 6, 75, 234, 237; teaching challenges 7
science4everyone project 21
Science and Plants for Schools 81
science-based questions 74

Science Processes and Concept Exploration (SPACE) project report 212
Science Sparks website 143
science subject leader *see* subject leader
science topics 1–2, 18–19, 25, 27–28, 32, 82, 111, 191, 202, 210–211, 216
scientific attitudes 7
scientific enquiries 2–3, 7, 16, 23–24, **24**, 32–36, 69, 77, 81–83, 89, 105–106, 172, 181–185, 198–201, 213–215, 231, 237; analogies to model current flow 198, 200; apparent movement of Sun 168–169; bicycle-chain analogy 201; Big Ben 183–184; categoric variables 107–108; categories of 105; changing materials 150–151; circuits, exploring 198; colour observation 182; continuous variables 108–110; day and night 166; discrete variables 108; electrical appliance, grouping and classifying 198; elicitation activity 77–78; first-hand observation 105–106; floating and sinking 214; friction 214–215; interpretion through dialogic talk 16–17; lenses 182; light to see object 182; nosiest classroom 183; observational drawing 78–79; pattern-seeking 105–107; patterns with reflections and echoes 184–185; phases of Moon 169–170; pitch of sounds 184; plant growth 82, **83–84**; rolling bottles 215; rope or hoop analogy 200–201; seasonal change 166–167; seasons, modelling 167–168; seeing sounds 184; solar system 170; sound travel through mediums 182–183; sunglasses 182; swings and roundabouts 213; toys–fair test 214; types of 35–36
scientific explanation 16, 115, 139, 175, 179, 197, 215
scientific ideas as indisputable facts 7
scientific knowledge 1, 4, 6, 13–14, 27–29, 34, 60, 97, 126, 180, 215, 229, 244; definition of 6; elements of 34; *vs.* 'everyday knowledge' 13; health needs 97; language used to discuss 7–8; tentativeness 6–7
scientific literacy 5–6
scientific models 10, 191
scientific processes 34–35
scientific reasoning 6; rejection of 7; styles of 7
scientific understanding 1, 47, 90, 102, 179, 202
Seacole, Mary 76
seaside collection 121
seasons 52, 54, 59, 139, 157, 159–160, 162, 164, 166–167; modelling 167–168; seasonal changes 48, 54, 103, 139, 144, 158, 160–161, 164, 166–167
secondary sources of information 24, 36, 61, 82, 84, 86, 89–90, 102–105, 127, 130–131, 138, 143, 150–151, 159, 166, 169, 172, 181, 194, 198
sedimentary lifestyle 119, 132, 135
seed dispersal and germination 82
seeds 16–17, 26, 49–50, 70–74, 77, 81–83; formation 82; germination 17, 71, 77, 81
selection, natural 44, 62, 90
self-assessment 25, 226
Send a Cow farming partnership 75
sensitive issue, teaching about 111–112

Index

sex education (SRE) 105, 111–112
shadows 37, 147, 159, 161–162, 165, 168, 176–178, 182, 185–188, 226; annotated drawing to explain 186; coloured 177, 187; movement 159, 169; puppets 121, 187; stage lights 182
shared attention 19
shared understanding 9–10, 31, 226–228, 231, 245
Shaw peer assessment case study 228
skywalkers 57
'slow wave' phases of sleep 19
'smart' clothes 203
smell 11, 23, 48–49, 56–57, 70, 78, 106, 145, 148, 207
smoking 91, 96–97, 111
snow box contents 147
social and cultural interactions 29
social construction 131, 133–135
social constructivist pedagogy 29–30
social constructivist (Vygotskian) theory 18
social plane and learning 9
socio-cultural views of learning in science 9
soil 15, 17, 48, 50, 55, 59, 61, 70–71, 74–75, 77, 82, 86, 115, 119, 122, 142
solar collector, temperature inside and outside 147
solar system 170
solid materials 49, 118–119, 121, 123, 139–140, 143, 148–150, 177, 182, 209, 214; liquids and gases, concepts of 148–149; mixture of 142, 151; sound travelling through 182–183; structure of 140, 150
sorting activities 25, 80–81, 110, 118, 124–127, 126–127, 132, 148, 153, 180, 213, 228–229
sound 1, 11, 22, 43, 48, 56, 58, 60, 131, 157–158, 175–189, 237; movement of materials caused by 184; pitch of 184; sources of 177, 180, 187, 189; symphony 58; travelling 182–183, 185, 187; travel through mediums 182–183; *see also* light and sound, learning about
sound-insulating properties of materials 189
source–sink model 196
space and Earth, learning about *see* Earth and space, learning about
space, portrayals of 162
SPACE project 8, 53, 62, 100–101, 122, 144, 212
spinners 218
Stanford, Nigel 184
STEM ambassadors programme 52, 75
STEM learning 246
stereotypes 5, 21, 54
string telephones lesson plan 188
student bridge 245
subject knowledge 2, 69, 91, 144, 157, 181, 204
subject leader 2, 4, 223, 231, 234–241, 239; becoming 239; and co-ordinator 235; management role of 235–236; monitoring and mentoring role of 236–237; professional development 234, 237–239; responsibilities of 234, 235, **235**
subject leadership 4, 234–235, 237, 239–241; and professional development 234; role importance 234; subject management to 235; support for 240–241

substantive knowledge 7–8, 36, 85, 176, 180, 203, 218
summative assessment: evidence for 226; and formative, relationship between 226; reliability of 226
Sun 24, 43, 57, 77–78, 97, 128, 141, 144, 147, 157, 160–168, 170–173, 177, 179, 182, 188, 195, 228; apparent movement of 168–169; and Moon 159–161, 164, 171–172; sunlight 17, 72, 77, 162, 167, 170, 185
sun box contents 147
sunflowers 49, 51, 73, 82, 85
sunglasses 182
sustainability 3, 20, 28, 50–51, 75, 117–118, 121, 143, 152–153, 163, 171, 203
sustainable development 43, 47, 50, 53, 58, 64, 69–70, 74, 143; agenda 43, 50; education for 143–144; goals 28, 43, 47, 50–51, 63–64, 74, 85, 111, 130, 138, 152
sustainable energy 202–203

talking 9, 22
TAPS project 25, 33, 85, 172; Focussed Assessment of science 218; lesson plans 84, 110, 172, 188, 203, 218; and PLAN resources 63; school self-evaluation pyramid 231; website 64
teacher assessment 30, 225–226, 228; active pupils 227–228; case study 228; data collection 30; data examination 30; definition of 225; focused 230–231; formative 225, 226; importance of 225–227; moderation 231–232; reliability of 226; responsive teachers 228–230; summative 225; TAPS project 31, *31*, 33
Teacher Assessment in Primary Science (TAPS) 25, 31, *31*, 33, 64, 84, 99, 110–111, 130, 152, 183, 188, 221, 223, 225–227, 226, 230, 240; assessment tasks 64, 84; focused assessment 230–231; 'formative to summative' pyramid 226–227, 231; on topic of living things 64; on topic of plants 84
Teachers in the Improving Science Together project 32
teachers' self-assessment question 51; animals including humans 96; changing materials 143; earth and space 162; electricity 192; forces 208; light and sound 178; materials 120; plant biology 74
teaching survey skills 60
technology 8, 24, 34, 44, 75, 192, 194–195, 202, 210, 216
technology centres 241
teeth 23, 37, 61, 92–93, 103–104, 103–105, 112, 151, 179
temperature, effect on plant growth 81
'theory of mind' 9
thinking 4, 8–9, 18, 23, 27–29, 31, 33, 35, 52, 55, 71, 81, 90–92, 99, 102, 110, 115, 121, 123–125, 129–133, 145, 148, 153, 157, 164, 171, 186, 188, 193, 202–203, 213–214, 216, 228–230, 238; creative 6, 35–36; critical 4, 29, 36; metacognitive 131–132, 151, 153; skills 35, 117–118, 123; suitable for primary school children **132**
Thomas, Micheal 25
Thunberg, Greta 43, 53, 145

Index

Time lapse video 87
TIMSS *see* 'Trends in international mathematics and science study'
tooth decay 93, 104, 106
'top-down process' 10
topics, situating 21
torches 37, 123, 166, 168, 170, 176, 178, 180, 182, 184, 194–195, 198, 202
Toy collection 121
toys 8, 23, 54, 80, 118, 121, 127, 163, 191, 198, 208, 214, 216–217
transition 4, 243–248; barriers 244; case study 247; projects 246–247; supporting 245–246; units 246
'Trends in international mathematics and science study' 6

values 5–8, 26–27, 58, 151, 193, 219, 230, 235
variables 24, 35, 37, 81, 106–109, 128–129, 132, 218–219; continuous 108–109; dependent 199; independent 146, 199, 219
variation 44, 50, 77–78, 83, 90, 100, 106, 108, 112, 214
Venn diagrams 124, 126–127, 198
vibration 180, 189
video clips 77
Vygotskian project 29

waste disposal 143–144
waste materials 144

water 10, 13, 16–17, 24, 37, 49–50, 55–56, 59–60, 64, 70–74, 77, 81–84, 91–92, 94, 97, 103–104, 112, 118–119, 121, 128, 132, 134, 139–152, 182–184, 198, 209, 214–215; cycle 86, 139, 141, 150; droplets 141–142, 150; effect on plant growth 81; level, change of 144; vapour 140–141, 148–149
weather 48, 52, 59, 115, 139, 146–147, 153, 160, 166
wellbeing 43, 64, 74, 89, 111, 243
Wellcome Trust's state of the nation report 234
Whole-class dialogic teaching 219
whole-school assessment 97, 223, 225, 227, 229, 231; pyramid-shaped model of 226
wildlife 52, 85, 103, 179
Wildlife and Countryside Act 65–66
Williams, Tanisha 76
wind box contents 147
woodland walk 60
word bank 125
working memory 10–11, 12
'working scientifically' 7; practical work 23; scientific enquiry 23, **24**; ways to 35–36
World Clock app 166
Worlebury St Paul's Primary 231
Wring, Geoff 193

yeast 49, 51, 143, 149

For Product Safety Concerns and Information please contact our EU
representative GPSR@taylorandfrancis.com
Taylor & Francis Verlag GmbH, Kaufingerstraße 24, 80331 München, Germany

www.ingramcontent.com/pod-product-compliance
Lightning Source LLC
Chambersburg PA
CBHW080612230426
43664CB00019B/2868